PURPOSES
OF ART . . . .

PURPOSES

HOLT, RINEHART AND WINSTON.......New York • Chicago • San Francisco • Toronto • London

ALBERT E. ELSEN

Indiana University

OF ART

FOR MATTHEW AND NANCY ELSEN

Cover Illustrations:
Donatello. *St. George*. Alinari-Brogi Photo.

Seymour Lipton. *The Sentinel*. Yale University
Art Gallery.

PREFACE

Years ago while still a graduate student I read the following statement by Ernst Cassirer in his *An Essay on Man*.

Human culture taken as a whole may be described as the process of man's progressive self-liberation. Language, art, religion, science, are various phases in this process. In all of them, man discovers and proves a new power—the power to build up a world of his own, an "ideal" world. Philosophy cannot give up its search for a fundamental unity in this ideal world. But it does not confound this unity with simplicity. It does not overlook the tensions and frictions, the strong contrasts and deep conflicts between the various powers of man. These cannot be reduced to a common denominator. They tend in different directions and obey different principles. But this multiplicity and disparateness do not denote discord or disharmony. All these functions complete and complement one another. Each one opens a new horizon and shows us a new aspect of humanity. The dissonant is in harmony with itself; the contraries are not mutually exclusive, but interdependent: "harmony in contrarity," as in the case of the bow and the lyre.

The influence that Cassirer's ideas had upon the plan of this book can be seen in the text and by a statement of its premise: *Art, which is the imaginative and skillful interpretation of experience in an esthetic object, has played throughout history important roles in men's attempts to master and enjoy their environments and to liberate themselves.* To illustrate many of the forms of environment with which art has been involved, a sequence of historical, rather than esthetic topics has been chosen. They touch upon such overlapping spheres of experience as the religious, political, economic, social, playful, esthetic, and psychological. In each of these spheres, it can be shown in support of Cassirer, artists have been called upon or chose to create "ideal worlds." The means by which societies of the West and East have sought to come to terms with their environment are

v

sampled by works drawn from many media. Within each topic the examples are usually arranged in their historical occurrence to convey a sense of art's chronology. Both the book's premise and its topics are to my knowledge unusual among introductions to art. The reader is given the intellectual basis for a different and viable means by which to look at art, begin to understand and re-integrate art's history, comprehend its relevance to civilization, and experience diverse aspects of humanity.

Art is not introduced in an historical vacuum. While dealing with the what, when, where, and how, the focus is here upon the *why* of art. No attempt is made to make art simple or to serve the casual reader who would give little time and thought to art. By its origin, character, and use, art is truly complex and demanding of one's time and attention. My aim is to help make this complexity intelligible and to suggest the rewards that come from seriously and patiently exposing one's self to art. Further, this book does not separate form and content, a false and in some ways fatal division so much in vogue in introductory texts and courses dedicated to what is euphemistically called art appreciation. Contentment with style or esthetics alone is to deny the richness of meaning that has made art meaningful and important in the past. To ignore content is to distort the exciting record of how through art men *have reacted to the world and the self*. Content must be seen in relation to purpose and to style. The whole art object benefits from being set into the context of even a small part of its originating environment and the continuity of problems and possibilities that have concerned artists over long periods of time. Art is thus more than visual experience, providing rich intellectual and emotional rewards, for it is not philosophy alone that has the capacity to demonstrate the polyphonic unity of culture. The history of art abounds in the harmony of contrarieties. If a simple common denominator exists to link all art, and the topics in this book, it is man the creator.

The ideas and plan of this book emerged and were tempered during the decade of the author's teaching life. They have been warmed by the fire and cooled by the apathy of students in a small liberal arts college, a large university, and audiences attending public lectures. The author makes no pretense of being a specialist in all of the areas or objects discussed. Certainly, Eastern art deserves better representation than I can now give to it. To my colleagues in art history, there may be times when it appears that predatory incursions have been made into private preserves. Unfortunately, introductory books on art both in the text and absence of bibliography generally ignore the excellence of a large body of art historical research. This resource has here been liberally drawn upon, or plundered if you will, but with recognition given to the scholars involved in a bibliography for each chapter. While hoping to encourage the reader to visit museums and galleries in order to experience art at first hand, the author also hopes that this book will interest him in the outstanding historical writings on art. Looked at in the extreme, a truly great work of art surpasses and survives the best and worst analysis. Exposure to historical literature will not abort the latent esthetic sensibility of any reader. By adding to this comforting thought the old maxim that art is long and life is short, I have chosen to write now still another in the growing introductions to art and to share with the reader the belief that we can never learn enough about what human beings can do with the spirit, mind, eye, and hand.

ACKNOWLEDGMENTS

The number of my creditors and the amount that is owed to them is such that what can be said here seems small payment for their generosity. My oldest debt is to Professor Lorenz Eitner of the University of Minnesota, sometime colleague and long time friend who believes in the topical approach. Between us there has been an interchange and mingling of ideas which at this stage makes attributions of originality difficult. Helping to reduce the errors of fact, ignorance about sources of information, and doubts about the entire project were colleagues Henry R. Hope, Theodore Bowie, and Diether Thimme. Heading the list of scholars who provided ideas and information in their writings and lectures from which I have drawn are four of my former teachers at Columbia University, Professors Meyer Schapiro, William Bell Dinsmoor, Julius Held, and Millard Meiss.

Gratitude must be extended to the many museums, photographic services, and private collectors who provided the photographs. Special thanks must go to Horst W. Janson, Walter Horn, and James R. Johnson for making available important photographs from their personal collections. I have also been the beneficiary of Willard Tangen of The Museum of Modern Art, New York.

This book has benefited from the fine, art history graduate students in the art department at Indiana University. Mrs. Peggy Gilfoy was an ideal research assistant, for both her resourcefulness and unflagging optimism. Jeromir Stephany, now at Eastman House in Rochester, and above all Alan Dubois did excellent supplementary photographic work. Finally, warmest thanks go to my graduate assistants who taught the discussion sections of the course from which the book emerged. They suffered outrageous projects, blue books and term papers but always gave valuable constructive advice. They should not be nameless: Michael Armstrong, George Bauer, Peggy Gilfoy, Margaret Harpe, Paul Harris, Phyllis Jacobs, Mazelle Kirkpatrick, Richard Knowles, Jan and Gerald C. Maddox, Tamara Thompsom, and Ellen Wood.

Bloomington, Indiana   A. E.
1962

Chronology of Text References to Western and Eastern Art
(All dates are approximate)

PREHISTORY				
Aurignacian	40,000–20,000 B.C.			
Magdalenian	16,000–10,000			
Late Neolithic: Early				
Bronze Age in Britain	1800–1400			
EGYPT				
Old Kingdom	3200–2160 B.C.			
Middle Kingdom	2160–1590		**CHINA**	
New Kingdom	1590–525		Shang-Yin Dynasty	1500–1000 B.C.
MESOPOTAMIA			Chou Dynasty	1000–221
Assyria	884–626 B.C.			
GREECE			**INDIA**	
Archaic	600–500 B.C.		Maurya	322–185 B.C.
Transitional	500–450		Sunga	185–80
Classical	450–400		**CHINA**	
Transitional	400–350		Han Dynasty	220 B.C.–A.D. 225
Hellenistic	350 B.C.–A.D. 300		**JAPAN**	
ROME			Protohistoric	A.D. 250–550
Republic	700–31 B.C.		**INDIA**	
Western Empire	31 B.C.–A.D. 400		Kushan, Later	
Eastern or Byzantine			Andhras Period	A.D. 50–230
Empire	A.D. 323–1453		Gupta and Successors	320–650

EARLY CHRISTIAN ART	
IN ITALY	3rd–8th century
HIBERNO-SAXON	7th–8th
CAROLINGIAN EMPIRE	8th–9th
ANGLO-SAXON; OTTONIAN	10th–11th
ROMANESQUE	1000–1200
GOTHIC	

North	12th–16th century		**CHINA**	
South	13th–15th		Sung Dynasty: North	960–1126
Flemish	15th		South	960–1280
RENAISSANCE (Italy)	1420–1515		**JAPAN**	
MANNERISM (Counter-			Fujiwara	1185–1392
Renaissance)	1515–1600		Ashigaka	1392–1593
BAROQUE	1600–1780		**CHINA**	
NINETEENTH CENTURY			Ming Dynasty	1368–1644
Romanticism	1815–1850			
Impressionism	1850–1885			
Counter-Impressionism	1880–1900			
TWENTIETH CENTURY				
Fauvism	1900–1910			
Expressionism	1905–1920			
Cubism	1907–1920			
Futurism	1910–1914			
Dada	1916–1924			
Surrealism	1924–			
Non-Illusionistic Art	1910–			
Abstract Expressionism	1941–			
Neo-Dada	1958–			

CONTENTS

ix

CHAPTER 1

ART AND MAGIC

In the early as well as late phases of many societies, art performed the vital function of securing for men successful participation in the world. In prehistoric, ancient, and medieval times, when art partook of the supernatural, men believed that religious and ritual painting and sculpture could effectively intervene for their benefit in the course of events. Through magical art it was possible to come to terms with life and death. There are cultures today, such as some in Africa and the South Pacific, in which art continues to fulfill this purpose. Western civilization, too, bears the traces of the influence of magical art of the past. Some of our most sophisticated literature contains references to the alliance between art and the supernatural. The Pygmalion myth and Don Juan's confrontation with the living statue of the man he killed in a duel are two examples. The Jewish and Christian abhorrence of idolatry that has persisted to the present is a form of reaction to the former legendary power that art possessed.

The works of art chosen for discussion in this chapter coincide with the beginnings or early stages of art in certain areas and societies. They come from caves, tombs, cult shrines, sanctuaries, and secret sites.

PREHISTORIC CAVE ART

The art of the prehistoric period was created between thirty and ten thousand years ago. The paintings in the French cave at Lascaux (Fig. 1.1) are estimated to be around fifteen thousand years old. The difficulties in providing exact dates for cave paintings are matched by the problems in interpreting the art itself. Naturally there are no written records to assist the archeologist, and he must rely upon the cautious study of these primitive tribes of today in which art has a religious or magical basis. More pertinent data is supplied by archeological investigations of the floor strata near the cave paintings, of the location of the art within the underground chambers, of what

1

1.1   Lascaux. Paleolithic cave painting, 30,000–10,000 B.C.

the paintings show, and of whether or not anything had been done to the images as part of tribal rituals. The poor ventilation, absence of light, and dampness of the deepest caves in which art such as that at Lascaux is to be found immediately suggest the prehistoric existence of sanctuaries devoted not to daily human habitation, but to rites and perhaps worship. A casual glance at the walls of Lascaux indicates that esthetic ornamentation was not the primary intent of the artists. Many of the painted animals, (Fig. 1.2), like the bison, deer, horses, and cows that constituted the principal staple of both the artist's repertory and his tribe's food supply, are to be found in both accessible and inaccessible places within the caves. Some locations, remote from the entrance, require arduous climbing, crawling, and squeezing through narrow apertures to obtain uncomfortable glimpses of the paintings and engravings. On some of the painted and engraved ceilings of these subterranean grottos, hundreds of images have

been superimposed upon each other in the same area, suggesting that there were privileged or sacred spots in which to locate art.

There is general agreement that the purpose of prehistoric art was magical in that the representation of the animals in some way partook of the reality of the beasts themselves. Further definition of the type of magic or use of the images is a matter of controversy among archeologists. Found elsewhere than at Lascaux are images which show unmistakable signs of having been attacked by pointed instruments, as if by sympathetic magic the hunters' cave ritual in the sacred cave insured their power over the quarry. A life-sized clay relief of a decapitated bear evidences the existence of such rituals, but does not prove the constant purpose of all cave art. Many of the animals show harpoons and lances aimed at their bodies. Most of the animals, however, are intact and healthy, and all of the females are gravid. The painting of pregnant animals may have been designed to insure the tribe's food supply. Grid-designed, polychromed squares near some of the animals have been interpreted as signifying either traps or tribal emblems. The human figure is often shown as a hybrid, the head or other parts of the body being those of birds or animals. Proposed identifications range from witch doctors to disguised hunters to prehistoric mythological figures. There are grounds for speculation that prehistoric man may have had a god, in fact a variety of religious beliefs, and that there may have existed myths as well as cults to protect the living from the dead.

It is impossible to look at these cave paintings without being struck by their intrinsic esthetic beauty and the skill of the hand that realized them on the rough stone walls. They suggest a mature artistic tradition in which the artist received part of his training from his experience as a hunter, where he had to rely upon keenness of eye and hand to provide his food. Small stones on which have been scratched copies

after a master drawing indicate that prehistoric art schools may have existed. Many of the polychromed paintings at Lascaux reflect a great sensitivity not just to the configuration of the animals but to color and modeling. The paint, made from ground minerals and charcoal and bound with gummy substances, may have been either scraped on with shredded bone or blown on through a hollowed bone. Animals were repainted, and in certain epochs the prevailing taste was for red or brown. A characteristic of the paintings found in the caves is the predominance of the side view of the animals. Foreshortening was a difficult concept for the artist, and the frontal view would also have meant the visual and perhaps magical loss of the main body and hind legs of the animals. It is from the side that the most distinctive features of the animal, so important for magical purposes, can be seen and rendered. There exists a painting of a woolly mammoth, for example, with its heart exposed as if on an x-ray

1.2 Lascaux. Paleolithic cave painting, 30,000–10,000 B.C.

plate, but this stress on the vital organs of the animal is the exception.

A wall from Lascaux may at first seem to have been painted on with no plan or consistency, but closer examination brings into focus series, like those of the reindeer and horses, which suggest that the artist may have been attempting to show more than one animal in the same area simultaneously. The confrontation of large bulls, or the back-to-back arrangement of different animals seemingly painted in the same style and time, suggests that prehistoric painting may have known the beginnings of groupings and situations, even if the latter were emblematic or ritualistic. The location of each animal and their overall dispersal depended to some extent upon the surface character of the wall. Ground lines were never drawn. It is possible that a certain rock formation evoked an animal image in the mind of the artist which he then drew, or that an outcrop or natural shelf served as a natural base for the figures. Again, we may only conjecture about the presence of esthetic intent at Lascaux.

EGYPTIAN TOMB PAINTING

Created several thousands of years after the execution of the paintings at Lascaux, the tomb painting of ancient Egypt showed a very different kind of wall painting, one which was nevertheless employed for magical purposes. The function of Egyptian tomb painting was literally to serve the wants of the deceased in the hereafter, to prevent his starvation or second death from thirst and to insure his comfort and link him with the living. In a wall painting from Thebes (Fig. 1.3), we see a well-run estate being surveyed, or the crops measured or harvested, food production recorded; at the far right is the standing figure of the deceased, for whose benefit the foregoing activities were undertaken. The deceased is always inactive—a passive watcher of typical earthly activities. Unique events are rare in Egyptian art. In Egypt the change to painting or use of models of objects, figures, and crops instead of burying servants, animals, and taking badly needed food from the living for the deceased was a

1.3 Thebes. Egyptian wall painting, Tomb of Memena, *c.* 1415 B.C. The Metropolitan Museum of Art.

1.4   Ravenna. San Appollinare Nuovo. Detail of nave wall showing mosaic of procession of virgin martyrs and the Three Magi, *c.* A.D. 500 (Photo: Hirmer)

tremendous step in civilization's advance. Through the murals we gain an insight into the differences between the tribal food-hunting societies of the cave age and the hierarchic food-gathering cultures of the Nile valley.

Setting aside the illuminating subject matter for a moment, the formal organization of the Egyptian wall into clear, accurately marked zones, bounded at the ends, top, and bottom of the wall by the edges, is itself a sign of a highly organized society. Ground lines support the figures. The surface upon which the painting has been done was artificially made and carefully prepared. The artists worked faithfully from pre-existing art and rules to insure the efficacy of their work. As in the cave paintings, the figures, objects, and animals are so disposed as to preserve their most identifying and useful features. The human figures have a frontal eye in a profile head, a frontal view of the shoulders, three-quarter view of the waist, and profile view of the legs. (The Egyptians, as illustrated in that portion of the mural showing scribes, were capable of foreshortening

the shoulders.) Egyptian art creates no illusion of depth. There is no suggestion of volume, and none of the figures, the settings, or objects suggest existence in any reality other than that of the picture surface. To render a scene that one would normally see as existing in depth, the Egyptians and most ancient artists used vertical zones so that no action, figure, or objects would be lost through overlap or diminution due to distance from the viewer. Egyptian funerary art was not intended for the eye of the living, however, but solely for the purpose of the dead in the next life.

EARLY CHRISTIAN MOSAICS

Taking a further step forward in time, to around A.D. 500, we can see in a detail of a wall from an Early Christian church (Fig. 1.4) the persistence of magical art. The wall and its contents have been more formally organized than in the Egyptian tomb. The illustration is of a climactic segment of a long procession that runs the length of the church, from the entrance to the area just before the altar. A group of feminine martyrs, carrying crowns, is preceded by the three Magi, who bring gifts to an enthroned Virgin and Christ ceremoniously flanked by angels. In one sense, this is an honorific theme in which the god receives offerings and allegiance from his followers. The magical-mystical aspect of the relief lies in the fact that the Christian Church conceived of the martyrs as being ever-present at the rite of the Eucharist. The art gives them an actual presence in the church. The ceremony enacted by the saints and Magi parallels that of the living congregation who move toward the altar to partake of the Eucharist. Professor Otto von Simson has shown how the "concept of imitation" of this ritual mystically joins the living and the dead into one event and dissolves the boundaries of time and space. It was for this, among other reasons, that the early Christian churches were known as "the House of Mystery."

To insure the vividness and apprehension of the subjects, the artist avoided overlapping the forms, rendered each in meticulous detail, and made the figures large in scale and uniform in movement. The value and radiance of the colored stones, glass, and gold of the mosaic medium contribute to the luminous mysticism and royalty of the conception and tend to dematerialize the wall itself. More than the Egyptian painting, the formal design of the Christian mosaic and its relation to the entire wall and columns of the arcade below signify the authority of the Deity.

THE SCULPTURE OF NEGRO AFRICA

What we lose by confrontation of African art in glass show cases or on electrically illuminated museum walls is its original context and use, its intricate involvement in secret rites, myths, and sites. Masks were often designed, for example, to be worn by a dancer moving to the accompaniment of music, by either fire or sunlight; thus, they were always seen from a distance. While acknowledging that there has existed a large body of African art whose magical purpose is at best tenuous or nonexistent, it is with ritual and prophylactic art that we are here concerned. The difficulties in generalizing about the basis and nature of African art lie in the variety and complexity of African societies whose unwritten traditions go back quite probably to prehistoric times. (African art in museums is usually less than two hundred years old, as the climate and impermanent materials permit quick decay.) For this reason specialized studies of individual tribes hold out the greatest hope for present and future understanding. From such studies, it is possible to advance certain generalizations which have so far borne up under the accumulation of new evidence.

The African sculptor was motivated even in his religious art by the desire to make a beautiful object. In some African societies the artist's work was seen and most appreciated by his fellow artists. The fact that the basis of much of African art lies in religion and magic should not make us clearly divide the artist's intent into neat categories of beauty and utility. It is often impossible to assess which parts of a war drum, headrest, or food vessel are designed for magical, which for decorative purposes. Not unusually, motifs that at some remote period were religiously symbolic have lost their original significance through generations of copying and alteration and are retained for their design enrichment.

Art was one of the vital means by which African tribes and the individual native could come to terms with both visible and invisible reality. Most African tribes believed in the existence of invisible forces or of a dynamic energy that pervades nature. A variant of this attitude has been called animism. Like the ancient Greeks,

1.5 French Sudan. Dogon female ancestral figure, wood. Collection Indiana University.

mental to magical art is the hope of its maker or possessor for increase, whether of his own vital forces, those of his tribe, or the crops and game upon which life depends. The making of fetishes and charms is a gesture of harnessing supernatural energy for either defensive or aggressive purposes. Art was thus believed capable of intervention in the course of life. Its efficacy rested upon the suspension of human disbelief. To criticize such thinking as "primitive" or "childish" is to forget its analogies in the history of Western civilization and the susceptibility of many in our present-day society to superstition, fetishes, and totems (hotels without a thirteenth floor, totems for athletic teams and nations, three coins in the fountain, knocking on wood, hanging football coaches in effigy, and so forth).

The visual appearance of African art shocks the eye accustomed to the naturalism, or fidelity to appearance, characteristic of Western sculpture since the middle ages. African sculpture is realistic but not illusionistic. Unlike the Christian sculptures of Christ to be discussed in Chapter 2, the sculpture of an African god or ancestor *is* its subject and not a reminder of it. Since the subject derives from mental images and not visual ones, the sculptor's seemingly arbitrary design is logical. In most cases, the sculpture cannot be matched against a living human or animal. The sculptor has inherited or invented distinguishing signs by which to conjure the presence of the god or spirit. Ancestor sculptures such as the Bauole carving (Fig. 1.6) are good examples. Some anthropologists believe that the departed ancestors of the tribe are considered its most important members. Ancestor sculptures are the abodes of departed chiefs or members of the clan, much like Egyptian funerary statues of the pharaohs. The dead reside among the living through art. The Romans made death masks and por-

some African tribes believed that spirits dwelled in or animated all of nature. African peoples early developed their own logical and closed systems whereby all phenomena and cause and effect were susceptible to detection by magic. Believing that life forces interact upon each other, many cultures used magic in order to insure beneficial results to themselves. Art as the carrier of magic (Fig. 1.5) was thus used in the worship of gods, spirits, and ancestors in the hope of placating the deities and taking on their power and prowess. Funda-

1.6 Ivory Coast. Bauole ancestor figure. Collection of the University Museum, Philadelphia.

and communion with the gods. When the dancer donned the mask, he gave up his individuality and literally, through impersonation, shared the identity and the power of the spirit. The ritual gestures and movements performed by the masked dancers put man in rhythm with the forces of his universe. The mask permitted secret and otherwise impossible communication with the other world.

The basis of the innumerable animal masks partially derives from totemism, in which the tribe identifies itself with certain animals valued for specific qualities, such as bravery. If the totem was a buffalo, only the horns need be imaged as a signal of its presence in the sacred object. When sacred objects were not in ritual use, they were frequently hidden or sheltered in shrines, entrance into which was taboo. A striking secret shrine door (Fig. 1.8) from the Senufoans reveals in its carving some of the ritual objects it protects and perhaps alludes to parts of ceremonies.

The shaping of African sculpture

traits of their ancestors and kept them in their homes for comparable purposes. A portrait likeness was generally not needed in African art, however.

Masks (Fig. 1.7) provide some of the finest and most spectacular African art. Their uses were several and included various celebrations, protection, performance of cult rites of passage such as those in ceremonies for the dead or initiates into manhood or womanhood, preparation for war, for play, invocation of the spirits to increase the food supply or insure the hunt. Simultaneously the masks provided security from

1.7 Katanga. Luba buffalo mask, wood. Courtesy of the Royal Museum of Central Africa, Tervuren (Belgium).

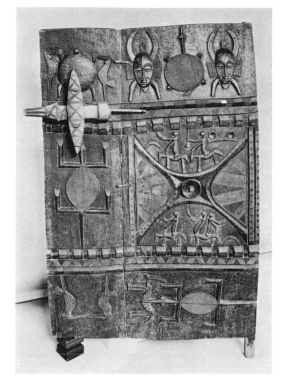

1.8 Senufo. Shrine door, wood. Collection of the University Museum, Philadelphia.

was thus an intricate blend of inherited forms and symbols and intuited signs that sculptors today find difficult or impossible to put into words. The love of musical rhythm enters into the sculpture in the sequences of curves and protuberances (Fig. 1.9). Exaggerations such as those of the genitalia may have been included to increase the work's potency, but the impulse to achieve a perfect design may have been just as strong. Figural movement is practically unknown in African art since it was unimportant in the purpose of the sculpture. The figures invariably assume a rigid frontality with great stylization in the joining of parts. There is an unmistakable sensuous pleasure in the round, smooth solidity of the forms, which often contrasts with the cicatrices or tribal scarification marks and ornaments of fashion. Various materials were affixed to wood both for ornamental and for magical purposes.

African esthetic cannot be slipped into a facile formula. While the African artist was definitely circumscribed in his work by the demands of his society to adhere to tradition, and for countless generations the same basic forms were perpetuated because of their satisfaction of security needs, the artist was far from frustrated. Often he was a respected member of the community

1.9 Africa. Songye fetish figure. Courtesy of the Royal Museum of Central Africa, Tervuren (Belgium).

1.10 China. Ritual wine vessel, bronze, Shang Dynasty. The Metropolitan Museum of Art, Rogers Fund, 1943.

whose services were eagerly sought after. As in other traditional societies, Egypt and Byzantium, for instance, the artist absorbed the beliefs and prototypal forms so that they became a part of him, and his contribution lay in their reinterpretation or refinement as well as in a demonstration of technical skill.

African sculpture is impressive in its variety and revelation of the emotional and intellectual forces recruited for its creation. From the masks, objects, and cult statues, we sense the verbally unexpressed mentalities and tastes of their makers. Linking the African peoples with ourselves is the artistic evidence of human speculation on the beings of nature and the nature of being.

CHINESE RITUAL BRONZES

In ancient China, judging by the art that has survived, the attention paid to the dead may have been greater than that paid to the living. As in Africa, Egypt, and Rome, worship of departed ancestors was considered important for the successful conduct of life. Sacred rituals using special objects were performed to insure rain and good harvests. The ornamented bronze ritual vessels (Fig. 1.10) dating from the Shang period in the second millennium B.C. held offerings of food and drink for the dead or grain and water for religious ceremonies. They rank with the most beautiful and finest bronze castings in the history of civilization. When used to propitiate an ancestor, the vessel might have the deceased's name inscribed on it along with that of the donor. There were over fifty types of ritual objects employed for such functions as the preparation and serving of food offerings. These objects have been found in tombs and may be considered as votives or vow fulfillments in the form of gifts to the departed.

Practically nothing is known of the Shang rituals although their intent seems to have included the insurance of resurrection, and the vitality and fertility of the donor and his tribe. Bronze was looked upon as a semiprecious medium and the ritual vessels were aristocratic objects. Both their shape and complex ornamentation were probably symbolic of concepts and power unknown to us today. The most frequent motifs derive from mythical and actual animals and birds—dragons, bulls, buffalo, snakes, deer, rams, owls, and cicadas, to name a few. Each motif had various associations or potencies which contributed to the total magical force of the vessel. It has been variously suggested that the dragon, for example, symbolized fertility, rain, clouds, and good omens; the cicada symbolized the regeneration of life. The owl seems to have been connected with the sun and heavenly fire, while the pheasant related to mother earth. Used in combinations these symbols were employed to meet different needs. When we search the ritual vessels for these motifs, we often find only vestiges or individual distinguishing features incorporated into the designs. As in African art, the original motifs underwent transformation but not necessarily loss of efficacy. The sculptors seemed to have compulsively filled every inch of the surface, often using for fill-in areas an abstract spiral form sometimes referred to as the "thunder pattern." Parts of the vessel, such as the handle or lip, were at times converted into animal or masklike forms, heightening the mystical nature of the object. Design sequences were adroitly adjusted to variously shaped fields and curving surfaces, always avoiding the cluttered and visually ambiguous. Frequently, as with the vessel illustrated, there appears to be a hierarchy of forms in size and relief, which may have alluded to the structure of the myths or beliefs from which they came.

JAPANESE HANIWA FUNERAL SCULPTURE

Between the third and seventh centuries A.D., protohistoric Japanese society placed small-scale clay funerary sculpture in the tumuli, or burial mounds, in which were buried tribal lords and emperors. These mounds, few of which remain with their sculpture complement intact, were surrounded by moats; from an aerial view, they are seen to have a keyhole shape. It seems possible that the humane and economically prudent use of ceramic "stand-ins" for human beings and animals to serve the needs of the deceased ruler may have come from China, which, like Egypt, had at one time practiced human immolation. In the third and fourth centuries low-fired, unglazed hollow clay cylinders, from which the name *Haniwa* comes, were set into the ground around the tumulus and filled with offerings for the dead. By about the sixth century, human, animal, object, and architectural representations were set on top of these cylinders and arranged in elaborate groupings on and near the mounds. These objects were the property of the dead, to serve them eternally. At the top of the mound, directly above the burial chamber and its sarcophagus, was placed a Haniwa replica of the deceased's house, thus providing him with a permanent residence. Gradually, around the house, there were added in successive periods and burial mounds, additional houses, granaries, livestock, weapons, human attendants, and guardian figures recalling the ruler's earthly estates. The ordering of these Haniwa groups may have been of a religious or ritual nature, but at present evidence for this is lacking. So ambitious were these Haniwa tombs that ceramic ducks were set into the moat. The horse (Fig. 1.11) was a favored subject as an aristocratic status symbol, and it was most frequently shown saddled and ready to be mounted. The horse's legs are frankly shaped as cylinders. Detail was kept to a minimum, and the design of the horse and other objects was intentionally simple, clear, and strong so as to be visible from a considerable distance. The sculptors worked quickly, giving vent to esthetic impulse during the modeling, which gives the art a fresh and varied quality. The eyes of the horse, like

1.11 Japan. Haniwa horse, tomb figurine, A.D. 300–600. Collection Indiana University.

those of human beings in Haniwa sculpture, were simply punched out of the clay. Legends grew up about the impressiveness and lifelike character of such horses. This may seem naïve to us, but for the viewer of the sixth and seventh centuries, unacquainted with detailed naturalistic art, the Haniwa sculptors provided the critical information necessary to establish the horse's identity. The living horse was looked at in terms of art rather than the reverse, as these old legends testify.

Far from being gloomy and funereal in mood, Haniwa art shows a broad latitude of lively expressions and gestures. Lacking are the dense formal designs and elaborate cryptic symbols of Chinese ritual objects. Little is known of the religious beliefs of the Haniwa period, which ended with the seventh-century advent of Buddhism and cremation. The art styles that produced the Haniwa horse and Shang ritual vessel impress upon us, however, their makers' divergent tastes and attitudes towards life and death.

EARLY MESOPOTAMIAN CULT SCULPTURE

In contrast to the Chinese and Japanese utilization of sculpture for the well-being of the dead, a third-millennium group of cult statues (Fig. 1.12) from the site of Tell Asmar shows early Mesopotamian concern for the living. These statues were found buried near the altar of a shrine and were undoubtedly originally arranged on the altar itself. Of what this original disposition consisted is not known. What is unique to Mesopotamia in the ancient world is that these statues include on one hand a god and goddess, and on the other, a priest and human worshipers, both groups in mutual confrontation. Art magically enacted the gods' epiphany to man, probably at the great New Year's festival when the human and the divine were believed to be the closest. (The ritual cups in the hands of the gods and some of the worshipers suggest this.) The tallest figure, 30 inches high, is Abu, the Lord of Vegetation, from whom men, plants, and animals obtain their life force. The second tallest figure, to his left, is the mother goddess. In front and slightly to the right of Abu is the priest, while the congregation comprises the remaining figures. Each sculpture was believed to have an independent and real existence. As alter-images of the actual congregation and priest, they attest to their subjects' devotion and worthiness to confront their gods. The awesome mystical nature of Abu is starkly realized by the sculptor's magnification of the eyes and by the bituminous black beard and immobilized frontal posture. The whites of the eyes were made from shell, and the iris was inlaid with black limestone or lapis lazuli. The relatively small scale of the figure conflicts with the concentrated magnetic pow-

1.12 Tell Asmar. Cult statues from Abu Temple, 3000 B.C. Courtesy of the Oriental Institute, University of Chicago.

er that it emits. The versatility of the sculptor is shown in his treatment of the quiet ecstasy suggested in the priest's face. The vividness of the sculptures as a whole and their design strength comes from the forceful schematization of the human form into geometrical shapes such as the cone and triangle. The assemblage of the body parts is additive and does not show organic integration. (Try to visualize the figures in movement.) This inorganic structuring of the body was, however, suited to the spiritual, trancelike state of the figures themselves. In the more naturalistic human form in Greek art, there is a concomitant beginning of a change in attitude toward art.

A GREEK VOTIVE FIGURE

The sixth century B.C. in Greece immediately preceded the brilliant Classical period and the lessening of the magical functioning of art. The sculpture of the *Calf-bearer* (Fig. 1.13) found near the temple of Athena in Athens helps us to visualize the developments which led to the distinction between the art of the supernatural and the mythical and the art of the material world. The life-sized statue was commissioned by a wealthy citizen as a votive to Athena. When the sculpture was made, around 570 B.C., art was still thought by the Greeks to possess a magical presence so that the donor's genius resided in his effigy. For additional security he had his name inscribed on the base. He has had himself shown bearing a sacrificial calf as an offering of good will to the goddess. In all likelihood the donor was satisfied that the sculptor had given his portrait likeness to the head of the statue. Compared to earlier Greek sculpture or to the Tell Asmar

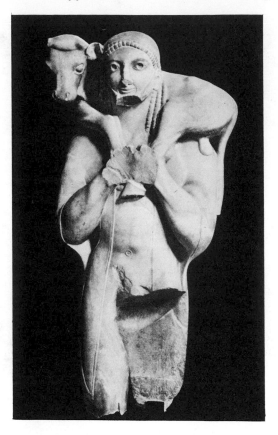

1.13   Athens. The Calf-bearer, marble, *c.* 570 B.C. Acropolis Museum.

immobile, the juncture of parts has become more fluid and closer to organic life. As the sculptured figure acquired greater mobility and anatomical detail during the Classical period, it was gradually divested of a sacred otherworldly nature. This process is reflected in the images of the Greek god, Apollo, discussed in the next chapter.

The purpose in selecting prehistoric cave paintings, funerary art from China and Japan, votive themes from early Christian, Mesopotamian, and Greek cultures, and fertility and talismanic motifs from Africa has been to suggest how art succeeded in assisting men to find and secure their place in the world. The arts have coordinated and fulfilled the human needs to know and to do, and to achieve a more successful participation in existence. The instinct to give tangible form, order, and beauty to concepts is as old and widespread as human history. Even when the artist was motivated by fear, he responded to esthetic impulses, which implies self-confidence in mastering his environment. Put in another way, while beauty was not separated from ritual or religious art, its creation nevertheless presupposed a certain secular pride and partial detachment from fear in the artist.

The necessarily limited number of examples chosen to illustrate the subject of art as magic suffices to initiate awareness of its extent and importance. The following chapters dealing with the gods, the Bible, religious architecture, and earthly rulers extend the evidence of art as magic into other areas.

group, the *Calf-bearer* evidences a more lifelike presence, the first steps toward bringing the appearance of art closer to the world of the living. (Originally the eyes were filled with colored stones; the "smile" was a device to animate the face. Viewed from different angles, the surface and volumes of the body have a marked sensuousness. Although the pose remains relatively

CHAPTER 2

IMAGES
OF GODS

No more important purpose has been served by art than its giving of a presence to gods. For millennia, art provided the visual reminders of celestial authority and made more intelligible in the eyes and minds of men the nature of their deities. The sculptured or painted presence of the god was the focus of worship and ritual, and also gave to the faithful a feeling of protection. Ancient Greek cities, for example, placed a statue of their god on the battlements to insure their defense. The god in material form also satisfied mortal curiosity and men's desire for familiarity and control over their gods. The act of making a sculpture or painting of a god was in itself an honorific gesture and, as we have seen, a means of coming to terms with the supernatural. The finished work of religious art also provided man with a visible ethic upon which to base or guide the conduct of life. Today we need not believe in the religions that inspired the old images of Apollo, Buddha, and Christ to be impressed and moved by them. Their greatness as works of art transcends time and the boundaries of religious beliefs. Nevertheless, unless we share to some extent the original concepts and emotions that produced this sacred imagery, we cannot fully recreate the awe, wonder, and gratification with which they were received at the time of their creation. To be content with only the visual or esthetic aspect of religious art is to miss the equally rewarding experience of learning about important human attempts to find and give form to the truth of existence.

APOLLO . . . .

On the temple of his sacred precinct at Delphi were inscribed the precepts of Apollo:

> Curb thy spirit.
> Observe the limit.
> Hate hybris.
> Keep a reverent tongue.
> Fear authority.
> Bow before the divine.
> Glory not in strength.
> Keep woman under rule.

In his study *The Greeks and Their Gods*, W. K. D. Guthrie has summarized Apollo's value to the Greeks by pointing out that Apollo is the very embodiment of the Hellenic spirit. Everything that marks off the Greek outlook from that of other peoples, and in particular from the barbarians who surrounded them—beauty of every sort, whether of art, music, poetry or youth, sanity, and moderation—is summed up in Apollo. Above all, he was the Averter of Evil (physical, as of disease, or exerting a less tangible influence), the god of purification and of prophecy. Any good Greek could see in Apollo the preacher of Nothing Too Much and Know Thyself. Under his most important and influential aspect may be included everything that connects him with law and order. Primarily he represents the Greek preference for the intelligible, determinate, mensurable, as opposed to the fantastic, vague, and shapeless. Apollo was also looked to as a god of nature and was known as "keeper of the flocks." He was the god of the palaestra, or gymnasium, having been the first Olympic victor. He presided over the transition into manhood and was a warlike god who carried a silver bow. Concomitantly he was thought of as the god of healing and was capable of purifying the guilty and cleansing sin.

The first artistic interpretations of Apollo were attempted during the Archaic period of Greek history. In the *Tenea Apollo* (Fig. 2.1) of the sixth century B.C., the god is shown standing erect, rigidly vertical and frontal, his body forming a perfectly symmetrical composition, the arms hanging at his sides, and one leg extended forward but with the bodily weight equally distributed on both legs. All of these characteristics are Egyptian in origin but were appropriate to the interpretation of Apollo as an authoritarian deity, in line with the Greek view of him as giver of laws. His complete nudity relates to his role as a supreme athlete. Nudity in Archaic Greek art was reserved for commemorative sculptures honoring athletes victorious in the Olympic games. The Archaic standing sculptures of Apollo were almost indistinguishable from the trophy sculptures erected for mortal, contemporary athletes. This ambiguity was caused by the idealization of the athlete, rather than creation of a portrait likeness of him. It is often only through inscriptions on the base that the identity of the standing figure may be ascertained. Thus, from the outset of his artistic appearance, Apollo was interpreted in terms of man and depicted in perfect physical form.

The pediment of the Zeus Temple at Olympia shows Apollo (Fig. 2.2) intervening in a legendary marital ceremony that has been disrupted by the drunkenness of the centaurs. It represents a developing idea of Apollo that parallels other changes in Greek art. The rigid frontal symmetry of the *Tenea Apollo* is broken by the profile position of the god's head and the extension of his right arm, a gesture calculated to restore order to the scene. The sculpture of Apollo, done at the beginning of the fifth century B.C., also departs from the earlier one in the lessening of the severity of modeling; the emphasis upon the corporeality of the god does not, however, obscure his great self-control in a situation of emotional and mental action. He thus epitomizes the faculty of rational conduct and restraint, as well as the enactment through his presence and gesture of law and order. The face and body of the statue have become more beautiful in terms of the actual human body. The proportions and bodily development, as well as the facial features, immediately set the god apart from the mortals and centaurs who surround him. The large scale and centrality in the composition are vestiges of older devices to insure the presence of an authoritarian concept.

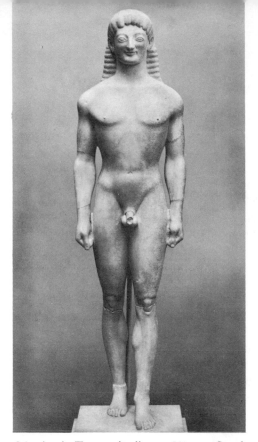

2.1 (top) *Tenea Apollo*, *c*. 550 B.C. Staatl. Antikensammlungen, Munich. (Photo: Kaufmann) 2.3 (bottom) Phidias, *Apollo*, *c*. 460 B.C. Kassel, Hessisches Landesmuseum.

2.2 (top) Apollo (detail) from the west pediment of the Temple of Zeus, Olympia, *c*. 460 B.C. Olympia Museum (Photo: Hirmer) 2.4 (bottom) *Apollo Belvedere*, fourth century B.C. Vatican Museum.

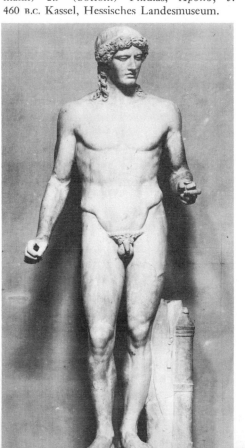

Although close in date to the Olympia Apollo, the sculptor Phidias's Classical *Kassel Apollo* (Fig. 2.3), carries even further the sensual possibilities of the body. The rigid central core or bodily axis of the earlier figures has been eliminated, and the weight is placed on the right leg in a hipshot pose creating a more active balancing of the body, one of the great achievements of Classical Greek sculpture. In this system of counterpoise, or contrapposto, the movement of each portion of the body is an ideal compositional counterpart to the Apolline tradition of harmony between spirit and body. The unblemished, richly developed nudity of the torso is perhaps a figuration of the ideals of personal and spiritual cleanliness of which Apollo was the patron deity. The strength of the still-idealized visage and the imposing physique, coupled with the pose, assist in the retention of a feeling of authority which has now become more humane than in the Archaic model. (This may correspond to the humane developments in Greek law, for instance, with respect to actual trial for homicide, which replaced the earlier family vendetta as a form of justice.) The perfect proportioning of the torso is a striking sermon in moderation and avoidance of physical or sensual excess.

The Hellenistic *Apollo Belvedere* (Fig. 2.4) depicts Apollo in actual movement with his left arm extended. It is believed that originally his left hand held the silver bow, his military attribute. (Other sculptures of Apollo show him with a lyre, signifying his patronage of the arts.) The movement permits illustration of Apollo's supreme physical control and, by implication, his intellectual grace. While retaining obvious idealized traits in the face and body, the *Apollo Belvedere* is the most lifelike and hence nonsacred of the sculpture we have seen, and this change corresponds to the religious and sculptural develop-

ments of Greece as a whole. This last figure also indicates why the religion of Greece declined in power. The gods are almost totally imaged in terms of man, permitting a fatal familiarity and identifiability between the god and the worshiper. This identifiability is apparent in spite of the fact that many of Apollo's attributes are beautifully incorporated within the sculpture. The handsome figure has an athletic and dancelike grace, retains the suggestion of purity of mind and body and of the faculty of wisdom so cherished by the Greeks. In all of the images of Apollo discussed here, the Greeks sought to interpret the beauty of his mind and morality by means of a beautiful human body. The conquest of mobility achieved by the sculptors, while powerfully evoking the nature of the god, may have caused the lessening of the efficacy of the god.

BUDDHA . . . .

Buddhism is composed of two sects. The Mahayana, or "Pious" sect, looks upon the Buddha as a god possessing the power of miracles and protecting the faithful from harm. The Hinayana, or "Rationalist" sect, looks upon Buddha as a great but human sage who provided a code of ethics that could deliver humanity from the sources of misery. One of the achievements of Buddhist art is that it has served both sects simultaneously. The meaning of the images of Buddha goes back to the first centuries B.C., when he was not shown in human form. He was replaced by symbols—his foot prints, the Wheel of Learning, the tree under which he achieved Enlightenment, an altar, or honorific parasol, recalling his princely origin. The faithful could achieve communion with Buddha by means of meditation on the symbols that induced his presence. When Buddha was finally given human form by the Gandhara artists, in the second or third centuries A.D., roughly eight centuries after his death, his body was read for concepts similar to those the symbols had conveyed. The tasks facing the early sculptors of the Buddha included the incorporation of thirty-two mystic signs of Buddha's superhuman perfection, such as the cranial protuberance, elongated ear lobes, a tuft of hair on his forehead which like the sun-dial halo signified his emission of light, spoked wheels on the soles of his feet to symbolize the progress of his doctrine and the power of the sun, and a series of ritualized hand gestures or mudras. Buddha's right hand pointed downward meant his calling of the earth to witness his triumph over evil and his enlightenment or dispensation of favors; his right hand raised was to dispel fear and give blessings. By joining his thumb and forefinger, Buddha set the wheel of his doctrine in motion. Of greater challenge to the sculptor was the metaphorical endowment of Buddha's body with the strength of the lion and his legs with the grace of a gazelle. The sculpture had to embody the sacred flame or fiery energy of the Buddha and his preterhuman anatomy. Finally, the sculptor had to impart to the statue that final state of serenity, perfect release, and deliverance from desire which Buddha achieved in Nirvana. According to his teachings, inward tranquillity was to be gained by first appeasing the senses, for only then could the mind become well-balanced and capable of concentrated meditation. The sensuousness of Indian art is partly explained by this attitude that the senses should not be denied, but should be used as the first stage in a spiritual ascent whereby the faithful could ultimately be purged of attachment to the self and the world's ephemeral delights and achieve a more perfect spiritual union with their gods and ideals. This confidence in the need and mastery of the sensual suggests that such Greek art as the

Apolline sculptures would have appealed to the early Buddhists.

Without question the seated Buddha statue is indigenous to India and is a native solution to the artistic incarnation of the Great Teacher and god. The seated position was favored, for in the life of Buddha it is recorded that after six years of penance Buddha at last came to the Tree of Wisdom where the ground was carpeted with green grass and there vowed that he would attain his enlightenment. He took up the seated cross-legged position with his limbs massed together, and he said, "I will not rise from this position until I have achieved the completion of my task." The model or prototype for the seated Buddha seems likely to have been the practice of yoga constantly before the eyes of the early Indian artists and recorded as having been the means of Buddha's achievement of Nirvana. The artist had to be acquainted with the practice of yoga, and may have employed it in the creation of his art. The objective of yoga is enlightenment and emancipation to be attained by concentration of thought upon a single point, carried so far that the duality of subject and object is resolved into a perfect unity. The *Bhagavad Gita* describes the practice of yoga:

> Abiding alone in a secret place, without craving and without possessions, he shall take his seat upon a firm seat, neither over-high nor over-low, and with the working of the mind and of the senses held in check, with body, head, and neck maintained in perfect equilibrium, looking not round about him, so let him meditate, and thereby reach the peace of the Abyss: and the likeness of one such, who knows the boundless joy that lies beyond the senses and is grasped by intuition, and who swerves not from the truth, is that of a lamp in a windless place that does not flicker.

Through yoga may be obtained

the highest state of self-oblivion. It involves highly developed discipline in muscular and breath control and the ability to clear one's mind of all superficial sensory preoccupation in order to concentrate upon a single object or idea.

The discipline of yoga seeks not only control of the physical body but cleansing and rebuilding of the whole living being. The human body transformed by yoga is shown free not only from defects, but also from its actual physical nature. The sensation of lightness, or release from the bondage of the body, induced by the practice of yoga produces the "subtle body."

One of the most beautiful of the seated Buddha sculptures comes from Sārnāth (Fig. 2.5) and was made in the fourth or fifth century A.D. It shows Buddha seated

2.5 Buddha Preaching in the Deer Park, A.D. 320–600. Archaeological Museum, Sārnāth. Copyright, Archaeological Survey of India.

upon the Lotus throne making the mudra of the wheel-turning as he preaches his first sermon in the Deer Park, where he first achieved enlightenment and to which he had returned. Below his throne (not shown in the figure) are reunited his followers and the symbolic wheel. The rear of the throne is ornamented with hybrid beasts and the foliate ornamentation of the sun disc. Minor flying deities flank the Buddha, not unlike the angels in medieval Christian imagery. The hierarchic formality of the whole indicates that the sculptor no longer deals with a specific event. The Sermon has been solemnized into a sacred symbol. The earlier, more individualistic and human interpretations of Buddha have been replaced by the idealized figure which was to be the basis of later imagery.

In the Deer Park Buddha, there is no reference to skeletal or even muscular substructure; the body appears to have been inflated by breath alone. There is no trace of bodily strain caused by the posture. The seat is firm and easy, indicating Buddha's mastery of yoga. The measure of Buddha was almost canonical at this time, being based on a basic unit called the Thalam, equivalent to the distance between the top of the forehead and the chin. The symmetry of the body makes of it a triangle with the head at the apex and crossed legs at the base. The face which wears the "subtle smile" includes the symbolic lotus-form eyes and ripe lips. The downcast eyes shut off his thoughts from the visible world.

Early standing sculptures of Buddha (Fig. 2.6), created in the late second and third centuries at Gandhara, display an obvious relatedness to early sculptures of Christ—both of which were indebted to Hellenistic and Roman free-standing figures. This indebtedness resulted from the invasions of India by Mediterranean cultures and its subsequent occupation by the Romans. Indian artists, working perhaps

2.6 (left) Gandhara. Buddha, third century A.D. The Government of India Information Services   2.7 (right) Mathura. Standing Buddha, fifth century A.D. Calcutta, Indian Museum. (Photo: Larkin Bros., London)

from Roman models, early produced a standing Buddha whose drapery and body balance recall some of the first-century B.C. Roman imperial sculpture, like the statues of the Emperor Augustus. The togalike robe is cut into naturalistic channeled folds so that we are aware of a counterpoised body structure beneath it. (It appears that Indian sculptures of royal personages also provided an early influence on free-standing Buddhist imagery.) Further Hellenistic influence can be seen in the face of Buddha which is a variant of the Apolline or Hellenistic ruler portrait type with the additions of the mystic signs. Eventually, in the succeeding centuries, notably in the fifth-century standing Buddha from Mathura (Fig. 2.7), the Indian artists departed more radically from Greek and Roman influence and developed a monumental standing Buddha more consistent with their religious ideals.

The Mathura standing Buddha is a sophisticated study in opposites. Against the vertical and immobile frontality of the body, the sculptor has designed an undulating sequence of drapery folds that prevent the eye from fastening on the boneless grace of the torso beneath. The transparency of the monastic robe illustrates the shining forth of Buddha's radiance. The hypnotic sequence of concentric discs and the ovoid head is relieved by the downcast eyes that intimate Buddha's withdrawal from earthly vision. The flat disc area with its ornamental foliate motifs is a foil for the sensual smooth volume of the head, while the rings of the halo and outline of the face and neck area play against the drapery rhythms. There is no abrupt transition or single detail to jar the eye or feelings; the totality of the design holds the eye soothingly within its borders and constantly returns it to the head of Buddha. The image is one of quiet authority that invokes love and respect without fear. The absence of bodily motion and anatomical exactitude deny achievements of late Greek and Roman art but do not disparage the skill of the sculptor. His models were increasingly drawn from previous artistic embodiments of the Buddha that had been successful in giving form to his faith.

While repetition of the images of Apollo and Christ frequently occur, Buddhist art for almost fifteen hundred years had experienced far greater adherence to a prototype. Part of the explanation of successive replication in Buddhist imagery stems from the belief in the magical efficacy of certain prized statues. Copies were thought to partake of the original's power. Further, the Buddhist artist was not encouraged to work from a living model and rely upon perception. It was his obligation to study great images, meditate on them, and then work out of his inspired memory. Buddha's beauty defied apprehension by the outward senses, and the artist worked from a mental conception in a way that had interesting parallels, as we shall see, in the art of Michelangelo.

CHRIST . . . .

It is now believed that the earliest Christian catacomb paintings date at the earliest from A.D. 200. No continuous tradition of art from the lifetime of Christ, based upon authentic images of Him to which later artists could turn for guidance, exists. The celestial countenance of Christ in the early Christian painting is based upon non-Christian sources, existing Christian art created after the second century A.D., and theologi-

cal views and developments; not until the late medieval and Renaissance periods were images of Christ a truly personal conception on the part of the artist. The first images of Christ, to be found in the catacombs and in funeral sculpture, show Him as the "Good Shepherd," a familiar image in Greek art in the Hermas figure, as well as the votive *Calf-bearer*. There is ample evidence to show that the Christians recognized and valued the similarity between Christ as the shepherd and Orpheus. The Greek mythological figure had much in common with both Apollo and Christ, as he was associated with salvation, sacrifice, love, and protection. The shepherd image was an ideal expression of the early Christian community, which was characterized by a close relationship between the priest and the congregation. The priest was seen as the shepherd, the congregation as the flock. The occurrence in art of the shepherd in nature was also fitting as the early Christian view of paradise was comparable to the Roman writer Vergil's descriptions of a new paradise, sylvan in character, a beautiful nature in which the soul could repose, ruled over by a gentle shepherd. Christ as the shepherd, whose coming Christian theologians saw in Vergil's prophecies, thus ruled over a bucolic world as if in a Golden Age. Second-century Christian saints also describe as a magnificent garden, the paradise in which the soul can find rest.

In a fourth-century sarcophagus (Fig. 2.8), the shepherd is surrounded by small winged figures harvesting grapes. Both the angels and the vineyard derive directly from pagan sources in which the grape harvest and wine alluded to premature death and regeneration. This explains the choice of theme for the sarcophagus of a deceased Christian who was well-to-do. Before the fifth century, Christian art mostly interprets what Herbert Muller calls "the

Historic Jesus," Jesus as the Messiah and not as a divinity. In the Lateran Sarcophagus, Jesus stands as the shepherd upon an altar, referring to his death and sacrifice for mankind. His resurrection provided the hope and optimism of the early Christian community and its converts.

The shepherd image may not have been without political significance. Some archeologists have pointed out that in catacomb paintings Christ has features resembling those in images of Alexander the Great. Other than this superficial resemblance, there is no stress on Christ's militant or royal nature. In general, the artistic prototype of Christ seems to have been late Greek and Roman sculptures of seated or standing philosophers associated with the contemplative or passive life. It was the custom for late Roman artists to depict pagan figures at the same time they were fulfilling Christian commissions. Sometimes sarcophagi were carved and completed ex-cept for symbols or faces; they could thus be purchased by either pagan or Christian clients and then finished.

In the fourth century A.D. Christianity received imperial support and was no longer the private religion of earlier periods. The Church was reorganized along the lines of the Roman Empire, and the priesthood became an autocracy. Theology and art were subjected to radical transformation and formalization. The external forms and cult aspect of religion criticized by the historic Jesus became prominent. In the sixth century, the Byzantine Emperor Justinian ordered an ambitious mosaic series for the apse of the church of San Vitale in the city of Ravenna, which he had just conquered from the Goths. The mosaic (Fig. 2.9) of the Enthroned Christ flanked by angels and Saints Ecclesius and Vitalis exists in the half-dome of the apse and reflects the transition from the historic Jesus to the theological Jesus. The Messiah has

2.8 Rome. Detail of the Lateran sarcophagus with Christ as the Shepherd, late fourth century A.D. (Photo: Hirmer)

been replaced by the Son of God, the humanity and humility of the shepherd by the impersonality of a celestial ruler over the hierarchy of religious government. The doctrines that lay behind this mosaic were not those taught by Jesus himself. At San Vitale the doctrine of the Incarnation and Second Coming informs the image. Like a Roman or Byzantine emperor, Christ holds an audience where he gives and receives honors. Bishop Ecclesius donates the church of San Vitale to Christ, while He gives the crown of mercy and martyrdom to Saint Vitalis. This is sacred art; the mundane values of earlier Christian imagery have been replaced. The event transpires outside of time and place, for the saints lived in different centuries. We see the outside of the church of San Vitale at the same time that the mosaic showing the donation is inside the building. Christ sits upon the heavens, but is mystically and simultaneously within the heavens. Beneath His feet flow the four rivers of paradise. The mosaic demonstrates how theologians had reconciled the divinity and authority of Christ with that of the earthly emperors who acknowledged obedience to Him. Christ rules the Heavens, while the emperor, Justinian shown in an adjacent but lower mosaic, rules the earth. The relative informality of earlier Christian imagery has been replaced by a complex series of artistic devices to convey the concept of Christ as the Second Person of the Holy Trinity. (Chapter 7 discusses Roman imperial sources of these devices.) Against the gold of the heavens, symbolizing the ineffable light of God, the youthful, beardless Christ sits attired in the imperial purple and gold. Contrasting with the attendant figures who must stand in His presence, Christ is frontal, larger; He is oblivious to those around Him. His ritual gestures of investiture and acceptance make a cross-shape of His body, accentuating His centrality in the image and in Christian dogma. The symmetry of numbers is echoed in the gestures of the satellite figures. While the mosaicists may have been inspired by St. John's descriptions of the radiance of Heaven, like John, they based the attributes and qualities of divinity upon their experience of the highest form of earthly authority known at the time, the magnificent court ceremonies of the earthly monarchs.

2.9 Ravenna, San Vitale. *Christ Enthroned*, apse mosaic showing Christ flanked by angels and by Saints Vitale and Ecclesius, sixth century A.D. (Photo: Alinari)

2.10 Moissac, Church of St. Pierre. *Christ Enthroned*, tympanum of west door, twelfth century A.D. French Embassy, Press and Information Division.

The esthetic form of art changed in accordance with developments in theology. The San Vitale mosaic embodies this esthetic as well as dogma. Each figure, for example, is sharply outlined, every detail clearly shown as if the viewer were standing close to each subject. The figures do not overlap and are all near the surface of the mosaic, which accounts for their great size. There is only a limited depth to the scene and no attempt to recreate atmospheric effects and the light and shadow of earthly experience. Absolute identification of the role and status of each figure had to be possible. The colors are rich and varied, but governed in their use in large areas by symbolism. The composition is closed, so that there is no suggestion that the frame cuts off any significant area or action. The figures experience, at most, limited mobility, their static quality designed to reflect a transcendent nature and to facilitate their meditative absorption by the reverent viewer. Thus artist and theologian combined to give a presence to dogma by creating imagery of an invisible, nonhuman world.

The great Byzantine images of Christ and those in the early Christian basilicas in Italy were to be found within the churches. By the beginning of the twelfth century, French Romanesque sculptors had transferred sacred images to the exterior, as we see in the great relief carved over the doorway to the church of Moissac (Fig. 2.10). But this did not immediately result in the conception of Christ as being of the world of the living. While adopting the ceremonial and sacrosanct properties of the San Vitale image, the Moissac sculptor powerfully added new ideas to the conception of the lordly Christ. Wearing a crown, Christ is a feudal king of kings, surrounded by Elders who are His vassals. His remoteness is reinforced by the great scale difference between His figure and the representatives of humanity. All glances are drawn to Him as to a magnetic pole. From His immobile frontal posture, the composition moves outward in waves. Angels and evangelical symbols, of intermediary scale between Christ and the Elders, but proportioned closer to Christ, serve to impress the onlooker with the hierarchical makeup of the universe and to bridge those in motion with the motionless Christ. Christ is here like the awesome Old Testament God. That which is mundane is extraneous to His world. The rendering of Christ is such that He is given a commanding and completely aloof presence. He is thus shown as Redeemer and Judge at the Second Coming. His beauty does not derive from comely proportions known to Apollo; it is of an entirely impersonal, unsensual nature, which appeals to thought and faith.

The twelfth-century Byzantine mosaic of Christ (Fig. 2.11) the Pantocrator, in the dome of the church of Daphne outside of Athens, focuses attention upon the face of Christ, His gesture of blessing, and His holding of the Bible. It is an image calculated to strike awe, reverence, and fear into the beholder. The face is severe, cli-

2.11 Daphne, *Christ*, dome mosaic, *c*. A.D. 1100.

maxed by the vigilance of the eyes. The celestial countenance is that of an immutable, stern judge who is both giver and upholder of the law. It is an impressive face, not beautiful in the classical sense, for it denies the importance of the flesh and stresses the power of the divine will. There is an unclassical imbalance in the Byzantine stress upon the eyes and the intensity of expression. No Greek sculpture of Zeus hurling his thunderbolt carries the wrath of which the Daphne Christ seems capable.

The legal and authoritarian aspects of the Byzantine Christ are continued but also relaxed in the thirteenth-century sculpture of the Beau Dieu (Fig. 2.12) from the French cathedral of Amiens. Christ stands between the main doors of the cathedral and below the scene of the Last Judgment. Beneath His feet are the lion and serpent symbolic of the evil Christ conquers. Both in His location and in His appearance, Christ has been made more accessible to the congregation. He stands before the doors to His house not as guard, but as host, like a gallant feudal lord. The humanizing of Christ into an aristocratic ideal is reflected in his new nomination, "the Handsome God," a title in many ways unthinkable at Moissac and Daphne. This garbing of Christ in a more physically attractive form accompanies His re-entrance into the world of the living and the reduction of the sacrosanct nature of the art itself. His face has dignity but tenderness, in contrast to the aquiline sharpness of the Byzantine Christ. The transition has been from the Byzantine Pantocrator, Lord of All the Universe, to the Gothic lord of men.

The Beau Dieu has an idealized countenance which should be compared with the head of Apollo from Olympia (Fig. 2.13). The Gothic head is noticeable for its sharp features and subdued sensuality, indicating an essentially Christian atti-

2.12 Amiens, Cathedral of Amiens. Detail of the Beau Dieu, thirteenth century A.D. (Photo: Giraudon)

tude towards the body. This is particularly noticeable in the treatment of the mouth. The more sharply ovoid outline of the Christ image, enhanced by the long tightly massed hair, the vertical axial alignment of the symmetrical beard, nose, and central part of the hair, give the deity an ascetic and spiritualized mien. Despite the generalized treatment of the forehead, cheeks, and hair, the Amiens Christ assumes more individualistic character than does the Olympian Apollo. The Apollo is totally unblemished by the vicissitudes of a mortal existence. It shows nothing of the asceticism, self-denial, and spiritual sublimity known by Christ. The eyes of the Gothic Christ are worked in greater detail in the area of the eyelid and have a more pointed upper arch than does the simplified perfect arc of the upper lids of Apollo's eyes. (Both sculptures originally had the iris painted in.) The Gothic Christ lacks the masklike calm of Apollo, whose creator had been exposed to a theatrical tradition in which the mask had been the carrier of the limited range of feelings that the face was permitted to express. Christ's face in turn lacks that aura of absolute physical

2.13 Detail of Apollo from the Temple of Zeus, Olympia, c. 460 B.C.

self-confidence (and consciousness) which
radiates from the visage of Apollo. Finally
it should be noted that the Gothic Christ
does not have the slight effeminacy of the
Greek god, which is perhaps related to the
rites or festivals enacted by Greek youths
on behalf of Apollo, and is in conformity
with certain Greek ideals of beauty which
do not make a sharp sexual distinction.

Comparison of a Buddha sculpture with the thirteenth-century head of
Christ at the French Gothic cathedral of
Reims, provides us with a summation of
two radically divergent tendencies in the
respective art forms of Christianity and
Buddhism (Figs. 2.14 and 2.15). The Buddhist head reveals the development toward
anonymity in the celestial countenance, a

refusal to glorify a specific individual. It
incarnates the spirit of Buddhism which
conceives of Buddha, "One—who is now
nothing," as representing a spiritual essence of religious attitude divorced from
any reference to a specific being.

The Buddhist face reflects the
ideal of a state beyond such perfect physical embodiment as we saw in Greek imagery. The smile on Buddha's lips recalls
his wisdom and sublimity, which he enjoys
in the Abyss or sphere beyond Nirvana.
The Reims Christ wears the marks of his
passionate earthly sojourn, the residuum of
care, in the worn surface of his face. The
brow is creased and the eyes wrinkled at
the corners, and we sense that the god has
a unique and dramatic biography. There

2.14   (left) Gandhara, Head of Buddha, fifth century A.D. Crown Copyright. Victoria and Albert Museum.
2.15   (right) Reims. Detail of Head of Christ, from The Coronation of the Virgin, thirteenth century A.D.

is no intimation of past life, of trial and pathos in the sculptured images of Apollo and Buddha. The Christian face speaks to us of a personal tragic drama. It displays and is capable of a far subtler span of feeling than the faces of either of the other two deities. The Gothic sculptor wished us to read tenderness, compassion, pain, and wisdom in the lines of the face. The Reims sculptor may have used a French king, perhaps King Louis IX (St. Louis), as his model, so that the god is now literally imaged in terms of man. The French sculptor has also put to use the mobile features of the face, the eyes and the mouth, to express these sentiments. The Buddhist culmination in art lay in its mastery of immobility of the face and body in order to catch the transcendent nature of the god. The eyes become gradually closed, shutting them off from the outer world. Those of Christ become expressive reminders of how the God on earth shared the dilemma of man. The Reims Christ is shown to us as a king, but not such a cosmic monarch as is found in Byzantine art. He represents the second half of the cycle begun in the catacombs when Christ emerged as a humble man, then as an emperor and ruler of Heaven. Now the cycle passes in the other direction, to terminate in the images of Christ discussed in the chapter on Rembrandt.

Western Christian art, like its theology, is dominated by the execution of its God. Buddha's death came tranquilly; for three days he lay on his right side with his head resting on his hand until he passed into the last Nirvana. Christ's physical and spiritual anguish on the Cross has no parallel in Buddhist or Greek art. One of the most impressive and personal interpretations of the theme of the crucifixion is that by Mathias Grunewald which occupies one of the main panels in the Isenheim Altarpiece (Fig. 2.16). Painted probably between 1513 and 1515, the altarpiece was intended for the monastery church of St. Anthony in Isenheim, Alsace. The monastery's hospital treated patients with skin diseases, like leprosy and syphilis. The first step in a new patient's therapy was to be taken before the painting of the crucifixion and to have prayers said at the altar for his healing. It was thought that skin disease was the outward manifestation of sin and the corrupted soul. The patient was confronted with the greater-than-life-sized painting of the dead Christ whose soulless body was host to the worst known afflictions of the flesh. Only Christ had the power to heal the sinner, for He had borne all of the sorrows of the flesh that garbed the Word. Previous regal, authoritarian, and beautiful incarnations of Christ were replaced by the image of the compassionate martyr. The vivid depiction of the eruptions, lacerations, and gangrene of the body were intended to excite the patient's identification with Christ, thereby giving solace and hope. From the late Middle Ages, partly because of widespread pestilence, there are countless examples in the art and literature of northern Europe of the faithful being enjoined to identify themselves emotionally with the passion of Christ. Grunewald probably drew upon the vision of the fourteenth-century Swedish saint Brigitta, who wrote,

> The crown of thorns was impressed on His head; it covered one half of the forehead. The blood ran in many rills . . . then the color of death spread. . . .
> After He had expired the mouth gaped, so that the spectators could see the tongue, the teeth, and the blood in the mouth. The eyes were cast down. The knees were bent to one side, the feet were twisted around the nails as if they were on hinges . . . the cramped arms and fingers were stretched.

Grunewald's image of Christ goes beyond this description in exteriorizing the body's final interior states of feeling. The

2.16 Grunewald, Crucifixion, Isenheim altarpiece, *c.* A.D. 1513–1515. (Photo: Bruckmann) Underlinden Museum, Colmar.

extreme distension of the limbs, contorted extremities, and convulsive contraction of the torso are grimly eloquent of Grunewald's obsession with the union of suffering and violence in Christ. In pathological fashion he has focused on the final rigidification of the death throes to the extent that either the hands or feet or the overwhelming face is sufficient to convey the death of the entire body. The brutal stripping of the living wood of the cross symbolically accords with the flagellation of Christ. Cedar, used on the vertical trunk of the Cross, was part of the cure for leprosy. The hopeful message of the painting can be seen in the contrast of the light that illuminates the fore-

ground and the murky desolate landscape behind, signifying Christ's triumph over death. John the Baptist, with his head miraculously restored and present at the Crucifixion, intones, "I shall decrease as He shall increase." Men are enjoined to humble themselves in order to grow anew in God. The static doctrinal and symbolic right half of the painting contrasts with the human suffering and emotion at the left among the grieving figures of John and the Virgin and Mary Magdalen. Grunewald's painting and views of religion seem to have stressed a communal response to tragic but elevating religious experience. Psychologically and esthetically, each figure, like the composition of the whole, is asymmetrical, the uneasy synthesis of polarities.

Images help to trace the changing views of Christ from those which saw in Him a humble messianic shepherd, through the kinglike God to be revered from afar, to the Godlike king who could be loved as a benevolent ruler, and finally to the Man of Sorrows whose own compassion evoked the pity of suffering humanity. The transition of sacred art proceeded differently in the cases of Apollo and Buddha. Apollo's effigy began as sacred art and terminated in profane imagery of a beautiful youth. Buddha's early interpretation progressed from humane individuality toward the sacrosanct impersonality of the sixth and seventh centuries. To comprehend the success of Greek, Indian, and Christian artists in their attempts to unite form and idea, one may interchange in the mind's eye the Reims Christ head and that of Apollo at Olympia, the Lotus throne of Buddha with Christ's position in the Moissac relief, or station the nude figure of Apollo in the Beau Dieu's position at Amiens, or finally, install the San Vitale Christ in the Antonite hospital chapel.

CHAPTER 3

RELIGIOUS ARCHITECTURE

The history of religious architecture is more than a record of styles and engineering achievements. It is a demonstration of the fact that architects have expressed or symbolized the most sacred values of their cultures. In a variety of ways, conceptions of heaven and the universe have been incorporated into the designs of religious structures. The architecture of the tomb, temple, and church, like the images of gods, manifests to the senses and intellect what lies beyond the visible. Such was the intent of the Buddhist burial mound in India, the temple in ancient Greece, the Gothic cathedral in France. Although sculpture was important to the adornment and meaning of these structures, our focus will be upon the ideologies and cultural meaning of the architecture itself.

THE GREAT STUPA AT SANCHI . . . .

The Great Stupa (Fig. 3.1) at Sanchi, in central India, consists of a hemispherical mound set upon a circular base, with a railed enclosure. At the mound's summit is an enclosed pavilion above which rises a tiered mast, or parasols. Inside the base and center of the stupa is a sealed chamber for the sacred relic. The sources of the stupa's form and meaning go back into the earlier history of India and of the Near and Far East. The stupa is derived from the burial mound, which may have originated in central Siberia at some early, as yet unknown date. The burial mound or barrow passed eastward into China and then Japan, where it took the form of the tumulus mound. Southwest from its probable point of origin, the barrow reappeared in India for the burial of rulers and holy men as well as for the preservation of sacred relics. It was in use at the time of Buddha in the sixth century B.C. Buddha's dying injunction to his followers to build edifices containing his ashes and relics as reminders of his teachings led to the erection of the original eight stupas, now lost. These stupas

3.1 Sanchi. The Great Stupa, 200–100 B.C. (Photo: Elisofon)

were built on the sites of the great events in Buddha's life: his birthplace at Kapilavastu; the Bo tree at Bodhgaya, where he achieved Enlightenment; Sarnath, where he preached his first sermon; and the place of his death, Kusinagra. Others protected his footprints and the stone slabs from which he taught. These stupas were the focus of pilgrimages and worship that enabled the faithful to recall and share in Buddha's triumph over evil and ignorance, thus being moved to emulation.

The Great Stupa at Sanchi was begun in the second century B.C. in the reign of the Sunga king Asoka. In the first century B.C., it was enlarged and enriched by the addition of the sculptured gates. The stupa was probably a copy of a lost prototype. As with Buddhist sculpture, the architectural replica shared the sacred values of the original. (This accounts for the widespread building of Buddhist stupas in southwest Asia.) Asoka's selection of the stupa form that had been used for royalty was appropriate in view of Buddha's princely origin and the concept of his being a World Ruler. The parasol was also an aristocratic symbol. Threatened with internal political and religious disunity, Asoka used

the Sanchi and other stupas to unite the various nature sects under the dominance of Buddhism by placing them on the older cult sites. The sculpture as well as architecture of the stupa at Sanchi reflects the assimilation of non-Buddhist art and cosmology.

The sculptured gates (Fig. 3.2), which may have developed from talismanic ones in towns, were covered with sculptures of minor and guardian deities impressed or recruited into the service of Buddha. The sensual figures of women entwined with trees represented tree goddesses, or Yakshis (see Chapter 12). Reliefs dealt with events in the life of Buddha, although he was not shown at this time in bodily form, or with princes who gave up all earthly possessions to follow Buddha. Birds and animals were symbolic of the elements or served as emblems of Indian rulers. Flower vases were fertility symbols, and miniatures of the stupa and the Wheel related to Buddha's death and his teachings of the Wheel of the Law.

The selection of the site and the laying out of the plan of the stupa were done with considerable ceremony and calculation. The stupa's orientation is close to

3.2 Sanchi. Eastern Gateway of the Great Stupa. (Photo: Elisofon)

new identity that permitted him to transcend earthly existence. The stairway that led to a platform at the top of the stupa's base may also have symbolized the spiritual ascent of the devoted. The stupa was never in darkness—torches illuminated it at night.

The base upon which the stupa's mound was raised derived from the old fire altars of the Indian Vedic religion. These fire altars were made of burned, and hence purified, bricks, each of which was carefully oriented in relation to the heavens. The human sacrifices were laid on the altar with their limbs similarly oriented. When a wealthy man died, he or his effigy, known as the Sacrificer, would be immured in the altar, head to the east and face toward heaven. The fact that Buddha's ashes were preserved in the mounds may have en-

the cardinal points of the compass, as its builders sought to put the structure in phase with the cosmos as it was at the particular time of the year in which the stupa was built. Mathematics and astrology, used throughout ancient sacred architecture, made the stupa a cosmic diagram (Fig. 3.3). The four gates symbolized the revolving ends of the swastika, the sun symbol; and the circular exterior railing, which separated the sacred precinct from the mundane, recreated the course of time and the stars. The circular area between the railing and the stupa's base was intended to permit the pilgrim, after he had entered the east gate, to circumambulate the stupa clockwise, thus tracing the movement of the sun. This rite was part of the mystical elevation of the worshiper, who when he entered the sacred precinct, partook of a

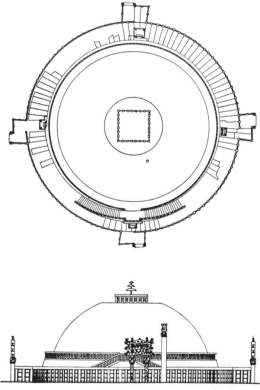

3.3 Sanchi. Diagram of the Great Stupa. Courtesy of Benjamin Rowland and the Pelican History of Art.

couraged the use of the old and sacred fire-altar form as a base.

The mound at Sanchi was solid except for the reliquary chamber, built of bricks, covered with concrete, and then plastered white. Other stupas were built of earth and masonry-faced, and often tiled or gilded with gold.

The hemispherical form of the mound lent itself to rich symbolic interpretation. The stupa mound was seen as the World Egg, the vault or dome of heaven which enclosed Meru, the World Mountain. Mount Meru is a mythical mountain central in Indian religious thought. Like the Egyptian pyramid and the Mesopotamian ziggurat, the Indian mountain symbol was sacred and symbolic of the earth and regeneration.

At the mound's summit the pavilion marked the house of the gods who ruled over earth. The stupa, like the pyramids and ziggurats, was a bond between man and the gods, earth and heaven. The tiers of the mast or spire derive from the Brahmist conception of the heavens' structure and the abodes of the thirty-six gods. It was from this symbolic architectural element that the pagoda originated. The spire itself was the World Axis; theoretically it rose from the watery underworld and continued through the relic or mortuary chamber and center of the World Mountain into the heavens. The stupa and its World Axis were thought to ensure plentiful water for the propagation of all life. Therefore in addition to its missionary function, the stupa had mystical power to shed benevolent influences upon the people and country in which it was located. The mystical mast was also thought of as the Bo tree, and the mound symbolized its fruit. When the shaft was placed above the ashes of Buddha or another holy figure, it symbolized the soul's ascent to paradise.

The presence of his relics made Buddha immanent through the stupa itself.

It became his second mystical body and deserving of veneration. The presence of the symbols of fire, water, earth, and heavens made of the stupa a miniature of the universe. These concepts in the minds of the pilgrims or would-be converts, who often traveled great distances to the stupa, must have deepened their reactions when they first approached the Great Stupa at Sanchi.

Even in its present imperfect state, the Great Stupa of Sanchi retains a quiet power suggestive of continued contemplation. Appropriate to its purpose, the stupa is a memorable but not monotonous form. As an object of meditative worship it has elegance and stability, relieved in its severity by the sculptured gates and summit elements. The stupa's original white surface provided a dramatic backdrop for the brilliantly colored gateway sculpture. The small-scale, prolix groupings of the sculptures effectively contrast with the few, clear armature shapes of the gates and with the monolithic form of the mound. The span confronting those who approach is thus from the minute and active to the monumental and motionless. A strong series of rhythmic concentric circles beginning with the outer perimeter leads the eye upward to the shining pinnacle of the mast. The various spacings of these circles, coupled with the sculptured gates, assist in conveying the true sense of the stupa's great scale. (It was 54 feet high.) Set upon a flat plain against the sky, it still commands attention and attracts movement toward it from all points.

THE PARTHENON . . . . . .

The meaning of the Parthenon (Fig. 3.4), a Greek temple built in Athens during the fifth century B.C., does not reside in its formation by cosmic symbols. The Parthenon's architecture does not literally represent the forms of myth and religion. It is nevertheless an inspired expression of Classical Greek higher values. Through analogies and the circumstantial evidence of culture, the Parthenon reflects the world view of Periclean Athens. The date of its building, 447–438 B.C., and its location on the sacred hill of the Acropolis in the city's center, are both important. During the Persian invasions of the 480's, a partially constructed temple dedicated to Athena, goddess of Athens, was burned and largely destroyed. After what seemed the miraculous defeat of the Persians, the Athenian Senate tardily authorized the temple's construction. The building of the Parthenon occurred in the flush of Greek confidence in Athenian gods, Athenian moral values, Athenian maritime mercantile success, and above all, Athenian culture. Ironically, the great temple also marks the beginning of the fateful decline of Athens' political power and of what several historians have felt was her moral corruption. Many in Athens protested the great cost of the temple as well as Pericles' impatient offer to pay for

it himself. To prevent the glory passing to Pericles, the Senate approved the project. The expenses were covered by contributions of the Athenian League, allies of that city state, by loot of Athens' piracy and wars, and by contributions of free citizens who with their slaves donated work on a daily basis. The smallness of the Parthenon in comparison with the size of Egyptian temples reflects the difference in the respective resources and to an extent, the absence of a powerful clergy in Greece. Nevertheless, for a city of one hundred thousand people, the Parthenon was an ambitious project. The Parthenon was a gift to the goddess of war and wisdom from free men who willingly submitted to her. It was a votive offering in return for past naval and economic success, for Athena was also the protectress of the navy.

The extent of community participation in honoring Athena is commemorated in the 525-foot frieze running from west to east outside the top of the sanctuary walls and above the second row of columns

3.4 The Parthenon. Architects: Ictinus, Callicrates *et al.*, 447–438 B.C. (Photo: Trans World Airlines)

3.5   The Parthenon seen from the West. Reconstruction by Gorham Phillips Stevens. The American School of Classical Studies, Athens.

at the entrances (see Fig. 3.9). The subject of this continuous relief is the Panathenaea that took place every four years to honor Athena's birthday. A procession of representatives of all Athens escorted the wheeled model of a ship from whose mast hung a newly woven purple woolen sail, or peplos. On the peplos were embroidered legendary battles in which Athena triumphed. When the procession reached the Parthenon, the sail was turned over to the priest, who hung it on the statue of the goddess in the sanctuary. In the relief the gods are shown seated as guests at the ceremonial banquet in the sanctuary. The relief depicts the sequence and putting in order of the procession which began in the city and included the marshals, magistrates, sacrificial animals, and libations carried by young girls, elderly citizens, youthful musicians, charioteers, and cavalry from the army. The 40-foot-high location of the relief, poor illumination, and partial obstruction by the columns indicate that it was primarily intended for the eyes of Athena. To accommodate mortal gaze, the sculpture is in higher relief at the top of the frieze.

The Panathenaea recalls the spirit in which the temple was built. Art was interwoven with the rituals of civic life accompanying dramatic festivals, athletic games, and religious performances. Public expenditure for art was conceded as necessary to enrich the lives of Athenian citizens. The ideal citizen of Athens was an active contributor to the affairs of the city. Within half a century this ideal was realized by Pericles, Sophocles, Aeschylus, Euripides, Anaxagoras, Socrates, Thucydides, and the sculptor Phidias, who oversaw the sculptural decoration of the Parthenon. In conjunction with Pericles, it may have been Phidias who assigned the architecture to Ictinus and an assistant named Callicrates. Many artists were recruited for the project (Fig. 3.5), and according to Plutarch, who wrote centuries later, such was the spirited

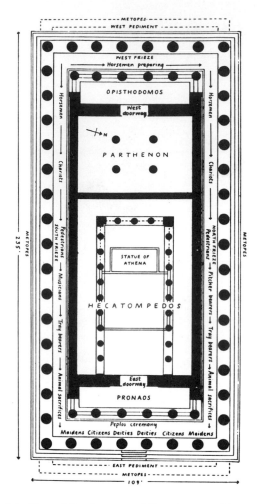

METOPES
WEST PEDIMENT
WEST FRIEZE
Horsemen preparing
OPISTHODOMOS
West doorway
Horsemen
Horsemen
Chariots
Chariots
N
PARTHENON
METOPES
METOPES
255'
Pedestrians
SOUTH FRIEZE
Musicians
Tray bearers
Animal sacrifices
Pedestrians
NORTH FRIEZE
Pitcher bearers
Tray bearers
Animal sacrifices
STATUE OF ATHENA
HECATOMPEDOS
East doorway
PRONAOS
Peplos ceremony
Maidens Citizens Deities Deities Citizens Maidens
EAST PEDIMENT
METOPES
109'

3.6 Plan of Parthenon and Panathenaean Procession. (After N. Yalouris)

rivalry among the workers and artists to excel in quality and speed, that to the amazement of subsequent generations the Parthenon was finished within the lifetime of those who inaugurated it.

The prime purpose of the Parthenon was to provide a worthy House of Athena. The temple form is the descendant of much earlier megarons, or houses of Mycenean kings, which had been built on the Acropolis before the time of the Parthenon. The temple was not a house in which a congregation worshiped. For this purpose an altar was placed outside before the eastern entrance. The temple housed

the gigantic 40-foot effigy of Athena garbed in military costume. Although it has been lost, we know that Phidias made this sculpture with gold for the dress and armor, and ivory for the flesh. A ship's mast was used for the interior armature. Entrance into the sanctuary was reserved for the priests and privileged laymen on certain occasions. The laity were permitted to look into the sanctuary through enormous eastern doors.

The orientation of the temple was worked out with considerable care, as was the case with all ancient sacred architecture. The temple runs roughly east and west. The central axis is slightly south of east, so that on Athena's birthday the rising sun shone directly through the doors onto her effigy. The location of the temple on the Acropolis was also calculated to permit the widest view from the city below.

The form of the Parthenon (Figs. 3.6 and 3.7) is that of the traditional Greek temple. It has a walled interior divided into two parts. The windowless eastern chamber housing the cult statue was known as the *Hecatompedos* or 100-foot, because of its 100-foot length. As seen on the plan, there was an interior two-step level colonnade which continued from the doorway behind the statue and created an aisle that permitted view of the statue from the rear. Natural illumination was provided by the huge doorway 32 feet high and 13 feet wide. Beneath the double-pitched roof was a flat ceiling of wooden beams. The sanctuaries of the Greek temples are historically interesting because they are large enclosed areas, even though their space was not consciously shaped with the expressive power of later periods, such as Imperial Rome and Gothic France. The statue of Athena completely dominated, if it did not crowd, the sanctuary. The second and smaller western room was the storage area for ritual objects, important votive offerings, and the

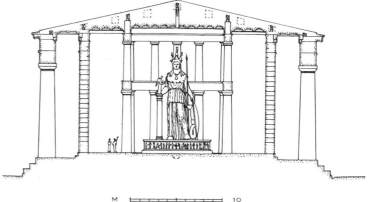

3.7 The Parthenon. Cross section (right) and detail of longtitudinal view of the sanctuary (below), omitting the storage chamber. Reconstruction by Gorham Phillips Stevens. The American School of Classical Studies, Athens.

M [scale] 10

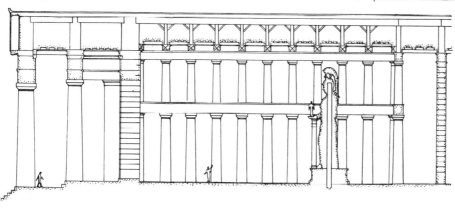

M [scale] 10

treasury of the Athenian League and the state. It was known as the Parthenon, "Chamber of the Virgin," from which the whole temple took its name.

The Classical Greek architects believed that the splendor of a temple should not be confined to the interior, and the most inspired part of the Parthenon's design is its exterior. This may be explained by the fact that the ritual was conducted out of doors and the temple was intended to be visually accessible. The worship of the Greek gods did not require the secretive ceremonials of ancient Egypt. The presence of important sculptural programs in the pediments and metopes also suggests that the temple was more extroverted than introverted in its address to the community.

The exterior pentelic marble columns were a shimmering white; metopes and triglyphs were brightly painted, and the horizontal architrave blocks above the columns were hung with military trophies.

The temple was mounted on a three-stepped base which set it apart from the earth and the viewer, much as a pedestal does for a sculpture. The height of the steps was intended to discourage their being climbed. The sanctuary's outer wall and gates were ringed by a handsome perimeter of columns. These columns and the horizontal architectural elements above them are of what is called the Doric order. The names and precise location of these parts are given in the diagram shown as Figure 3.8.

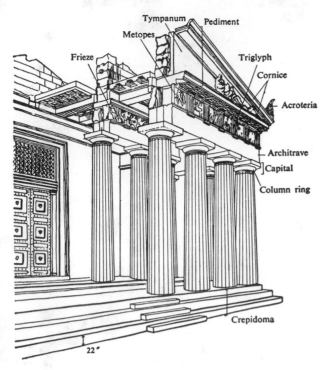

Frieze — Tympanum — Pediment
Metopes
Triglyph
Cornice
Acroteria
Architrave
Capital
Column ring
Crepidoma
22'

3.8 The Parthenon. Sectional Drawing. (After N. Yalouris)

VALUES EMBODIED IN THE PARTHENON

The Parthenon tells us more about the human than the metaphysical nature of the Greeks. Even in its ruined form it reminds us of the power of human intellect and of the Greeks' reverence for Athena as the goddess of wisdom. The words of the fifth-century Athenian philosopher Anaxagoras could have been inscribed upon the Parthenon: "All things were in chaos when mind arose and made order." The temple affirms its makers' belief in a rational unity of reality and is analogous to the Greek view of the world as ultimately knowable, static, and symmetrical. A little over a century before, temple sculpture had imaged the demonic and evidenced traces of apprehension, if not fear, of the unknown. The Parthenon expresses man's confidence in himself, in his place in the world, and in the dignity of his gods, who were human

as well as divine. To translate these generalities into the specifics of the temple it is important to take in the whole of the architecture. The Parthenon, like Classical sculpture, was designed according to the Greek ideal of eurythmy, or the good and pleasing appearance of the whole. It gave the impression of compactness and completeness. Its beauty lay in the impossibility of adding, subtracting, or altering any part without disrupting the whole. Its ideal rhythm consisted of a lucid repetition of similar elements, like the columns that in themselves have a harmonious stability. Oswald Spengler has described the classical as that which can be taken in at a single glance. The Parthenon's design gives itself readily and easily to the eye. We are immediately aware of parts, their tidy disciplined relation to other parts and to the whole, not unlike the relationships making up the polis, or Greek city-state. Each part has its own identity, as seen in the nomenclature of the Doric order. If separated from the totality, the part and its location could be quickly identified. Parts with corresponding identity have a like measure and proportion to the whole, constituting the Greek ideal of symmetry. Given one half of a Greek temple it would be possible to predict or reconstruct the other half. Beauty and nature were interpretable to the Classical Greeks in terms of a conceptually perfect human body. Such a body was composed of harmoniously disposed and interrelated parts and was symmetrical. The capitals of the columns effect a subtle transition from the vertical to the horizontal in the manner of a finely modeled torso in sculpture. The taste for a round, tapered, and fluted column is indicative of a preference for the animate and sensitive proportioning found in the best fifth-century figure sculpture. The intervals between the column axes can be expressed in terms of a column diameter and the width of a man's shoulders. The very scale of the Parthenon is more humane than is that of the mammoth Egyptian temples. Like the perfect human form, the form of the Parthenon is based upon a mathematical module and a consistent set of ratios. There was an Athenian foot, and Professor William Dinsmoor's meticulous measure of the Parthenon has revealed Ictinus' use of mathematics rather than impulse to achieve the structure's unprecedented and perfected visual harmony. The ratio of the temple's height to its width on the east and west is 4 to 9, its width to its length is also 4 to 9, and that of the column diameter to the interval between columns is 9 to 4. The seventeen columns on the long sides are two times plus one the eight columns on the east and west, again giving a 9 to 4 relation. With but one module and ratio, the architect was able to calculate mentally all of the proportions and dimensions of his entire building. (One sheet of parchment cost a day's wage.) It is likely that Pythagoras' work in numbers and his belief that everything could be expressed by them influenced Ictinus. Numbers were believed eternal and incorruptible because they existed outside of the senses. Looking patiently at the Parthenon permits both the visualizing and the intuition of its proportional system, which induces a strong sense of equanimity and of the structure's rightness.

Further separating Ictinus' Parthenon from earlier Greek temples are the excellence and thoroughness of the optical refinements. There is not a straight line in the entire building. Each step is curved convexly, forming the perimeter of a tremendous circle with a diameter, according to Professor Dinsmoor, of 3½ miles. The purpose of this curving edge was to correct the optical distortion of sagging that one experiences when looking at a long straight line parallel to the earth. The entire upper area of the temple above the columns had a similar curve. The columns have been concentrated near the corners in order to provide a visual arrest when the eye moves along the peripheral colonnades. (It also serves to align the triglyphs and metopes with the columns in such a fashion that two triglyphs can meet at the corner.) The four corner columns have been thickened so as not to appear spindly or narrower than the others when seen against the sky. The columns themselves have been given an entasis, or slight swelling, as they rise from the base, to prevent the optical distortion of concavity induced by uncorrected vertical lines. The columns are tilted back slightly to prevent the illusion that the building is falling forward. Use of these optical correctives, which required a consummate knowledge of mathematics, prevented the beauty of the temple from being impaired by the fallibility of the human senses; the eyes do not deceive the mind in the experience of perfection.

The Parthenon was further enhanced by the superb sculpture in the form of a continuous frieze (Fig. 3.9), metopes, two tympana areas, and decorative acroteria or roof sculptures. (These included lion heads and a sculpture group at the apex of the pediment, all of which have been lost.) The metope sculptures (Fig. 3.10), which dealt not with the recent Persian war but with legendary victories won by the ancestors of the Athenians over the Lapiths, Centaurs, and Trojans, lent animation to the horizontal and vertical lines of the temple. The metope figures are in strong relief and in a wide variety of movements at variance with the axes of their frames. Some of the figures slightly overlap their borders, which reduces the severity of the edges. The tympana contained sculptural representations of the birth of Athena from the brow of Zeus on the east, and the victory of Athena over Poseidon on the west. These sculptures were supervised by Phi-

3.9 The Parthenon. Detail of the Panathenaic frieze.

3.10 The Parthenon. Detail showing triglyphs and metope. (Photo: Hirmer)

dias. Many of them were painted and in the round. Isolated, each figure has an autonomy, but within a group, it fits into the whole. Despite the magnificence of these sculptures, they did not overbalance the temple as a whole but served as a crowning religious and esthetic element.

Just as the Parthenon pays tribute to the high ideals and ordering instinct of the Classical Greek mind, so does it also recall the limitations of that art and its culture. Ictinus was respectful of tradition but not a slave to it. Within definite limits he refined and improved what had come before, but he did not revolutionize Greek temple architecture. The engineering of the Parthenon is extremely conservative; its post-and-lintel system was millennia old. The Greeks knew of the arch and the dome but associated certain traditional forms with their sacred buildings, and there was no such structural chance-taking as in later Rome or the medieval period of western Europe. It is recorded that Ictinus, like other great artists of his age, wrote a book about his work. Typical of Classical Art is the desire to codify what is perfect. There is no esthetic or engineering advance beyond the Parthenon in Greek architecture. The Greek ordering impulse found it hard to adapt to the tensions and changing times that followed. The cool aloofness and exquisite closed perfection of the Parthenon, like Classical sculpture, do not partake of the qualities of variety, unexpected emotional warmth, and psychological range encountered in ancient daily living. Professor Herbert Muller points out that the Classical Greeks had no respect for empirical knowledge, no sense of history (as shown by the metope mythical reliefs). There are many links missing between the Parthenon and life in fifth-century Athens. The sculpture and architecture sequences never achieve the profound interdependent psychological and formal cohesiveness in groupings found in later western medieval art or in normal human relationships.

Perhaps it is coincidental, but part of the downfall of Athens was her inability to sustain successful enduring alliances with other countries. Political misfortune and disunity caused the initiators of the Parthenon, Pericles and Phidias, to fall from power, the latter ironically and falsely imprisoned for stealing gold from Athena's statue. Longer than the city-state that produced it, the Parthenon and its noble but limited ideals have endured as a beautiful abstraction. Before moving to the Gothic cathedral, remember Spengler's observation that the Greeks' mode of worship was a pious observation of form, not soaring aspiration.

The Gothic Cathedral . .

The best approach to the Gothic cathedral in France is that of the medieval pilgrim who, traveling on foot to a city such as Chartres, first saw the distant cathedral spires across the fields. Physically, esthetically, and spiritually, the cathedral still dominates the town (Fig. 3.11). The cathedrals that rose above the medieval houses glorified not only Christ and the Virgin, but also the cities that erected them. The cathedrals symbolized man's awareness of the divine as well as his own self-consciousness. The very phenomenon of cathedral building presupposed the extensive development of cities in the eleventh and twelfth centuries. These cities in turn reflected important stages in European economic growth, the accumulation of wealth, and organization of labor, administrative efficiency, developments such as horseshoe

3.11 Chartres Cathedral viewed from the city.

nails and pulleys in mechanics, transportation, and communications, and the establishment of relative political stability. There also emerged significant intellectual resources and activity outside the monasteries.

During the twelfth and thirteenth centuries the one-hundred-mile area around Paris was covered by what one medieval writer called a "snowfall of cathedrals." Cathedral building was an economic expenditure surpassed only by war. Today it staggers the imagination that a city such as Chartres, having a probable population of ten thousand in the twelfth century, should undertake, over a period of less than a century, the erection of a single structure that today would cost in excess of seventy-five million dollars. While satisfying civic pride, the Gothic cathedral was above all a gift to God. The rivalry between French cities to outdo one another in size and magnificence of their cathedrals was undoubtedly motivated in part by secular concerns,

such as economic benefits, but the deep and measureless religious faith and optimism of the builders was the prime mover. Like their cities, no two cathedrals are the same. In addition to their size, the sheer variety of the Gothic cathedral's architecture prohibits us from writing about a fixed type as we could about the Greek temple. This variety is in itself evidence against the view of the unity, conservatism, and lethargy of medieval society. There was only one Church, however, and the cathedral symbolizes basic spiritual unification. The so-called Gothic period is one of consistent change; architectural styles seem constantly in process, reminding us of the vitality as well as discord of the Middle Ages.

The word *cathedral* comes from the latin *cathedra*, and means that the bishop's seat is within. The bishops and their urban dioceses affirmed rivalry with the monasteries and their ascetic world-denying doctrines. The richly ornamented and elaborately designed exteriors of the cathedrals reflect a more affirmative attitude toward life on earth and recognition of the civil community than do the introverted monastic churches. From no matter which prospect within the town one views or approaches the cathedral, the forcefulness and compelling variety of its design make themselves felt. There was no prescribed approach, no sacred way by which the worshiper had to proceed to the front of the House of God. In their original state, the cathedrals were not isolated by the open square completely girdling the building that we see today (Fig. 3.12). A cathedral might have squares on the west and north or south, but usually the city's secular buildings encroached directly upon the walls of the cathedral, on its chapter house and cemetery. This tight proximity of the secular and the sacred parallels the role that the cathedral played in the community.

The Gothic cathedral was more

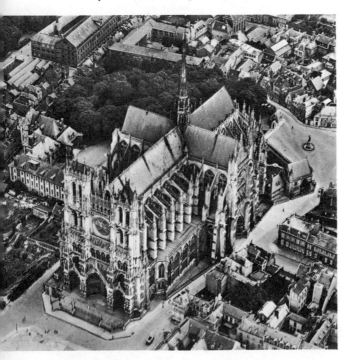

3.12 Amiens Cathedral. Seen from the air.

than the religious focus of its society. Its bells regulated the day's secular activities just as the significant events in the life of Christ, the Virgin, and the saints provided the calendar for great fairs, festivals, and the performance of the mystery plays. The cathedral met the public's needs and love for splendor and spectacle, serving as the backdrop and stage not only for its daily religious drama, but also for public festivals that were often irreverent in nature. Public explosions that occurred in the Feast of the Fools were looked upon by churchmen as safety valves against the severe prohibitions of Christian dogma. It was thus that on specific occasions, gambling and sausage-eating at the high altar were permitted, donkeys were worshiped in the sanctuary amidst the incense of burning shoe leather, or the laity might elect a mock pope, dress up as monks, and pervert the church service. The House of the Father served at times as a playground for his children. During the important fairs that brought wealth to the city and funds for the cathedral's construction, the Church-owned and tax-free property was used by the merchants. The city of Chartres was able to build its cathedral because of income from secular fairs that attracted people from all over France, and also because of the wealth attracted by the sale of indulgences, gifts to enshrine the sacred relic of the Virgin's Cloak, and the enormous sums accruing to the bishop and deacons from land holdings and tithes. It was not unusual to have business transactions conducted within the nave of the cathedral, and on occasion, wine was sold in the crypt of Chartres. The building of the rood screen between the nave and eastern portion of the church was partly due to the need for privacy by the priests when they celebrated the mass. The silence that we encounter today in the cathedrals contrasts with the clatter of voices about which the

priests complained in medieval times. The cathedral nave served severally as a lecture and concert hall, as a repository for important civic documents, as an arsenal, a municipal museum, and a trysting place. In many instances the bishop or deacons owned only the eastern portion of the church and not the nave, which belonged to the city.

THE ARCHITECTS

The fact that we do not know the names of many architects who worked on the cathedrals does not support the view that they were anonymous in their time, or of the "folk," or priesthood. The names of many medieval architects have survived because of the medieval distaste for anonymity, the great esteem in which master builders were held, and the means by which they were honored. Some architects, like Robert of Luzarches of Amiens and Hugh Libergier of Rheims, were entombed in their churches and their images engraved on the burial slab. Some were given degrees, for instance, a doctorate in stonework. The name of the architect might be inscribed in a floor medallion at the end of a labyrinth incised on the nave's pavement, like that at Chartres. By crawling along the labyrinth on their knees, those who could not make the pilgrimage to Jerusalem were able to make the journey symbolically and, not coincidentally, pay their respects to the builder. The master builders of the cathedrals, the equivalents of present-day architects, frequently came from distinguished lay families, were trained by their fathers, and had roughly a middle-class and free status. They seemed to have been pious men of good moral character and education who were relatively well off financially. They had opportunity for travel as their services were often vied for internationally. Their education was in the craft of masonry or carpentry, Euclidean geometry, drafting, Latin and French, and various secrets of building that were passed on from one generation to the next. Much of their education was empirical, and for centuries Gothic architecture developed by trial and error. The notebook of a thirteenth-century architect, Villard de Honnecourt, reveals a broad curiosity that encompassed machines, sculpture, furniture, details of buildings, and animals. The master builder could be versed in the making of objects and ornaments, furniture and fortifications, as well as churches and castles.

The function of the master builder was to conceive the plan in consultation with a priest or the Church canons, decide how the edifice was to be built, and oversee its construction. He was often responsible for selecting materials; he procured the labor, estimated costs and amounts, settled labor disputes, and saw to the welfare of his artisans. By the thirteenth century the master builder needed only to give orders.

Because of prohibitive costs, plans were not drawn on parchment until the fourteenth century. Earlier, drafting of details or sections was usually done on plaster slabs or wood, and these were not saved. Not until the fifteenth century, with Brunelleschi's Pazzi Chapel, was the totality of the building planned entirely step by step in advance. Many of the details of building and sculpture were left to experienced and trusted masons, carpenters, and sculptors. When an architect died, his successor respected what had already been done, but while he might continue unfinished sections according to the original plan, he might also introduce new ideas. Chartres cathedral lacks a homogeneous style; its sponsors did not insist upon any architectural consistency other than excellence. It is a peculiarity of the Gothic style that it is capable of absorbing such a heterogeneity of modes.

While the cathedral impresses us with its richness of symbolism, the basic problems confronting the master builder were practical. He had to adapt his plan to demands of the liturgy and the performance of the canonical offices; provide for the proper disposition of the relic and several altars; facilitate movement of the congregation, and make provision for the delivery of the sermon.

THE MEANING OF THE GOTHIC CATHEDRAL

The extent to which conscious symbolism entered directly into the form of the cathedral is difficult to assess. The architects were literate, educated townsmen in contact with the intellectual, spiritual, and lay leaders of the community. They consulted with Church canons, bishops, theologians, and priests on the theological program for the sculpture. The meanings of measure and light as interpreted by great theologians of the past were also an available resource, but that these interpretations were consistently and systematically translated into prime elements of architectural design is conjectural. Of great influence were the already existing religious buildings, as well as the practical problems of erecting and supporting enormous vaults over one hundred feet from the floor of the nave. Official handbooks of Church symbolism did not exist for the artist to consult. While there were twelfth- and thirteenth-century important writings by such men as Durandus, they were not dogma, and the literary symbols contained within the treatises gave no assistance in matters of style or, in many cases, of the shapes of parts. The cathedrals inspired reverent fantasies in many writers who worshiped within them, and their several interpretations of the same architectural features are after the fact of their having been made and are not consistent. What adds to the wonder of the cathedrals, and their intellectual greatness in history, is that the architects did give symbolic form to the highest ideals and a great portion of the spirit of their age. Acquaintance with the Gothic cathedrals makes us aware of their profound and sometimes elusive connection with societies that produced the Crusades, the feudal system, and universities and that enriched the history of science and philosophy, contributed significantly to jurisprudence, and fashioned the poetry of the troubadours. To comprehend the meaning of the Gothic cathedral in its broadest and deepest sense, all of these activities would have to be explored, as modern scholarship is now doing with exciting results. Only a few references to these discoveries can be made here, however.

The Gothic cathedral was the House of God, but unlike the House of Athena, the deity in tangible form did not dwell within. The cathedral was an ambivalent symbol of Christ, the heavenly Jerusalem, and the universe. Its magnificence in terms of the treasure expended upon it was deemed appropriate to its function as an offering from the faithful and as the spiritual residence of Christ or the Virgin. It was through the cathedral that man was made aware of the invisible and infinite, and that the divine became immanent. The master builder sought to contrive a setting that would so attune the thoughts and feelings of the worshiper that he could realize the most important event of his life, the soul's communion with God.

MEANINGS AND ORIGINS OF PARTS OF THE CATHEDRAL

The West Façade. All of the major parts of the cathedral have a history that extends back into the Middle Ages or, in some cases, into antiquity. Their assimilation into the cathedral was a process not

only of formal adaptation and change, but of meaning (Fig. 3.13). "The Gateway to Heaven," as the west façade was called, may trace its history back to Syrian churches of the sixth and seventh centuries and to Roman Imperial palaces faced by twin-towered portals. As the late Baldwin Smith has shown in a brilliant study, towered gateways were used as entrances to royal cities and abbeys in Carolingian times and were the locus of impressive ceremonial receptions for the king's advent. Christian artists, in mosaics, ivories, and manuscript illuminations, used a bejeweled twin-towered portal to signify the idea of

3.13 Chartres Cathedral. Façade. Courtesy of the French Government Tourist Office.

3.14 Chartres Cathedral. Detail of Rose Window, west façade.

a triumphal gateway and the House of God. The translation of the early Christian basilica into a twin-towered edifice must be seen in the light of Charlemagne's revival of Roman political symbolism and his desire to show his supremacy over the Church as well as the state. The emperor's symbolical participation in the Church service and his exalted authority were indicated in the towered façades of Carolingian and certain Romanesque churches by a solarium, or balcony, on which was located his throne and behind which was placed a large circular window. Sun symbolism was equated with the king as well as with Christ. By the late thirteenth century, however, the symbolism of the west façade was entirely transferred to Christ. Nevertheless the façades of such Gothic cathedrals as Chartres with their recessed portals that had evolved in Carolingian times, their "galleries of kings," their circular windows, and their towers still bear the impress of earthly kings.

The Circular Window. The origin and meaning of the great circular window of the west façade has been explored by Helen Dow. This English scholar has

shown that circular windows go back to Babylon and had been known in Europe since Roman times. Unlike the misnamed Gothic "rose windows," with few exceptions the circular windows lacked stone tracery until the building of the Church of St. Denis around 1140. The basic form of the rose window (Fig. 3.14) found at Chartres may have originated in old schemas of the Wheel. The great Byzantine chandeliers, or polycandelons of pierced metal discs, were used in France by the twelfth century as either hanging or standing lamps. Lamps lent themselves to the sun and light symbolism that had accrued to Christ in the Middle Ages. Its circular form was rich in meaning, signifying virtue, eternity, God, or the Church. The great circular window also took the form and associations of the Wheel of Fortune by which Christian virtue could be contrasted with the vicissitudes and transient nature of earthly existence. Ezekiel's vision of the wheel made the window appropriate to the Scriptures. The prominence of the window as well as its form symbolized the eternal and righteous eye of God. (The word *nave* means *ship* in Latin, the window being, therefore, the ship's guiding eye.) Light and justice seem to have been two of the most important meanings of the window. As in its use by Charlemagne, the window surrounded by the many sculptures of saints conveyed the concept of a king surrounded by his armies. The full meaning of this interpretation becomes apparent when the sculptural program of the west façade of Chartres is explained.

The Sculptural Program of the Chartres West Façade. The purpose of the sculptural programs occupying the honored positions around and immediately above the doors and in the stained-glass windows was to manifest Church dogma. That these sculptures were didactic or self-evidently symbolic is questionable, for it seems that the faithful relied upon the spoken word for their instruction in dogma, and hence in the meaning of art. That theological programs were actually planned and carried out in cathedrals has long been known. Adolph Katzenellenbogen has contributed an outstanding study of the sculptural program of the west façade of Chartres (Fig. 3.15), showing that the contents of the three tympana, or semicircular relief panels over the doors, present Christ in his dual nature of God and Man, and as the source of divine wisdom.

At the far right Christ is shown seated on the lap of the enthroned Virgin, indicating Her role in His incarnation. In the pointed vaults flanking the tympanum are representations of the seven liberal arts; grammar, dialectic, rhetoric, arithmetic, music, geometry, and astronomy. These are the intellectual means by which to attain an awareness of divine wisdom. The Virgin, esteemed as the seat of wisdom, be-

came an inspiration and guide of these arts, indicating the growth of humanistic study within the medieval Church. The left tympanum shows the Ascension of Christ. Its flanking vaults contain symbols of the zodiac and of manual labor. The concepts illustrated here are that of Christ's transcendence and rule of time and that of the active life of physical labor that, balanced with the contemplative life of learning, led the faithful towards a knowledge of God. The central tympanum shows the second advent of Christ and the Last Judgment.

Immediately below the tympana, on the rectangular lintel, are arranged the twelve prophets who prophesied Christ's second coming and assist at the Judgment. Flanking the doors of the Royal Portal are the jamb figures whose purpose is to proclaim the sympathetic concord that exists between the Church and state and between the Old and the New Testament, and the illustrious lineage of the French monarchy. It was common practice in the Middle Ages

3.15 Chartres Cathedral. Royal Portal, west façade, mid twelfth century. Courtesy of French Cultural Services.

to show past or present kings and queens of France as important personages from the Old and New Testament. This emphasized that royalty was a defender of the Church and enhanced their public esteem. In art, heroes of the Church and state, not their actual deeds, were shown. The implication was that the virtuous qualities of the Old Testament royalty had been continued by the monarchs of France. This was part of the medieval preoccupation with searching for parallels between the present and past, the old and new, the visible and invisible. The jamb figures, which date from about the mid-twelfth century, have a columnar alignment, and their appearance and purpose suggest that they form a second wall by which the Church is strengthened and defended. One must pass between the predecessors of Christ on the jambs before reaching Him; this signified the old leading to the new. To pass through the door was to move toward God through Christ, for Christ said, "I am the door. Whoever enters me will be saved." The gallery above the circular window contains effigies of French kings, hence the name "gallery of kings" (see Fig. 3.13). The gallery itself may have derived from the earlier medieval and ancient palace "window of appearances" in which the ruler presented himself to the public. Where the kings protected the western front of the church, the bishops were imaged as defenders of the flanking sides.

The Bay System. The bays are the rectangular cubelike divisions that include each vault and four piers. Professor Walter Horn has traced the origin of the bay system (Figs. 3.16 and 3.17) in medieval churches to early medieval secular wooden architecture used for all-purpose structures, episcopal tithe barns, and houses. A few bay-divided timber churches survive from the Middle Ages. In many of the sections of medieval Europe, residences, mar-

kets, and barns were structurally interchangeable. Tithe barns were often of tremendous size, and their construction in regular units permitted considerable lengths. The early Christian basilicas did not possess bays, and their entrance into religious architecture, probably during the ninth century, is another important example of religious architecture drawing upon secular sources. (The Christian basilica itself had derived from Roman public buildings.) The addition of the bay to the basilican form skeletalized and partitioned the interior into similar parts, thus opening up important possibilities for expressive design articulation and for the use of geometrical or arithmetical schemas to organize the inside. The bay system was valued by the builders because of its familiarity and ease of handling. It met the Gothic needs of multiplicity of parts and of the hierarchical implications of the bay order.

THE PLAN AND MEASURE

As in ancient and earlier medieval times, the orientation of the Gothic cathedral was meant to place the building in harmony with the universe (Fig. 3.18). The apse, containing the altar that symbolized Christ's tomb, was oriented consistently to the east, which signified rebirth. The western end was traditionally associated with death and evil, and it was on this entrance that the Last Judgment was carved. The north was identified with cold and darkness, the world of the old order. The south signified the new dispensation. In addition to its symbolic value, the demands of the liturgy caused retention of the old cross plan; it facilitated procession through the nave, provided a large area for the choir east of the transept and ample space for the altar, and made feasible side aisles to accommodate the pilgrims who came to venerate the relics in the chapels. The basic

3.16   Mereville, France. Market hall, fifteenth century. Courtesy of Walter Horn. (Photo: Roberts)

3.17   Chartres Cathedral. View of the nave looking toward the apse. (Photo: Marburg)

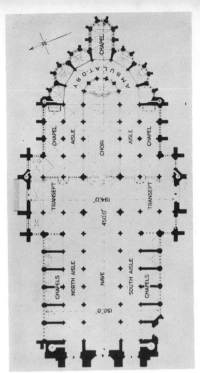

3.18 Amiens Cathedral. Plan.

plan of the Gothic cathedral had emerged in Carolingian times with the addition to the basilican nave, aisles, apse, and occasional transept of the crypt, choir, and radiating chapels. The strong internal divisions of the church's plan signified the hierarchical order and authority of the clergy and its relation to the laity, who were prohibited access to the choir and altar areas.

Scholars who have taken pains to draw accurate ground plans of medieval churches have found that in certain cases it is possible to discover scientific organization. One of the trade secrets of the master builder was a module on which he established both the scale and the proportions of his building. It seems doubtful that entire Gothic buildings were organized according to a single or consistent geometrical or arithmetical progression, but by the fifteenth century Brunelleschi was to do so in his Florentine buildings.

Using any polygon, the master builder worked out the problem of building a tower and effecting the transition from a square base to a round spire. While all builders recognized the use of geometry as an aid to building, there were undoubtedly some who by temperament sought to use it extensively in a way that guaranteed them "true measure" and thereby heightened the cathedral's symbolic analogy to the measure that cemented the universe. Otto von Simson argued strongly for the latter instance in his study of Chartres. His findings showed a basic proportion of 5 to 8 was utilized in the plan and elevation of the cathedral. (Stretched ropes or measured poles belonging to the builder were used.) Von Simson supports his argument by the fact that God was frequently referred to and even imaged as a geometer. Church literature before and during the time of the cathedrals is rich in its religious interpretation of numbers and geometry; to cite but two examples, the triangle symbolized the trinity, the square the relation of the Father to the Son. In mystical numerology, almost any number could be interpreted as revealing some aspect of divinity or dogma. Numbers and geometry were thought to be important means by which the intellect and workings of God could be made intelligible to human understanding. We see the Gothic designer's taste for enumeration in towers, windows, piers, balustrades, arcades, statues, doors. The parts of the cathedral lend themselves to counting, but not to a single program of interpretation or numerical translation. Qualitatively, rather than in a literal quantitative way, the master builder again realized a vital preoccupation of his time.

THE INTERIOR AND LIGHT

The dedicatory services performed in the sanctuary of the cathedral drew upon three principal Biblical sources to link the building to the past. The first was the Temple of Solomon (Chronicles II, 2–6), the second was the Temple of Ezekiel, and the third was the description of the Heavenly Jerusalem by St. John. While the Bible does not describe what Solomon's temple looked like, it does record its covering of gold and precious gems, and this description may have influenced St. John. It is the latter's writing that presents the most striking analogy to the celestial city:

And the building of the wall of it was of jasper; and the city was pure gold, like unto clear glass. And the foundations of the wall of the city was garnished with all manner of precious stones. . . . And the city had no need of the sun, neither of the moon, to shine in it; for the glory of God did lighten it.

Other Biblical sources speak of glass walls, and the increased use of stained glass in the twelfth and thirteenth centuries may have been an attempt to strengthen the analogy of appearance between the church and the Heavenly Jerusalem. The cathedral's exterior reflected much of the religious and secular history of life on earth. The interior is the mystical heart of the cathedral where God's epiphany takes place.

To enter into the initial darkness of the cathedral from the sunlit exterior is to re-experience the medieval worshiper's sense of movement from the mundane to the celestial world (see Fig. 3.17). Perhaps the most exalted efforts of imagination and inspired creation of the Gothic builders are the internal colored light and idealized space of the cathedral. Light and color are both form and symbol, the style and content of Gothic religious architecture. The suffused polychromed glow never permitted, when the churches had their original complement of windows, total revelation of the space, detail, or significantly, the measure of the interior. There was no comparable space or light in any other type of medieval building. The space and light and the music of the cathedral interior transported the worshiper from familiar sounds, illumination and shadow, scale, textures, and distances, into a world of intricate melodies of sound and color, changing vistas, elusive surfaces, and heights not determined by his own measure. The quick change from sunlight to darkness impelled the visitor to retard his pace and devote himself to penetrating and searching what seemed veiled from the eyes. The stained-glass windows were intended to keep out almost all the exterior light and all references to the earthly world. Their task was to elevate and enlighten the mind and soul. Seen from the floor of the nave, windows sixty feet away did not lend themselves to easy reading, and details of the rose window are unintelligible. Within the relative obscurity of the interior, the sonorous reds and blues could be fully apprehended by the eye, and gold achieved finer luminosity. The piers, walls, and vaults reflected the diffused shifting colors of the windows, contradicting the nature of the stone.

The brilliance of the original cathedrals, however, was not confined to windows alone. In the thirteenth century, Durandus wrote:

The ornaments of the nave consist of dorsals, tapestry, mattings, and cushions of silk, purple and the like. The ornaments of the choir consist of dorsals, tapestry, carpets and cushions. Dorsals are hangings of cloth at the back of the clergy. Mattings, for their feet. Tapestry is likewise strewed under the feet, particularly under the feet of Bishops, who ought to trample worldly things under their feet. Cushions are placed on the seats or benches of the choir.

But it was the light from the windows that inspired the greatest awe and inspired praise by Church theologians of the cathedral's "bright" and "lucid" structure. God was perfect light into which no mortal eye could look. The light man could see was only a pale reflection of God. Light was the source and requirement of beauty, the means by which God manifested His presence and creativity to man. Light passing through the windows symbolized the Incarnation of Christ. Light symbolism was inherited, from earlier Christian churches, and was known and used in ancient times. The power and uniqueness of its use in the Gothic cathedral inspired the great Abbot Suger, builder of St. Denis, to record his mystical ascension to God by means of meditation on the light of his cathedral.

> Thus when—out of my delight in the beauty of the house of God—the loveliness of the many-colored gems has called me away from external cares, and worthy meditation has induced me to reflect, transferring that which is material to that which is immaterial, on the diversity of sacred virtues; then it seems to me that I see myself dwelling, as it were, in some strange region of the universe which neither exists entirely in the slime of the earth nor entirely in the purity of Heaven; and that, by the grace of God, I can be transported from this inferior to that higher world in an anagogical manner.

STYLE

In addition to colored light, soaring spaces, and complex views within the cathedral, other distinguishing components of the Gothic cathedral style include the pointed and occasionally rounded arches, the ribbed vault, and the flying buttress, all having been known or developed during preceding architectural periods. These elements are usually joined in strong rhythmic numerical sequences. The subordination of parts to larger parts and of larger parts to the whole has a strong feudal and hierarchic character. The same elements and sequences recur in various scales and admixtures with other motifs. It is difficult to separate the parts from their contexts because of their sequential arrangement and

3.19 Structural diagram of a Gothic cathedral.

the density of the sequential groups. Nevertheless, the viewer is always conscious of looking at the parts of a greater but incomplete whole. Unlike the Parthenon, no single prospect permits comprehension of the cathedral's total design. Like Gothic sacred music, the composition of a cathedral is polyphonic: the simultaneous combination of a number of parts each constituting an individual melody that harmonizes with the others. There is some evidence to suggest further analogy in the use of mathematics to proportion musical and architectural structures. Surveys indicate, however, that many builders did not feel obliged to perpetuate older traditions and practiced their own variations of proportions to achieve more impressive visual harmonies.

To a greater extent than in early medieval architecture, the Gothic cathedral reveals its skeletal armature, the multiple play of its forces, and dispositions of thrusts and weight (Figs. 3.19 and 3.20). The massive walls of the militant Romanesque churches were largely dematerialized by the increased replacement of stone by glass between the main piers that support the vaults. The cradling action of the flying buttresses involves the external structure in a new way and lends a muscular appearance to the exterior.

The plan of a Gothic cathedral (Fig. 3.18) shows the enclosure of the nave and aisles to be a continuous series of points, a regular constellation of piers, connected by thin, parallel walls. While the medieval architect may not have used the word or have thought of space in terms of the modern architect, he had a great feeling for the effectiveness of certain distances between walls. Villard de Honnecourt's notebook shows a primary concern with graphically designed screenlike walls (Fig. 3.21). No doubt much of the physical character of the cathedral was determined by the engineering functions of load and support; the building's width was probably related to what the builder felt he could safely vault and buttress. It is too limited a view, however, to look upon the architect's

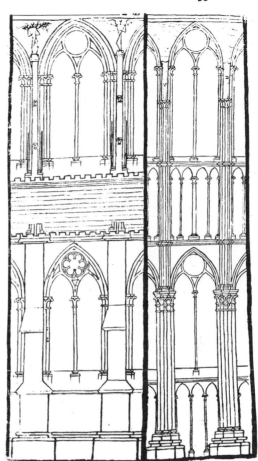

3.21 De Honnecourt. Sketch of exterior and interior elevations, nave of Reims Cathedral.

3.20 **Chartres** Cathedral. **Exterior view of the** buttresses from the south side.

intent as being only a structural tour de force. Many design decisions, such as the addition of pinnacles to buttresses, the clustering of slender shafts to the main piers, the use of pointed arches, and probably the ribs of the vaults, were intended to enhance the whole and increase its expressiveness. (Fig. 3.22). There is greater articulation and sculptural treatment of the piers than is necessary for their function as support, for example. The proportioning of nave arcade, triforium, and clerestory resulted from esthetic and perhaps symbolic decisions intended to bring the building closer to visual and intellectual perfection. Much

3.22 Chartres Cathedral. View of the vaults at the crossing of the nave and transept.

of the emotional experience of entering a cathedral is the rational and intuitive re-experiencing of the builder's logic, which he took pains to make available to the senses. The master builder's rich inventiveness with three-dimensional form, his several adjustments, alterations, and additions made beyond structural necessity, have occa-

sioned the view that in the Gothic cathedral function follows form.

The engineering and design evolution of the cathedral generally meant better vault buttressing, more intricate vaults for visual purposes, greater consistency in using oblong bays, stress of the vertical design, and a strong trend toward a greater multiplication and homogeneity of parts.

This tendency towards homogenization and consistency can be seen in the increased unification of the spaces of the aisles and the nave, the contraction of the transepts, the single roof line, and the extension of the buttress design from the sides completely around the apse. There was a less blocklike organization of the interior spaces and a more graceful, though less powerful, progression from the nave to apse. Units involved in a series, such as columns, lost the individuality of the Romanesque period, acquiring similar decoration, proportion, and scale. Even stone cutting became more uniform. Elements aligned vertically took on a common axis and family of shapes, and there was a general reduction of the contrast between horizontal and vertical in favor of the latter.

The great number of fields for sculpture continued throughout the Gothic period. Statues are found not only above and around doors, but in arcades, on buttresses, pinnacles, and towers. Theological programs were reserved for the lower privileged areas around the main portals. The Romanesque tendency of animating capitals, the endings of arches, waterspouts, spires, and areas under the choir seats through human, foliate, and animal forms was maintained. The impression is gained that as cathedral architecture itself became more sculptural, it conveyed its maker's increased affirmation of his place and confidence in the world.

CHAPTER 4

THE

SACRED BOOK

From the fall of Rome until the fourteenth- and fifteenth-century development of easel painting and the printing press, the handmade illuminated and miniature-filled book was the carrier of much of the most important painting and content in Western Christian art. The historical worth and intrinsic beauty of the medieval manuscript are insufficiently recognized by the general public today. We have come to associate great painting with that done on walls and easels, both executed on a fairly large scale. Monumentality in art does not depend upon sheer physical size nor the medium the painter employs. The concept of sacred art, which includes medieval manuscripts, is also alien to present-day experience.

Illuminated medieval manuscripts are precious records of the civilizing history of human society during the so-called Dark Ages. They reveal the varied development in art that prepared the way for Renaissance painting. They evidence the imagination and skill with which medieval

peoples came to terms with their religious environment. Far from being merely a public record of medieval man, this form of medieval painting is also a valuable reflection of his private nature.

SIGNIFICANCE OF THE
SACRED BOOK . . . .

Christ is the only god whose attribute is a book. Early Christian art includes images of a bejeweled throne on which sacred writings have replaced the figure of Christ. Many medieval Christian images show Christ holding a gem-encrusted Bible. Figure 4.1 shows a late tenth-century manuscript in which Christ is depicted giving the sign of benediction with His right hand and holding the sacred book with His left. Christ is shown seated upon the heavens with the earth as His footstool. The extreme formality of the arc alignments and the axial symmetry of Christ comprise a mystical and formal epiphany for the viewer. Al-

4.1   Christ seated upon the heavens. Gospels from St. Maxim, Trier, late tenth century.

though of great importance, the book is secondary to the vortex design in the navel area, possibly a symbolical reference to Christ's divine birth.

The sumptuous type of medieval illuminated manuscript, that used for liturgical purposes, often possessed magnificent book covers on which were set precious stones, pearls, carved ivory panels, enamels, and elaborate gold and silver work. These covers were treasures in themselves, often donated by kings or queens. The precious materials were not intended primarily for visual delight, but rather to create an appropriate binding for the sacred text and to symbolize mystical truths found in the Bible. The color, luminosity, and perfection of precious stones were interpreted as divine attributes or as symbolic of the blood of the martyrs, the Virgin's purity, the radiant presence of God, and so on. In some cases, medieval Christian patrons supplied pagan gems carved in antiquity. The gems were suitably baptized, the pagan spirits exorcised and made Christian.

Medieval artists and patrons did have an esthetic, but it was predominantly religious. Beauty was equated with God. We know from medieval churchmen as well as alchemists that gold was thought to possess magical powers; the color and radiance of gold were the most appropriate light symbolism of the period. Legends sometimes grew up about the miraculous powers of these books, particularly those that had been the property of saints.

A superb example of the magnificence of these book covers exists in the Morgan Library (Fig. 4.2). They were made around 870, possibly in or near Reims. Within a carefully composed geometrical format, reliefs in bossed gold show Christ on the Cross, grieving angels, and above Christ's head, the contracted forms of Mary and John. The thinness and malleability of gold permitted intricate details of the agitated angels and handsome relief modeling of the figure volumes. The quiescent Christ contrasts with both the movement of the attendant figures and the dense variegation of the gems and their setting. The precious stones and pearls are mounted on arcades and lions' feet and are set off by filigree borders.

The key to understanding the reverence accorded the medieval illuminated Bible lies in the meaning of *the Word*. The Gospel of St. John begins: "In the beginning was the Word, and the Word was with God, and the Word was God." The words of the Bible were therefore sacred, and it was the task of the artist to "clothe" the word in the richest and finest manner of which he was capable. Many manuscripts contained gold or silver writing on purple-dyed parchment. In a German book written at the end of the tenth century are the words, "May the Lord clothe your heart

4.2 The Crucifixion. Book cover from the Lindau Gospels, Reims or St. Denis, *c*. 870. Pierpont Morgan Library Manuscript No. 1. Courtesy of the Trustees of the Pierpont Morgan Library.

with this book." The precious nature and garment accorded to the book were in a real sense gifts to God from the faithful.

The meaning of the word in Christianity helps to explain why illuminated manuscripts made of it a cultured and imaginative object to a greater extent than had the ancient scrolls and pagan books. No earlier writings demonstrate ornamentation of the letter, specifically the initial, of a comparable calligraphic beauty. While many ancient books were written in handsome scripts, the manuscripts themselves were not the objects of imagination or fantasy as were medieval Christian manuscripts. Ancient writing knew no privileged words, except for the names of Roman emperors, and the task of writing was

considered to be menial and fit only for slaves. With Christianity, the practice of writing passed from slaves to the priesthood. Certain words and letters did have special value or emphasis to the medieval monk scribe who gloried in the task of writing the Gospel from and for God. For the Christian, the act of writing was in itself sacred.

A medieval Bible was not produced for the private pleasure of a wealthy secular patron. The layman, in fact, did not own hand-illuminated books until the later Middle Ages. Even the royalty that commissioned the most elaborate manuscripts seldom owned the book or appreciated all of its intricate beauty. The book was meant not for the eyes of the public, but for God

4.3 St. Erhard celebrating the Mass. *Uta Codex*, Ratisbon, 1002–1045.

complex religious ordering of life and the universe, and the book reveals the source and basis of that order. The sacred book was more than a collection of stories; *the book was Christ*.

In some medieval churches the Bible was suspended from the ceiling above the altar by gold chains. It was carried in religious processions, and in the East it was placed upon a throne. Usually the Bible stood on the altar, flanked by candles and incense burners. The candles symbolized the light shed by the Gospels. A detail of an early eleventh-century manuscript made in Ratisbon shows Saint Erhard celebrating the mass (Fig. 4.3). To his right can be seen the sacred book, painted in gold, resting on the altar next to the Eucharistic objects. When the book was used during the mass, it was kissed by the bishop. When it was read from, the knights drew their swords as a gesture of their defense of the Scriptures and the people put down their staffs. During investiture ceremonies, the sacred book was laid on the neck of the candidate, indicating that Christ is the head of the bishop, for example, who is about to assume the leadership of the Church.

Clearly the art within the decorated book also is sacred. (Chief exceptions are the nonreligious themes that appear in the margins of the texts.) The miniatures and figure-rendering in medieval manuscripts give a first impression of unreality and naïveté. It should be remembered that the artist was making images of sacred subjects, mystical, in other words, that were as vivid and real in his mind and the minds of the congregation as life on earth.

THE PRODUCTION OF MANUSCRIPTS . . . . . .

At some time between the second and fourth centuries, the book form, or codex,

and for his servants in the Church. (There are many instances in art, such as the sculpture and painting in Egyptian temples or the sculpture and stained glass of the Gothic cathedrals, of works visually inaccessible to the public but exposed to God.)

The sacred book was a privileged object owned by the priest, abbot, or bishop as representative of the Church of God. The congregation was separated from the book just as it was remote from the sacred objects on the altar. They submitted to it for their religious instruction, and the gospels along with the sacraments assumed a core position in medieval Christian life. It is difficult for us to comprehend the dramatic experience of the congregation when the sacred book was produced during the mass, at coronations, or for special blessings. The Gothic cathedrals make manifest the

evolved and replaced the papyrus scroll, a single horizontal sheet with its ends attached to sticks and columns of writing. The ancients had occasionally included text illustrations or technical diagrams in their scrolls; those found in the Egyptian *Book of the Dead* and in Greek and Roman scrolls dealt with medicine, science, and mythology. Roman illustrations were primarily wall paintings reduced to miniature size. With the development of the vellum book that, unlike a scroll, opened from the side, the artist was offered an entire page, a framed picture; composition could be as elaborate as he desired. Vellum also permitted painting upon both sides of the page.

The sustained and imaginative development of the illuminated book stemmed from decorated initials made by Irish monks in the sixth century and from illustrations made by Byzantine artists of Constantinople and Syria. (Bibles had been brought to Ireland by Roman missionaries.) The earliest West European development of book illumination took place in England during the seventh and eighth centuries, principally in Northumbria. During the reign of Charlemagne, illuminated book production accelerated beyond the rate of the previous two centuries in France and England. The Carolingian Renaissance gave the great impetus to illuminated book production in western Europe. In the eighth, ninth, and even tenth centuries, there were specific, clearly defined locales and geographical sources for book production; thereafter production was widespread throughout Europe, and during the eleventh and twelfth centuries, an enormous quantity of manuscripts was produced. The mobility of artists and the books themselves during this latter period makes tracing their origin more difficult.

A great variety of illuminated books was produced during the Middle Ages. Sacred books consisted not only of the Bible, but also of excerpts from the Bible, like the Gospels or the Psalms, calendars of the religious feasts, prayers, blessings, commentaries, and sermons. Generally these books had ornamented covers, frontispieces, canon tables, or tables of concordances of the Gospels, less frequently a full page devoted to the cross, portraits of the evangelists or saints, illuminated initials, and miniatures illustrating the texts. The examples used to illustrate most of the foregoing are drawn from different manuscripts produced at different times and places and are but a slight sampling of the inexhaustible wealth of imagery to emerge from medieval writing rooms.

The notion of the medieval artist as self-effacing and resigned to oblivion is fictive. There exist hundreds of signatures of artists, many accompanied by short prayers, at the end of books, in which the artist asks for praise, avows his reverence, and curses the ardors of his labor and the obdurate nature of his tools. ("I've come to the end, curse this pen and damn this ink.")

Parts of Sacred Books . .

THE FRONTISPIECE

From a great Bible made at the monastery of St. Martin at Tours, France, during the first half of the ninth century comes a painting of the Abbot Vivian presenting the finished manuscript to the Carolingian king (Fig. 4.4). This depiction of an actual historical event is the exception rather than the rule in medieval manuscript painting. The king is shown enthroned in what must be an apse of a church. Abbot Vivian and the other monks are shown in a semicircle before the king, and the artist ingeniously managed to show their faces as well as their backs. The frontispiece commemorates the king's patronage and the

4.4 Abbot Vivian presenting the Bible to Charles the Bald. Vivian Bible, Tours, *c.* 850.

use of the Bible as a gift, indicating the supremacy of the emperor over the Church. The artists of the Tours school were deeply imbued with an awareness of the world of rank and protocol and evolved important devices to interpret these subjects. Rather than putting the spectator on the level with the monks, thus obscuring part of the king's person, the artist chose an elevated viewpoint that exposes the entire scene. The disposition of the figures and their gestures, as well as the pose of the king and his central placement, are governed by the rules of the ceremony itself. From images such as this we learn the appearance of Carolingian church interiors.

Another donation scene (Fig. 4.5) is in a German manuscript of the late tenth century, the *Gero Codex.* We see the scribe presenting the Bible he has copied and em-

bellished to his patron saint, Peter. Peter is shown enthroned, larger in scale than the scribe, placed exactly beneath an arch of a building that symbolizes a church, and his gesture is made without an accompanying facial sign of recognition of the monk's presence. The head of St. Peter may have been copied from a late Roman sculpture of a pagan subject. The separation of the monk's feet from any ground line does not signify that he is "jumping for joy." By this time in European art, painting had ceased to attempt any suggestion of three-dimensionality. With the absence of space or depth, the figures acquire a relative flatness and weightlessness. Medieval painting was a symbolical as well as mystical art, whose power did not depend upon a duplication

4.5 Scribe presenting the Bible to St. Peter. *Gero Codex. Sacramentary of Gero, c.* 970.

4.6 Coronation of Henry II by Christ. Sacramentary from the Cathedral Treasury of Bamberg, Ratisbon, 1002–1014. Munich, Bavarian State Library.

of the world of appearances. The fact that the figures overlap the architecture under which they at first seem to stand or sit is justified on the basis of clarity and avoidance of cutting or segmenting the figure, gesture, or action.

Some of the great German manuscripts made for eleventh-century Ottonian emperors possess magnificent coronation images for frontispieces, celebrating events in which the book itself played an important part. When Charlemagne's tomb was opened in the tenth century, the body was found seated upon a throne with the coronation Bible open upon its lap. This Bible was used in turn by Ottonian kings at their coronation. A page (Fig. 4.6) showing the coronation of the German king Henry II, painted in Regensburg between 1002 and 1014, depicts the arms of the king being

supported by his patron saints or representatives of the Church. Seated above and behind him is the figure of Christ, who blesses the new king with His right hand and places the crown upon his head with the left. The use of gold and brilliantly colored patterns, the geometric composition and careful ordering of right and left, up and down, center and subsidiary areas, makes this page exciting testimony to the power, wealth, and tastes of the court. It also demonstrates the successful alliance of the Ottonian kings with the Church of Rome, an alliance that greatly influenced the course of medieval history.

THE CROSS PAGE

During the seventh and eighth centuries, some English and French manu-

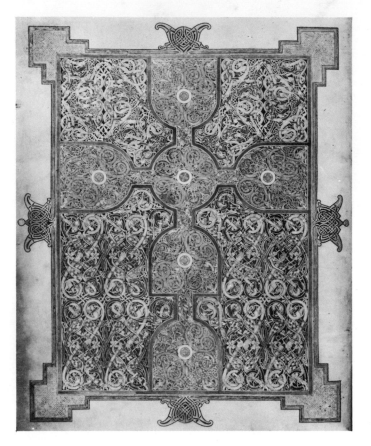

4.7 Cross page. *Lindisfarne Gospels*, late seventh century. Copyright The British Museum, London.

scripts included pages devoted to the Cross. In the cruciform page of the *Lindisfarne Gospels* (Fig. 4.7), the Christian Cross is seen against a densely filled field of interlaced forms. The conjunction of flowing lines and strict geometry may have been symbolic of the bringing of law to the lawless, for the interlacing has been subordinated to the limitations and shapes of each area by the straight linear boundaries and right angles provided by the Cross and its frame, a Roman Christian heritage. But this is only conjecture, for while the monks had converted the Saxons and Celts to the Cross, they themselves had been converted to pagan art. Old barbaric associations of magic may have carried over into the manuscript painting along with the artist's desire to make the richest and most powerful presentation of the Cross.

The Cross page died out in the eighth century, but a painting of some three hundred years later (Fig. 4.8) seems to continue ideas implicit in earlier works. The mystically mesmerized Saint Valerian makes his gesture of blessing in such a way that his whole body is a cross fixed centrally within the frame. Behind him, symbolically in dark colors against the light of the saint, are menacing bestial forms. The all-consuming faith and trancelike withdrawal of the saint insure his survival and glory in a world of evil. This moving art image illustrates the medieval conception of the holy man who must live in a dark and hostile world.

IMAGES OF EVANGELISTS

In many medieval Gospel books the evangelists were portrayed at the beginning of the scriptures for which they were responsible. Generally, the evangelist was shown seated, usually in a side view; his symbol (the lion for Mark, eagle for John, ox for Luke, and winged man for Matthew) was often shown above him. In a late seventh-century Irish manuscript, the *Echternach Gospels,* the evangelist St. Mark is not shown in person but is represented by his lion symbol (Fig. 4.9). Despite its remoteness from a literal leonine image, here is a strongly imaginative equivalent. The sharpness of the lines that construct the body suggest that the painter may have been influenced by metalwork. While the artist may have been unaware of true anatomy, he imparted a lively movement and ferocity to the beast. The design of the entire page is one of the strongest in manuscript art. The frame has an active life, intruding into the central area and being played off against the lion. The writing partakes of the color and calligraphic qualities of the lion; the whole takes on a powerful consistency and discipline.

Of great importance to Western medieval art was the coming together in manuscript painting of the figure-centered Mediterranean tradition and the nonfigurative style of the north. The evangelist portraits provided the initiative for this synthesis in the seventh and eighth centuries. A page of an Irish Gospel Book of the eighth century, the *Golden Codex of St. Gall 51,* evidences the assimilation of the two traditions (Fig. 4.10). In the frame area are the motifs from northern pagan art— knotted forms, spirals, fantastic four-legged animals, geometric shapes, rows of dots. The figure of the saint, still of paramount importance on the page, has had imposed upon it the northern taste for incisive curvilinear outlining, flatness, and arbitrary proportion. There is no sense of a body existing beneath the drapery. Despite the rigid frontality and symmetry of the figure, its absence of flesh color and portrait features, the synthesized saint possesses a

4.8 (left) St. Valerius. *Codex Gertrudianus.* Reichenau, *c.* 980. 4.9 (right) Symbol of St. Mark. *Echternach Gospels,* late seventh century.

4.10 (left) The evangelist John. *Golden Codex of St. Gall 51*. Ireland, eighth century. 4.11 (right) The evangelist Matthew. *Ebbo Gospels*. Reims, *c*. 830.

powerful presence. Later, within the eighth century, as a result of the Carolingian Renaissance, the Mediterranean and Classical figure style gained ascendance.

The origin of the Carolingian evangelist portraits probably goes back to late Greek and Roman sculptures and paintings of seated philosophers. The seated posture had acquired in antiquity connotations of the contemplative, as opposed to the active, life. Additional sources may have been Ravenna mosaics of the sixth century that depicted all four evangelists seated and accompanied by their symbols. Unlike the ancient philosophers, who were shown dictating, but never actually engaged in the inferior act of writing, the images presented by medieval artists include the inspired, pensive, puzzled, aloof writer. The artist could identify himself

with the evangelist, as both were involved in writing the words of God.

One of the most exciting evangelist portraits (Fig. 4.11) in medieval art is from the *Ebbo Gospels*, produced near the city of Reims around A.D. 830. Nowhere in ancient art do we ever find so emotional an image. Saint Matthew is interpreted as a deeply inspired figure. His inner agitation, as well as the artist's own passionate enthusiasm, can be seen in the energetic drawing and nervous rhythms of the garment—qualities that overflow into the landscape and the frame. The reserve or detachment of Classical philosophers is unknown to this artist who charges with excitement his color, composition, and the frame itself.

In contrast, an evangelist figure (Fig. 4.12) from an English manuscript of the early eleventh century, the *Gospels of*

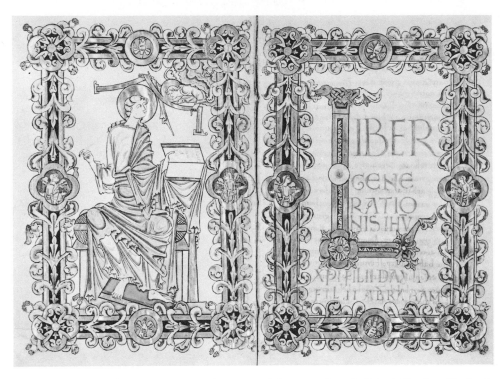

4.12   The evangelist Matthew and the first page of the *Gospels of Judith of Flanders*. England, early eleventh century. Courtesy of the Trustees of the Pierpont Morgan Library.

Judith of Flanders, presents a cool and elegant appearance. The elongated figure of St. Matthew and his gold-edged garment convey dignity and restrained spirituality. The activity of the garment and frame is more expressive than the man's features or gestures. Expressiveness in medieval painting was not confined to gestures and facial expressions, but can be seen in the drawing of the entire composition.

An early eleventh-century artist working on the island of Reichenau, on Lake Constance, Switzerland, produced an image of St. Luke in which the evangelist is shown in an ecstatic and hypnotic trance (Fig. 4.13). In the evangelist's lap are the five Books of the Old Testament. The prophets in these books are grouped about the evangelist's symbol. The symbolic meaning of the image lies in the belief that the Old Testament prophesied the coming of Christ and that the evangelists were the new heralds of His coming. The trancelike state of the saint is appropriate to the time and place in which the image was painted. Monastic reform under the Ottonians called for greater observance of intense piety and renunciation of worldly pleasures. St. Luke is presented as a model of mysticism. We see simultaneously the saint and his vision, which is in the image he appears to support, not unlike Hercules upholding the world. The miniature itself has a mesmerizing effect with its rigid symmetry extending down to the enormous eyes of the saint. The arch is a symbol of heaven, the drinking animals refer to those nourished by the Scriptures, and the brilliant gold background transports the scene outside of time and place.

THE ILLUMINATED INITIAL

Writing was a privileged art in medieval Christianity. The written word came to have considerable personal interest for the scribe, and between the two evolved an intimate personal relationship. St. Augustine, writing of the advantages of the

4.13   The evangelist Luke. Gospels from Bamberg
Cathedral Treasury, Reichenau, eleventh century.

priestly life, spoke of the opportunity to
participate in the creation of the book and
the meditation upon the Word. The results
of this relationship between scribe and
letter can be seen in the great changes in
the appearance of writing and the structure
of the written page that took place from
the sixth through the ninth centuries. The
increased beauty of the writing indicates
that the scribes did not always worry about
the legibility of the text, which was usually
known by heart. The variety of scripts, the
difference in scales of the lettering on the
opening page of a Gospel, the variety of
colors, and the assignment to certain initials
of elaborate decoration create a hierarchical
structure based upon increased valuation of
words stressed in prayers, the liturgy, and
chants or privileged because of their loca-

tion. In contrast to the uniformity of Greek
and Roman writing, no two pages of a
medieval text look the same, as can be
seen in the illustration from the *Book of
Kells* (Fig. 4.14). Beginning at the finish
of the sixth century, the initial was separated from the main body of the text by
being enlarged, set into the margin, and
formed by different lines and colors. The
illuminated initial gradually took over the
margin of the page and began to intrude
upon the text itself, as in the *Lindisfarne
Gospels* (Fig. 4.15), until, around 800, the
initial took over the entire page. The illuminated initial opened to the artist an entirely
new world of meaning. The ornament or
imagery that enhances the initial is not illus-
trative of the text, but is the product of
pure fantasy. Its justification probably lay
in the belief that the magical power of the
word required commensurate visual garb.

During the Romanesque phase of
manuscript art, the initial became the outlet
for the private sentiments of the monk and
his immediate environment. Scenes of sadism, masochism, brutality, and conduct not
generally associated with Christianity overflow initials and margins. The great *Winchester Bible*, produced in England during
the twelfth century, contains rich deposits
of this type of imagery (Fig. 4.16). The
two versions of the first Psalm are presented jointly, with the initial *B* filled with
episodes from the Old Testament that prefigure those in the New Testament. At the
upper left, David is about to slay a bear
and rescue a lamb from its jaws. The
antitype at the right shows Christ exorcising a demon from the mouth of an afflicted
man. At the lower left, David is shown
pulling open a lion's mouth to release a
lamb, while at the lower right Christ, accompanied by the Archangel, harrows Hell
by binding the hands of the devil and prying open the leviathan's jaws with the end
of his cruciform staff. The initial has itself

4.14 (left) Page from the *Book of Kells*, *Mark* 13:17–22. Northumbria, *c*. 800. 4.15 (right) Page from the *Lindisfarne Gospels*. Lindisfarne, late seventh century. Copyright The British Museum, London. 4.16 (below) Two initials from Psalm I, *Winchester Bible*. England, twelfth century. (Photo: Sollars)

become the field for illustration, with the figures and action so composed as to move energetically within and on the curved frame. All of the scenes stress the open jaws. The juncture of the two arcs of the *B* is an animal mask from whose jaws emerge intertwined ornament that in turn refers us to the entanglement of David and the beasts. Violence is performed on or by the jaws; they are identified with salvation and evil. This oral fascination has been traced to Anglo-Saxon literature, for example, *Beowulf*, with its monsters. The illustration from the *Winchester Bible* is but one of many instances in medieval religious painting and sculpture in which mordant themes are encountered.

The initial had become a type of safety valve for the artist of a religion that was strongly prohibitive. It gave free play to demonic instincts, tastes for rapacious energy, labyrinthine forms and processes. This type of art gives us an insight into the inner torment and uncertainties of medieval religious life as well as into the delight of the artist in the movement and freedom found in secular life. (The acrobatic figures in English initials may have derived from actual performances of *jongleurs*—sideshow artists.) Comparable license was taken by medieval sculptors who carved the capitals for monasteries and cathedrals, bringing to life the excluded world of monsters and phantoms of irreligious imagination. It must be remembered that there was no artistic outlet for secular fantasy other than religious art. The intimate dialogue between the artist and his work, marginal to be sure in medieval art, was to become central in later periods.

STORYTELLING MINIATURES

Beginning with the ninth century, there was a revival of storytelling in miniatures, a genre found in late Roman art.

Frequently the artist had older manuscripts or copies of late Roman work from which to work. Copying in manuscript art was not considered dishonorable, but on the contrary was an important and venerable practice; originality was not the aim of the artists. Copying, however, did not preclude a display of individuality, and the Carolingian copies of what are now lost Greek and Roman prototypes display important differences from the original styles.

Not all of the decoration of medieval manuscripts was painted. Many manuscripts contain outstanding drawings. Such manuscripts were not intended for royalty or great public ceremonies but were what might be called nonofficial art, for the private contemplation of the monks. The single most important medieval manuscript decorated with drawings is the *Utrecht Psalter*, produced in or near Reims from about 833 to 835. It contains over 166 illustrations of the Psalms and thousands of figures and objects, drawn in brown ink on the text pages without being separated by a picture frame. The original source of the *Utrecht Psalter* was probably a lost Greek manuscript made several hundred years before. There was great freedom in the copying of the earlier manuscript, and the artists of the *Utrecht Psalter* felt free to infuse their drawing with an energy and impulsiveness not found in the original. The drawings contrast strongly with the uniformity of the letters, and the compositions are more loosely structured than are the columns of text. The artists did not literally interpret the Psalms, but often added to them or contrived fanciful metaphors. The movement and structure of the drawn figures are much freer than those found in the painting of the time. The *Utrecht Psalter* comes close to being encyclopedic in the manipulations of figures and groups, and we can observe the artist's enthusiasm for landscape forms despite the

4.17   Illustration of Psalm CII, *Utrecht Psalter*. Reims, *c.* 833–835.

absence of the total integration we associate with landscape painting. The Psalter contains many images of the Hell Mouth, seen in the illustration of Psalm CII (Fig. 4.17), which were to influence later art. The manuscript as a whole was one of the most influential in medieval times because of the quality of execution and richness of subject matter.

Eleventh-century German artists such as those who produced the *Golden Codex of Echternach* (Fig. 4.18) rank among the finest storytellers in the history of art. Unlike Roman artists, the Ottonian painters conceived of the entire page as possessing an integral design. The placement of the figures or groups in each zone is thought out in terms of the whole page. The climactic moments of the adoration and the presentation in the temple take place on the right side of the page with the most important figures located beneath symbolical arches. The chronology of the events is broken in order to give the most important events the privileged locations. Medieval art permits us to see simultaneously the inside and outside of a building. The open doors signify that the action or location of figures is indoors. The Ottonian artists created strong rhythmic designs and broad gestures played off against single-colored backgrounds. While color is used symbolically in connection with the principal figures, it is also skillfully balanced off the colors on the three zones. There is a distinctness and terseness in Ottonian miniatures that recalls the actual narrative style of the Bible.

Versatility and imagination went into manuscript miniatures, for instance,

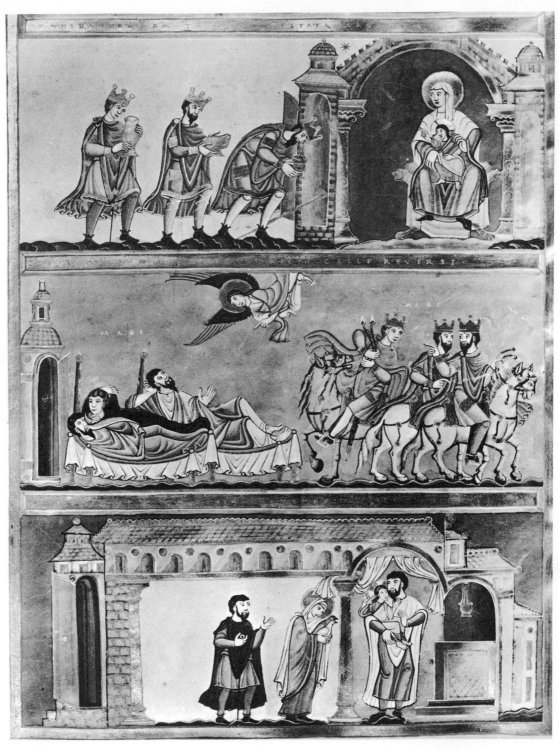

4.18 Epiphany: Kings arriving with gifts; Divine warning and departure; presentation in the temple. *Golden Codex of Echternach*. Echternach, 962–1056. Courtesy of the German National Museum, Nurnberg.

4.19 *Christ on the Sea. Gospels of the Abbess Hitda of Meschede.* Cologne, eleventh century.

the eleventh-century painting of Christ on the Sea of Galilee (Fig. 4.19). Through the tilt of the dragonlike ship that seems about to swoop out of the frame, the undulating composition of the sail and ship that play against the pulse of the sea, and the anxious looks of the disciples, the painter has realized a spirited image of individuals in distress. The dormant figure of Christ is the one stable area in the entire work. Even the frame has received impulsively flecked touches of gold.

While the medieval artist was unaware of the mathematics of perspective and the science of anatomy, the power of his fantasy and skill as a draftsman and composer created invaluable works of art as well as religious images.

CHAPTER 5

THE SYNTHESIS OF HEAVEN AND EARTH IN FIFTEENTH-CENTURY ART

FLEMISH ART . . . .

The value of man and of his earthly world were affirmed in the Middle Ages, long before the emergence of the Italian Renaissance. In the thirteenth and fourteenth centuries, medieval art evidenced its absorption of secular values and awareness of human worth. At the end of the Middle Ages, in fifteenth-century northern France and Flanders, what is today Belgium, there was a rapid development of illusionistic or naturalistic painting with an unprecedentedly high correspondence between sensory experience and what was painted. Flemish painting represented the movement to abandon many medieval attitudes and artistic devices for the interpretation of religious subjects. The extent to which this movement had progressed in less than three centuries can be seen by comparing a twelfth-century stained-glass window panel from Chartres (Fig. 5.1) and Campin's Merode Altarpiece (Fig. 5.2). No longer in consistent use were such symbolic attributes as halos and abbreviated settings. Also

abandoned was the constant surface adherence of the Chartres figures caused by the linear contours, flat, bright colors, absence of depth, and bodies without weight or volume. Use of generic facial types for the angel and the Virgin was replaced by portraiture. Fifteenth-century art rejected a remote mystical world that the Flemish viewer could not penetrate and that barred him from identification of himself and his values. The celestial sphere of the Chartres window had been replaced by what appeared to be a spotless mirror of early fifteenth-century Flemish life. This art did not abandon religious subject matter but continued the attachment of the artist and patron to the medieval Christian tradition. Essentially the objective of the Flemish artists was to fuse mystical religious content with orientation toward the visible, material world.

The motives for this shift in northern European art included the desires of the artist to image the real world as he saw, touched, and walked through it, experiencing its beauty with all his senses. The af-

74

fluent Flemish cities, such as Bruges, Tournai, Ypres, and Ghent, seemed appropriate incarnations of the heavenly city as well as the means by which to express sentiments previously excluded from art. The Church did not resist the new realism but sought to utilize it for its own purposes. Because of the vividness and familiarity that naturalism could give to invisible holy personages, the new art seemed a strong instrument for the exposition and support of dogma, which itself had become more tolerant of earthly existence. Unforeseen by the Church was the fact that the artist could not negate his private and nonreligious feelings when he painted religious figures and the interiors and landscapes in which they moved. Thus the new art of the late Middle Ages was an uneasy synthesis between religious and secular values with, in fact, an undertone of conflict eventually settled in favor of the latter. This synthesis

5.1 Chartres Cathedral. West central window, Annunciation panel, twelfth century. Faces restored 19th Century. (Photo: Johnson)

5.2 Campin. Merode Altarpiece, *c*. 1420–1430. Courtesy of The Metropolitan Museum of Art, The Cloisters Collection.

was the beginning of the disengagement of art and beauty from religion.

The key to this synthesis was the *symbol*, or the tangible sign of the invisible. One of the most brilliant scholars to study this period, Erwin Panofsky, has pointed out that the artists' and theologians' problem was to disguise religious symbolism under the cloak of real things, reconciling the idea of the symbol with empirical probability. Over a thousand years of Christian tradition had to be conciliated with the new naturalism and made into "corporeal metaphors of things spiritual." The use of the symbol was abetted by the fact that all of reality came to be thought of as saturated with meaning. The process of looking at a Flemish painting becomes one of gradual penetration beyond the superficial into submerged layers of meaning. The following works of art have been chosen to illustrate the forms taken by the Flemish synthesis of heaven and earth.

One of the earliest and most important fifteenth-century Flemish paintings to illustrate the symbolic synthesis of the mundane and theological is Campin's Merode Altarpiece. In the left panel the donor, a businessman named Ingelbrecht, and his betrothed kneel in a walled garden. Through the open gate can be glimpsed a street like those in Tournai, where the painting was done. The figure standing behind the open gate has been variously interpreted as the painter himself, a servant, or the marriage broker who arranged the betrothal of the patron and his wife. (The wife was added after the painting was completed.) The garden and its flowers were simultaneously traditional symbols of the Virgin and familiar adjuncts to Flemish middle-class urban houses. The partially open door serves to link the left and center panels, but its rendering makes ambiguous the exact relationship of the donor and the scene to the right. We do not know if he is an actual eyewitness to the event. The

Annunciation to the Virgin in the central panel is depicted for the first time in art in a fully appointed middle-class parlor. Only the angel and the small child carrying a cross on rays of light overtly announce a supernatural event. The child and cross replace the dove in this Annunciation scene; they signify Christ's incarnation and passion. In her physical appearance, posture, and surroundings, the Virgin is a middle-class type. Her virtues are those prized in both the Virgin and the ideal Flemish housewife. Her sitting on the floor evokes her humility; the immaculate care of the room and its contents alludes to her cleanliness; the reading of the Bible and theological literature signify her piety and awareness of her role. Meyer Schapiro has observed that what is seen in the room is a metaphor of what takes place within the Virgin's body. The handsome bronze laver, hanging in the niche above the angel's head, recalls the Virgin's body as an immaculate vessel. The lilies are associated with her purity. The candle's wax and wick become the flesh and soul of Christ. The absence of flame from the candle and fireplace is explicable on the basis of the divine light that enters the room through the closed window. Light had been the mystical metaphor of Virgin birth for centuries prior to this painting. In the words of St. Bernard, "Just as the brilliance of the sun fills and penetrates a glass window without damaging it, and pierces its solid form with imperceptible subtlety, neither hurting it when entering nor destroying it when emerging: thus the word of God, the splendor of the Father, entered the virgin chamber and then came forth from the closed womb." If extended, the rays of light would meet the side of the Virgin's head, consonant with the view that she conceived through the ear.

The meaning of the tiny infant carrying the cross links the middle panel to the third panel, which shows Joseph steadfastly at work in his carpenter's shop. On the table before Joseph is a mousetrap, its presence plausible as a household object of cleanliness. Its theological meaning, as Schapiro has shown, explains Joseph's role as earthly husband of Mary and the meaning of Christ's incarnation. Medieval theologians explained Christ's assumption of the flesh as a plan to redeem humanity from the devil—"The Deity was hidden under the veil of our nature, and so as is done by greedy fish, the hook of Deity might be gulped down along with the bait of the flesh [Gregory of Nyassa]." Joseph was used to conceal the birth of Christ from the devil, and Campin has shown him as neither too old to have fathered a son nor too young to disturb the faithful, but at the right age to deceive the devil. The mousetrap was a theological symbol explained by St. Augustine: "The devil exulted when Christ died, but by this very death of Christ the devil is vanquished, as if he had swallowed the bait in a mousetrap. He rejoiced in Christ's death like a bailiff of death. What he rejoiced in was his undoing. The cross of the Lord was the devil's mousetrap; the bait by which he was caught was the Lord's death."

The block into which Joseph is boring holes may correspond to contemporary fishing bait box lids and to spike boards attached to the ankles of Christ in fifteenth-century Dutch paintings of His carrying of the cross.

To look at the Merode Altarpiece only in terms of its complex symbolism is to neglect Campin's ability as a painter. The panels are marvels of lucidity by which figures and objects impress themselves upon the eye. The composition, like the painting's meaning, is a synthesis of medieval and new devices. The elevated viewpoint and careful alignment of shapes tend to orient them toward the old surface pattern even while creating the illusion of rooms and objects seen in depth. The strewn objects on Joseph's workbench and the table between the angel and the Virgin manifest this double character. The inconsistency of scale permits complete re-creation and visibility of objects seen in depth—the window lattice and shutters, the well, seen through the window over Joseph's right shoulder, that repeats the shape of the mousetrap. The rightness of Campin's compositional sensitivity is sensed by trying to take in the whole of the Annunciation panel at one time and then mentally moving any object slightly out of position. Campin seems to have conceived of the painter's purpose as being both a reconstitution and a more perfect ordering of reality.

Both the Joseph panel of the Merode Altarpiece and Jan van Eyck's small painting of *St. Jerome in His Study* (Fig. 5.3) might easily be taken for secular subjects. It is such painting that inaugurated secular, or genre, art. Van Eyck, asked by a Roman cardinal to paint St. Jerome, surrounded the translator of the Scriptures with all the accessories that would be found in a scholar's study. The cardinal could identify himself with the saint as a leader of the Church, while Van Eyck, a man of considerable learning, could admire Jerome's intellectual achievements. Among the objects associated with scholarship are books, writing materials, and the astrolabe, an instrument used in astronomical study. The two superimposed disks of the astrolabe were inscribed with drawings of the stars and earth so that the relations of the two at any time could be established. Van Eyck was a mapmaker and, judging by the wealth of meaning in his painting, an avid reader of books. The painter's task was also that of a translator of the Scriptures into the vernacular of his society. Medieval manuscript portraits of the evangelists show how Van Eyck humanized the saint. He is shown neither in a trance nor in ecstatic inspiration, but in quiet consuming concentration, the heavy weight of the

5.3 Van Eyck. *St. Jerome in His Study*. Courtesy of the Detroit Institute of Arts.

head felt in the wrist of the supporting hand. A soft light illuminates the casual pile of books on the shelf and clutter on the writing desk. The meticulous reproduction of objects contrasts with the naïve rendering of the lion, St. Jerome's attribute. The clumsy leonine body, which lacks the vitality of the Echternach lion, was no doubt a result of Van Eyck's not having seen the live animal and having to work from inaccurate art models. Van Eyck could accurately render anything with which he was familiar—the light's reflection, textural uniqueness, or craftsman's art.

The five-by-eight-inch size of the painting attests to the origin of Flemish wooden panel painting in manuscript art. Rarely did Flemish artists paint on the scale of the Italians, who created considerable mural art. Painting such as Van Eyck's is effective because of its modest scale, which demands close viewing of its microscopic detail. The compositions do not consist of large, easily read liaisons between shapes. The quality of a precious object imparted by the St. Jerome panel resides in the small, concentrated areas of saturate luminous colors and the hardness of surface in both the painting and its contents. Only by looking long and closely at the painting can one savor the sophisticated scale modulations of the forms. Van Eyck's painting permits focus on the smallest metal bolt without blurring of the adjacent areas. From the most minute form, one may take in increasingly larger forms of the books, hour glass and lectern, the strong box that serves for a desk, the cardinal, his chair, and the draped shelves. The largest form is never completely contained within the painting, perhaps to remind us of the infinity of variety and size created by God. Flemish painting reverses earlier manuscript art by revealing God in worldly terms.

Desire to re-create the brilliance as well as detail of the visible world was probably the strongest incentive for Van Eyck's improvement on the old medieval technique of superposing layers of linseed oil over tempera painting; Van Eyck and Campin combined their pigment with oil rather than egg as in tempera painting. The glazes intensified the color and permitted reworking and admixture of colors because the medium dried slowly. This technique was ideal for the simulation of light and its reflection. The oil-treated surface was semitransparent, and the natural light that fell on it is partially repelled and partially absorbed, further adding to the jewellike quality of Flemish art. In a large painting like Van Eyck's *Madonna with Chancellor Rolin* (Fig. 5.4), all of the shapes were first drawn on smooth plaster or gesso ground applied to the carefully joined wooden panels. Tints of hand-ground mineral or earth color were applied directly to the gesso and then in layer after layer of glazes, so that the color acquired depth and volume as well as luminosity. Color became less detachable from the figures, and objects seen in depth tended to lie less consistently upon the painting's surface than in earlier manuscript art. Van Eyck wanted the illusion of three-dimensional sculptural roundness to extend his painting's verisimilitude to nature. He had been a painter of stone and wooden sculpture, which at the time was more naturalistic than painting. The sculptural incisiveness of his drawing was allied to his developments in color.

Van Eyck's passion for accuracy and the success of his painted illusions may incite the criticism that his is unimaginative art. Such criticism does not take into account that the most exact transposition onto a two-dimensional surface of a three-dimensional object, space, and light requires more than manual dexterity. To begin to comprehend the nature of fantasy

in the art of Van Eyck, consider for a moment the subject and whole painting of the *Madonna with Chancellor Rolin*. Van Eyck has created a large luxurious interior inhabited by imposing figures behind which an inexhaustible panorama extends beyond the limits of sight and imagination. Every detail is empirically verifiable, and yet the totality is a scene never beheld by Van Eyck or anyone else before the painting was finished. As a gesture of self-confidence in his spiritual merit, or wish-fulfillment, the chancellor of the Burgundian dukes has caused himself to be granted an audience in the heavenly chateau of Christ and the Virgin. Although inspired in sculpture and architecture by archeological sources that Van Eyck mistakenly believed were from the time of Christ's stay on earth, the final design of the interior knows no earthly counterpart. Through the colonnade is seen a walled flowering garden, metaphorical of the Virgin and her residence. Two unknown and intriguing fig-

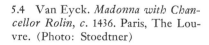

5.4 Van Eyck. *Madonna with Chancellor Rolin, c.* 1436. Paris, The Louvre. (Photo: Stoedtner)

ures with their backs to the spectator look out upon a crystal clear river that divides an earthly city on the left, identified as Maastricht in Belgium, and the heavenly metropolis on the right. It is no accident that Christ's fingers which give the blessing are tangent to the symbolically seven-pillared bridge between the two cities, for the Christ Child was the divine link between heaven and earth.

Van Eyck's making of his art was activity in sympathy with God's creation of the world. The life born in the painting is at once based on, yet remote from, his own. Van Eyck has established himself as its sole executor, selecting, rejecting, refashioning what is to enter it. All material substance has been painstakingly and lovingly explored, given a heightened surface materiality and fixed into a complex order. The painting contains a thousand glittering points to be discovered and enjoyed. To be shared with the painter is his wonder at optical perception as seen in the fact that small objects near the eye may block out objects of far greater magnitude that are behind them in the distance or the fact that the eye cannot at once take in all that is living within the sweep of its gaze. Thus the wealth of a lifetime's accumulated visual and intellectual experience is given a new imaginative cohesion and existence on a rectangular surface measuring twenty-six by twenty-four and one-half inches.

To comprehend Van Eyck's re-created world the viewer is always obliged to commence with or return to almost atomical detail. The face of the seventy-six-year-old chancellor, for example, betrays his hard and ethically questionable career; Van Eyck has reconstructed him beginning with the pores. There is a hint of wit in the painter's having made adjacent to the chancellor's brow the distant obdurate hill, while above the head of Christ are placed the spires of the heavenly Jerusalem whose effulgence provides His halo. Although

aware of the fallibility of his patron, Van Eyck's painting, like all of his art, is a radiant expression of optimism in the order of life, of faith that because of Christ's sacrifice the earth will again know paradise. He respects earthly rank as a counterpart to celestial authority, and his imagery is aristocratic in form and content. Van Eyck and Campin reflect the divergent tastes and conflicting attitudes that existed in their time between the aristocracy and the middle class. The Virgin in the Merode Altarpiece cannot be interchanged with the *Rolin Madonna*, for example.

More man-centered in the expression of his religious sentiments than Campin and Van Eyck was the Flemish painter Roger van der Weyden. He opposed their shared focus of figures and objects and particularly Van Eyck's pantheism. Roger's *The Descent from the Cross* (Fig. 5.5) is unusual in Flemish painting because of the total weight of expression and composition borne by the figures alone. To insure its full and immediate impact upon the viewer, Roger compressed the action within a shallow boxlike space much like the sculptured altarpieces of the period. His intent was to provide an image for pious meditation whereby the worshiper could empathize with Christ and His followers. The subject is the lowering of Christ's body from the Cross. The theme is that of passion and compassion. The artist's purpose has been best summarized by Otto von Simson in a fine study of this painting: "The Christian artist must seek to approach God through the affect of compassionate love. He must seek to awaken these affects in others in order to help establish the bond of similitude between God and the contemplator of His image. This is the religious mission of the emotionalism of all Gothic art." Roger's painting grows out of the compassionate emphasis and the concern with the tragic in Christianity that had arisen at the end of the Middle Ages.

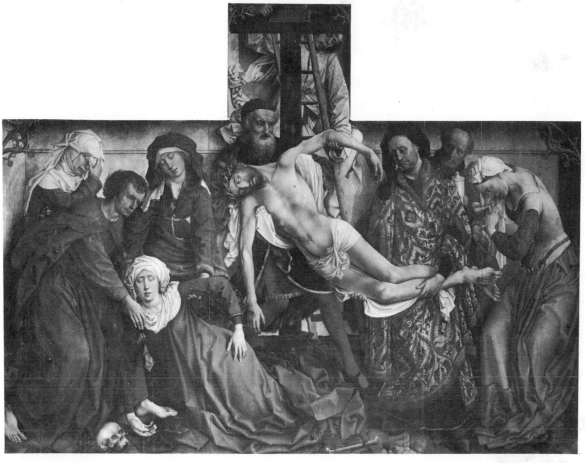

5.5 Van der Weyden. *Descent from the Cross*. Madrid, The National Museum of Prado.

The critical act of the worshiper's self-identification with the grief-stricken followers of Christ hinged upon lifelike rendering. It is not only their outward physical appearance that Roger achieved with such power, but also the refined range of states of feeling that they manifest. This range includes varying degrees of active and abstracted participation in the moment —from the deathlike swoon of the Virgin, who mystically shares the death of Christ in her role as co-redeemer of mankind, through the levels of awakening comprehension of the event seen in the figures supporting Christ, to the full capitulation to lament in the Marys, and finally John's calm resignation as he foresees the consequences of Christ's death. The bodies as well as the faces make transparent their possessors' inner state. At the right, for instance, Mary Magdalen is seen in a suspended movement caused by total loss of self-consciousness. The emotional and psychological unity of the participants is marvelously embodied in the composition itself; the placement and alliteration of the limbs join the whole in forceful rhythms. This multiple form of unity was essential to the intent of Roger—to have the whole congregation share in the experience. They, like the mourners in the painting, were to come to life through Christ's death.

Of a different temper and outlook is Dirck Bouts's painting of the Last Supper (Fig. 5.6). The altarpiece's subject was commissioned by the Brotherhood of the

5.6 Bouts. The *Last Supper*. Central panel of Altarpiece, *c*. 1464. Louvain, Belgium. (Stoedtner)

Blessed Sacrament in Louvain in 1464. The disciples are assembled for the solemn and sacred moment when Christ blessed the bread and the wine. Bouts painted not only the origin of the sacred rite, but also a humane ethic by which the brethren could imitate Christ and the disciples. The supper is set in a large contemporary Flemish hall, modestly dignified and immaculate in appearance. No obvious attempt was made to refer to Judas' betrayal. According to tradition, Judas sits diagonally across from Christ and is otherwise distinguishable only by his darkened complexion and markedly downward gaze away from Christ. The painting's expressiveness comes from the cumulative build-up of the parts and complex interrelation of figures and environment. Bouts has underplayed the contrasts

between the formal and the informal that enrich his style. These include the random appearance of the table's objects and the geometric regularity of the floor tiles; the isolation of the figures and the continuity of the architecture, the judicious spacings between shapes and frequent tangencies that unite them as if on a common surface. Behind the airless, measurable space of the room, segmented by the windows and doorways, are to be seen earthly vistas of infinite dimension. In contrast to earlier religious painting, Bouts's large-scale setting slightly dominates the figures because of their relative immobility. The quiet mood evoked by the sunlit hall is consonant with the weighted stillness of the disciples that is their basic means of unification. The link between the figures and the architecture has been thoughtfully calculated in order to complete the composition and perhaps intimate an invisible rapport between the animate and inanimate. The curve of the disciple's back at the lower right, for instance, repeats that of the hood of the fireplace behind Christ. The pantry opening serves as a frame for the double portrait, possibly of Bouts's sons. The disposition of the figures around the table is analogous to the sequence of windows, arcades, and the end wall. The figures immediately to Christ's right and left, however, are more closely aligned with the background shapes. Nowhere is this integration stronger than between the slightly enlarged figure of Christ and the objects behind Him. He is joined with the axis made by the panels that close off the fireplace, replacing the old halo and its cross. The lintel and chandelier extend the axis upward. (The chandelier was a metaphor of Christ, as discussed in the section on the Gothic cathedral.) This central axis contains the meeting points of the diagonals of the floor, table, and ceiling so that the rationalization of space partakes of mystical symbolism. Christ's head, gestures, and the bread and wine complete the axis. With familiar secular accessories, Bouts was able to symbolize the theological centrality of the Eucharistic rite. The figure of Christ shows the least mobility of all, and despite the worldly context, Bouts has shown Him as belonging to a higher spiritual order.

Superficially, Bouts's figures appear puppetlike. As he saw them, however, the disciples did more than cast shadows. Their slightest movement betrayed an awkward, peculiarly human angularity, and they were most graceful when at rest. Each manifests a personal inward concentration. Their grace is spiritual, not physical. They are models of simplicity and purity, in the later Middle Ages adjudged to be the virtues necessary to emulate Christ.

It is likely that the figure standing to the far right is the painter himself. This was not an unprecedented inclusion, as we saw in the illustration from the *Gero Codex*. Roger van der Weyden had earlier portrayed himself as St. Luke drawing the Virgin. Nevertheless, Bouts affirmed the esteem in which the painter was held by Flemish ecclesiastical and secular patrons. While his inclusion was prideful, the painter has shown himself as an attendant, respectfully apart from the sacred meal. He is thus a servant of Christ in a double sense.

Even when the artist did not literally show himself, his painting might be a self-portrait. Hugo van der Goes's *Adoration of the Shepherds* (Fig. 5.7) contains explosive tensions and alternating serenity and turbulence that shed light on the artist's withdrawal to a monastery and eventual suicide. The painting's large scale and ambitious composition rivaled the greatest works of such predecessors as Jan van Eyck and Roger van der Weyden. Van Eyck's amplitude of setting and particularization of detail are present in the *Adoration*, as is Roger's insistence upon strong

emotive demonstration. Van der Goes's painting is, in fact, a great summation of Flemish achievements climaxed by the bold intrusion of the painter's personality. From the rich deposits of theological literature, Van der Goes mined the symbolism of the painting.

Joseph is given prominence by being placed in the right foreground in front of a large pillar that is part of a ruined stone edifice. His literal and figurative stability in the painting and his membership in Christ's earthly family make his connection with the pillar appropriate. He kneels and pays homage to the scrawny new-born babe, who lies on some straw in the center of a circle formed by attendant angels, the shepherds, and the Virgin. The pillar may relate to the apocryphal tradition that had the Virgin leaning against it during the night when she gave birth to the Christ Child, a situation analogous to that of the birth of Buddha, whose mother stood beneath a tree and grasped it for support during childbirth. Van der Goes used the medieval device of scale discrepancies between the figures to set the angels apart from the mortals.

There is no shed for the Christ Child, but the ruined stone building relates to the decay of the Synagogue, the changing of the old order for the new which is signaled by the child's birth. Panofsky has shown that a building in the background contains the insignia of David, indicating that it is his vacant house. The wheat on the ground at the center and bottom of the picture alludes to Bethlehem, "the house of bread," and the words of Christ, "I am the bread which came down from Heaven." The flowers, which include the lily, iris, and columbine, refer to the blood of the passion, the pain that pierced the Virgin's heart, and her grief and sorrow.

The presence of the ox and ass, standing behind the manger in the stone building, had a far different meaning than it does today. In medieval times the two animals had radically different connotations, partly because of a sentence in Isaiah, "The ox knoweth his owner and the ass his master's crib." This was taken to mean that the ox recognized the Saviour while the ass did not. The ass was often used as an anti-Semitic symbol referring to the Synagogue, which was at times personified as a woman riding an ass. In older images the ass is sometimes shown as eating, biting its tail, or

tearing at the swaddling clothes, indicating its own stupidity and, by implication, that of the Jews in failing to recognize the Saviour. Van der Goes has shown the ass eating the straw of the manger. The ox is sometimes shown as engaged in a tug-of-war with the ass for the swaddling clothes, protecting the babe with its horns, or kneeling before the child, indicating a total epiphany.

Van der Goes has given the shepherds considerable importance in his paint-

5.7 Van der Goes. *Adoration of the Shepherds*, 1475. Portinari altarpiece, central panel. Florence, Uffizi Gallery.

ing, paralleled in the increased roles they played in the mystery plays where the authors had to fabricate dialogue for them because of their popularity with the audience. Van der Goes treats the annunciation to the shepherds and their appearance at the child's side in synoptic fashion. (The annunciation takes place on a hill in the right-hand corner of the panel.) The faces of the shepherds are a striking contrast in excitement and ascending levels of comprehension as they realize what they are witnessing. They are given an intensity of expression which borders on the fanatic. This study in psychological reactions to a situation, while contained in a religious context and marginal within the picture, holds the seeds for later art, which divested such studies and moments from Biblical incidents and set them in purely secular situations. After its completion, the Portinari Altarpiece was sent to Italy, where it caused considerable and influential interest.

Flemish art of the fifteenth century included fine works of religious and secular sculpture, of which few have survived. A reliquary of Charles the Bold (Fig. 5.8) was made by a gifted goldsmith. The records of the church of St. Lambert in Liège show that it was given by the Burgundian duke as expiation for extensive damage to the church. He has had himself shown kneeling and holding his gift of a reliquary in which is housed St. Lambert's finger. The Duke's sponsor, St. George, backs him up and doffs his helmet in a courtly gesture of courtesy, as if presenting his charge to the saint. The entire work is less than twenty-two inches high; it was made of gold with inlaid enamel on a silver gilt base. The craftsmanship of this sculptural treasure makes us miss all the more what has not survived from the period. The finest painters and craftsmen were employed by Charles the Bold for extravagant

5.8 Reliquary of Charles the Bold, 1467–1471. Liege, Cathedral of St. Paul.

secular undertakings. One of the most famous spectacles was the wedding of Charles to the sister of the English King, Marguerite of York, in July of 1468, described by Baron van der Elst on the basis of chronicles of the event.

A forty-foot tower was set up, painted with heraldic devices and adorned with mechanical boars, wolves, and donkeys, to be operated by puppeteers so that they danced and sang . . . Inside the hall was lighted by bronze chandeliers shaped like castles. They were surrounded by artificial forests, where wandered extravagant Gothic monsters . . . A table was set for the bride and groom and for the most important guests under one canopy. Down the center stretched a huge lake framed in silver. In its waters floated thirty ships each so marked as to represent a territory of the Duke's domain. Some of them were seven feet long and rigged like the galleons that dropped anchor . . . before the port of Bruges and Damme. This marvelous fleet of carriers brought food to the guests seated around the table. Small boats were loaded with lemons, olives, rare fruits, and spices. After the main course dessert was brought in, borne aloft on the shoulders of the retinue of servants. The sweets were pastries in the shape of castles with very real bastions and battlements. Cooks and chefs had to be as skillful architects as the designers of the chandeliers. . . . From one of the huge pies emerged a whole band of musicians vigorously playing their instruments.

Italian Art . . . .

Although he painted early in the fourteenth century, the Florentine artist Giotto is the point of departure in the effort of fifteenth-century Italian artists to unite in perfect harmony the world's divine and earthly aspects. Giotto was able to project Biblical subjects into his paintings in ways that made the supernatural plausible and intelligible to all. He divested religious art of its aristocratic aloofness and theological abstraction, and he reduced reliance upon symbolic accessories and gestures. As his contemporary Dante was to literature, so was Giotto to painting. The divine was translated by them into a new vernacular to facilitate simple devotion. To his own age, Giotto's great achievement was the lifelike appearance of his subjects, in contrast to the art of his contemporaries. The criterion was not the direct matching of Giotto's paintings with the real world, but with the art that had gone before. While it

is difficult today to appreciate this difference, Giotto remains a brilliant interpreter of the Bible whose mastery of composition was indivisible from his abilities as a narrator. *The Raising of Lazarus* (Fig. 5.9) is one of a series of large mural paintings adorning the Arena Chapel in Padua; it was painted in 1305–1306. Dead for three days, the putrefying Lazarus was brought to life by Christ. To those who first looked upon this painting, it seemed that Giotto had brought new life to art.

To read the story within the painting is to retrace the major compositional movements. At the left, as if having turned from the disciples, Christ effects the miracle through the magnetism of his gaze and gesture of his hand. There is no distracting object behind him. The gold background traditionally used in most art of this time has been replaced by blue sky, which immediately sets the action on earth. So powerful is the eye of Giotto's Christ that it impels the viewer across half the painting to the figure of Lazarus. A second bridge between the resurrector and resurrected is formed by the gestures of two intervening figures. The two arm movements of the figures on the exact center who serve as intermediators, are not symbolic but are instinctive, showing Giotto's relaxation of the figure's adherence to stereotype. Even when Giotto's people are motionless, they impress us as sentient beings. Gesture is precious coin for the artist who expends it judiciously; Giotto never squanders it. It must build the action and forcibly link or pace the composition, never distract by trivial movement or ostentatious detail. Not only the arm movements of the principals lead from Christ to Lazarus, but also the powerful but simple directional arrangements of the draperies, which retain a medieval quasi-independence of the body. Those on the figure behind Lazarus, whose face is veiled to ward

5.9 Giotto. *The Raising of Lazarus*, 1305–1306. Padua, Arena Chapel.

off the smell of putrefaction, brake the eye's drive to the right and refocuses its attention on Lazarus. The small bending figure of the man who has removed the lid of the tomb is so placed as to guide our attention to the kneeling figures of the women, who return the elliptical movement of the action to Christ. The figures are bonded together by ties that reflect a rich internal life and simple physical grace.

At all times the viewer's concentration is held within the frame. The painting's frame is like that of a window through which we look into a clear shallow space, sufficient for the firm sculpturesque vol-

umes that displace it. The frame works with the figures, serving as a measure and foil for their large scale, erectness, and resulting dignity. The size of Giotto's figures and their broadness of modeling in relation to the large framed area they occupy is such that to reduce the scale to that of a Van Eyck or a manuscript painting would be to destroy the visual power of the painting. Within the frame, the intervals and solids of the figure series make the total composition like a musical chord. Against the figures is set the diagonal of the simulated hill in the background. Its shape is like a graph of the action, which begins at the left and climaxes at the right. Working at a time when artists were still uncommitted to naturalistic scale and detail, Giotto was free to shape the landscape in ways that would accentuate his dramatic focus and aid in welding the figures together. As seen in this painting, Giotto's was a man-centered world in which Christ appeared as a man among men. The hope that his art held out was both in the humane vision of Christ, and in the temperance, humility, and solemnity assigned to man, who is shown as worthy of redemption. Giotto's rendering of the figure's form is integral with the spiritual values he assigned to his ideal of humanity. The painter made a historically influential equation between the weighty mass of his figures and their moral worth. The magnetic quality of the figures is owed to their materiality. The stability of their movements and disposition within the scene convey the impression that men have a meaningful part in a larger order.

More than one hundred years after the creation of Giotto's Paduan paintings, the Florentine artist Masaccio contributed to a fresco cycle of St. Peter in a chapel newly built by a silk merchant named Brancacci. No artist in the intervening period had grasped the full import or extended the ideas of Giotto as did Masaccio in his fresco of *The Tribute Money* (Fig. 5.10). The Brancacci chapel became the fountainhead of ideas and inspiration for many artists who followed, including Michelangelo, who supposedly had his nose broken there during a quarrel. The events depicted by Masaccio are those attending the arrival of Christ and the disciples before the gates of Capernaum, where a toll was asked of them. St. Augustine interpreted this event as a foretelling of the toll that Christ was to pay upon the Cross for mankind. At this moment, for the first time Christ singled out a disciple, Peter, to participate in a miracle. Following Christ's in-

structions given to him in the center, Peter, at the far left, takes the coin out of a fish's mouth, and he pays the publican at the extreme right. As in the work of Giotto, the main group is assembled in the center and close to the lower edge of the painting. Although the fresco was high up on the wall, our viewpoint is about on a level with the heads of the group. The setting is new; the scene takes place on a broad plain before an extensive mountain range, seen in atmospheric depth, and a full-scale entrance to the city, drawn in correct linear perspective. While the human form still dominates in the painting, it has been set into its natural context. As if affirming this relationship, Masaccio's figures cast shadows upon the ground, conveying a marked sense of their relation to earth and exposure to natural light. (The painting has suffered from restoration and darkenings due to dirt and fire.)

What Masaccio was to achieve as a young painter, a few years before his death at twenty-eight, was a similitude to nature which no previous Italian artist managed. While giving greater naturalistic drawing and color to his figures and their setting, Masaccio never carried his similitude to the extremes of the Flemings. Characteristic of many of the painters to follow, Masaccio omitted intense detailing of parts in order to preserve the compositional fluidity of the whole. Never undertaking the portraiture of Roger nor landscape cartography of Van Eyck, Masaccio did not literally mirror the visible world. His building blocks were the study of such qualities as the reflection of light by broadly treated volumes, the relation of solids to voids, and the rhythmic interplay of the human body with the forms of nature and architecture. The figures around Christ belong to an impersonal ordering and do not display spontaneous volitional movement. Masaccio, like Giotto, was persuaded that the passive

5.10 Masaccio. *The Tribute Money, c.* 1427. Florence, Church of the Carmine. (Photo: Alinari)

but intense state of being could be as important as extroverted action. The enactment of a strong gesture is tied to its relevance in creating an action that is significant for the moment and for the compositional bond. Masaccio modernized but did not basically alter Giotto's ideal of a stable world governed by powerful laws.

This modernization took the form of a greater awareness of and skill in rendering the anatomical makeup and coordination of the human figure. The corporeal body asserts itself even when sheathed in draped folds. Masaccio wrote the early entries in the encyclopedia of figural movement to which those who followed in his century were to make extensive and significant contributions. This release of the human body from a kind of limbo of inertia was as important for the future secularization of art as was the Flemish celebration of the man-made object. Masaccio utilized newly discovered gestures and postures modestly but tellingly in enriching the human role in religious drama. Subsequent artists with greater anatomical and physiological knowledge nevertheless came to copy Masaccio's figures, recognizing their timeless

expressiveness, but not always sensing their coordination with the total design of his compositions. The strength of Masaccio's treatment of the faces of the disciples augments the intrusion of the human into what had been the exclusive domain of the divine. There are good grounds for belief that Masaccio did not paint the face of Christ, this weaker conception having been done by Masolino. Like many who followed, Masaccio drew strength from empirical as well as theoretical inspiration, and while the faces of his human characters gained in intensity and plausibility, that of the adult Christ because of His divine nature became troublesome. This dilemma is a sign of the transitional nature of the fifteenth century, which stood with one foot in the medieval period and one in the modern. Noteworthy are the great fifteenth-century portraits of secular subjects, a few faces of saints (perhaps because of their humanization), but renderings of Christ's face as eloquent as that at Daphne are rare.

What imparts excitement to the fifteenth century is the artists' pursuit of objective correspondences to nature that released tremendous energies; gave rise to a pervasive spirit of free inquiry that in turn nourished venturesome, fresh ideas; and produced brilliant individual styles. A galaxy of talents crowned Italian art before the century was half spent. Masaccio and Veneziano, the sculptors Donatello and Ghiberti, and the architects Brunelleschi and Alberti, the latter being primarily a theorist, evolved theoretically and empirically scientific bases for the means of representation. For most of the century these discoveries did not dogmatically straitjacket the artist. Further, these abstract devices for rendering and ordering—perspective, proportion, anatomy, and the study of light—were not the sole prerogative of either sculpture or painting. Secular criteria were established for the formation and judgment of all art. The rationalization of the means by which the artist could master the imaging of the visible world coincided with the aggressive urban middle-class's drive to systematize business conduct, explore the earth's surface for more efficient mercantile success, and exalt manmade goods. Body and mind were to be in felicitous coordination, and this ideal enhanced the attraction of the ancient Roman sculpture known in that century. For most of the century, ancient art served as a repertory of postures rather than subjects. The revival of ancient themes garbed in the form of Roman art came late in the century. The supernatural was still respected; however, priority was given in art to the sensorily verifiable experiences, like the clear measurable shaping of space and vital energetic bodies, as well as the convincing re-creation of familiar settings in home, city, and landscape. The artist continued to rely upon imagination for his basic conception, but he was now armed with new constructive and expressive means to suit his own taste and that of his time for the emulation, but not literal imitation, of all that was material and measurable.

Almost contemporaneous with Masaccio's *Tribute Money* is Donatello's relief sculpture *The Feast of Herod* (Fig. 5.11), made for the fount in the Baptistery at Siena. Donatello drew upon the newly discovered device of systematic perspective in order to create the appearance of the relief's orderly recession into depth. The diagonals of the steeply sloping floor converge to a point marked by the elbow of the seated figure who gestures towards the severed head of John the Baptist. The diagonals of the upper part of the relief meet at a point slightly above, on the cornice of the wall behind the banquet table. Donatello designed an ambitious imaginary architectural background consisting of three separate halls to extend the illusion of a palatial setting. It permitted him to expand the action to include the deliverance of John's head to Herod's servants in the most remote hall. In the middle hall is a musician who accompanies the dance of Salome. The right profile of the figure looking toward the musician resembles that of emperors found on Roman coins and reminds us of Donatello's interest in ancient art. In the foreground, Donatello left the center of the scene empty except for a few objects on the table. Seemingly, the action has been divided into two areas. At the left around the head of John is the explosive radial grouping climaxed by the horrified figure of Herod. No artist of his century surpassed Donatello's ability to dramatize the workings of the human mind in situations of great tension. He brought to art a great awareness of crowd psychology which vivified and united his figures with a range and depth of feeling unequaled at the time. These qualities were suited to the subject which shows not the sacred moment of martyrdom, but the animated group response to a sadistic murder. The reactions of the figures to the apparition of John's head polarize around expressions of attrac-

5.11 Donatello. *The Feast of Herod*, baptismal fount, 1425–1427. Siena Cathedral. (Photo: Brogi)

tion and repulsion. Donatello bridged the gap between the two foreground groups partially by means of the triple arches and the table, but also, most important, by the fanatical stare of Salome suspended in her dance. Just to the left of Salome's almost classical profile is the horrified figure who leans away and hides his face from the gruesome spectacle. The disparity of these two reactions is seen against those of curiosity or obliviousness to what has happened. The frame of the relief no longer limits the action as figures move behind it at the left and right. Not unlike the framing device on a camera, that of the relief is used by Donatello to pick out the critical area of a field too large to be totally encompassed. Within the frame is a wealth of sensations that includes contrasting textures of the flooring, walls, cloth, flesh, and hair; and a range from figures almost in the

round that seem to bulge into our space to the etched detailing of the architecture. The entire relief was originally gilded, and the brilliant gold helped to unite this variety. In his boldness, Donatello failed to compensate for the out-of-scale shadows that the frame and high-relief figures, such as Salome, cast on the area behind them. No earlier relief was so loaded with the ambitious and complex objectives attempted by Donatello.

The Venetian painter Domenico Veneziano drew insight and inspiration from Donatello and the insurgent art of his time to produce his master work, the *Madonna and Saints* (Fig. 5.12). Flanking the enthroned Madonna and Child at the left are Saints Francis and John the Baptist, while at the right are Saints Zenobius and Lucy. This is a devotional and honorific painting of a type frequently found in ear-

5.12 Veneziano. *Madonna and Saints*, 1440. Florence, Uffizi Gallery. (Photo: Alinari)

lier Italian art but here transposed into a fresh conception. The hierarchic symmetry by which divinity is honored is tempered by the forceful individualization of the saints. They belong at once to a timeless hierarchy, but have acquired personalities and states of feeling that prohibit their total submission to an impersonal order. We may speak of the saints' heads as portraits in a more exact sense than in discussing Masaccio or Giotto.

St. Lucy is shown in profile, a favored view both because of its ancestry in ancient numismatics and medallions and because of its use in secular portraits of the time. To St. Lucy is given serene elegance and contemplative composure. Her profile serves to draw the glance back into the painting and toward the masculine, rugged, and pensive head of St. Zenobius. No attempt was made to flatter the saint; the extent of the minute articulation of his features and strong modeling of the robes suggests that Veneziano was influenced by sculpture and Flemish painting. Both the

pose and facial conception of St. Francis convey the painter's feelings about his arduous self-denial and humility. The figure of Francis is strong enough to be seen by itself as a moving image. It possesses the quality of strong inner piety the Italians admired in Flemish art. Within the larger painting, however, it serves as a counterweight to Veneziano's most inspired conceit, John the Baptist. Ironically, the saint has been used as an interlocutor between the viewer and the Mother and Child. He himself is the most magnetic figure in the painting. Donatello's creation of a psychotic type of St. John lay at the root of Veneziano's interpretation. Much may be read in his face—suffering, compassion, the gift of clairvoyancy, and oblivion of self. That these things radiate simultaneously from his countenance testifies to more than Veneziano's masterful, inspired drawing. It indicates his recognition that the small area between the chin and forehead may record the essentials of a man's life. Taken as a whole, John has a late medieval head and the firm body of an ancient Hellenistic athlete.

So strong is Veneziano's over-all design that it does not disintegrate under the weight of the attention given to the heads. The handsome and spacious architectural setting is largely responsible for this unity. Its design according to correct linear perspective creates a lucid stereometric space that clarifies the location of each form within it. Despite Veneziano's use of advanced techniques of representation, there is still a medieval ambiguity to the foreground space of the saints, for the arches behind them appear to touch the top of the frame, suggesting that the saints are under the arches. The spatial hollows created by the niches and arches accentuate the massive volumes of the figures which are carefully set before them. Veneziano had a sculptor's sensitivity to the interplay of solids and voids. The severe clarity and simplicity of the architecture never conflicts with the gestures of the saints but serves to underscore their slightest movement. Veneziano's painting is a graphic demonstration of architectonic design, by which the figures are consistently related to the axes of the frame and architectural content of the scene, thus insuring stability and immediate legibility of the whole design. For the first time in Italian painting, Veneziano introduced a convincing representation of brilliant sunlight, which shines from a single source on the rear wall just to the left of the heads of the Virgin and Christ. The light provides not only warm illumination of the background, but a contrast with the cool foreground area.

Shortly after Veneziano's painting was completed, Andrea Castagno painted a fresco of the Last Supper (Fig. 5.13) that was the prototype for several later fifteenth-century versions of the same subject. Although the subject is Biblical and the fresco's location was in the refectory of a Florentine church, Castagno's interpretation is in human and mundane terms. The disciples and Christ are shown seated at a long table in a severely beautiful pavilion whose design is based upon contemporary architectural tastes. Marginal evidences of

5.13 Castagno. *Last Supper*, 1445–1450. Florence, Sant'Apollonia. (Photo: Stoedtner)

the increased interest in ancient art are the simulated bronze sphinxes at the ends of the bench and certain details of the architecture. Through linear perspective, Castagno created the forceful illusion of the pavilion's recession behind the end wall of the refectory. Within the resulting space of the room and seen against its coordinate system of verticals and horizontals are the impressive figures of the disciples. The initial appearance of the group resembles what might have been a social gathering, common to both Castagno's society and that of the ancient Hebrews whose principal evening meal was an almost public occasion for the assembling of friends and a public speaker. Castagno shows the moment when Christ has prophesied His betrayal. Judas is singled out by his placement across from Christ and by the absence of a halo. Because of Castagno's adherence to laws of perspective, Judas is actually larger in scale than Christ, who sits further in depth, a technique never seen in medieval art.

Christ has not, in fact, received the emphasis that is given to the disciples who flank him and ponder the significance of his announcement. The group of Peter, Judas, and Christ is set off slightly by the accentuation of the marble pattern in the wall above their heads. The natural light that enters the room through the windows at the right falls equally on all present. The individualization of the disciples is accomplished by their rugged countenances, the variety of their rhetorical postures, and lack of restriction by the framework of the architecture. Despite the relative passivity of the figures, Castagno's ideals of latent muscular energy and cool hard-edged sculptural surfaces assert themselves. It was painting such as this which in its time was said to bring the dead and the past to life by giving them a vivid physical presence.

In view of their preoccupation with reason and physical laws, the most challenging religious subject for Italian artists was the miracle of the Resurrection. The *Resurrection of Christ* (Fig. 5.14) painted by Piero della Francesca, a one-time assistant of Veneziano, demonstrates how faith and reason joined to produce what may be the most profound painting of its age. Under a cool matinal light Christ is risen, while at His feet, deeply gripped by sleep, lie the recumbent soldiers. The supernatural conversion is expressed in such subtle and diverse ways as to reflect the concentrated effort of a superior intelligence. The partially ruined halo is extraneous. The supra-human nature of Christ is established by more significant means. Much of the shock immediately induced by the painting comes from the unexpected appearance of hieratic symmetry in a natural setting. Piero's passion for geometry as form and symbol explains the design of the base of the tomb and the head of Christ in an isosceles triangle. At its apex Piero painted the most powerful head of Christ of the entire fifteenth century. In this head and specifically in the hypnotic area of the eyes is condensed the most crucial mystery of the Christian religion. Through the eyes Piero conveys the concept of the risen Christ awakening into a world beyond mortal vision. The rigidity of His face and pose and His obliviousness to his surroundings suggest a spiritual or psychological rather than physical transformation. True to the account of the Resurrection, Piero shows Christ in human form. His body still has material weight, as seen by the pressure of His leg on the tomb's edge. The dark areas around the eyes speak of the Passion and the long entombment. Death is treated by Piero as a form of sleep, which gives additional meaning to the dormancy of the pagan guards, as yet unenlightened by the miracle.

By means of contrast Piero suf-

5.14 Della Francesca. *The Resurrection of Christ*, 1460. The Sansepolcro Gallery. (Photo: Alinari)

fuses his message throughout the entire painting, and all the contrasts involve the figure of Christ. He divides the painting into vertical and horizontal, right and left. But as in medieval art these directions must be viewed from Christ's standpoint. The landscape to Christ's right is one of winter and, like the wound in his right side, indicative of death. The tree trunk nearest the banner is a rhyme of His body, and so are the branches of both sets of trees to Christ's head. To Christ's left is the springtime of nature, alive and verdant through His sacrifice. Thus the landscape signifies the world before and after His coming. The convergence of the trees on both sides toward the figure of Christ insinuates His relation to the state of the earth. (The mound at the viewer's far left serves to balance the head of Christ and hold the focus within the frame.) Piero's Christ is the God of all that lives. In Piero's paintings that show Christ before death, He is a submissive gentle figure. Resurrected, He is a masculine militant being. The firm musculature, stance, and suggestive erectness of his standard convey this. The last contrasts with the diagonal spear held loosely by the sleeping soldier. It is conceivable that Piero painted himself as the sleeping soldier whose head seems to rest against the edge of the tomb. If this is true, it was done to suggest a personal and further contrast of the human and the divine.

Close reading of such forms in Piero's art as those of the soldiers reveals his belief in the use of variants on geometric shapes as well as anatomy to structure the body. Each figure is joined at some carefully chosen point with another figure or object in the background. There are two perspective viewpoints—one slightly below the soldiers, one on the level with Christ's head. This selection, along with his use of geometry and the study of volumes as shaped under light and shadow, was activated by an awareness of the expressive-

ness, not the neutrality, of his means. The true descendant of Giotto, Masaccio, and Veneziano, Piero believed that beauty was achievable through the artist's imposition of a more perfect order onto the superficial appearance of nature. Piero's criterion of reality in art, like that of most Italian painters, was the degree to which the final painting corresponded to the Idea within his imagination or soul. He did not share the belief of the Flemish artists that reality could be apprehended by direct sensory or emotional experience.

Today it is customary to look upon art and science as incompatible and to differentiate between artists and scientists on the basis of temperament. Their broader cultural and disciplinary unity is ignored. In fifteenth-century Italy, many artists contributed to the study of natural science. The artistic and scientific temperaments were viewed as in alliance. The development of mathematical perspective was carried out by artists. The study of human anatomy by artists was in advance of that taught in the medical schools from inaccurate textbooks. Beginning probably with Castagno and assuredly by the time of Pollaiuolo, artists undertook actual dissection of the human body in order to study the relation of its structure to its functioning. One of the appeals of ancient sculpture was that it provided what was thought to be accurate information on physiology and musculature, and provisioned the artists with expressive posturings by which to increase the expressiveness and animation of their figures. Although religious personages were endowed with new and more lifelike properties as a result of this enthusiastic scientific study, in the works of such artists as Pollaiuolo the body itself is celebrated as a model of energy, strength, and robust action.

Pollaiuolo had made purely secular studies of the naked figure in strenuous movement (*Battle of the Ten Nudes*, 1470)

5.15 Pollaiuolo. *The Martyrdom of St. Sebastian*, 1475. Reproduced by Courtesy of the Trustees, The National Gallery, London.

and was one of the first Italian artists to join Classical form with Classical subject matter (*Hercules and Anteus, c.*1470). In his *The Martyrdom of St. Sebastian* (Fig. 5.15), fascination with the expressiveness of the same body and pose seen from multiple perspectives is clear. Forms are carefully arranged around St. Sebastian so as not to overlap. Pollaiuolo was one of the first painters in his century to show the actual exertion of physical strength by muscular action. The human figure now completely breaks the old mold of symbolical and rhetorical gesture. Pollaiuolo was unable to give graceful resolution to the energies and movements of his figures, who seem overdeveloped and often static. As a sculptor, Pollaiuolo was more successful, for in paintings he could not resolve the new conceptions of the body with space. He used a plateau arrangement and elevated viewpoint for the figures, which tends to flatten the foreground area. The deep landscape backdrop behind the plateau has no esthetic or dramatic ties with the foreground. The figure of St. Sebastian has a certain sentimental and soft quality which does not permit it to dominate the scene by any means other than its elevation. In sum, Pollaiuolo's painting is impressive in its parts, but not in the whole, and for its vigorous espousal of secular values, not its communication of exalted religious ideals.

The reasons for the lack of complete success in the Pollaiuolo's *Martyrdom of St. Sebastian* and Ghirlandaio's *Adoration of the Shepherds* (Fig. 5.16) lie partly in the increased complexity of secular demands which had to be synthesized with those of religion. Both paintings, particularly Ghirlandaio's, reflect the extent to which Italian art of the third quarter of the fifteenth century was filled with contradictory objectives in form and content. The *Adoration of the Shepherds* took shape from a wide variety of current public tastes.

5.16 Ghirlandaio. *Adoration of the Shepherds.* 1485. Florence, Sta. Trinita. (Photo: Alinari)

Painting a few years after the importation to Florence of Van der Goes's *Adoration of the Shepherds*, Ghirlandaio drew liberally upon Flemish naturalism but not upon its symbolic meaning. By temperament and taste he could not fire his figures with the spiritual fervor that exalts the Van der Goes painting. The shepherds in the Florentine painting seem tame in comparison to their Flemish counterparts, perhaps because they were portraits of the artist's patrons. Joseph is given a transparent theatrical gesture, and the ox and ass made innocent onlook-ers. The Christ Child is given more weight and ample proportions. To meet the growing interest in archeology, the shed has been supported by pseudo-classical piers, the manger converted to an ancient sarcophagus (symbolically not inappropriate), and a triumphal Roman arch straddles the road at the left. As a projection of Florentine social life and customs, Ghirlandaio has shown a procession winding down the hill as if coming from the city to welcome a visiting dignitary. It was known in Ghirlandaio's time that the Roman triumphal arch was the locus of ceremonies in which the ancient city honored the advent of a ruler. Like their Flemish counterparts, Ghirlandaio, Castagno, and Leonardo da Vinci made decorative accessories such as shields, helmets, and floats for the many pageants staged by Florentine rulers.

The review of Ghirlandaio's ambitious content must be followed by a brief assay of his composition. He failed to interweave the foreground and background, and despite the ample space he has constructed, his principals cling to the area nearest the surface of the painting. The area behind them is like an expendable backdrop, interchangeable with another setting. Ghirlandaio did not grasp the integrated vision of the Flemish painters, and in departing from that of his own Italian predecessors, he incurred problems resolved only by later artists, for example, Leonardo da Vinci. Summary of the basic differences between Italian and Flemish painting in the first three quarters of the fifteenth century permits judgment of the strengths and weaknesses of Ghirlandaio's painting.

Beginning with Giotto and continuing through Piero della Francesca, Italian style was characterized by a compact and immediately perceivable unity through the large fluid continuity of the figures who dominated their environment. Organic design resulted from the smooth interdependent functioning of figures and environment. Flemish style was characterized by a less mobile, if not static, complex additive ordering of the microscopic through the telescopic in which the setting often rivaled the human being in importance. The Italians delighted in the sensual relation of large, firm distinct volumes against each other and credible space. The Northern artists favored dense groupings of contrasting rich tones of color and light, and intricate linkages of the edges of shapes lying at varying depths from each other. The Flemings val-

ued all that was given to the senses as a sign of divine meaning, and they searched for individuality in nature. Their criterion of realistic painting was largely a quantitative one of measuring and matching the subject against the painting. Italian art sought the abstract principles behind the appearance of nature, like harmonious and beautiful form. Its criterion of painting was qualitative in that the painting was to be measured against the idea or theoretical conception that lead to its formation. Flemish art arrived at convincing spatial illusion through the trial and error of observation; the Italians first developed it empirically and then through theory. The Italians favored the good and pleasing appearance of the human form with supple coordination between mind and body. The Flemish accepted the unathletic but natural movement that often accompanies profound inner feeling.

In the sixteenth century Michelangelo illuminated the differences between the art of the two areas and revealed his own prejudices:

Flemish painting will, generally speaking, please the devout better than any painting in Italy, which will never cause him to shed a tear, whereas that of Flanders will cause him to shed many, and that not through the vigor and goodness of the painting but owing to the goodness of the devout person. . . . In Flanders they paint with a view to external exactness of such things as may cheer you and of which you cannot speak ill, as for example saints and prophets. They paint stuffs and masonry, the green grass of the fields, the shadows of the trees, and rivers and bridges which they call landscape, with many figures on this side and many on that. And all this . . . is done without reason or art, without symmetry or proportion, without skillful choice or boldness, and finally without substance and vigor.

CHAPTER 6

THE SYNTHESIS OF HEAVEN AND EARTH IN SIXTEENTH- AND SEVENTEENTH-CENTURY PAINTING

Art as Religious Propaganda . . . .

Since its inception, Christian art has had the function of propaganda; in fact, it can be contended that all religious art serves the purpose of propaganda. "Propaganda" is to be here interpreted as the dissemination of religious information and views through the medium of art. One of the most spectacular religious utilizations of art was in the Counter-Reformation artistic program of the Roman Catholic Church, which evolved in the second half of the sixteenth century and reached fruition during the seventeenth. This program was intended to counteract the Protestant Reformation and its assaults upon not only the Holy Roman Catholic Church, but also its art. The Council of Trent, which sat in the north Italian town of Trento from 1545 to 1563, was an arm of the Inquisition instrumental in crystallizing Church policy with regard to internal reform, as well as in

plotting of strategy against the northern Protestant heretics. In the last year of its session, the Council set down its views on art. In essence, this program reaffirmed the Church's belief in the importance of art, opposed idolatry, espoused the didactic purpose of art and its provisions for an ethical model for the faithful, decried indecency in religious paintings and sculptures, and insisted upon decorum, respect, and accuracy in interpreting theological or spiritual subject matter. The implications of the Council of Trent's view included an anti-Humanistic attitude, a type of Counter-Renaissance, favoring an appeal to the emotions of the believer in the manner of Ignatius of Loyola's *Spiritual Exercises*. (These exercises involved a self-induced ecstatic trance or meditation, comparable to yoga, in which the individual lost all self-consciousness and through visions identified himself with the feelings or state of his object of worship. Ignatius felt the stigmata of Christ during one of his trances.) Another implication of the Council's views was to stress the supernatural, or suspension of the rational, thus giving rise to a number of works of art dealing with miraculous themes. Truth before beauty and the strengthening of existing Church doctrines by artistic provision of visual proof are two final and essential outgrowths of this action by the Church.

To insure the carrying out of their decree, the Council instituted censorship of art by agents of the Inquisition. The most famous case brought before these agents, the Holy Tribunal sitting in Venice on July 18, 1573, was that of the Venetian painter Paolo Veronese who had painted a questionable version of the Last Supper (Fig. 6.1). The transcript of the trial illustrates among other things the uneasy synthesis of the spiritual and the secular in the minds of the judges as well as the painter. When questioned about his profession, Veronese answered as follows:

A. I paint and compose figures.
Q. Do you know the reason why you have been summoned?

A. No, sir.
Q. Can you imagine it?
A. I can well imagine.
Q. Say what you think the reason is.

A. According to what the Reverend Father, the Prior of the Convent of SS. Giovanni e Paolo, whose name I do not know, told me, he had been here and Your Lordships had ordered him to have painted [in the picture] a Magdalen in place of a dog. I answered him by saying I would gladly do everything necessary for my honor and for that of my painting, but that I did not understand how a figure of Magdalen would be suitable there for many reasons which I will give at any time, provided I am given an opportunity.

Q. What picture is this of which you have spoken?

A. This is a picture of the Last Supper that Jesus Christ took with His Apostles in the house of Simon. . . .

Q. At this Supper of Our Lord you painted other figures?

A. Yes, milords.

Q. Tell us how many people and describe the gestures of each.

6.1   Veronese. *Feast at the House of Levi*, 1573. Venice Academy of Art. (Photo: Alinari)

A. There is the owner of the inn, Simon; besides this figure I have made a steward, who, I imagined, had come there for his own pleasure to see how the things were going at the table. There are many figures there which I cannot recall, as I painted the picture some time ago. . . .

Q. In this Supper which you made for SS. Giovanni e Paolo what is the significance of the man whose nose is bleeding?

A. I intended to represent a servant whose nose was bleeding because of some accident.

Q. What is the significance of those armed men, dressed as Germans, each with a halberd in his hand?

A. This requires that I say twenty words!

Q. Say them.

A. We painters take the same license the poets and the jesters take and I have represented these two halberdiers, one drinking and the other eating nearby on the stairs. They are placed there so that they might be of service because it seemed to me fitting, according to what I have been told, that the master of the house, who was great and rich, should have such servants.

Q. And that man dressed as a buffoon with a parrot on his wrist, for what purpose did you paint him on the canvas?

A. For ornament, as its customary. . . .

Q. Did any one commission you to paint Germans, buffoons, and similar things in that picture?

A. No, milords, but I received the commission to decorate the picture as I saw fit. It is large and, it seemed to me, it could hold many figures.

Q. Are not the decorations which you painters are accustomed to add to paintings or pictures supposed to be suitable and proper to the subject and the principal figures or are they for pleasure— simply what comes to your imagination without any discretion or judiciousness?

A. I paint pictures as I see fit and as well as my talent permits.

Q. Does it seem fitting at the Last Supper of the Lord to paint buffoons, drunkards, Germans, dwarfs, and similar vulgarities?

A. No, milords.

Q. Do you not know that in Germany and in other places infected with heresy it is customary with various pictures full of scurrilousness and similar inventions to mock, vituperate, and scorn the things of the Holy Catholic Church in order to teach bad doctrines to foolish and ignorant people? . . .

A. Illustrious Lords, I do not want to defend it, but I thought I was doing right. I did not consider so many things and I did not intend to confuse anyone, the more so as those figures of buffoons are outside of the place in a picture where Our Lord is represented.

. . . . .

After these things had been said, the judges announced that the Paolo would be obliged to improve and change his painting within a period of three months from the day of the admonition and that according to the opinion and decision of the Holy Tribunal all the corrections should be made at the expense of the painter, and that if he did not correct the picture he would be liable to the penalties imposed by the Holy Tribunal.

Veronese's answers give a sixteenth-century definition of painting based upon the composition of figures which were to be read. Like a dramatist, the artist had to envision why each figure was present and what he would logically be doing. Veronese claimed for the artist the same license given to the poets when it came to filling a large space with ornament and enrichment. He had to rely on stories and information outside of the Bible to bring the past event to life in terms of his own time. His criteria were his ability and personal judgment of fitness, fortified by what he had seen in great art of the past. The great scale of his painting and the sumptuous setting and supper were reflections of Veronese's personal delight in contemporary Venetian social customs.

A fellow Venetian, Tintoretto, while not insensitive to the secular life around him, was able to paint religious images fully in keeping with the ideals of the Counter-Reformation. Against the Protestants, the Roman Catholic Church affirmed that to participate in the Eucharistic rite was to partake mystically of the blood and body of Christ. This belief impelled Tintoretto to paint the Last Supper in a way to express the miraculous meaning and origin of this rite.

Tintoretto's art also exemplifies a Counter-Renaissance attitude that looked upon the style as well as the content of such painters as Leonardo da Vinci as too worldly in orientation. Comparison of Leonardo and Tintoretto's versions of the Last Supper (Figs. 6.2 and 6.3), a century apart in date, reveals the ideological and esthetic gulf that separated the two men and their periods. Preoccupied with the study of internal human motivation, Leonardo chose to portray the moment when Christ foretold His betrayal. This permitted a virtuoso display of his findings on how expression was conveyed by face and gestures and how different personalities reacted to the stimulus of shock. The supper takes place in an austere room, illusionistically treated to continue the refectory in which it was located, a setting that permitted display of Leonardo's mastery of the science of spatial organization and the effects of certain lighting conditions. Tintoretto's setting is a rustic inn, and the meal is less like the formal banquet or social occasion seen in the earlier painting. The inn's illumination is almost melodramatic, to accord with the mystical sacramental moment chosen by Tintoretto. To achieve his effects, Tinto-

retto made small sculptural figures and set them into an open-ended box and then moved different lighting over the model (The best basis for analyzing the form of such art is the style principles evolved by the late Heinrich Wölfflin.)

Leonardo's form is closed, or completely contained within the limits of the picture area. The vanishing points and figural action lie either at the center of the painting or within its borders. Tintoretto's form is open in that the space, light, shadow, and action seem to extend out of the frame at several points. Leonardo organizes his figures and the banquet table in such a way that they seem to exist in an imaginary plane parallel to the picture surface, holding the viewer off from the action. Tintoretto's figures and banquet table exist on a diagonal with the picture surface and are thus recessional in character. It is easier to isolate individual figures, objects, or units within the Leonardo than in Tintoretto. Leonardo's work shows multiple unity, as opposed to unity. The potential isolability of Leonardo's figures is owed to the clear edge that bounds each form and the relative evenness of the light, or clarity of shape and illumination. The more indivisible relationship of Tintoretto's figures is a result of the overlapping shadows and of the construction of the figures by color as well as by light and shade. Tintoretto's composition includes the qualities of obscurity and painterly construction. Leonardo's range of light and dark exists primarily in a middle register, avoiding strong contrasts in large areas. The dramatic and mystical effects of Tintoretto's composition are realized through strong value contrasts in major areas. Leonardo, in the manner of other Renaissance painters, avoided clashing colors placed close together. Tintoretto used strong disparities between colors to enhance the visual excitement of his pictures. He employed multiple and irra-

6.2 (above) Tintoretto. *The Last Supper*, 1594. Venice, San Giorgio Maggiore. (Photo: Alinari)
6.3 (below) Da Vinci. *The Last Supper, c.* 1494. Milan, Santa Maria delle Grazie.

tional light sources, as opposed to Leonardo's more natural and even distribution of light. Tintoretto designed space so as to draw the viewer into the picture with a swift rush. He then balanced off this inward thrust by the large foreground groups and the shapes of the angels overhead that pull the eye forward again. Leonardo used the edges and perspective focus of the architecture to lead the viewer into depth, and the head of Christ, in the foreground, to bring him back into an area near the picture plane. There is a meaningful focusing on Christ in both paintings. Leonardo had Christ's head coincide with the perspective vanishing point and the rational fulcrum of the work, while Tintoretto bathed the silhouette of Christ's head in the most intense light of the painting. For Tintoretto, light thus replaced perspective or geometry as the principal bearer of religious truth.

The most mystical of the Counter-Reformation painters was El Greco, who believed in the irrational basis of Christian dogma and the necessity of achieving a uniquely personal style to embody his private visions. The events in his paintings are not shown in fifteenth-century Italy, according to the rational perception of a detached observer, but are emanations of an ecstatic visionary who sought to show in one explosive moment things that defy intellectual comprehension. For this reason his *Resurrection of Christ* seems antidotal to that by Piero della Francesca. Figure 6.4 shows the mystical levitation of Christ's body as it rose from the invisible tomb. The position of Christ's feet assist in this feeling of ascent and also recall the posture of his crucifixion. El Greco was concerned with the metaphysical more than the psychological. The cold eerie light of the scene originates from Christ's transfigured person. His effortless movement upward contrasts with the effects of the awesome force of the mystical light that

has upset the sleeping tomb guards, dazzled those who awaken, and exalted the witnesses who comprehend the transformation. Through gestures at once rhetorical and symbolical, El Greco demonstrated the forceful process of spiritual enlightenment and the significance of the Resurrection. The gesture of Christ's right hand is the sign of the completion of what had been

6.4 El Greco. *Resurrection of Christ*, 1584–1594. Madrid, Museo del Prado.

ordained, while its counterpart in the large figure at the lower right is one of simultaneous recognition and supplication. The extreme luminosity, the elongation, and the inconstant silhouette of Christ's body reduce its corporeality and eliminate the suggestion of militancy seen in Piero's God. All that in Piero was tangible and substantial has been made elusive and immaterial. The stability of Piero's composition, its implied triangle verticals resting on solid horizontals, all locked within a square format, has been replaced by an unstable irregular lozenge design in a vertical frame. Just as the mystical nature of El Greco's Christ was freed from the logic of matter, so is the event abstracted from specific earthly place and time.

The strength of El Greco's religious message did not weaken his inspired inventiveness as a painter. Great artists of the past and his own time had early taught him lessons in drawing, color, and composition. As his art became more introspective, however, he imposed upon himself unprecedented artistic problems; the success of their solution could not be judged by the work of others. El Greco's *The Legend of St. Maurice* (Fig. 6.5) now appears as a beautiful accomplished fact. The rightness in the solution of its problems obscures their original existence. Before summarizing the painting's subject, which raised these problems, it is useful to recall that the didactic message of Counter-Reformation art often took the guise of instructing the faithful in the art of dying for their beliefs. The Protestants were critical of the Church's veneration of its numerous martyrs. To affirm the sacred act of the martyr and to encourage world-wide missionary work, Roman Catholic artists were enjoined to recount the historical sacrifices of the martyrs. The story chosen by El Greco is that of the wholesale execution of a Roman legion which with its commander, Maurice, had been converted to Christi-

anity. Refusing the emperor's ultimatum to renounce their faith, every man in the legion was beheaded on the spot of what is today St. Moritz, Switzerland. El Greco stressed the moment of decision when the legion officers surrounding Maurice considered the ultimatum. Accordingly, almost one third of the painting's surface is devoted to this small group in the foreground. The upper part discloses angels who descend from heaven holding the crowns of martyrdom. To the smallest, most restricted area at the left is consigned the execution of the entire army.

El Greco boldly juxtaposed the largest and smallest figures in the entire painting. By means of the medium-sized angels placed at the upper left and the large standard at the right, he set the eccentric composition solidly within the frame. The sculptural firmness of the foreground officers is replaced as the eye moves rapidly into depth by the diaphanous character of the tiny figures in the distance who are less tangible than the clouds. El Greco took extreme license with figural proportion and space construction, and by compression of the action attained a heightened visual impact. A special grace was given to the large figures to set them apart from ordinary men. What appears as their affected movement meant to El Greco that the martyrs possessed a rare spiritual coordination of body and soul.

Essential to the style of these paintings by El Greco is the total absence of straight edge, evenly illuminated surfaces, continuous closed silhouettes, repose, and measurable space. Every shape seems in the process of change; rarely is the eye permitted to rest. Figures and clouds swell from tapered points, and rocks and pennants are edged in writhing contours. It is possible to follow the drawing action of the painter's hand in the irregular cloud and flag forms. His thinking was focused on the particular objects he was painting as well as on the adjacent areas so that rarely is a figure or object seen in isolation. No dominant sustained vertical or horizontal axis structures the composition. Unity is finally the result of a close fitting together of oscillating or irregular parts, often at obtuse angles to each other or else in parallel series.

That there was no homogeneous Counter-Reformation style can be seen by the fact that along with El Greco's paintings those of Peter Paul Rubens were highly acceptable to the Church. The Greek and Flemish artists were contraries in temperament and style. Rubens was able to reconcile a love of the flesh with love of the spirit. His mythological pagan types, kings, peasants, and religious personages are interchangeable, sharing a common robust virility, effulgent healthiness, and appetite for living. The deeply introverted El Greco distrusted the carnality of the body with a medieval fervor, while Rubens seems to have been fulfilled through the sensuous painting of the flesh. The energy in El Greco's painting is mystical; that in Rubens' is muscular. When Rubens painted his *Raising of the Cross* (Fig. 6.6), he involved his subjects in the arduous mechanics of raising a huge object freighted with a herculean body. For Rubens, both life and the taking of it required a massive expenditure of physical as well as spiritual effort. El Greco evokes unshed tears of anguish, Rubens induces the sweat of pain. What El Greco shows lying beyond touch, Rubens addresses to our finger tips. While St. Maurice

El Greco has been called insane, and more recently misguided attempts have been made to suggest that he suffered from eye defects. Neither was the case. His unique art was the product of years of development and lucid calculation and passionate religious conviction. El Greco might have declared that his external vision was normal, but it was his "inner eye" that was abnormal.

6.5 El Greco, *The Legend of St. Maurice*, 1581–1584. Madrid, Museo del Prado.

and his captains tread lightly on the earth, Rubens' race of giants grows from it. Rubens' Christ has known heroic physical exertion, that of El Greco only spiritual exercise.

Comparison with El Greco may mislead the reader into doubting Rubens' religious sincerity. Mystical asceticism has not been the only producer of great religious art. Rubens was passionately devoted to the Roman Catholic faith and spent a life time enriching the splendor of the altar with his paintings. Like the fifteenth-century Flemish artists before him, Rubens saw no contradictions in his response to the attractiveness of the material world or

6.6 Rubens. *The Raising of the Cross*, 1610–1611. Antwerp Cathedral. Copyright A.C.L. Brussels.

In Rubens' work, the foreground brilliance and posturing of the nearest figure draw us upward to the saint and back down into depth at the left where the devil quits the church. The diagonal in depth was a consistent stylistic device by which Rubens told a story, achieved dramatic and visual climax, and held his composition in forceful resolution.

The vigorous movement and sensual appearance of Rubens' figures are born in the rhythms of his brush and the creamy substance of his paint. To enjoy El Greco's color is to appreciate rare admixtures of tones, predominantly cool colors under a sometimes shrill light, restraint in the build up of heavily pigmented areas, and by comparison with Rubens, a less obtrusive trace of the brush. Showing warm light and lush sequences of opacity and transparency, Rubens' colors and glazes create the im-

the mythological past. He had optimistic confidence in himself and in the right and power of the Church. Like the Roman Catholic rulers and ecclesiastical patrons who paid for his secular art, he saw no sin in the healthy enjoyment of what lay without dogma. When he painted religious subjects, such as *Saint Ignatius Exorcising Demons from the Church* (Fig. 6.7), he was attentive to the spirit of his theme. Just as St. Ignatius had recommended projecting oneself into the state of the subject of worship, Rubens' painting draws the viewer into the church to share the excitement of the miracle and the new hope of the sick who have been cleansed of the devil. Such projection is difficult if not impossible in the construction of El Greco's paintings.

6.7 Rubens. *Saint Ignatius Exorcising Demons from the Church*, 1619. Vienna, Kunsthistorisches Museum.

pression of pulse and blood lying just beneath the flesh. Rubens' brush was swept with bravura across a form or was delicately touched to a tiny area demanding a highlight. The viewer looking at a Rubens painting can sense the physical as well as esthetic pleasure that the artist enjoyed as he worked. It is not difficult to comprehend Rubens' full involvement in the materiality of the medium that permitted him to re-create the sensuous world he loved.

The virtuoso seventeenth-century artists achieved illusions in a wide variety of media of a staggering range of subjects. The most gifted sculptor of the century and most ardent in his devotion to the aims of the Church was the Italian Gian Lorenzo Bernini. Among his other talents were playwriting, stage design, painting, and architecture. His most spectacular production in sculpture is the *Ecstasy of St. Theresa* (Fig. 6.8). St. Theresa was a sixteenth-century saint who recorded her visions. One of these, available to Bernini, describes the event portrayed in the statue:

I saw an angel close to me, on my left side, in bodily form. This I am accustomed to see but very rarely. Though I have visions of angels frequently, yet I see them only by an intellectual vision, such as I have spoken of before. It is our Lord's will that in this vision I should see the angel in this wise. He was not large, but small of stature and most beautiful—his face burning as if he were one of the highest angels who seem to be all of fire. . . . I saw in his hand a long spear of gold and at the iron's point there seemed to be a little fire. He appeared to me to be thrusting it at times into my heart, and to pierce my very entrails: When he drew it out, he seemed to draw them all out also and to leave me all on fire with a great love of God. The pain was so great that I cried out, but at the same time the sweetness which that violent pain gave me was so excessive that I could not wish to be rid of it.

6.8 Bernini. *Ecstasy of St. Theresa*, 1646. Rome, Church of Santa Maria della Vittoria. (Photo: Alinari)

Bernini chose the moment between thrusts of the spear with the saint writhing in paroxysms of pleasure and pain. The erotic nature of both the vision and the sculpture is patent, but in keeping with the religious purpose of making the situation as vivid as possible. Bernini practiced the *Spiritual Exercises* of St. Ignatius of Loyola in order to absorb himself as deeply and accurately as possible into his subject. The nature of the vision excited his interest, particularly the coexistence of conflicting psychological states, imaged on the face of the saint with consummate virtuosity. Treating stone as if it were the wax of the models from which he worked, Bernini created the illusion of clouds, cloth, and flesh. The marble was warmed by light which entered from a concealed yellow glass window. There was no previous sculptural parallel to Bernini's deliberate

6.9 Dal Pozzo. *Allegory of the Missionary Work of the Jesuits*, 1691–1694. Central portion of the ceiling, Sant'Ignazio Cathedral, Rome.

and controlled use of light as both form and mystic symbol in his composition. The sculptural group is set behind a proscenium arch, and in the background golden shafts serve as radiant backdrops. Sacred sculpture and painted altarpieces, such as that by Roger van der Weyden, had served as religious theater before. Bernini transformed the chapel where the sculpture was housed into a sphere in which the differences between art and reality were suspended.

So important was the Counter-Reformation concept of the religious vision that an increasing number of churches had their vaults illusionistically painted in grandiose compositions that permitted the faithful to look upwards directly into heaven. One of the most powerful paintings was Andrea dal Pozzo's *Allegory of the Missionary Work of the Jesuits* (Fig. 6.9). It celebrated the work and sacrifice of this order on all of the continents and demonstrated the reception in heaven of its leader and martyrs. Pozzo transformed the vault to give the impression that the church soars upwards an additional two storeys and is without any ceiling. Against the illusion of massive stable architectural elements, columns and arches, Pozzo floated clusters of figures in a remarkable series of foreshortenings so that no matter from what point the observer looks, the scene is in perspective. There are no clear zones of light and dark. The entire scene is suffused with radiance, accelerating the eye upward with no prolonged restraint. The message of the painting is that to the faithful heaven is directly accessible. As with the Gothic cathedrals, Pozzo's work and its meaning is best experienced in conjunction with the religious music of that time, which was also calculated to release the congregation of the living from their earthly existence.

Turning from Pozzo's painting to Caravaggio's *The Supper at Emmaus* (Fig. 6.10) means moving backwards almost a century. Caravaggio's view of religious art that best met the needs of the people proved more appealing to the intelligentsia than to the masses, and the tradition that gave birth to Pozzo's style represents a drastic but more popular alternative. Ironically Caravaggio's painting of religious subjects had a strong influence on secular or genre painting of the seventeenth century. The painting of *The Supper at Emmaus* was intended for the guest room of a convent. It shows the two disciples Cleophas and Peter Simon seated with Christ, whom they had taken for a fellow pilgrim and invited to eat

6.10 Michelangelo Amerighi Caravaggio. *The Supper at Emmaus*, c. 1598. Reproduced by courtesy of the Trustees, The National Gallery, London.

with them. The cockle shell on the disciple's tunic signifies that the men were pilgrims, like those who frequently used the convent's guest rooms. Caravaggio shows the moment when Christ reveals Himself by His blessing and breaking of the bread. Coupled with the revealing gesture of Christ is the clarifying action of the strong light that poetically embodies the illumination of the minds of the disciples. Their reaction is violent, in contrast to the darkened face of the uncomprehending innkeeper. Caravaggio's message was simple, intended for the least sophisticated and humblest viewer: The common man may have direct knowledge of his God. The miraculous can occur without angels, halos, or opening of the skies. Christ's epiphany takes place in the heart of the faithful. The modest dress and table fare were obvious means by which to remind the faithful of Christ's humility. Not unlike the Flemish painters of the fifteenth century, Caravaggio detailed every surface evidence provided by his subjects, from the contrasting complexions of the figures to the worm holes in the fruit. Caravaggio attached mystical feelings to the most tangible items. Unlike the Flemings, Caravaggio placed the action against a plain background and spotlighted only the figures and table. He involved the viewer more intimately in the scene through the violent foreshortening of the gestures and precarious balance of the fruit on the near edge of the table. The disciple at the left is so turned as to draw the eye immediately to the hand of Christ and thence to His face, the table, and the figure at the right. The strenuous extended gesture of the latter, which seems to push into our space, is paralleled by the angle of the table before him, thus harnessing the number of strong movements that otherwise would mitigate each other. Caravaggio has demonstrated the expressiveness of which the profile is capable. Often using models taken into his studio from the street, the painter was at his most forceful in painting rugged or picturesque types and most disconcerting to the public when he attempted the head of Christ.

Many Church officials, and it would seem the general public, found Caravaggio's painting vulgar or lacking in decorum and unnecessarily impoverishing the holy personages. He was criticized for painting distracting objects, such as the still-life arrangement of the table, which undermined the drama of the moment. Because he avoided elaborate and traditional didacticism, Caravaggio's work was also condemned for not being self-explanatory. To those unacquainted with the story, the supper may have seemed like a secular event. And in fact, the seventeenth century was to see a further obscuring of the lines that separated religious from secular painting.

The Table in Baroque Secular Art . . . .

More than in the centuries that preceded it, seventeenth-century European painting broadened its base to include varied and intimate secular subjects. Simultaneously with the great religious art produced in this century, art that responded to the curiosity of artist and patron about the daily living of the peasant and middle classes increased in the Roman Catholic countries as well as Protestant Holland. Building upon sixteenth-century secular art, the seventeenth century produced important secular art not only from intellectual resources, such as ancient literature, but also from encompassed folk traditions, exploring the unethical, irreverent, sexual, vulgar, comical, and passive aspects of human conduct. The people chosen to populate what are called "genre" paintings were given more human dimensions than those possessed by figures in Renaissance art. Where the Renaissance had discovered the means to render the actual and ideal outer appearance of men and their serious contemplative moments, during the baroque period the painter's knowledge of and concern for expressing the emotions and workings of the mind became paramount. The range of animation of which human beings are capable comes much closer to being realized in seventeenth-century art than in fifteenth-century. This new focus and enlivening of human activity had important consequences for the form of painting.

Genre painting resists strict limitations. It may overlap into spiritual art, allegory, and historical painting. At the core of genre painting is the omission of a climactic or historical moment in favor of activities that are part of the stream of quotidian existence. Generally, it deals with types of persons in types of common occurrence, but frequently a painter will go beyond typification into portraiture or choose unique moments in the life of his subjects. Early genre painting was based upon a growing tolerance of art, a basic optimism and affirmation of earthly existence, and curiosity about the way large segments of humanity pass their days. While this art form eschews the ritual that was so much a part of religious and political imagery, it nevertheless may focus on the rituals of daily life in the home. Partisanship or social conscience was not the motivation for depicting the peasant life. The misery, oppression, and tragedies of the peasants or the lower middle classes did not find their way into seventeenth-century art. Genre art was not democratic, for it affirmed class distinctions. Favored themes were those of diversion, customs, or quiet revery which did not threaten the established social order but provided the upper classes with vicarious experiences. The middle class as well as the aristocracy bought this type of art. Relative political and religious security enjoyed by the monarchs and Roman Cath-

olic Church in Europe during the seventeenth century was responsible for a relaxation of demands on the painter. Roman Catholic countries witnessed the phenomenon of painters doing both official work for the Church and the courts and genre painting for prominent churchmen as well as the laity. In Holland, specialization came into being during this century, so that artists painted only landscapes, portraits, still lifes, or genre art, depending upon their success with the market. Genre art, which was rarely commissioned, symbolizes the double edge of freedom and material insecurity that accrued to the artist during the baroque period. In Holland, by midcentury the market was overloaded, and painters were forced to take on additional jobs or give up painting altogether.

While there is much of esthetic value that we admire today in seventeenth-century genre art, the general public who bought or speculated on art was guided primarily by fidelity to appearance and cannot be considered as connoisseurs. The form of genre painting was not entirely uninfluenced by either religious or noble painting, but the artist nevertheless had great license in the making of his paintings. The format of genre art is smaller than that of the grandiose paintings done for the Church or the royal courts. It was intended for the more modest scale of the home and for greater intimacy of viewing. The proximity of the figures to the picture's surface and the emphasis upon costumes, object accessories, locale, and facial or gesticulatory expression invited close reading and prolonged reflection.

An object frequently found in baroque genre painting is the table. In religious art the table was used occasionally to hold the books of a church scholar or devotional objects of a saint, but is more widely identified with the Last Supper. Not only did the table serve the purpose of the enactment of an important sacred drama, but Renaissance painters had utilized it as a means to link the past with contemporary social customs, as we have seen. In genre painting the table becomes the locus of various occasions for people coming together as well as for individual activity.

Such an occasion where the table serves as a meeting place for a segment of the community is the wedding feast in the painting (Fig. 6.11) by the sixteenth-century Flemish artist Peter Brueghel. Though not the first, Brueghel was the most gifted genre painter in his century in depicting the daily life of Dutch peasants. What little biographical material is available indicates that he was not a peasant, but a rather highly educated townsman whose paintings were bought and admired by kings and many of the intellectual elite of his day. A

humanist, Brueghel saw his art as a means of recording his study of man, not in terms of ancient writers and philosophers, of the coordinate system of the Church, but in the light of advanced contemporary secular theories and his own empirical experience. Brueghel's art reflects his astuteness as an observer, not criticism of nor compassion for the peasantry. He saw the peasant not as the symbol of fundamental wisdom but as basically unreasoning, passively submitting to forces greater than himself. The peasants are always involved in inherited activity, work, customs, and traditions. Brueghel's figures are motivated by simple, uncomplicated drives, enacting their existence automatically, often with energy, if not with great cheer. (Smiling peasants are rare in Brueghel's paintings.) Brueghel's

6.11 Brueghel. *The Peasant Wedding*, c. 1565. Vienna, Kunsthistorisches Museum.

subjects, whether Biblical or genre, share the phenomenon of recurrence as if the artist had sought and set down certain eternal constants in life. Not content to be a reporter, Brueghel brought to art lucid analysis and a genius for storytelling that elevates his *Peasant Wedding* from a prosaic event to good theater. The earth was Brueghel's stage and those upon it his characters. In this painting the set is a grain-filled barn after the harvest. An overflow of guests comes to celebrate the personal harvest of the farmer's daughter, who sits both coyly and smugly beneath a symbolic crown hung upon a green cloth. The fullness of the grain stacks and the bride are meaningful allies as are the groom and the fertility symbol of the crossed sheaves which hang before his eyes. Art historians could not find the groom, but the literary historian Gilbert Highet, who has given the best reading of the painting, identified him as the dark-clad, intoxicated figure in the center, just to the left of the rear figure holding the door that serves as a tray for custard pies. The ill-mannered groom and his glaring parents seated across from him are wealthy townspeople, and as Highet points out, Brueghel encourages our speculations on both the wedding night and life ever after of the bridal couple, although the painting's evidence makes the future clear. A few of the subthemes in the drama are the priest's earnest pleas for subsidy from the recalcitrant landlord at the far right, enjoying the occasion less than does his dog; the longing gaze at the distant food of the bagpiper, and the contrast between the bride's brother filling a jug at the left and the little girl cleaning her plate. The former's activity reminds us of Christ's changing of the water to wine at the marriage of Cana. In fact, the diagonal composition of the long table and triangular grouping in the left foreground can be found in sixteenth-century paintings of the Last Supper. These objects also assist in maintaining our detachment from the action. The ample figures are hard-edged in firm outline, so that the pile of empty jugs in the basket invites an ironic comparison with the peasants who made them and the piled-up figures in the doorway at the upper left who also wait to be filled. The bright clear colors never impede the study of the detail and keenly observed awkward gestures of each figure. For Brueghel, painting was to be equally pleasing to the mind and to the eye.

The table appears in the Spanish artist Velázquez' *Water Carrier of Seville* (Fig. 6.12) as an adjunct to business, serving as base for an earthenware water jug. A brilliant painter of Spanish royalty, Velázquez spared no talent in portraying a street vendor named El Corzo, his young clients, and the modest objects. The mundane act of selling water has been solemnized by the painter into an almost sacramental event, and it is not improbable that Velázquez had the sacrament of the Eucharist in mind. There is no intimation of the noise and jostling of the streets. The boy drinking is in shadow, while in strong illumination the vendor and boy receiving the glass silently share an unspoken meditative union. Both in content and in form Velázquez has changed small coin into gold. The individuality of El Corzo, the youth holding the glass, and the jugs rises above typicality and impresses them on the memory. The still tractable face of the youth contrasts with the traces of hard use in the face of the older man and the jug upon which his hand rests. There is no overt attempt at pathos. The large objects and three-quarter length figures, close to the viewer, show restrained dignity and powerful affirmation of their worth. Immobility adds to their eloquence. The effect is obtained through a formal closure of shapes holding the eye within the frame. A rough ovular form is created by the placement and linkage of the large jug with the shadow of the smaller

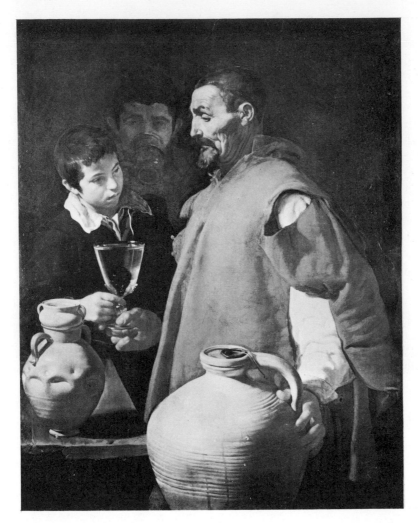

6.12 Velázquez. *Water Carrier of Seville*, c. 1619. Wellington Museum, Apsley House, London. Crown Copyright.

and the hand of the man, the small jug's tangency with the boy's wrist, the glass and the boy's right arm leading to the head and those of the other two figures, and then the smock's curvature that returns the eye to the large jug and anchors the oval to the frame at the right. A few tones, chiefly gray, terra cotta, white, and flesh-colored, are applied to large areas in deft nuance, reserving for the glass and droplets of moisture on the jug the most brilliant lights. The lucidity of the lighting and firmness of the drawing in the forms are countered by the subtlety with which the paint itself has been applied.

In the painting of *The Cheat* (Fig. 6.13) by the French artist Georges de la Tour, done around 1630, the table has become the setting for intrigue, deceit, and downfall. The card game had entered into art in the sixteenth century and been used by Caravaggio and his followers to illustrate the calling of St. Matthew. Caravaggio had also painted a *Gyp at Cards*, reflecting not only the sporting instincts of segments of Roman society, but also their pleasure in a bold display of dishonesty. La Tour's use of this theme followed a stay in Rome where he may have encountered the idea. The subject may be related to the story of the prodigal son, favored by Church authorities, who supported the sacrament of penance against the Protestants. Both the painting and the card game are highly contrived. The players are outfitted in what for that time were outlandish costumes. The

6.13 De la Tour. *The Cheat, c.* 1630.

deck is stacked against the young man in such a way that if the aces don't get his money, wine and the courtesan at the table will. The cheat has an affected air of nonchalance, tempting the susceptible youth to look at his cards while reaching for his ace in the belt. Just the eyes and hands are sufficient to tell the story. All hand movements have a suave boneless ease serving to enact the deception and tie the figures together visually. The shadowing of the cheat's face recalls that of Judas in earlier versions of the Last Supper. The dark deed, however, is performed in daylight which coolly illuminates the firm, smooth, continuous volumes of the bodies and the sparkle of the shiny accessories. The airless environment makes possible the meticulous clarity of detail of the types who themselves seem all surface and no depth.

The table identified with the unity and humility of the family can be seen in Louis Le Nain's *Peasants at Supper* (Fig. 6.14), painted between 1645 and 1648. The table is the means by which the family comes together each day and shares the quiet pleasures of home, hearth, and board. Absent from the painting, however, are the noise, movement, and disorder that would be found during or even after the evening meal. There is no overt rapport between the figures. Those in the foreground look at us, and those in the darkness gaze into the fire. Le Nain, perhaps seeking to exalt the probity of the peasant, cast him into an artificial mold. Each figure is consciously posed. The child at the lower right, like the objects carefully placed near him, serves as a visual stabilizer to the composition. Each person is carefully turned so as to counterbalance another figure, eliminating any impression of volition or spontaneity. The general air of decorum in the peasant hut is shared with official painting of French royalty. (Compare Rigaud's portrait of Louis XIV, Fig. 7.20). Le Nain stressed the peasant's reflective capacity and graceful composure rather than his life of arduous labor or moments of energetic relaxation. The painting's strength lies largely in the realization of the materiality of the figures, objects, and setting. The hardness of the

6.14 Le Nain. *Peasants at Supper*, 1645–1648. Paris, The Louvre. (Photo: Giraudon)

bodies and garments is whetted by the soft gradients of shadows and the way the light rebounds from the durable surfaces. Le Nain shows a certain detachment, a refusal to become deeply and emotionally involved with his subjects, but he holds them aloof with respect, and his searching eye achieved coordination with his brush.

The hesitancy of seventeenth-century French genre painters to engage in extravagant demonstrations of emotions contrasts with the flamboyant tastes of the Flemish painter Jordaens. In his *The King Drinks* (Fig. 6.15), the table is again the cause of family assembly. The occasion comes from Flemish folklore and is the feast celebrating the day of Epiphany, during which the entire clan assembles for feasting and drinking. Shortly before Epiphany, "King's tickets" were sold in Antwerp. The old man in Jordaens' painting has made the lucky draw of the tickets at the table and is reigning monarch. His drinking signals the explosion of festivity. He has assigned to each relative a mock

title for his "court"—the "Singer," the "Cock," the "Doctor," and the "Spinster." Jordaens epitomizes that aspect of baroque art which delighted in situations where the individual, consciously or not, loses control and abandons himself to feeling. In paintings such as this the seventeenth century introduces laughing figures; before, only angels or the Madonna smiled as signs of divine grace. The impetus for laughter in *The King Drinks* and many other baroque paintings is alcohol and the dominant mood of abandon. The family table has become the setting for an orgy. The Renaissance and sixteenth century might show mythical figures such as satyrs and nymphs having a riotous picnic in an ancient wood, but the seventeenth century brought the theme directly into home or tavern.

Both in form and content, this is a painting concerned with the five senses. The figures make or respond to noise, like the bagpipes that abound in the country, concoct grotesque expressions to shock the eye, fondle sensuous objects, inhale a variety of smells, and submit the palate to a staggering array of foods and drink. In a way, this painting is also a study of cycles, stressing the contrasting flesh of young and old, the range of expressions from anticipation to satiation, and the intake and outlet of wine. Jordaens displays his virtuosity in demonstrating the number of ways people may be seen with their mouths open. The face is given a great mobility bordering at times on the caricatural. The artist's insight into the ritual rather than spontaneous character of the event manifests itself in the forced nature of some of the jeering faces.

The painting itself is an assault upon the senses and tastes of the viewer. Strongly flavored with reds, blues, and yellows, its silhouettes heave and defy stability. The dark jacket of the standing figure to the "king's" left serves as foil and anchorage for the agitation. The costumes and flesh of the figures accustomed to appeasing their appetites are painted so as to stress their appeal to the touch as well as the eye. Although depicting a scene at once hilarious and vulgar, the artist reserves his good taste for the actual painting. Above the "king" are the words, "It is sweet to be admitted to a friendly table."

Such a proverb written above

6.15 Jordaens. *The King Drinks*, 1625–1650.

6.16 Brouwer. *The Smokers, c.* 1630. The Metropolitan Museum of Art, The Michael Friedsam Collection, 1931.

Adrian Brouwer's *The Smokers* (Fig. 6.16) would provide wonderful irony. A Flemish painter active in Holland, Brouwer was preoccupied with the boisterous public life around the tavern table. His small paintings catalogue drinking bouts, brawls, cooking, eating, and gossiping, gambling, toothpulling, and painful operations on feet and, in one instance, his own back. His subjects appear to be poor townsmen rather than peasants. He defiantly devoted entire paintings to gross types with bulbous inflamed noses and gaping mouths, or sleeping drunks with delusions of exalted status. His self-portraits show discoloration and deterioration in his own face due to alcohol. Brouwer's *The Smokers*, probably done in the late 1630's, is his own avowal of manliness and the ethic of being one's self. He can drink and smoke with the best, take practical jokes, and withstand pain, and not give a damn for whoever looks at his painting. Naturally dis-

dainful of contemporary theories on composition and drawing, Brouwer sketched coarsely, but his characters and his paintings preserve the disorder of the tavern with its atmosphere freighted with stale smells and murky lighting. The paint is applied ruggedly and with gusto, again affirming his distaste for the effeminate and precious. His strokes and tones convincingly weave the garments and flesh that belong to those poor in pocket, but rich in the love of earthly pleasures.

While for some Dutch artists, influenced greatly by Caravaggio, the table meant the melodramatic enactment of debauchery or perverse conduct, Pieter de Hooch satisfied his countrymen's middle-class taste by showing tables in settings of propriety and quiet sociability. His paintings frequently show tables in arbors, intimate courtyards, or neat interiors around which are gathered well-bred gentlemen who play an honest game of cards, imbibe with discretion, or converse wittily with pleasant hostesses. One of de Hooch's finest paintings is *The Mother at the Cradle* (Fig. 6.17). Here the table, although set off to the side, is identified with domesticity, the care and vigilance of the wife for the children and the home. This ideal of insulated constant security is measured out not alone in the relation of the mother to the cradle, but in the cool geometrical rightness and sun-warmed atmosphere of the rooms. Everything is in its correct place to make up an ideal home and a beautifully arranged painting. Even the dog has turned his body at a right angle so that he is aligned with the receding angle of the floor tiles and is tangent to the door frame, taking the eye into depth and toward the mother. Through the door and windows come not the sounds and sights of Holland's political anguish, but only a dream-like stillness, reassuring heat of the sun, and the fragrance of well-tended gardens.

Toward the third quarter of the seventeenth century in Holland, Vermeer

6.17 De Hooch. *The Mother at the Cradle*, 1659–1660. Berlin, Kaiser Frederick Museum.

further restored peace and civilized culture to the table. Constants in his art are sunlit corners of elegant whitewashed rooms with carefully disposed tables, paintings, chairs, and handsome passive women. It is as if Vermeer's young women had come to exemplify Dutch culture shortly before the disastrous wars of the 1670's. They are shown standing near or seated at sturdy tables, making lace, reading, writing, in animated conversation with military suitors, admiring themselves, or sleeping. They are comforting images of sedentary feminine diversion. *A Woman Weighing Gold* (Fig. 6.18), painted in the 1660's, juxtaposes a painting of the Last Judgment against the form of a girl holding a balance. A devout converted Catholic, Vermeer may have regarded as symbolic the painting and its placement in relation to the girl. It is possible that the idea is of the religious conscience of the girl who is faithful to her responsibility. She stands below the figure of Christ in the position and area that the Archangel Michael would assume as he weighed the souls of the resurrected. The

6.18 Vermeer. *A Woman Weighing Gold*, *c*. 1660. Courtesy of the National Gallery of Art, Washington, D. C.

violence and terror of the day of judgment and of the painting make an ironic contrast with the stilled life in the room. (It is historically interesting to see a painting of a religious subject no longer over an altar, but hung in a private home.) Balance is not only the theme of the painting, but the key to Vermeer's compositional ideas. The woman is arranged in the setting, not unsympathetically, like the other objects so that her hand and the scale must be taken in with the picture frame behind them, and seen against the open box and the girl's left hand. The casually arranged cloth on the table serves to draw us to both the source of light and the girl. The tangible rigid armature formed by the right angle of the table against the wall and the alignment of the woman with the painting provide a measure of the movement of the light and its refusal to be shaped into clearly defined patterns. Vermeer needed only a restricted segment of the visible world to reveal life's poetic potential.

Vermeer's private life conflicted with the tranquillity of his paintings. Before his death in 1675 he suffered financial problems, and his widow filed for bankruptcy. With great difficulty she succeeded in regaining possession of the painting that is known as *The Artist in His Studio* (Fig. 6.19). It is a painting of what appears to be an artist's workshop, a frequent genre subject of the time. A seated artist is painting a young model who holds a book and trumpet, symbols of fame. The table appears in the room in connection with art. On it are objects, a cast and sketchbook, that may symbolize the arts of sculpture and architecture. Scholars have shown that the wall map is of the Netherlands in the sixteenth century, before Holland achieved its independence. The artist's elegant costume is also of that century, suggesting that this is not an actual self-portrait. The half-drawn drape is an old device by which to suggest revelation of a past event. The

painting is thus not directly about Vermeer's studio and own lifetime, but is a nostalgic evocation of the more affluent and ideal working conditions enjoyed by Dutch artists the century before. The painting of the studio model in the guise of fame may have been an ironic personal statement by the artist skeptical about the future esteem of his own work and aware of the artificial nature of fame itself.

To realize this wishful image of an ideal, Vermeer gave the totality of his gift as an artist. From the painting we can begin to comprehend the imagination and inspired effort of the artist that went beyond the amazing technical achievement of simulating appearances. The fact that the viewpoint, angle of light, and placement of objects were all calculated before brush met canvas does not detract from Vermeer's excellence, for these preliminary decisions were esthetic judgments in the fullest sense of the word—the room arranged in terms of art. The eye moves into the painting slowly and logically from the large foreground shapes at the left to the artist at the right, and then to the model, with each area precisely manifest in its distance from other objects and the viewer. The careful but not obvious avoidance of simple alignment by parallel edges or right angles enriches the visual design and impels us to see each object in relation to another. Contrasts stress the idiosyncrasies of each shape, but do not destroy the feeling of inner rapport between all within the painting. There are several conjugations of strong rhythmic sequences, like the ceiling beams, the brass chandelier curves culminating in the Hapsburg eagles, the horizontal vignettes of Dutch cities on the sides of the map, the black and white striping of the artist's blouse, and the alternating floor tiles. Against these sequences can be seen the random sparkle on upholstery nails in the chairs and in the fabric of the drapery. The drape holds all of the painting's colors

6.19 Vermeer. *The Artist in His Studio*, 1665–1670. Vienna, Kunsthistorisches Museum.

in less concentrated hues with the exception of a small patch of blue that matches the color in the model's dress. Its dense saturate pattern contrasts with the airiness and more open schema of the room itself. Shadows never obliterate, but also force us to find new revelations of tones and shapes. The composition is anchored at the left by the half-lighted drape seen against the most brilliant light on the wall behind it, and at the right by the judicious alignment of the edge of the map, the chair, the right easel leg, and the segmented black tiles that lead into the painting. Like the seated artist, we are expected to weigh in our minds the rightness of each stroke in terms of the stuffs, luminosity, and hue of the object brought into being. The mahlstick held by the artist is to steady his hand, and Vermeer's art is a brilliant demonstration of wrist painting.

In the manner of Van Eyck, Vermeer reconstructed his world in terms of the smallest ray of light and the fragment upon which it fell. Unlike Van Eyck, Vermeer's compositions were free of hierarchical demands of religious subject matter so that he could bring to the arrangement as well as to the detail a full revelation of his aspirations.

CHAPTER 7

IMAGES
OF KINGS

In the ancient world art was one of the most important means of making concrete for the public the abstract concepts of kingship. The average man in antiquity usually knew his ruler through art rather than through the king's physical presence. The burden of giving a presence to the divinity or omnipotence of the king fell to the artist, who relied not only on a likeness of his subject, but also on certain prescribed and traditional artistic devices to interpret attributes in a way clearly decipherable by the people. The symbolism of authority was extended in the mind of the populace to architecture which related to the residence, appearance or epiphany, and ceremonies in honor of the ruler. The historical repetition of Egyptian symbolism in the Mediterranean world and that of antiquity in the Middle Ages was not motivated simply by the appeal of design in painting, sculpture, and architecture. Symbols and devices were absorbed by succeeding cultures and used to inform their own art that glorified kingship of an earthly or heavenly monarch.

THE KING AS DEITY

The Egyptian pharaoh was divine. He was the descendant and heir of the sun god, the ruler of the sky. An Old Kingdom statue of Khafre (Fig. 7.1) seated upon a throne includes the carved image of the hawk god, Horus, who is lord of the sky, directly behind the head of pharaoh. The hawk's wings embrace the headdress of pharaoh, symbolic of the origin and divine protection of the ruler. The pharaoh is shown rigidly frontal, a timeless pose repeated without deviation for over three thousand years of Egyptian history and the ancestor of the twelfth-century enthroned Christ at Chartres. The transcendence of the pharaoh over mortality is revealed through his aloof and immutable posture. There is no bodily movement or expression. The stiffness and immobility of the human body were the means by which the sculptor, working with human anatomy, imaged the separateness of his king from mortals. In short, pharaonic imagery that deals with cosmic kingship sought to be as unnatural as possible. The only alteration

124

7.1 Giza. The pharaoh Khafre, *c*. 2560 B.C. Cairo Museum. (Photo: Hirmer)

in the position of statues of the pharaohs is from the elbows down; the ruler is sometimes shown holding a staff of office or the crook and flail, the attributes of authority held by the lord of the underworld, Osiris. His tasks were to be a shepherd and judge of his people. The sacerdotal nature of pharaonic imagery parallels the ceremonious nature of Egyptian court life and the formality of the kings' public appearances. Such courtly protocol combined with its development in Persia was to be taken over by the later Roman emperors and the Christian Church.

For three thousand years, pharaohs were imaged in paintings and relief sculptures that proclaimed godlike character and protection of the people. Shown in battle, at the hunt, in the company of other deities, and officiating at state ceremonies, the pharaoh's effigy was placed on the walls of tombs, palaces, and temples. One of the

greatest of Egypt's rulers, Ramses III, who lived in the fifteenth century B.C., followed tradition, using the outer wall of a great temple as a political billboard. He had himself shown hunting wild bulls (Fig. 7.2). This was not a secular theme of frivolous sport, for all activities engaged in by the pharaoh were religious, symbolic of his fight against evil. Wild beasts as well as enemy tribes were viewed as the partisans of Seth, a malefic underworld god. While the benevolent hawk god Horus flies above him, the pharaoh coolly dispatches the fleeing animals with his spear. The reins tied to Ramses' waist seem unnecessary because of the perfect discipline demonstrated by the chariot's horses. The symbolically smaller-scale troops also seem superfluous, for Pharaoh's personal victory was inevitable. The raised and extended front legs of the horse were a victory symbol throughout the ancient Near and Far East. The fallen inverted buffalo beneath the horses is interchangeable with bodies of dead warriors in reliefs of war. So effective was this combination of gallop and fallen prey that it persisted in imperial imagery into the nineteenth century and recurred with new connotations in Picasso's *Guernica* (see Fig. 15.12). The relief of the hunt also demonstrates fine synthesis of naturalistic observation and rendering, in fishes, reeds, and buffalo, and of the stylized or schematic formula by which Ramses and his retinue are depicted. The intrusion of pictographic writing extolling the pharaoh demonstrates that the event and art transcended time and space unification and possessed a higher reality.

WARRIOR KINGS

A hunting relief from a seventh-century B.C. Assyrian palace shows the king, Ashurnasirpal shooting a lion poised on the rear of the royal chariot. Assyrian

7.2   Egypt. *Ramses III hunting wild bulls*, *c.* 1200 B.C. Medinet Habu, Vol. II, pl. 117. Courtesy of the Oriental Institute, University of Chicago.

palaces abounded in symbolically repetitious reliefs of imperial war-waging, hunting, and religious ceremonies. The great size and number of the reliefs were intended to impress visiting emissaries with the king's might. Assyrian kings were not deified; they were mortals, who demonstrated their right to rule through physical prowess, actually jeopardizing their lives by hand-to-hand combat with their foes. The king's acclaim depended in part upon acknowledging the courage of his oppo-

7.3   Nimrud. Ashurnasirpal II killing a lion, *c.* 850 B.C. Courtesy of the Trustees of the British Museum, London.

nent, who was given a chance to attack. The relief shown here (Fig. 7.3) indicates the type of hunt the king might wage, utilizing captured lions that, if recalcitrant, could be goaded into fighting by the noise of cymbals and irritating wounds. Deliberate in his aim despite the beast's proximity, the king is about to apply the fatal shot to the brain. The muscular character of Assyrian kingship is reflected in the relief modeling, which contrasts with the flatter bone-and-sinewless Egyptian forms. The overlapping of figures and objects in depth and their abundance of detail, schematized as it is, show a more earthly orientation in Assyrian art than in Egyptian imperial art. Even the small portion of the relief illustrated here permits us to enjoy the rhythmic composition. Serving as compositional rhymes, the lion at the left and the horses also demonstrate phases of the hunt. The symbolic leap over the dead lion is also thoughtfully handled in terms of contrasting silhouettes and of compactness and extension of forms. The king and charioteer serve as compositional and narrative fulcrums. The profile view was favored in antiquity for its clarity of exposition and usefulness in rendering animals and figures in movement.

The richest legacy of imperial imagery bequeathed to history is in Roman art. The transition of Rome from a republic to an empire is reflected in two sculptures of Roman rulers. The first (Fig. 7.4) is of emperor Augustus and was made shortly after 20 B.C. The second (Fig. 7.5) dates from the late fourth century A.D. and is probably of Emperor Marcian. Augustus' statue was found in his wife's villa and is known as the Prima Porta Augustus; the bronze cast of Marcian is called the Barletta sculpture because of the east coast Italian city in which it is located. Augustus is shown in military uniform as befitted the Imperator. His gesture is that of the com-

mander-in-chief exhorting his troops. On his breastplate beneath the approving figure of Jupiter is the scene of a Parthian chieftain voluntarily returning captured eagle standards from Roman legions, a historic diplomatic feat achieved by Augustus, signifying his peaceful rule. The figure below symbolizes Mother Earth, and the overflowing horns attest to the material prosperity under Augustus' rule. The dolphin by his leg alludes to the belief in the divine origins of the emperor's family, and the Cupid rider alludes to Venus and fertility. Thus brought together on the breastplate are an actual historical event, divinities, and allegories that demonstrate the universal Roman Peace for which Augustus was famed. Although deified by some of the provinces he conquered, in Rome itself Augustus chose to remain its first citizen, or princeps, nominally subservient to the Senate in nonmilitary matters. His effigy is that of a handsome, athletic, dignified, but humane ruler, given to clemency as well as war. His weight is gracefully balanced in a manner reminiscent of the Greek *Spear Carrier* (Fig. 10.1). The figure is poised and seems easily capable of further movement. Originally, a bronze version of this sculpture may have stood in a public place where an actual crowd venerated it.

The Barletta statue was also erected in a public place. It is a rare survivor of the full-length imperial statues of the time. Unlike that of Augustus, Marcian's effigy towered over the crowd, impressive in its greater than life-size scale. No longer mortal and bowing to an earthly power, Marcian is shown as divine and wore a crown. Both emperors were military, but Marcian's statue is more militant. The quality of human mercy is replaced by the severity of the later divine uncompromising guardian of the Empire. In the original state, the Emperor probably held a sword (now he is shown with a cross), thus giving

7.4 Rome. The *Prima Porta* statue of Augustus, and a detail of the head, *c.* 19 B.C. Vatican Museum. (Photo: Anderson)

comfort to his many non-Christian followers and evoking fear in his enemies. The sword and the orb of the world replace the program of Augustus' armor and foreign policy. The relaxed fluidity of Augustus' movements is replaced by a durable stance and a rigid arrangement of the limbs and body. The sensuous softness of Augustus' form has given way to a tough unyielding surface and more masculine treatment of the drapery. The feet and legs alone predict the qualities of the upper portions of the bodies in their breadth, weight, and relation to the base.

Both sculptures are portraits of the rulers. The head of Augustus echoes classical Greek tastes—it shows physical beauty, controlled and slight informality of the hair, easy movement in the features, con-

stant composure. The bronze head of Marcian has a geometric, blocklike, axial symmetry enhanced by the charismatic fixity of the enlarged irises. There is no casualness in the hair beneath the crown, no tactile savoring of the beard. Augustus' portrait does not belie his ability to speak eloquently and to extemporize. The fixity of Marcian's mouth reminds us that on public occasions the late Roman emperors spoke in formulas or gave prescribed signs, avoiding spontaneity and the trivial gestures that would have marred their godlike impersonality.

Between the Barletta and Prima Porta figures in date are two other works of imperial art that reflect political and artistic changes. The equestrian statue of Marcus Aurelius (Fig. 7.6), made between A.D. 161

7.5 Barletta. Statue of Emperor Marcian (?), and a detail of the head, c. A.D. 400. (Photo: Hirmer)

and 180, survived medieval demolition of Roman imperial statuary because it was mistakenly believed to be the first Christian emperor, Constantine. Originally, a fallen barbarian lay beneath the horse, and Aurelius' gesture is one of clemency to his foes. In his left hand he held a globe. Freestanding sculptures of a figure on horseback in Aurelius' time were the prerogative of the emperor. So esteemed were this and other artistic effigies of the emperor that laws were written concerning abusive language and other human conduct prohibited in its vicinity; violation meant severe punishment. Occasionally public executions were performed before the monument, and a prisoner on trial could touch the statue, claiming sanctuary and right of appeal to the emperor.

Aurelius' horse is rendered in scrupulous detail so that the bronze cast still conveys the modeled veins and creases in the flesh visible to someone standing below. The head of the Emperor however, is less detailed. To accommodate the gaze seen from below and at a distance, the hair portions are deeply drilled and the planes of the face broadly modeled. There is a general lessening of particularizing and portrait quality, making of the figure and its gesture more of an ideal embodiment of the near-deific status of the living Emperor.

Toward the end of the second century A.D., the gladiator-trained Emperor, Commodus, had himself depicted as the Hercules (Fig.7.7), thus proclaiming himself immortal. Some of the debased Roman emperors donned animal skins and entered the Colosseum arena to attack women. Nero had assumed the role of a living god in the first century, setting off a long tradition that in America resulted in Horatio Greenough's sculpture of George Washington as Zeus and Lincoln's enthronement in a Roman temple. Commodus' statue reflects the vanity that caused him to shoot five hippopotami with a bow and arrow from his box at the Colosseum before a cheering multitude. It also indicates the growing power of the army over the Senate in electing and maintaining an emperor. Commodus' bloody murder after a short and sanguine reign did not diminish the drive to deify the living ruler of Rome. In his sculpture the artist has not completely endowed him with the godlike frontality of the Barletta statue, but the pose of the head and its alignment with the knotted claws and emblematic crest are close to it. The almost effeminate delight in simulating the textures of flesh, hair, and animal skin, is inconceivable in the ascetic Barletta figure.

IMPERIAL PORTRAITS AND RELIEFS

Reliefs showing the emperor with groups change from those showing isolated figures. Like their Assyrian predecessors, Roman emperors were shown in a wide variety of reliefs and paintings of battles, hunts, and courtly civic functions. One of the most beautiful and impressive reliefs of the Augustan age is the *Ara Pacis*, Altar of Peace, constructed and carved between 14 and 9 B.C. Built on the Field of Mars, a military parade ground outside Rome, it was in-

tended to publicize the Emperor's foreign and domestic policy. The Emperor and family are shown on one of the exterior sides with the procession led by the priests either at the founding or completion of the altar. Only a detail of the relief is shown here (Fig. 7.8), but it demonstrates the informality of the group arrangement and the indistinguishableness of Augustus, who is probably the figure at the left, the left half of whose body has been lost. Like other members of his family, the Emperor wears a laurel crown, but neither in posture, gesture, or position is his eminence stressed. The image Augustus was literally projecting was that of the ruler who was anxious to restore sincere religious observance and

7.6 Rome. *Equestrian Statue of Marcus Aurelius, c.* A.D. 161–180. (Photo: Stoedtner)

the unity of the family. Dilatory temple at-tendance and juvenile delinquency were not unknown in Augustus' time. The sculptor has given us strong portraits of members of the imperial family, priests, and senators, observing the individuality of their garments, footwear, stance, and move-ment. So natural and casual are the figures that some have part of their feet projecting over the edge of the relief's base, augment-ing the illusion of recession in the back-ground.

Over three hundred years later, a great triumphal arch was erected near the Colosseum and Forum to commemorate the victorious arrival of Constantine at Rome. It was adorned with new and old relief sculptures taken from other monuments. Two of the new reliefs (Fig. 7.9) showed Constantine receiving homage from the Senate and distributing gifts, according to tradition. Unlike the figures of the Augus-tan relief, those of Constantine shock the eye with their stunted bodies, large heads, and repetitious gestures, geometric align-ment, and total loss of individuality. The figures are flattened out and have lost all sensual appeal. From surviving monumen-tal sculptures of the time, it is known that sculptors of consummate skill continued to work for the Emperor. The reliefs were relatively small and were not intended to fulfill the same functions as, for example, the over sixty-foot-high full-length statue of Constantine that was placed in his ba-silica. Although the best talent available at the time did not work on the relief, it nevertheless has a certain power and suc-ceeds in expressing the courtly ideals of the time. Within the Emperor's presence all ac-tivity was conducted according to strict ritual. The historic importance of these re-liefs lies in the culmination of the drive to-ward a centripetal centrality of composi-tion with total focus upon the unflinchingly frontal and centralized figure of the em-

7.7 Rome. *Commodus as the New Hercules, c.* A.D. 185. Conservatori Museum. (Photo: Alinari)

peror. No previous ancient culture had re-alized so completely the artistic devices now at the service of the ruler. Official taste was indifferent to organic life of flesh and blood. Ideas superseded emphasis upon out-ward form, and the external sensual life of the body glorified in Greece and early Rome passed into eclipse. A new and posi-tive esthetic evolved in accord with hieratic and spiritual ideas that would have been outraged by such an interpretation as that of the Altar of Peace. A predominantly ur-ban, sophisticated taste produced the Con-stantine statuary and Barletta figure, and provided the base for such medieval Chris-tian imagery as in the Ravenna apse mosaic of Christ.

The eastern portion of the Roman

7.8 Rome. Field of Mars. *Ara Pacis*, relief of Augustus procession, *c.*
14–9 B.C.

7.9 Rome. Detail of the Arch of Constantine showing a frieze with the
Emperor in the center, early fourth century A.D. (Photo: Alinari)

Empire, known as Byzantium, was founded by Constantine in A.D. 330, with its capital in the city that bore his name, Constantinople. Earlier Roman imperial devices for imbuing art with the majesty and deeds of the ruler were continued and refined in the centuries that followed. Art workshops were part of the Palace of the Emperor in Constantinople; the ruler, who held the monopoly on many precious materials including purple dyes, could insure that royal art would continue to remind his people of perpetual victory and divinely sanctioned rule. Coins, public statues, ivory reliefs on boxes, consular credentials, textiles, paintings, and mosaics, army standards, and such precious objects as silver disks bore the imperial effigy for a thousand years. The emperor was always shown in majestic authority, whether fighting, hunting, officiating at public ceremonies, or attending the public games in the hippodrome. The so-called *Barberini Ivory* (Fig. 7.10) is an outstanding example of the image of the early Byzantine ruler. A semiprecious medium imported from India and Africa, ivory had the advantages of softness for delicate and detailed carving, durability, and the ability to take paint. The Barberini panel was probably part of a series commemorating military and diplomatic triumphs of Emperor Anastasius I; it was made around A.D. 500. The triple register design is a schema that can be traced back to the fourth millennium before Christ in Egyptian imperial imagery, notably the *Narmer Palette* (Fig. 7.11).

In both objects, the top zone is symmetrical, its uncompromising formality being reserved for images of supreme deity. The Egyptian gods in the form of bulls precede their later anthropomorphosis. On the ivory, a frontal bust of Christ appears in a medallion held by angels. The Christians had simply replaced earlier Roman pagan images of the Emperor with their God and preserved the hierarchic format. The second zone of the ivory shows the Byzantine Emperor on horseback, his standard significantly overlapping an Asiatic chieftain. His stirrup is supported by an allegorical figure of Earth. The flanking figure of an official presents him with a statue of victory. On the palette, King Narmer is shown in ceremonial gesture, mace in hand, about to destroy his adversary with one stroke. (Reflecting a Christianizing influence, by the time of the *Barberini Ivory*, Byzantine emperors had reduced the number of battlefield images and those in-

7.10 Byzantium. The *Barberini Ivory* showing Emperor Anastasius (?) on horseback, *c.* A.D. 500–520. Louvre, Paris. (Photo: Hirmer)

7.11 Egypt. *The Narmer Palette*, fourth millennium B.C. Cairo Museum. A cast of the original, Courtesy of the Metropolitan Museum of Art.

volving cruelty.) While subordinate to their respective gods, both rulers assert their importance through their great size in the areas they occupy. Further, Anastasius is shown in an almost frontal pose, tactfully not competing with Christ. He is relatively central within his field, for one flanking official is missing. In the lowest, most inferior register both pieces contain the greatest mobility and symbolically significant, least ordered portion. The enemies of Narmer flee or are dead, their disarray contrasting with the pharaoh's solemnity. Below Anastasius at the left are barbarians who bring tribute and emissaries from India bringing gifts that include ivory. The relief carving in both works is of the highest quality, precise, clear, and adept in adapting political demands to compositional ones. The art of intervening centuries impresses itself upon the Byzantine relief in its greater sensuousness, variety of movement, and body perspectives.

To the unfamiliar, Byzantine art may appear stiff, repetitious, and unfeeling. There is no display of human warmth in the imperial images, no dialogue between the figures; they seem to be lined up like milk bottles at a carnival sideshow. Exposure both to Byzantine history and to Byzantine art assists discrimination between finer and lesser objects. Accustomed to no alternatives, Egyptian, Roman, and Byzantine artists took their roles for granted and created inspired art within the imposed tight limitations. Much of the power of Byzantine art, like that of earlier Rome, derives from its complete realization of political and religious ideals. The Barberini panel and the silver *Disk of Theodosius* (Fig. 7.12), made at the end of the fourth century, show the possibilities of art outside a democratic society. Wearing the imperial diadem, Theodosius is enthroned beneath the center of a gabled and arcaded structure that may have symbolized a façade of the

palace. Left and right are his sons, the princes Honorius and Arcadius, holding orbs symbolic of rule over the earth. At the flanks are members of the imperial guard. An official kneels to receive a gift or investiture of power from the emperor. According to custom, no one looks at the official. His hands are covered, showing his unworthiness to touch the divine person of the emperor. In the area below is the goddess of Earth with cornucopia symbolizing abundance under Byzantine rule. At this time Christian emperors were not averse to using pagan symbolism. The emperor's omnipotence is shown by his great hierarchic scale, centrality, and location beneath an arch symbolic of heaven. These attributes are more important than the personality or features of the ruler, hence the impersonality of the image. The artist is again depicting an abstract idea. An eyewitness description of an audience held with a Byzantine emperor by Liudprand of Cremona in the tenth century illuminates the environment that the artist was expressing, but not describing. Having been led into the audience chamber of the emperor, Liudprand wrote:

Before the seat stood a tree made of bronze, gilded over, whose branches were filled with birds, also made of gilded bronze, which uttered different cries, each according to its various species. The throne itself was so marvelously fashioned that at one moment it seemed a low structure and at another it rose into the air. It was of immense size and was guarded by lions, made either of bronze or of wood covered over with gold, who beat the ground with their tails and gave a dreadful roar with open mouth and quivering tongue. Leaning on the shoulders of two eunuchs I was brought into the emperor's presence. At my approach the lions began to roar and the birds cry out. . . . I lifted my head and behold, the man whom I had just before seen sitting on a moderately elevated seat had now changed his position and was sitting on the level of the ceiling.

Unfortunately, no images of this marvelous throne and audience hall have survived. The genius that contrived the tree and lions lives only in Liudprand's words. But close study of the composition, gestures, degree or type of movement, and color of any such political imagery, even though unfamiliar, can re-create the general ideas intended by the artist. As is true in all art, there is no divorce in imperial imagery of form and idea.

The influence of Byzantine imperial imagery was felt all through the Middle Ages. One of its strongest manifestations is in tenth- and eleventh-century Ottonian manuscript art depicting the Germanic emperors. An Ottonian emperor had married a Byzantine princess who brought to her husband's court works of art, and possibly artists, which helps to account for eastern influence in western Europe. The Emperor Otto II had himself shown in a manner reminiscent of Theodosius (Fig. 7.13). Allegorical figures of four nations bring gifts to the impassive ruler sitting beneath an architectural canopy, itself a celestial symbol. The perspective of the canopy is crude and inconsistent. To preserve the ruler's centrality and completeness, however, the artist logically omitted the fourth column and permitted the king's form to overlap the front columns. To have rendered the depth of the painting from the viewpoint of the spectator outside of the picture would have been to place him in a position superior to that of the ruler. Conventions or schema were used without concern for fidelity to appearance, only suitability to the theme. The sure rhythmic drawing of the four women, the certainty in the lines of the canopy, and the imposing proportion of the emperor in breadth and height are assurances of the artist's excel-

7.12 Byzantium. The *Disk of Theodosius* showing an investiture of an official, *c.* A.D. 390. Academy of History. Madrid.

7.13 *Emperor Otto II, c.* A.D. 985. From the Gregory Registry Manuscript.

7.14 Fujiwara no Takanobu. *Portrait of Mina-moto Yoritomo*, A.D. 1185. Jingoji, Japan.

lence. Only enough detail to demonstrate the opulence of the royal robes and severe elegance of the architecture and throne was needed. The event occurs outside of time and place; hence the artist does not work from appearances.

The Ottonian portrait shares certain properties with the Japanese portrait of the great Shogun, Minamoto Yoritomo, by Fujiwara no Takanobu (Fig. 7.14). Both were iconic images of power. Takanobu, however, joined to the impersonal symbols and stiff forms of the commander-in-chief's ceremonial costume a facial likeness of his subject. Yoritomo is shown seated on a cushion throne, as he would be seen in the place of honor during a formal ceremony in the audience hall of a palace. This imposing portrait was painted on silk shortly after 1185, when Yoritomo overthrew the pleas-ure-loving Fujiwara regents and the em-

peror retired from active rule. Yoritomo brought the samurai, the warriors, into power and created the Baku-Fu, or military government, of Japan that lasted until the nineteenth century.

Takanobu's painting inaugurated the portrait tradition in Japanese art. The style was a continuation from previous periods. It comprised large crisp silhouettes, clear ornamental patterns, flat-toned, tex-tureless flesh painting, and an austere airless surrounding. Mineral colors were mixed with glue, giving opaque, unmodeled surfaces. By western standards, the lines seem impersonally drawn, but they reveal occasional deft changes in value while preserving a serene but wirelike quality. The subject's hands and feet are not shown. The Shogun's individuality thus resides in the small, immobilized shapes of the eyes, nose, and mouth. The pose of the head and hair style are traditional, as are the symbols of office and power, the sword and scepter. Nevertheless, the injection of traces of Yoritomo's personal features is evidence of encroachment of the samurai's taste for naturalism as opposed to the abstract facial types of previous periods. Just as the samurai continued aspects of the pre-existing courtly art style, so their code of conduct, Bushido, was based upon such earlier sources as Zen Buddhism, Shintoism, and Confucianism.

In Yoritomo's shogunate the code of Bushido came into ascendance. Yoritomo's portrait is therefore of a Japanese feudal ideal of the perfect knight, or samurai. Takanobu seems to have illustrated this code in many respects. The samurai was disciplined in the strict course of rational conduct, "Rectitude is the bone that gives firmness and stature . . . without rectitude neither talent nor learning can make of a human frame a samurai." The knight was expected to possess all the martial virtues, such as the moral and physical courage that comprise valor, and to be imbued with the spirit of daring in the cause of righteousness. Benevolence, fortitude, and great endurance were also held to be princely virtues. True gracefulness was to be achieved by an economy of force. The samurai knew unswerving loyalty to the state, not to the individual. From youth he was exposed to a Spartan system of nerve training so that he would at all times exhibit stoic composure and calm presence of mind. "A truly brave man is ever serene." The absence of animation in the portrait expresses the samurai view that it was unmanly to show facial emotions and that strong character was possessed by "he who shows no sign of joy or anger." Culture was also part of his training. The samurai revered, and might even spare, an opponent who in the heat of battle preserved the presence of mind to compose or recall an appropriate couplet.

Yoritomo's portrait, which hung in a palace, may have been intended for worship. More likely it was a memorial to his military and administrative genius, to be venerated by later generations of samurai. The concept of the ruler's portrait as providing a reminder of ethics would thus be shared by East and West.

STATE PORTRAITS

The finest sculptural portrait of a fifteenth-century Italian Renaissance ruler is that of Lorenzo de' Medici, done by Verrocchio around 1478 (Fig. 7.15). It is a painted terra-cotta bust that bears impressive witness to the duke's power and excellence. The extent to which Florentine style was able to impart ideals of authority is further demonstrated when the bust is seen along with the Medici Palace (Fig. 7.16), built by Michelozzo in 1444. With both in mind, it is helpful to consider Machiavelli's statements in *The Prince*, written in 1513 and first published in 1532. Although later

in date, these precepts were influenced by Machiavelli's knowledge of Lorenzo and the tradition out of which he came. Their relevance to art can be seen in the importance the writer has placed upon appearances:

> We . . . encourage such Princes to fortify and guard their own Capitol city. . . . The Prince ought to go in person and perform the office of a commander . . . have no other aim, nor thought, nor take anything else for his proper art, but war. It is necessary for a Prince, desiring to preserve himself, to be able to make use of that honesty, and to lay it aside again, as need shall require. Wherefore a Prince ought not to regard the infamy of cruelty, for to hold his subjects united and faithful . . . a Prince [ought] to serve himself of the conditions of the Fox and the Lion . . . and let him seem to him that sees and hears him, all pity, all faith, all integrity, all humanity, all religion . . . for all men in general judge thereof, rather by sight than touch, for every man may come to the sight of him, few come to the touch and feeling of him. A Prince ought to endeavor in all his actions to spread abroad a name of his magnificence and worthiness. He ought in the fit times of the year entertain people with Feasts and Masks.

Skilled in the arts of war and politics, Lorenzo was also a man of culture, and he gathered in his court a brilliant circle of philosophers, men of letters, and artists, such as the young Michelangelo. On a more modest scale than the Roman emperors, the Medici also staged ambitious public pageants for the city of Florence. The similarity and expressiveness of the design qualities common to the Medici Palace and the Verrocchio bust merit analysis. Both the bust and palace have firmly enclosed volumes and three clear zones strongly separated by horizontal forms. Both have a completeness capped by overhanging shapes that arrest the eye from further movement upward. Each part is distinctly formed and

7.15 Verrocchio. *Lorenzo de' Medici*, 1478. Courtesy of the National Gallery of Art, Samuel H. Kress Collection. Washington, D. C.

7.16 Michelozzo. Palazzo Medici-Riccardi, 1444. Florence. (Copyright Stoedtner)

set within a rectilinear coordinate system. Both artists have utilized repetitive sequences and alignments that bring into balance vertical and horizontal elements. There is no frivolous ostentation nor effete accessories. Bust and palace have a rugged impenetrability and spring from solid stable bases. Sharing a common ideal, both artists created firm and handsome public façades. What lies behind them is not readily given to our eyes.

The deification of Louis XIV was a full-time project for the army of artists, musicians, writers, and poets gathered at the great court of Versailles in the seventeenth century. Among this brilliant coterie was the sculptor Bernini who in 1665 carved the magnificent bust of King Louis XIV (Fig. 7.17) that remains in his bedroom at Versailles.

In his memoirs, Louis set down his views of the ideal Christian king:

> As he is of a rank superior to all other men, he sees things more perfectly than they do, and he ought to trust rather to the inner light than to information which reaches him from outside. . . . Occupying, so to speak, the place of God, we seem to be sharers of His knowledge as well as of His authority.

Bernini carved his ideals of kingship, which perfectly accorded with those of Louis. The person of the King lent itself to the sculptor's ideal so that there was no need to flatter any features. The bust forms an impressive contrast to Verrocchio's sculpture of Lorenzo de' Medici. Whereas the latter rests solidly upon a broad base, the eyes turned down, the entire figure geometrically veined, Bernini's King is poised in the air above a cloudlike sweep of drapery that swirls upon a narrow base. The upper portion of the body is unself-consciously posed in a three-quarters view, staring into space or as if responding to an "inner light." The long wig billows and curls about the serene countenance. The highly polished marble radiates with light, reminding the spectator that Louis was the Sun King. This bust demonstrates the reasons for the construction of the great palace of Versailles.

Versailles symbolized the complete centralization of power in one man. Versailles, which cost the lives of thousands of men, became not only the residence of the Imperial court, but also the seat for the entire governmental administration. The main building of the palace, over six hundred yards wide, was a completely self-contained city just by itself. It contained living quarters, business offices, kitchens, banqueting halls, ballrooms, rooms of state, and even its own theater. There was no palace in France or Europe to rival it. For members of the French court or high government officials, not to live at Versailles was tantamount to exile.

Aerial views of Versailles (Fig. 7.18) illustrate the symbolical relationship of the palace and its environment. On one side lay the city of Versailles that had been built up as the palace grew. There great avenues slashed through the city and converged upon the main parade grounds before the palace. Just as in ancient times, all roads now converged upon the capital of the world. The central road came from Paris and, like the palace, was built upon the same axis as the Champs Élysées and the Louvre, over nine miles away. The public side of the palace faced the town and the people, the source from which the king drew his finances and manpower. The funnel shape of the city plan reflects this activity. The rear section of the palace was addressed to many square miles of private gardens, the area of private pleasure reserved for the King and his court. Here, Louis's rule over nature was made patent by the rigid but beautiful geometry of the gardens, planted according to the plans of LeNôtre. The palace, which significantly stood on the highest ground, was thus the fulcrum between two worlds, public and private, of man and of nature.

The approach to the palace was through the traditional Court of Honor (Fig. 7.19). This gigantic court recessed toward the center of the palace in a series of stages. Moving toward the main entrance, a visiting ambassador would not enter a fortified, blocklike castle, but would be gradually embraced and surrounded by long elegant palace wings that reached out like hospitable arms to draw him in. In the innermost courtyard, marble busts of Roman emperors were mounted on the walls. Exactly in the center of the palace, above the main doorway, was the King's bedroom which led to a balcony from which Louis could make public appearances and observe military reviews. The "balcony of appearances" that had begun in Egypt was here given its most resplendent setting. Such a balcony was used in this century by Mussolini and Hitler.

The bedroom was the most important room in the palace. All of the King's movements from the moment that he arose until he retired were governed by ceremony. The nobles of France served him in a variety of ways that included the much-sought-after honor of attending him as he dressed or disrobed in his chambers. The weakening of French nobility is sometimes considered to be symbolized by the competition among the dukes and barons for the honor of drawing the King's bathwater, and laying out his stockings, or slippers. It is difficult to envisage the French nobility that built the great medieval castles or chateaus

7.17 (left) Bernini. *Bust of Louis XIV*, 1665. Versailles.

7.18 (below) Air view of the palace at Versailles. Courtesy of French Embassy, Press and Information Division.

7.19   Court of Honor, Versailles. (Photo: Alinari)

of the fifteenth and sixteenth centuries performing such tasks.

Within the palace, Louis had an army of artists and artisans lavishly decorate the ceilings and walls with extensive murals depicting events in the lives of the gods to whom Louis felt akin. The famous Gobelin tapestry and ceramic industries were founded as royal monopolies to supply Versailles with miles of tapestries, carpeting, and moldings. Over one hundred-forty types of colored marbles were assembled from all over Europe for the wall and stairway decorations. Yards of stucco and marble sculptures of gods, nymphs, nudes, and naturally French royalty, were carved and set in the rooms and gardens. No expense was spared in making this the artistic center of the Western world. In fact, it became the model for European royalty, and today many palaces in Germany, for example, Nymphenberg, outside of Munich, are scaled-down variations of Versailles. The Palazzo Medici-Riccardi would have been as inappropriate to Louis XIV as Versailles would have been to Lorenzo de' Medici.

Louis had no need for a fortified residence. His armies ruled all of France and much of Europe. He did not need rusticated masonry walls to evince his strength. The huge windows, from floor to ceiling, and great Venetian mirrors in the famous Hall of Mirrors were as expressive of the Sun King as the thick walls and barred windows of the Florentine palace were of the Renaissance rulers. Since Louis was the Lord of Light, his earthly palace became an incarnation of this concept.

The gardens were designed to be used by the six to seven thousand people who lived at the court. On the upper levels of the gardens, Louis held fabulous banquets that were often accompanied by brilliant displays of fireworks. Over thirteen hundred waterspouts were built for the many fountains, each designed around a marine motif. In shaping the water, Louis showed his rule over nature, as he did in the clipping of hedges and boxing of trees. Long garden prospects shaped even the space. Great open-air stairways, whose design went back to those built by Bramante

7.20 Rigaud. *Louis XIV*, 1701. Louvre, Paris. (Photo: Alinari)

at the Vatican and by Michelangelo on the Capitoline Hill, not only carried the promenader from one level of the garden to another, but gave the sensation of leading directly to the clouds. The gardens and palace of Versailles were a private city that demanded the most advanced and skilled mathematics and engineering of the time to build.

The most expensive portrait ever painted is reputedly that of Louis XIV by Rigaud (Fig. 7.20). It is believed that the artist received in excess of seventy thousand dollars for it. Rigaud's work is the logical culmination of state portrait development. Full-length, it abounds in references to the vocation of the subject. There are yards of purple, ermine-lined robe emblazoned with fleurs-de-lis. The king stands as the epitome of confidence and manly grace, his left hand on his hip and his right holding his scepter of office. His shapely legs are carefully exposed, revealing their trained suitability for the dance. Although the high-heeled red shoes may strike the modern observer as effeminate, the king was nevertheless proud of his manliness and his embodiment of the etiquette that he demanded of his courtiers. The full-length portrait does not permit a close inspection of the face, but forces the artist and viewer to dwell on the accessories and splendor of the king's office.

A formal portrait of Adolph Hitler (Fig. 7.21) equals in skill Rigaud's portrait of an earlier monarch. The eye-level of the viewer is intentionally placed well below the figure of *Der Führer* so as to increase his physical stature. He is in uniform, backed by a gigantic sculpture of a powerful youth holding an eagle. The setting recalls ancient pharaonic imagery with the hawk god and other portraiture that shows the ruler in the presence of deities. The shadow on the sculpture mitigates the levels of reality. The only module for the figure of Hitler is life-size sculpture. He is shown outdoors, and in the foreground are building blocks and instruments, a sign of the building of the New Order. Off in the distance on a low horizon can be seen the outline of a stadium, the incubator for Nazi youth who recognized Hitler as their spiritual father. The painter gave Hitler a visionary aspect by posing him in a three-quarters view and directing his gaze upward as if he were contemplating the future. The artist avoided an uncompromising frontality which would have brought por-

7.21 Ehrler. *Adolph Hitler*, 1939. Whereabouts unknown.

traiture full circle and back to the image of the pharaoh. As in the older portraiture upon which this is based, the painter was interpreting the abstract ideas of the Third Reich rather than the personality or mood of his subject. This painting shows how a legend of Hitler's strength, invincibility, and immortality could have grown up in Germany. Nothing in the handling of the figure suggests compromise, humility, or compassion.

CHAPTER 8

THE PROVISION
FOR PLAY

Such basic manifestations of human society as myth, religion, language, law, commerce, art, and science were permeated in their beginnings with the element of *play;* this is the thesis of *Homo Ludens, A Study of the Play Element in Culture*, by the late cultural historian Johan Huizinga. As defined by Huizinga, while it is basically fun, play can be serious and meaningful as a significant social function. It transcends the immediate needs of life, and its essence depends upon imagination, intensity, and the strict following of rules. Irrational, play exists outside of good and evil, truth and falsehood. Play may involve contests, races, performances, dancing and music, pageants, masquerades, and tournaments. (The Western high noon "walk down" is the last descendant of medieval play forms of mortal competition.) Beauty can be produced by or involved in play, and life may be adorned or amplified by it. Play is a voluntary activity, but it may become an obligatory cultural function when transformed into a rite or ceremony. Ritual is a form of serious play bound up with obligations and duty and is a matter of shows, representations, and dramatic performances. Ritual, magic, liturgy, sacrament, and mystery have on many occasions grafted themselves onto play. Play is "played out" within certain limits of time and place. Thus Huizinga:

All play moves and has its being within a playground marked off before hand either materially or ideally. . . . The "consecrated spot" cannot be formally distinguished from the playground. The arena, the cardtable, the magic circle, the temple, the stage, the screen, the tennis court, the hall of justice, etc., are all in form and function playgrounds, *i.e.*, forbidden spots, isolated, hedged round, hallowed, within which special rules obtain. All are temporary worlds, within the ordinary world, dedicated to the performance of an act apart.

In his book, Huizinga touches only marginally on the purposes served by architecture in providing culture with its sacred and profane playgrounds. This section will treat architectural examples that

8.1 Salisbury. Stonehenge, aerial view from the northeast, *c*. 1800–1400 B.C. Crown Copyright Reserved. (Photo: A. K. St. Joseph, University of Cambridge)

support the spirit, if not always the letter, of Huizinga's thesis. It will also show how the images of kings or political authority extended into secular architecture. With the concept of the playground, it will be possible to bring a new unity to important and diverse works of architecture without overburdening the reader with engineering nomenclature and statistics.

SACRED PRECINCTS

One of civilizations earliest surviving sacred playgrounds (Figs. 8.1 and 8.2) was built between 1800 and 1400 B.C. at Stonehenge, near Salisbury, England. The sacred enclosure is ringed by a 320-foot quarry-ditch and bank within which are two large concentric circles of upright stones and stone-holes. Within these are two horseshoe-shaped stone series. These rings were built over a long period of time and at one point may have surrounded a wooden shrine. A few trilithons, two vertical stones topped by a horizontal stone cut to fit the curve of the circle, remain. Prob-

ably imitative of wood structures, these stones may have been a symbolic fence, a frame for ritual, or a spirit abode. To the northeast, or lower right in the aerial photograph, over two hundred-fifty feet from the center of the circle and connected to it by a causeway, is the "sunstone." Originally a wooden gate stood between the

8.2 Salisbury. Conjectural restoration of Stonehenge after the final rebuilding, *c*. 1400 B.C. (Drawing: Alan Sorell)

"sunstone" and the circle, creating a formal approach and entrance. In the center of the innermost horseshoe is a grounded thin stone slab conjecturally referred to as the "altar stone." The ring of white patches that lies near the girdling ditch consists of shallow holes containing some evidence of cremation, indicating that at some time Stonehenge may have served as a sacred burial ground. In ancient times, holes in the ground were often considered openings to the underworld and were used as depositaries for offerings to netherworld spirits.

The orientation of Stonehenge probably gives a clue to its symbolical purpose. On the first day of the summer solstice, the sun rises directly above the sunstone for someone standing in the exact center of Stonehenge. On a straight line running southwest from the sunstone, through the now lost gate and the precinct's center, is the great central trilithon. On December twenty-first, the first day of the winter solstice, the setting sun is framed by this trilithon. On this date, the congregation and priests may have entered the precinct through the northeast gate and then faced the spectacle of the fading sun. This may have been the great occasion for ceremonial funerary rites. In certain ancient cultures the door had connotations of life and death and the winter solstice was identified with the death of the sun. What tribe or people built Stonehenge is not known. The astonishing exactness by which the massive stones are oriented (it is possible that in their original completed state they divided the year into four parts), coupled with the skill and organization needed for quarrying, transporting, cutting, and erecting them, indicates a high level of intelligence and social organization.

Thus early in human history, a plot of earth was marked off and endowed with a special order which set it apart from wilderness. The symbolic orientation strongly intimates that man used this sacred area as a link between himself and the spirit world, and thus Stonehenge is related to the laying out of holy ground for religious buildings and rituals in East and West. We do not know the nature or origin of the rituals at Stonehenge, but Huizinga's comments about the function of play are relevant: "In the form and function of play . . . man's consciousness that he is embedded in a sacred order of things finds its first, highest, and holiest expression."

By the sixth century B.C., the Greeks had evolved elaborate sacred playgrounds; these took the form of temple precincts where men could be in the company of their gods. The most important Greek temples were usually enclosed by walls which also protected satellite buildings to service the needs of the gods and their temple residences. One of the most beautiful precincts was that of Delphi (Fig. 8.3), built upon the side of a mountain on

8.3 Delphi. Model of the temple of Apollo and the amphitheatre of Dionysius, sixth century B.C. Metropolitan Museum of Art.

8.4 Polyclitus the Younger. Theater at Epidaurus, fifth century B.C.

what may be the most spectacular natural site in the world. The Delphi precinct was devoted to Apollo and Dionysius, and included a temple for the former and an amphitheater for the latter. Here the famous Delphic Oracle was consulted by cities and nations from all over the ancient Mediterranean world. Delphi was considered by the Greeks to be the center of the world. Like the sacred enclosures in India, China, and Japan, Delphi was the scene of ritual observances and holy festivals. Its architecture included a stadium, permitting the performance of athletics along with drama. Handsome treasury buildings supplied by various Greek cities lined the sacred way, or approach to the temple, and were set off by the beauty of groves of trees and colonnaded walks which made of the whole a miniature and ideal city. The precinct was built up over a long period, adjusting the locus of its buildings and avenues to the contours of the hill and to some extent to the principal monuments, but never was there a single over-all master plan or ordinance that made a uniform architectural style mandatory. Like ancient Greece itself, Delphi is impressive in the completeness and individu-

ality of its parts, but it knew no strong binding alliance of the whole. As at the Parthenon, part of a consecrated playground on the Acropolis in Athens, the devotees and priests remained in the open air. In antiquity, all places of assembly in the outdoors were within the provinces of architecture, with the landscaping, sculpture, and painting used to adorn the precinct giving to it the dual role of open-air hall of fame and art museum.

THEATER, ARENA, AND BATHS

The origins of the roofless theater that was an important component of the temple precinct probably go back to village festivals and fertility rites enacted on circular threshing floors. By the second half of the fourth century B.C., theaters had developed from temporary wooden bleachers to permanent stone installations geometrically and impeccably designed and set into the natural curve of a hill. One of the most beautiful theaters visually and acoustically is that designed by Polyclitus the Younger at Epidaurus (Fig. 8.4). Its three parts are the horseshoe auditorium, pitched at two different slopes to improve

148 THE PROVISION FOR PLAY

the acoustics, the circular ring, or orchestra, and the stage, or backdrop, which partially closed the horseshoe design. The auditorium was divided into wedge-shaped sectors of stone seats accessible by stairways. The Greek chorus occupied the orchestra in the center of which an altar to Dionysius was sometimes placed. So perfect is the theater's design that the sound of a pebble dropped on the stone at the center of the orchestra can be heard in the last row. The design of the stage, or *skene*, is uncertain; it may have had two levels providing storage and dressing areas, an armature for painted scenery, and a raised level for the actors when the play called for them to be separated by height. Both the Greek theater and the dramas written for it reflect the transition from religious to secular concerns over a period of centuries. Many Greek theaters in time came to be used for public meetings other than those attending the enactment of tragedies and comedy. In this respect, the original "sacred spot" of the theater as Huizinga would have defined it came to be compromised.

In its design and purpose the theater at Epidaurus signified one of the great, peaceful, and civilized contributions of Greece to mankind. Its antithesis in form and purpose was the Roman Colosseum (Figs. 8.5 and 8.6), whose sanguine history incarnates the predatory side of ancient Rome. "Bread and circuses" for the Roman public was the maxim of Roman rulers from the time of Julius Caesar. The imperial dole provided grain and oil for as many as two hundred thousand Roman citizens. For circuses, the emperors sanctioned as many as one hundred seventy-five red-letter days, or holidays, on which the populace was treated to gigantic spectacles. Such spectacles had begun as religious observances honoring the souls of the dead but by the second century A.D. had degenerated into public orgies of mass slaughter. The

single monument that best commemorates the Roman uncivil playground is the Colosseum, built between A.D. 70 and 80 by Vespasian and his son Titus on the site of an artificial lake on Nero's palatial estate. The Colosseum was inaugurated in A.D. 80 by the killing of five thousand animals in its arena. Within the three succeeding centuries, this figure paled beside the expenditure of five thousand pairs of gladiators and eleven thousand animals in one day, or the bill of two and one half million dollars for gladiators paid by Marcus Aurelius for one series of games. The martyring of Christians was numerically a minor item on the arena's bill of fare. To supply the bloody ludic lust of the Roman populace, whole continents were scoured for wild animals and barbaric tribes, and thousands of criminals and military captives were executed on the Colosseum's sands.

While many of the architectural forms and principles used by the Romans had been known earlier, no previous culture had brought so many ideas and techniques together on such a grandiose scale. Where the finest styles and most perfect buildings had previously been reserved for the gods and kings, the Romans made the finest architecture available for public use. The development of the arch, buttress, barrel and groin vault, and the masonry and concrete dome were Roman contributions motivated to serve the needs of the living. The design of the Colosseum was the product of highly civilized intelligence and execution.

The building stands above the ground, covering six acres and forming a complete exterior oval of 615 by 510 feet and containing an arena of 281 by 177 feet. (In the Middle Ages, a small city was built inside the Colosseum.) It probably accommodated fifty thousand spectators. Its partially ruined exterior shows its three tiers of arcades, the upper two of which were

8.5 Rome. The Colosseum, exterior view, *c.* A.D. 70–80. Courtesy TWA. (Photo: Emit)

8.6 Rome. The Colosseum, interior view. Courtesy Italian State Tourist Office. (Photo: Emit)

filled with sculptures. Above the arcades was a wall punctuated by windows, shields, and the supports for ships' masts that held the ropes for the canvas awning that shaded the spectators. Sailors manned catwalks to manipulate the awning, at times painted like a billboard of political propaganda. The external 160-foot-high wall gained muscular and rhythmic design emphasis by the columns engaged to the piers of the arcades. Travertine marble with metal clamps covered the outer wall. At ground level, eighty arcades gave access to the building; seventy-six were for the general public, one each for the emperor and the Vestal Virgins, or priestesses, one for the Door of Life through which the opening procession of combatants marched, and one for the Door of Death which disgorged the bodies of the slain. The exterior had a handsome masculine simplicity in the stark clarity, vigor, and expressive design of its serial openings and horizontal courses.

The open-air auditorium was supported on a great internal brick, stone, and concrete skeleton of piers, arches, vaults, and corridors. This network permitted quick entrance and exit of the masses whose tickets showed them their entrance arch and seat designation. The concentric, continuous vaulted galleries on the second and third levels permitted shaded strolling during intermission.

The arena was separated from the spectators by a high stone wall; directly above the wall were the emperor's podium and seats for the senate. Archers, nets on this podium wall, and a second temporary wooden wall within the arena protected the viewers from energetic wild animals. The seating arrangement followed the hierarchical makeup of Roman society with the lowest class at the top. Ironically, during the baroque period, Roman Catholic painters drew their ideas for the seating in

Heaven from the plan of the Colosseum.

Beneath the arena, with its floor of sand, often covered by wooden boards, was a network of rooms, cages, ramps, and elevators, run by counterweights and pulleys, that brought the beasts directly into the field. Elaborate sewers served not only for the disposal of blood and waste, but also for draining water when the arena had been flooded for mock naval battles. The natural springs that had fed Nero's lake serviced the Colosseum. On a given day the arena might in the morning contain a miniature fleet in combat, and in the afternoon artificial mountains and forests through which animals and hunters would stalk each other. The ingenuity, energy, and ambition of the Colosseum stage managers came to be increasingly taxed and drawn to perversion as the centuries went by and the public demanded new and bigger thrills.

The Colosseum and its slaughterhouse function are not the sole means of understanding Imperial architecture and Roman society. No other government provided its people with as extensive, practical, or handsome architectural facilities with which to enjoy life. The Roman Imperial bathing establishments, or *thermae*, provided recreation in the healthiest sense. While Rome had hundreds of small public baths, there were eventually nine major thermae that could serve several thousand people at a time. Roman concern with personal hygiene goes back to its earliest history. By the time Emperor Caracalla built his enormous bath, there was a long tradition whereby all Romans set aside at least the late afternoon to go to the thermae and there tend to both body and mind. The Imperial baths were in truth miniature cities, microcosms of the Roman urban life. All are in ruins, but those of Caracalla, built in A.D. 211, were typical.

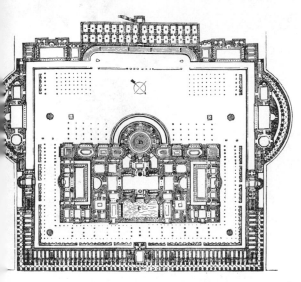

8.7 Rome. The baths of Caracalla, reconstructed plan, A.D. 211.

The baths of Caracalla (Figs. 8.7 and 8.8) were built upon a great walled platform 1080 feet on each side covering 270,000 square feet; outside of the complex were shops. Underground were furnaces that heated the water and steam for warming the gigantic rooms, great hypocausts or ducts, and service corridors through which horsedrawn vehicles could pass. Within the upper walled area were colonnades, gardens, fountains, sculpture, lecture halls, and libraries (in the east and west semicircular sides of the plan), athletic fields, and the great central complex of bathing halls, dressing rooms, and grand concourse. For the first time in antiquity, sports and bathing were brought together, permitting both exercise and cleansing of the body. The cultural facilities permitted audition of new plays and of speeches, examination of art objects, and reading. Juvenal's prayer for "a healthy mind in a healthy body" could thus be realized. Further, the baths were ideal for socializing and the exchange of news and political views. Personal reputations and political fortunes were, needless to say, at stake during mixed bathing in the nude.

A bathing ritual began with skin-scraping and a "dry bath" of steam; then followed immersion in a domed hot pool on the south, passage to the central "warm hall," or concourse, for cooling off and conversation, and finally a dip into the cold pool, open to the air on the north side of the complex. The warm hall contained an estimated sixteen hundred people at one time. No previous society had provided such extensive *indoor* facilities for civic enjoyment.

This conquest, or creation, of internal space was made possible by engineering. Enormous brick and concrete vaults were raised upon huge buttressed piers. The groin vault, the intersection at right angles of two barrel vaults of equal

8.8 Rome. The baths of Caracalla, reconstructed interior. (Copyright Stoedtner)

diameter, permitted carrying of the structural load upon four piers. This freed great wall areas for fenestration, as is seen in the Gothic cathedrals. The Romans were not only masters of space design, but also of the use of lighting. Light fell not upon rude concrete, but upon marble and mosaic floors and pools, polychromed marble walls, gilded stucco and coffered ceilings. Exteriors were often stuccoed and painted to simulate marble, for the Romans lavished their art upon the interior, as did the Early Christian churches of the fourth century. Within the baths the average Roman received delight and grandeur for the eye, endless gossip for the ear, culture for the mind, the means for making fit or pampering the body and satisfying the soul (the basement of the Caracalla baths included a shrine to the god Mithras).

The emperors built and supported admission to the baths to keep the political allegiance of the public, but it is the formal design of the environment created by the buildings that puts the Imperial stamp on the baths as well as on all great Roman public monuments. The shaping and control of vast impersonal interior space and its vistas, the precise ordering of the sequence of room functions and their scale, all garbed in the costliest materials are as much an image of Imperial authority as was the emperor's own effigy.

FORUM, SQUARE, AND BOULEVARD

The connotative imperial discipline of Roman design and its use of space for human congregation and movement is also to be seen in the public forums which served as governmental and cultural nuclei for the cities. The great Roman Forum (Fig. 8.9), while built over many years and lacking in the symmetry of the typical Roman forum, is still another example of the playground. Built upon the site of the leg-

8.9 Rome. The Forum, reconstructed by Becchitti.

endary battle of the Romans and Sabines, the Roman Forum is a large area closed off from the rest of the city and its traffic by a periphery of buildings and monuments. It was accessible through a triumphal arch. The myriad buildings and objects mirrored activities that took place in the Forum—a basilica or large enclosed public hall of assembly for judicial and commercial purposes, temples, Senate council chambers, library, rostrum for orations, and artistic trophies culled from military victories abroad. Striking columnar sequences confronted the eye from every prospect and abetted the cohesiveness of the whole. Despite the number and diversity of the buildings, each was so set off as to preserve its individuality and create a series of perspective climaxes. The central area of the forum was largely free of permanent monuments, providing a stage for parades and processions, and acting as theater for large audiences for public speeches and plays, contests, religious ceremonies, funerals, and public punishment. It was on the Forum rostrum that Mark Antony delivered the funeral oration for Caesar. Despite the plethora of activity within it, the forum was always hallowed ground, symbolic of communal unity and the maintenance of civil order. The late Camillo Sitte commented: "The place of the forum in cities corresponds to that of the principal room of the house. It is to the city the principal hall, as well arranged as it is richly furnished." Descendant of the Greek agora, or open-air civic meeting places, the forums were less devoted to the union of gods and their followers and more to union of men with their fellows.

In the cities of medieval Europe, the ancient Roman forum concept was transformed and perpetuated as the square (Fig. 8.10). Although medieval cities had fewer and smaller buildings within which play activities could be performed, the open-air square, usually in the heart of the city, performed many functions that were ludic in nature. Even today, there are performed in the square contests, pageants, and plays which date back to medieval times. The famous Pallio, the biannual

horserace in Siena, soccer in the Piazza della Signoria in Florence, and the honoring of the Holy Blood in Bruges are examples. Medieval manuscripts and old woodcuts show civic squares being used for knightly tournaments; Peter Brueghel painted the mock and festive combat between the partisans of Carnival and of Lent in a Flemish square, and Giovanni Bellini depicted a religious procession proceeding around St. Mark's Square in Venice.

The typical Roman forum was based upon strict geometric forms and axial symmetry and was usually constructed at the behest of one ruler during his lifetime. Medieval squares did not come from the drawing board. Often formed over a period of centuries, with little attempt at regularity, symmetry, or uniformity, they show strong esthetic consciousness. They were not squares in the

8.10   Venice. St. Mark's Square.

literal sense. They were spaces of human scale closed in by a variety of buildings and having discrete entrances and exits which usually abutted the square at the corners. The angularity of the square's sides tended to increase the sense of its size and visual interest. Often the proportion of a square, its width to its length, was keyed to the proportions of the major building, such as a cathedral, that fronted on it. In many cities the cathedral was not free standing, and on its exposed sides were usually one or more squares interconnecting with one another, each with a relatively specialized function, including different types of markets, for example. Crucial to the successful design and function of medieval squares was the lack of permanent central monuments and fountains that force traffic and play activity to bend around them. When fountains and statuary were included in a square, they were assigned to the periphery, freeing the internal area for changes of settings—from market stalls to tournament equipment or stages. Many European squares were flanked by arcades that shaded pedestrians and vendors and encouraged the leisurely noon and twilight social promenades that have for centuries been part of European customs. Beginning in the nineteenth century, many of these medieval squares came to be used as the out-of-door portions of cafés.

A spectacular example of a cathedral serving as the occasion and backdrop for the design of a magnificent square is the piazza in front of St. Peter's in Rome (Fig. 8.11). It was designed by the sculptor-architect Gian Lorenzo Bernini in the seventeenth century. Seen from above, the square's keyhole shape resembles a pair of arms reaching out from the cathedral's façade in a symbolic embrace. Bernini actually compared them to the invisible moth-

8.11 Bernini. St. Peter's piazza and colonnades, begun 1656. Rome.

erly arms of the Church, "which embrace Catholics to reinforce their belief, heretics to reunite them with the Church, and agnostics to enlighten them with the true faith." Practical functions also fortified Bernini's final design decisions: the square had to incorporate existing fountains and an obelisk, provide a dramatic and dignified approach to the church for pilgrims and processions, hold the thousands who came to receive the Pope's Easter benediction from a balcony above the main door and his blessing from a window in the papal apartments on the square's north side. The covered colonnades that separate the huge open space of the square from the narrow medieval streets around it contain two passageways for pedestrians and one for carriages, thus giving protection from sun and bad weather for processions, visitors, and pilgrims.

Like its medieval predecessors, Bernini's piazza was not a literal square. Unlike the medieval squares, it was of a formal, geometrical and drawing board origin, free-standing from adjacent buildings and having permanent monuments in its center. The handsome rhythmic colonnades reflect a sculptor's sensibility to solids interacting with space and the power of alternating light and dark areas. Bernini's instinct for the dramatic, attested to in his stage designs, can be felt today by anyone who enters the square through the colonnades and suddenly feels the space sweep strongly away from him and then move climactically towards the church. Medieval intimacy of scale was set aside for a more impersonal and imposing effect.

The same authoritarian spirit that inspired Bernini's square motivated the nineteenth-century design and ruthless imposition on to a medieval city of the famous Parisian boulevards (Fig. 8.12). Fearing the handicaps to the military and police that the old Parisian streets afforded during

times of political uprising, King Louis Napoleon and his adviser Baron Haussmann created a strategic network of long, broad, straight, connected boulevards that permitted the rapid transport and display of government forces and would, if need be, have allowed cannons to be fired the length of the avenues. A secondary, more enlightened motive for the Parisian boulevards was to transform Paris from the medieval "black city" described by Victor Hugo into a modern city of light, making it the pleasure capital of the world in form as well as in spirit. Handsomely tree-lined boulevards divided horse and carriage traffic from pedestrians, in effect a class division. The elegant fashion shops and broad sidewalks of the boulevards encouraged windowshopping and the sidewalk café. The apartment buildings lining the boulevard, which tended toward greater uniformity than houses on medieval squares, had large windows and balconies from

8.12 Paris. Boulevard des Italiennes, 1864.

which to obseve the ceaselessly varied movement on the streets below. (The consequences for painting are discussed in Chapter 16.) Parade and promenade, uniform and high fashion, spectacle and spectator all found their place on the boulevards. As the Forum had been the poor man's living room in ancient Rome, the nineteenth-century boulevard became the public as well as aristocratic playground.

SECULAR AND SACRED GARDENS

Today the political symbolism of baroque squares and boulevards is forgotten. Few remember that public parks have a history, that they originated as private gardens for kings and nobles. Some of the most beautiful playgrounds in history were originally conceived as lavish private gardens for the exclusive use of a privileged few. No present-day public park has known the cost and utilization of advanced technology and the finest art that can be found in the old palace and villa gardens of Europe and the Far East. Though surviving in an altered and incomplete state, the gardens of the Villa d'Este at Tivoli near Rome still reflect the magnificence of their sixteenth-century origin at the command of that period's most secular Roman Catholic cardinal, Ippolito II d'Este. With the aid of architects, masons, archeologists, sculptors, and French fountain experts, the Cardinal laid out on the sloping hill beneath his villa a geometrically designed complex (Fig. 8.13) that comprised myriad fountains and pools, walks and stairways, grottoes, a cross-shaped pergola that

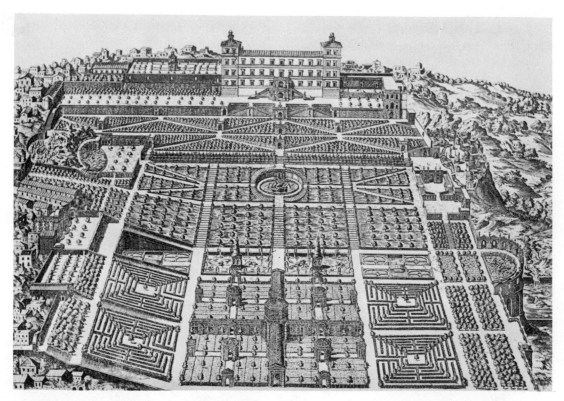

8.13   Tivoli. Villa d'Este Gardens, an engraving of the projected design by E. Duperac, sixteenth century.

quadrated herb and flower gardens, labyrinths, and artificial forests of trees which increased in density as they neared the villa. There were even secret gardens and a tennis court to the cardinal's residence. The axial grid layout of the paths and orderly pattern of the trees contrived an artificial environment that flattered the power of its owner. The importation of trees and plants involved considerable cost as well as taste. Diversion of river waters into the gardens and fountains was made possible by skilled hydraulic engineers. (The Tivoli citizens lost some of their water supply and were barred from the benefits of plumbing.) Archeological excavations in the nearby ruined villa of the Roman emperor Hadrian supplied the gardens with actual antique statuary of pagan gods and goddesses, as well as with models for contemporary sculptors who adorned the fountains and grottoes with nude figures in anything but Counter-Reformation attitudes. Likewise inconsistent with the cardinal's vocation were concealed devices that without warning sprayed unsuspecting guests with water. More important esthetically were the variety and beauty of the fountains whose appearance and sound were gauged to their location. Lining the paths close and parallel to the villa is the Lane of One Hundred Fountains; water issues from vases and boats, spraying upward or pouring down into troughs on two levels. The Fountain of the Dragon exploded jets of water sounding like cannon shots, while another had a metal tree with singing bronze birds chased by the appearance of a mechanical screeching owl. Fountain noises were achieved hydraulically and patterned after ancient treatises on pneumatics. Perhaps the most spectacular water and sound spectacle was that of the Fountain of the Organ (Fig. 8.14), described by the French writer Montaigne during a visit in 1581:

The music of the organ, which is real music and a natural organ, though always playing the same thing, is affected by means of the water which falls with great violence into a round arched cave and agitates the air that is in there and forces it . . . to go through the pipes of the organ and supply it with wind. Another stream of water, driving a wheel with certain teeth on it, causes the organ keyboard to be struck in a certain order so you hear an imitation of trumpets.

Hearing and smell receive delightful sensations, but it was to the eye that the garden was principally addressed. Water was sculptured into seemingly endless shapes, ranging from geysers, fan shapes, and spitting torrents to bubbling cascades and dribbles. In his fine history of the gardens, David Coffin points out their demonstration of man's dominance over stone, water, and verdure, and how "during the deadly hot Roman summers the gardens were to bathe all one's senses, visual, aural, and tactile, with the refreshment of water."

The Tivoli gardens were to have a widespread influence on the later courts

8.14 Tivoli. The Fountain of the Organ, Villa d'Este gardens.

of Europe and upon such gardens as those at Versailles. It is only in relatively recent times that the public has been allowed access to such delights as the grounds at Versailles and the Tivoli in Copenhagen.

Almost one hundred years before Cardinal d'Este built the Tivoli gardens, a superior monk of the Zen Buddhist temple of Ryoanji, outside Kyoto, had a sand and rock garden laid out in a rectangular three-walled court bordered by the veranda of his house (Fig. 8.15). Possibly derived from a lost Chinese prototype, this is the oldest and most beautiful garden of its kind in Japan. It constitutes a consistent contrast with that of Tivoli. Physical access to the rock garden, for example, was prohibited to all but the monk gardener who cleaned and raked the sand. It was a silent, spiritual garden, a field for pious speculation that led to enlightenment for the monks who

sat upon the veranda. Uncannily disposed in twos, threes, and fives on a 30-by-70-foot smooth sand surface are fifteen meticulously chosen irregular stones with coarse moss at their base. In the manner of certain Chinese and Japanese landscape painting, the garden is meant to be seen from an elevated and mobile viewpoint with no horizon line. (Originally the mud walls were painted white.) The emptiness in this garden may have had metaphysical significance in terms of suggesting the immanence of the creative spirit, or Tao.

Lacking an obvious formal axis, the stones' placement may have depended upon a mystical triangularity, but certainly upon exquisite esthetic intuition. From all possible prospects on the veranda, the size, texture, color, movement, and spacing of the stones are in visual accord. Japanese painters, poets, and philosophers as well as

8.15   Kyoto. Sand and rock garden, Ryoanji temple, *c.* 1500.

professional gardeners designed gardens of this and other types. The mystical nature of the Ryoanji gardens permitted those in communion with it to visualize the rocks and sand either in their actual state or as islands, analogies to Buddha and his disciples and to the protection of her cubs from an enemy by a tigress faced with the fording of a river. The garden was named, "The Garden of Crossing Tiger Cubs." Seen under mist, the glistening surfaces of the stone and moss against the deeper hues of the sand lent themselves to further imaginative projection. The lesson to be learned from the garden was that of the underlying harmony of all life in the universe, not, as at Tivoli, man's self-glorification at the expense of nature.

Even when the Japanese garden was part of palace grounds, it preserved its rustic, informal, natural quality. The garden at Katsura (Fig. 8.16), the imperial summer palace at Kyoto, is the loving creation of gardeners who were fine artists. Mingling ponds, mounds, beaches, and groves, the Katsura gardens are totally unpredictable on the basis of any one part. The ritual tour enjoyed by seventeenth-century royalty followed prescribed water routes or the discrete paths and stepping-stones contrived to appear as integral parts of nature. Constantly changing views unfolded to the eye just as textures subtly changed underfoot. Except for the buildings, the gardens possess no reference to human scale or activity, so that one moment they are seen in their normal identity and in the next may appear as endless depths, sea, and mountains. Worn stones and moss and aged trees preserved the viewer's impression of being surrounded by timeless serenity. Impeccably cared for, the garden's correct informality is preserved by the elimination of mud, unsightly collections of leaves, and the disrupting action of wind. In such an environment, men could cleanse their minds of mundane concerns.

The building most appropriate to such a setting is the tea house (Fig. 8.17) in which the *cha-no-yu*, or traditional tea ceremony, is performed. Usually a one-room structure surrounded by a small scale garden, at Katsura the seventeenth-century tea pavilion, the Shokintei, contains additional rooms. The tea house satisfies Huizinga's definition of the playground in the fullest sense. A religious ritual practice by Zen monks before the image of Buddha, *cha-no-yu* became secularized into a form of socialized meditation, but preserved the rules and solemnity of its origin. A few invited guests assembled at the garden gate and in prearranged order passsed leisurely through the garden, cleaning their hands in a rude stone waterbasin, and usually entering the tea house through a low door which was a symbol of humility and the democracy of the ceremony. In an alcove of the austere tea room woud be hung a single painting, a simple flower display, or a beautiful object that, after thoughtful inspection by the entering guests, served as a source of discussion. Following strict ritual, the host prepared the tea with intentionally crude but handsome utensils. Simplicity and naturalness were the notes struck by the environment, the tea objects, the gestures, and the subsequent conversation that ideally never touched on business or politics. The original severity of a religious exercise was supplanted by genteel estheticism. From the temple the tea ceremony passed to a deceptively simple, light, wooden-framed structure topped and stabilized by a heavy thatched roof. Between the exterior wooden supports were rough, mud covered lath walls and semitranslucent rice-paper screens. Openings in the wall were intentionally irregular, both for visual effect and to guide the light more effectively for the tea ceremony. At great cost, the

8.16 Kyoto. Gardens and tea house, or Shokintei, at Katsura, seventeenth century.

8.17 Kyoto. Interior of the Shokintei showing the hearth and a tree trunk used to support a partition.

owners of the tea room constructed a building that gave the impression of austere rusticity and imperfection. Devoid of interior furniture, the guests sitting upon the rice mats over the floor, the tea room gives the impression of emptiness.

Arthur Drexler has explained the significance of this quality of "emptiness" according to Zen and Taoist ideas as the means of expressing the sole reality:

> The purest style of tea house architecture . . . claimed to be concerned not with the material of the building itself, but with the emptiness within. . . . It was important to produce a space that would reflect the transiency of things in this world . . . and to this end asymmetrical compositions were preferred: only what is incomplete is still within the process of life and is therefore imperfect.

This worshipful attitude toward imperfection extended to introducing an untreated tree trunk as a partition support in the room, thus linking those within to nature without. Further, at Katsura, sliding wall panels open the tea room to a poetic vista within the garden. This harmony of internal and external space in Japanese architecture has influenced contemporary American domestic architecture, but the "family room" does not qualify as a playground in the same sense as the tea room.

THE MODERN ARENA

The twentieth century has shown a return to the Roman practice of building a variety of large public playgrounds that are both in and out of doors. Once again the most advanced technology is being placed at the disposal of society as a whole. It is the engineer, rather than the architect, who has provided the incentives, means, examples, and in some cases the esthetic itself of enclosing vast unobstructed space for large-scale human activity and enjoyment. The great engineering and design developments of the Italian Pier Luigi Nervi and the American R. Buckminster Fuller have involved large secular utilitarian structures. Unlike their Roman counterparts, the structures of Nervi and Fuller are not symbols of government or propaganda for rulers. Although governments and business have supplied the occasion and funds for specific projects, the incentives and research of the two men have been independent of official sponsorship. Their art is a tribute to the free use of intellect, intuition, and sensibility.

Nervi's Small Sports Palace (Figs. 8.18 and 8.19), built in Rome for the 1960 Olympic Games, provides a striking contrast to the Colosseum. The Romans protected spectators from the sun by huge sails strung on ropes; Nervi spanned the large arena with a reinforced concrete dome. The Romans built large domes for their temples, palaces, and baths, but none on the scale possible to Nervi and other modern architects. Nervi, for example, developed a method of spraying fine steel mesh with concrete to produce thin, elastic slabs that could be variously shaped according to the structural and esthetic problem. His big domes are further reinforced by metal rods and mortar that joins the prefabricated sections. The high ratio of strength to weight is the result of thin concrete building units with great resistance to compression and metal reinforcing armatures with high tolerance of tension. Concentration of load and reinforcement largely dictate Nervi's designs, but he has pointed out that he cannot completely predict or mathematically calculate the structure's performance beforehand and must rely in part upon intuition. The curving, crisscrossed, exposed concrete ribs of the Small Sports Palace dome literally graph the lines of stress and force transfer in the

8.18   Nervi. Small Sports Palace, 1960. Rome. (Wide World Photos)

8.19   Nervi. Small Sports Palace, interior. (Wide World Photos)

structure. At the dome's edges, fanshaped ribs collect the load and transfer it to Y-shaped exterior buttresses. Where the Romans felt compelled to overlay their engineering skeleton with plaster and marble, Nervi prefers the revelation of the structure's lucidity. Structure and final shape are thus indivisible. Nervi feels deeply that a good structural solution has an inherent beauty and strong sensory appeal. He has said, "The esthetically satisfying result of the interplay of ribs placed in this way is a clear reminder of the mysterious affinity to be found between physical laws and our own senses." Thus Nervi fulfills a personal ethic concerning the rightness of his work for its purpose, media, and times.

Fuller's view of architecture begins with the general problems of space enclosure and temperature control, solutions to which can be applied to individual cases. Fuller is best described as a comprehensive designer, a synthesis of inventor, mechanic, economist, and strategist, dedicated to providing new and advanced standards of living for all people. No other figure identi-

fied with modern building has shown Fuller's awareness of and ability to use the total resources of technology and industry. His structures are designed for mass production, and many can be assembled in a matter of hours. Many are demountable, and all can be packaged and transported. No modern designer consistently gets more out of a pound of material in terms of strength to weight ratio, cubic volume of space covered, and manpower time for consruction. A brilliant example of Fuller's ideas is the 145-foot Kaiser Aluminum dome at the Kaiser Hawaiian Village (Fig. 8.20). The parts were manufactured in Oakland, California, and flown to Honolulu. Within twenty-four hours not only was the auditorium structure completed, but an audience of 1832 people came to a symphony concert in it. (The structure's acoustics are excellent.) The auditorium is a multipurpose structure. Absence of permanent interior partitions permits its use for myriad recreational and cultural events. Many similar domes are being erected throughout the world to serve not only recreation, but

8.20 Fuller. Kaiser Aluminum dome, Kaiser Hawaiian Village. Honolulu. (Kaiser Aluminum Photo)

also business, government, military, and domestic needs.

The dome is preferred by Fuller because it encloses the greatest area with the least surface, and can be designed to be self-supporting and resistant to both internal and external pressures. Based upon spherical geometry, Fuller's structural principles are best described in the unprecedented patent accorded his design in 1954:

A frame of generally spherical form in which the main structural elements are interconnected in a geodesic pattern of approximately great circle arcs intersecting to form a three-way grid. . . . My "three-way grid" of structural members results in substantially uniform stressing of all members, and the framework itself acts almost as a membrane in absorbing and distributing loads. The resultant structure is a spidery framework of many light pieces such as aluminum rods . . . sheets . . . which so complement one another . . . as to give an extremely favorable weight-strength ratio, and withstand high stresses.

The basic building component, or cell, of the Hawaiian dome is the tetrahedron, a four-sided pyramidal shape with approximately sixty-degree angles, more efficient structurally than ninety-degree angles. Combined with other tetrahedra, the dome has an alternating concave-convex surface and a grid of interlocking hexagonal patterns made by aluminum bars. Like the expanding ripples caused by a pebble dropped into a pond, the load of the dome is shed radially. The structural investment of strength thus controls the paths of energy into the most economical system. With his structural ideas, Fuller has obtained the greatest performance per pound of material employed, which is of maximal importance in an age when shelter may have to be shipped to other planets by rockets. Only within the past few years has there been inter-

national recognition of the importance of Fuller's achievement. This achievement is an example of how architecture has become more than the art of building and must now be viewed as the art, science, and social science of creating a synthetic environment for human activity and enjoyment.

In the United States the most important and interesting attempt at the revival of a cultural and recreation center is the Lincoln Center for the Performing Arts in New York City (Figs. 8.21 and 8.22). Minus the temple and religious focus, the Lincoln Center brings to mind the ancient precinct at Delphi. The Center's seven theaters, concert halls, and educational buildings are designed to attract artists from all over the world and an estimated annual audience of 3,200,000 people. In place of the Delphi treasuries that held votive gifts to Apollo, the Lincoln Center includes a library-museum of the performing arts. The Lincoln Center is a collaborative effort of leading architects; aided by experts and musicians from all over the world, they created auditoriums with the most successful time-tested and advanced acoustics and flexible stages. Ironically, the builders claimed to use the most advanced ideas in structure, but all of the buildings are steel-framed boxes placed behind grandiose arcades of molded concrete. The ten-story arcade before the Metropolitan Opera House is at the same time imposing, but its future effect upon people standing before it is hard to foresee. Not unlike the Roman designers of the Colosseum, the American architects overlaid their structures with columns and arcades, and the plazas in the center have covered walks reminiscent of the Roman forums. One area of the Center is set aside as a tree-lined park with a reinforced concrete bandshell. The greenery and modest scale of the shell provide some relief from the severity of the monumental buildings.

8.21 (above) New York City. Model of the Metropolitan Opera House, Lincoln Center for the Performing Arts. Copyright Ezra Stoller Associates. 8.22 (below) New York City. Model of the exterior design, Lincoln Center for the Performing Arts. Copyright Ezra Stoller Associates.

Unlike their Roman predecessors, the modern architects made no provision for incorporating sculpture as an integral part of the building design. Paradoxically, as the work of engineers like Nervi and Fuller have approached the esthetic of an austere architectural beauty, the architects have moved in the direction of the pristine geometrical shapes of the engineer, adamantly avoiding any nonarchitectural decoration of building exteriors. The scale of the buildings, rigorous formality of the plan, coolness of the forms, the parade-ground tree alignment, the vast spaces between buildings recall devices used by Roman and baroque emperors, and even by not long dead modern tyrants, to impress their authority upon the public. Thus, authoritarianism may derive from architects as well as governments.

CHAPTER 9

THEMES FROM NATURE

A landscape painting by Hsü Tao-ning (Fig. 9.1) signifies that by the year A.D. one thousand Chinese art possessed a consistent and integrated world view with a focus on nature, not man. Landscape painting had developed from magical funerary functions and animistic beliefs and had passed into the service of Confucianism and then Taoism. Chinese pictorial writing was the source of painting, and all artists were first trained in calligraphic brushwork. Artists were frequently scholars, poets, and philosophers, and their painting was aristocractic rather than public art. Although its esthetic beauty was appreciated, landscape painting remained closely tied with mysticism and its function of facilitating the beholder's communion with the reality of the universe. It demonstrated the belief that all things in nature, no matter what their size, were of worth.

Hsü Tao-ning's painting is not the literal recording of a specific mountain site. It shares many qualities, however, with the mist-shrouded, ragged, soaring peaks of northern China, and fishing in a mountain stream is as timeless as it is universal in that country. Never in Chinese and Japanese painting was the artist enjoined to imitate surface appearance. Literal imitation was thought vulgar, an impediment to true insight and the genuine spiritual and esthetic experience of nature through art. A sign of a great painter was his ability first to fathom the meaning of what he was painting and then to impart wisdom to his art. For this reason, Chinese and Japanese painting was based upon the copying of the work of venerable masters. Nature was shaped according to types, signs, and symbols in order to convey thought and feeling. The painter learned by heart the various ways to render mountains, water, and trees, the principal ingredients of landscape art. Despite typification that extended to every stroke that the artist might make, the sublime artist, as he was regarded by those who followed, was able to transmit his unique personal reactions to a given subject. The ideal mode of painting was one that gave the appearance of effortlessness (made pos-

9.1   (facing page and above) Hsü Tao-ning. *Fishing in a Mountain Stream*, Museum of Fine Arts, Kansas City, Missouri. (Chinese scroll paintings were intended to be viewed from right to left.)

▶

(Opposite) *Fishing in a Mountain Stream*. Enlargement of third motif from the right. Collection of William Rockhill Nelson Gallery of Art, Atkins Museum of Fine Arts, Kansas City, Missouri.

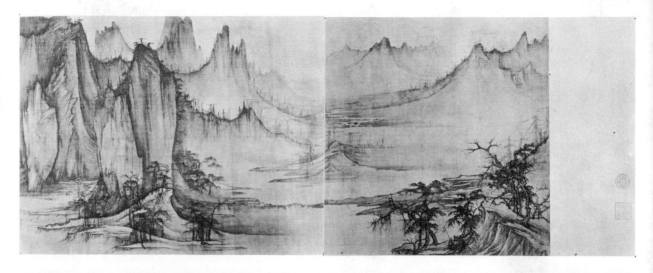

sible in part by mastery of types and strokes), in which the artist could figuratively allow his landscape to paint itself. To do this, he had to be able to empathize with the subject he was painting and be a part of the vital movement, flexibility, or toughness of the water, trees, and mountains. Painting was a form of deep and serious spiritual communion with nature, permitting the artist and the compatible beholder to realize a sense of oneness with the perfect unity, creative energy, and spirit essence of the world from its infinite space, to the mountain, and down to the smallest pebble. The great purpose of painting was to provide the soul with joy. A city dweller who possessed a landscape painting was supplied with a source of religious experience and release from urban cares. The role of the viewer was to attempt a communion with the painting identical with that of the artist and nature. The painting had to be experienced with reverence, humility, and intense concentration so that the viewer could enter into the scene, traverse its paths, fish its waters, walk its shores and paths, feel the resilient strength of the bamboo oppressed by the wind and the exhilarating loftiness of the mountain peaks.

The hand-scroll painting, developed by such tenth- and eleventh-century masters as Hsü Tao-ning, is one of the great vehicles of Oriental painting and the finest format for their landscapes. These paintings were never to be viewed in their entirety and rarely by more than one or two people. The scroll was to be unrolled a little at a time in sympathy with the temporal progression of a traveler through a landscape. Thus, a succession of motifs is revealed in an area about two feet wide. The classical format of the scroll painting inaugurates the scroll with the depiction of ground near the bottom of the silk, or paper, as if inviting the viewer to enter. In the next passage, the viewer is led into the middle distance by a path or stream, and subsequently to the distant peaks, and finally back again. This is repeated with variations throughout the whole. At any point, the viewer can look to his right, from whence he has come, or to the left, the area still before him. Some scrolls took as their subject the course of a river from its source to its termination in the sea. There are no human dramatic scenes, no climactic events as we know them in the West. Man is not the measure of the universe in this art; he plays an important but small role in the unfolding of time.

The construction of a Chinese or Japanese landscape painting does not assume a fixed position of a spectator rooted to one spot outside of the painting. The paintings were constructed from many viewpoints. Usually the artist began at the top with the most distant forms, like the faint outlines of mountain peaks, and then, in the manner of Chinese writing, worked downward and forward toward the bottom. The total spatial construction depends upon the moving focus of the traveler within the scene. The painter wanted the effect of endless measureless space extending beyond the limits of the frame and the eye, a space in which all things in nature lived. This space could be suggested by pale washes of ink or entirely unpainted silk or paper. The space was illuminated by no strong single source of light but rather by an over-all diffused light concentrated more in certain areas than in others. Shadows were rarely shown.

Color was seldom used in Oriental landscape painting; ink was preferred. Free of descriptive function and seeking to infuse his painting with qualities not given directly to the senses, artists found ideal the gradients achievable with ink.

In China and Japan, Zen Buddhist painters developed a technique of ink-splash

9.2 Sesshu. *Fisherman and Woodcutter*, late fifteenth century.

painting. During long meditation, the artist conjured up the vision of his painting in his mind and waited for the moment of perfect unity with it, in terms of Zen, "enlightenment." When he achieved this instantaneous revelation, his task was to set it down as rapidly as possible in order to sustain the ecstatic vision. The ink was then literally splashed on to the surface, in conjunction with controlled stroking. A Japanese master at this type of painting was the fifteenth-century Sesshu. In his painting of *Fisherman and Woodcutter* (Fig. 9.2), a dozen quick strokes insinuate the environment. There are varying degrees of form definition. The relative intensity of the ink establishes what is near and far, and the traceable movements of the brush create forceful directions for the eye as well as suggesting the nature of the substances in the landscape. This type of painting was not for amateurs, but demanded firm, disciplined control of the brush, a sure sense of values, and great sensitivity to spacing. Only what was caught in the web of the artist's consciousness emerges. Once the idea was fixed on paper, the brush was spared. The artist signed his name with a woodblock, and often he, a priest, or a poet might inscribe a message or line of poetry directly onto the painting. Often paintings were inspired by poetic passages. The placement and weight of the dark black ink emphasizes the total composition. The writing and the position of the figures shows the sureness required of the artist in locating his forms within the space of the painting, for he had no continuous network of edges or groundlines to guide him.

There are important similarities as well as differences between the painting of nature in East and West. The sixteenth-century Flemish painter Peter Brueghel, like his Oriental counterparts, was a man of culture in close association with geographers, philosophers, and writers who shared many of his views and who most appreciated his paintings. Landscape development in the sixteenth century was related to other forms of exploration. There is a view that Chinese landscape painting also had its roots in geography. Brueghel, like many Chinese

9.3 Brueghel. *Return of the Herds, c.* 1560. Vienna, Kunsthistorisches Museum.

painters, traveled widely, storing in memory and sketches a vast repertory of motifs. His finished paintings were not of specific locales but were attempts to incorporate a cosmic view of the infinite extensiveness, depth, height, timelessness, change, and order of nature. The purpose of Brueghel's art was to demonstrate what he understood about nature and man's relation to it. Like Hsü Tao-ning, Brueghel found the world governed by laws over which man had no control and to which he passively submitted. In *Return of the Herds* (Fig. 9.3), men and animals bow before the impending storm. Man loses his individuality against the overwhelming backdrop of the world in which he lives. The face of nature, not man, acquires expressiveness and individuality. Brueghel, again in the manner of Oriental painters, had an animistic

view of the earth, but he conceived of it as a great organic body as described in the words of the philosopher Nicholas of Cusa who lived before him: "The earth is a great animal, the rocks are his bones, the rivers his veins, the trees his hair."

The large mountain to the right in *Return of the Herds* has a gaping cavern in its side, like an enormous wound. Brueghel often sketched cracks and fissures in rocks, and evidences of erosion and decay in nature. But he was also attracted to evidences of regeneration, and this painting was one of a cycle, devoted to the seasons, that pictured the death and rebirth of the land. Oriental artists before Brueghel had done cyclical paintings of the same subject, but in the form of Brueghel's painting, important differences appear. He painted a continuous earth surface and sky, and gave a greater tangibility to space. His viewpoint was more consistently that of an external observer in a fixed position. He sustained a complex integration of the many parts of the scene and covered the entire surface with paint, drawn forms, and particularized textures. Like Hsü Tao-ning and Sesshu, Brueghel wished the viewer to lose himself in the painting by searching out its smallest parts—the village at the mountain's base, the harvested fields, and gallows—and to discover that it was not the human beings that imparted important drama to the scene. Man's efforts to change the face of nature have produced little more than fly-specks.

Brueghel organized his landscape with a clear, firm, continuous foreground that falls away into the lower valley in a series of overlapping areas. Zigzag diagonals lead the eye to the greenish-blue hills below the horizon. The dark cloud cover returns us to the foreground. The partially seen foreground trees at the right and left create a framing effect never found in the Oriental landscape scrolls. The composition may also be read as a foreshortened, roughly ovular form beginning in the foreground with the herd, curving back from the left

along the mountain range to the horizon, and then coming back to the lower right by the large, scarified mountain and foreground tree. Not only does this design assist in holding the vista within the frame; it also carries the connotations of recurrence, like the cycle of which this painting was a part. Chinese scroll landscapes of mountain ranges tend toward a largely lateral orientation with no such recurved movement toward the viewer as is found in Brueghel's work.

A distinguishing talent of Oriental painters was the ability to evoke the elusive qualities of a landscape seen in a mist. One of the most beautiful examples of this type of painting is on a folding screen; it is the depiction of a pine wood (Fig. 9.4) by Tōhaku. His inspiration came from the early morning view of pines around Kyoto. With but three or four ink tones, leaving vast areas of the paper untouched, he induced the appearance of a forest suspended in a soft vaporous atmosphere. The one tree given a distinct focus serves as a stable basis for contemplation as well as composition. The strokes do not imitate the surface appearance of the tree but convey qualities of the sharp, compact, vertical

9.4   Tōhaku. *Pine Wood*, folding screen, early seventeenth century. Tokyo, National Museum.

9.5 Seghers. *Mossy Larch Tree, c.* 1635. Copyright Foto-Commissie, Rijksmuseum, Amsterdam.

clusters of needles and the asymmetrical, individual posture of every tree. Each screen panel is complete yet adds to the scope and depth of the whole. Fugitive as thought, the painting at one point offers what is tangible and solid, and then lets shapes melt into the measureless. Here are mingled the painter's love of a scene daily delighted in, perhaps his esteem of the pines as analogues of human dignity and durability, and awareness of a religious immanence in nature.

Tōhaku died in 1630, within a few years of the time when a Dutch artist named Hercules Seghers made his etching *Mossy Larch Tree* (Fig. 9.5). It is possible, but not probable, that Seghers may have seen the work of Oriental artists as a result of the Dutch East India Company's contacts with the Far East. Seghers' small etching, roughly four by seven inches, bears a deceptive and superficial resemblance to the aged, picturesque trees in Chinese and Japanese painting. The moody isolation and morbid undertones of Seghers' print, consonant with his other etchings and paintings of wild, uninhabitable, rocky landscapes, show little analogy to the form of Oriental art. Not enough is known of Seghers' personal life to say definitely that this tree is a personal melancholy metaphor, but taken with the body of his work, it gives ground for the speculation that there may be some private connection between the two. Seghers was drawn to ruin and decay, and the etching medium, unknown to Oriental artists, in which the metal plate is bitten into by acid on all parts not protected by a repellent, lent itself to the exposition of his fantasies. In the *Mossy Larch Tree*, no firm armature nor solid connection with the ground exists. What can be seen of the trunk is a dense succession of discontinuous light and dark spottings resulting from the plate's corrosion by acid. Because of its semitransparency and disposition of weighted branches lying parallel to the surface, the almost phantom skeletal form of the tree seems to hover within the space. The dark areas were raised above the surface during the printing process when the moistened paper was forced into the etched areas of the plate. This slight relief helps to materialize the tree's substance within its nebulous environment. The peculiar quality attained by a sharp instrument drawing on metal appealed strongly to Seghers for the delineation of the grotesque angularities of branch endings and the loose, raveled strands of the moss.

The technique which underlay Tōhaku's painting and Seghers' etching is but one of many basic differences between their work and Monet's *Bordighera Trees* (Fig. 9.6). Monet did not select from nature properties that could be transcribed into lines or clear, firm boundaries. When Monet confronted the trees he was not concerned with hidden essences, philosophical symbols, or memory images. He was concerned with sensations of sunlight and color directly experienced at the moment and place he painted. Chinese and Japanese landscapes lack the brilliance of Monet's sunlight.

Tactility, mass, solidity, continuity, and occasionally identity of objects are usually absent from Monet's paintings. The painting's fabric is composed entirely of an over-all accumulation of small divided touches of bright color. Monet's painting shows discontinuous edge, continuous touch. The spectrum of his colors and the mixture of his tones in a square inch of *Bordighera Trees* has no counterpart in Eastern painting. A square inch taken from the bushes at the lower right contains in dispersal many touches of green; a few flecks of red, the complementary color in-

9.6 Monet. *Bordighera Trees*, 1884. Courtesy of the Art Institute of Chicago, Potter Palmer Collection.

duced in the eye by its exposure to green; yellows and whites from the sun and reflected light; violet induced by the yellow, and some oranges and blues from areas either seen through the bushes or adjacent to them. The strokes do not follow movements in nature itself; each seems different from the others. This technique was not acquired from a tradition, but developed from Monet's earlier painting and his encounter with the landscape as he worked quickly to fix with the brush what was fleeting to his sight. The inventiveness and energy of his painting is clear at every point on the canvas. The tree trunks from root to branch show no formularized pattern but express sheer discovery of the action of light upon color and form. No part of the surface is unpainted. The ground is covered with the thick tangled web of Monet's strokes, heavy-laden with oil pigment. Monet did not compose his painting by arranging his landscape like furniture. He made the whole work together through the equivalence of visual weights or densities of color in each area. In his personal study of the effects of mixed color on the eye of the beholder, Monet learned which tones expand and which contract, which

advance and which recede, how a few highkeyed areas counterbalance deeper tones. Not color in the abstract, but nature's color excited Monet. The landscape was not an excuse but the reason for him to paint.

In contrast to Sesshu's landscape, *Bordighera Trees* shows finite space that does not swallow up those who live within it. It is a personal space directly relatable to the location, viewpoint, and feelings of the man who painted near the Bordighera trees. His excitement, betrayed by his brush, comes from direct confrontation of the scene in nature. In a fifteenth-century landscape, part of an altarpiece by Jan van Eyck, there is a gem-strewn earth symbolizing the second coming of Paradise. Not until four hundred years later in Monet's luminescent, sun-soaked landscapes is a comparable optimism encountered. Monet painted for himself a second, secular Eden which insulated him from the shocks of history and personal trials and allowed him to devote himself to the creation and admiration of beauty.

Weather and water were movingly interpreted in such Japanese painting as Sesson's *Wind and Waves* (Fig. 9.7). The

9.7 Sesson. *Wind and Waves*, sixteenth century. Collection of Mr. Nomura, Tokyo.

absence of any horizontal line and the conjugation of curved forms aligned in one direction instill the feeling of the wind's presence. The precarious tilt of the boat and the recurved thrust of the tree in the foreground imply the power of what is unseen. A few stylized strokes coalesce into wave forms, but it is the vast undefined area of the painting that represents the magnitude of nature's force. Sesson did not attempt to emphasize the human drama by placing the boat in the foreground. (The medieval treatment of Christ on the Sea of Galilee [Fig. 4.19] creates an interesting contrast.) Chinese and Japanese artists saw in the bamboo and pine that bowed before the wind a model of ideal human conduct. They emphasized less the danger of the moment than the habitual means by which men and trees accommodate the adversity of wind and waves and submit to cosmic forces.

Nothing in Chinese or Japanese painting is comparable in form or subject to Leonardo da Vinci's series of drawings depicting cataclysms. Where Sesson showed a typical storm, Leonardo created a vision of the world's destruction in a tumultuous roaring convulsion. Leonardo's religious paintings reflect his admiration of order and the harmonious existence of man with nature. But his note books and drawings reveal his preoccupation with disorder and his belief that the world was a precarious balance of powerful forces. Were these forces unleashed, he believed, the termination of all life would be accomplished with greater violence than in the Deluge.

Leonardo made scientific studies of a wide variety of phenomena, such as water and rock formation, in order to comprehend and possess all of nature. He felt the need for direct optical study and objective recording of what he saw. The scope of Leonardo's interest was so broad that there were no stereotypes of drawing for him to imitate even if he had so desired. The cataclysm drawing reproduced here (Fig. 9.8) shows Leonardo's own devices for tracing the movements of water, wind, and dust. A mountain undermined by the action of water is disintegrating, and its

9.8 Da Vinci. *Drawing of a Cataclysm, c.* 1516. Windsor Castle.

surface, scoured by powerful winds, reveals the ancient marks of earthquakes on
its sides. As the mountain unpeels and col-
lapses, in the center clouds of dust-filled
air and water move outward in centrifugal
waves. Accompanying the sketch were
long, vivid, and precise written statements
detailing the sequence of destruction, the
psychological and violent reactions of men
and animals to disaster, and the "pitiless
slaughter made of the human race by the
wrath of God." These statements and
drawings show that Leonardo was haunted
by visions that may have been induced by
widespread prophecies that the world
would end at the end of the fifteenth century. It was not contrary to Leonardo's
scientific temperament to give expressions
to these highly emotional visions, for they
were executed with considerable logic and
disciplined exactitude. Witness one of his
descriptions of the Deluge:

> First of all let there be repre-
> sented the summit of a rugged mountain
> with certain of the valleys that surround
> its base, and on its sides let the surface of
> the soil be seen slipping down together
> with the tiny roots of the small shrubs, and
> leaving bare a great part of the surround-
> ing rocks. Sweeping down in devastation
> from these precipices, let it pursue its
> headlong course, striking and laying bare
> the twisted and gnarled roots of the great
> trees and overturning them in ruin. The
> mountains becoming bare should reveal
> the deep fissures made in them by the an-
> cient earthquakes; and let the bases of the
> mountains be in great part covered over
> and clad with the debris of the shrubs
> which have fallen headlong from the sides
> of the lofty peaks of the said mountains,
> and let these be mingled together with
> mud, roots, branches of trees, with various
> kinds of leaves thrust in among the mud
> and earth and stones. And let the frag-
> ments of some of the mountains having
> fallen down into the depth of one of the

valleys, there form a barrier to the swollen
water of its river, which having already
burst the barrier rushes on with immense
waves, the greatest of which are striking
and laying in ruin the walls of the cities
and farms of the valley. And from the
ruins of the lofty buildings of the afore-
said cities let there rise a great quantity of
dust, mounting up in the air with the appearance of smoke or of wreathed clouds
that battle against the descending rain.

It is significant for Leonardo that
the world's end did not come with the Last
Judgment and that there was no question of
salvation. In other drawings, Leonardo
showed the destruction of cities and men as
if revealing that, in contrast to nature,
society and culture weighed lightly in the
valence of the universe. Into these visions
came the artist's misanthropy, pessimism
about a natural harmonious order, and deep
personal disquiet.

The seventeenth-century French landscape artist Poussin restored nature to a
noble orderly setting for the enactment of
grandiose classical tragedies. Its mood is
directly determined by the human drama
enacted within it. The funeral of Phocion
(Fig. 9.9) is a subject drawn from Plutarch
and concerns the Athenian general Phocion, unjustly executed by the state he had
loyally served. At his request, Phocion's
body was carried from Athens to his native
city to be cremated and his ashes scattered
on the earth. The solemnity of the carrying
of Phocion's body is to be read in the mien
of the litter-bearers and the gravity of the
landscape. Basing his ideas on Greek and
Roman rhetoric and music, Poussin conceived of art in terms of modes by which to
interpret happy, calm, or sad events. To
control the effect of his art, he did not allow his own feelings to influence the act of
painting, which was governed only by adherence to these modes. Nature and art
were thus constrained by Poussin's intel-

lect. Poussin felt it the painter's task to impose his will on nature and art, to study everything within the painting, avoid the spontaneous and the trivial, and to control each stroke. He believed, as did the French philosopher Descartes, that reason could determine the true nature of physical order. Nature appears in Poussin's painting as an unopposed harmony, not unlike an aspect of a mechanistic universe. Nature's order was the model upon which Poussin based his painting, showing ancient Classical architecture juxtaposed to trees and mountains. The calm stability of the landscape is more clearly articulated and perfected by the walls, columns, and pediments of the city.

Much of the scene's tranquillity comes from the soft late afternoon light that falls on the landscape from the left. This lighting was partially a device to indicate that the event took place in the remote past. It illuminates the critical parts of the story and creates light zones that gently alternate with soft shadows and lead the eye into depth. Poussin insisted upon extreme values of light and dark being smoothly joined by intermediate ones. He provided a measurable and logical transition from the darkened foreground to the distant most brilliantly illuminated horizon. The dark foreground areas hold the viewer apart from the scene in order to evoke a detached, sustained awareness of the action and the painting's structure. Poussin further avoided rough edges, jarring angles, or unamicable color combinations to effect graceful passage from one area to another. His colors were mostly dark browns, greens, and grays, with the strongest colors, the reds and whites, reserved for small areas where it was essential to identify the figures. The large trees at the right and left and the clouds were used as the subtle coordinates and containers of the action, providing within the frame a second, natural frame-work for the scene. In the right foreground area is a group of stone ruins that provides visual anchorage for that portion of the canvas, but also reminds us that Poussin constructed his entire painting as if using building blocks with each shape and shadow having an unalterable position in the whole.

The painter's definition of art was, "It is an imitation made on a surface with lines and colors of everything that one sees under the sun. Its end is to please." He did not embody this definition, for his painting is based on literature and is a conceit, or conception of the mind, not a scene directly encountered. He favored drawing over color in the construction of form, and did not reveal colors as they actually appear under sunlight. His vision was highly selective, and his painting was strongly addressed to the intellect.

Poussin's definition of art was more perfectly realized in the nineteenth century by Cézanne, who admired the older painter. This admiration was directed towards Poussin's logical method, his systematic means of setting down his thoughts. Unlike Poussin, Cézanne was strongly committed to reproducing strong sensations of color, light, and air, a lesson he learned from the Impressionists. In *Mount Sainte-Victoire* (Fig. 9.10) he painted what he saw; he emphasized consistently lines and colors of surfaces; and he directed the whole toward delighting the senses. Cézanne made no demands upon literary erudition. By the 1880's, he had given up somber, figural dramas in landscape settings, and the mountain became a personal obsession and the climactic focus of his paintings from nature. Meyer Schapiro defines this attraction on the basis that the mountain externalized Cézanne's "striving and exaltation and desire for repose." No single form, but an idealized nature as a whole may have held out somewhat the

9.9 (above) Poussin. *Funeral of Phocion, c.* 1648. Paris, The Louvre. 9.10 (below) Cézanne. *Mount Sainte Victoire,* 1885–1887. London, Courtauld Institute of Art.

same appeal to Poussin. The mountain in the *Funeral of Phocion* was for Poussin, as for the Chinese, the residence of public gods.

Cézanne's landscape painting involved more of a struggle than that of Poussin in putting nature into order. Cézanne's harmony involves the difficult and arduous balancing of unlike forces; stability and instability, energy and repose. Poussin made careful plans for a painting and could foretell how it looked before it was finished. Each shape such as a tree or building probably was painted to completion before the whole was finished. Cézanne's method was more empirical and relied upon momentary intuitions and judgments. He repeatedly worked over the whole painting and would alter what he had painted or what he saw if it did not fit into the total esthetic structure. Unlike Poussin, Cézanne's landscape cannot be separated into isolable parts or tidy zones. Cézanne's building blocks are simultaneously color and drawing, and they fuse, overlap, or grow out of each other. In the fields, for example, he used a segment of a line to firm up a section that otherwise would have been spatially ambiguous or needed a sense of direction. He was at once concerned with presenting a stabilized view of nature in depth and with achieving a coherent surface pattern. The left-hand area between the pine trunk and the frame shows this concern. In isolation, the section, lacking any specific object reference, appears to be a succession of colored patches which alternately move forward and backward but in consistent reference to the surface. Put back into its original context it falls into place and contributes to the valley's recession. Cézanne coordinated the foreground shape of the tree trunk in its edge, color, and axis with the adjacent areas on either side. Just above the horizon line, he painted sections of pine branches whose agitation

reinforces the mountain's immobility. Suitably, the mountain is the only object seen in its entirety. The branches also bring the viewer's eye back to the foreground. Unlike Poussin, Cézanne tolerated strong juxtapositions of warm and cool colors, saturate and dilute tones, such as those found in the sky area. The actual stroke directions of Cézanne's brush are more essential to the painting's construction than to the imitation of textures in the landscape. They indicate the direction in which a solid moves into depth such as the foothills of the mountain, energize a large area such as the sky, and accelerate or decelerate the eye's movement through the painting, as in the fields. Cézanne sought an equilibrium between emotional and intellectual response to nature and painting but never did he domesticate the former to the extent that Poussin did. Cézanne preserved the irregularity, energy, and contradictions he found and admired in nature, and his emotional excitement with the scene comes through clearly in the final painting.

Landscape painting underwent great changes in the works of two French artists; two Dutch painters, too, showed striking developments. Jacob van Ruisdael was a contemporary of Nicolas Poussin. His *Wheatfields* (Fig. 9.11) however, shows a divergent attitude toward nature. The only importance of literary subject matter and the human figure in Van Ruisdael's work is to contrast their insignificance with the immensity of nature. The landscape is not the projection of the moods of men within the painting. Indeed, Nature's indifference to man seems to comfort the Dutch painter. He shows wheatfields, human attempts to cultivate nature, but he accentuates the wild scrub vegetation along the road, the eccentric stances of the trees, and the shifting shapes of enormous cloud formations which defy human alteration. Characteristic of Van Ruis-

9.11   Van Ruisdael. *Wheatfields*, *c.* 1650. Courtesy of the Metropolitan Museum of Art, Bequest of Benjamin Altman, 1913.

dael's style are the rough silhouette and tangled mass of vegetation in one or more areas. In other paintings Van Ruisdael dealt with morbid themes, pessimistic meditations on man's mutability reflected in ruined buildings and graveyards overgrown by wild foliage. Van Ruisdael resisted Poussin's belief in the intellectual encompassment, measure, and orderliness of nature.

To instill the extensiveness of earth and sky into his painting, Van Ruisdael used a point of view slightly above the foreground so that over two-thirds of the canvas is devoted to the sky. Sun and shadow-laden air are almost tangible. All of the drama of Dutch landscape painting takes place in the sky. Painters never showed the battles that were waged against the Spanish.

Their landscapes were as insulated against current events as were their still lifes and domestic scenes.

In *Wheatfields* the road is put almost at the viewer's feet to lead him more directly and quickly into the landscape. Poussin avoided the emotional involvement Van Ruisdael felt was so essential. By alternating zones of shadow and golden light, Van Ruisdael controlled the pace by which the eye moves through the landscape and senses its profundity. The forward roll of the clouds counters the inward thrust of the earth so that the composition has a foreshortened wedge-shape as opposed to Poussin's disposition of areas largely parallel to the surface. Van Ruisdael gave to his painting a vivid sense of nature in movement, its processes of growth and decay, the shift of light as the sky changes, and the violent force of winds that propel the clouds and contort the trees.

Van Ruisdael was stirred by the wars within nature herself, between the forces of life and death and man's feeble attempt to conquer land and sea. A solitary individual, Van Ruisdael used his painting to come to terms with a great impersonal, indomitable force outside of himself.

The painting of nature was an even more deeply personal instrument for Vincent van Gogh, so much so that his *The Plowed Fields* (Fig. 9.12) may belie the painter's intent. Writing from St. Remy to the painter Émile Bernard in December 1889, Van Gogh described a painting that is probably the one reproduced here:

> The sun rising over a field of young wheat, lines fleeting away, furrows running up high into the picture toward a wall and a row of lilac hills. The field is violet and yellow green. The white sun is surrounded

by a great yellow halo. Here . . . I have tried to express calmness, a great peace.

What a shock the last sentence is! The viewer is pulled immediately and violently by the arrowlike flight of the fields into the painting's depth but not to another and prime focus of the scene—the sun. Compounding the painting's tension between perspective and spiritual focus is the leftward tilt of the land, which also competes with the pull of the sun. The sun is the only stable form in the entire work, but it is at the right and very top of the painting, the most difficult point of access. No previous landscape painter had looked and painted the actual sun so directly. This act by Van Gogh was as startling as that of the medieval artist at Daphne who painted the face of his god. For Van Gogh it was from the sun's force and brilliance that nature, art, and he himself gathered vigor and life. In his last years, the basis of his being lay in attaching himself, through hard work in

9.12   Van Gogh. *The Plowed Fields*, 1889. Collection of Robert Oppenheimer.

his art, to man, the soil, and the heavens. He wrote of "plowing on my canvases as they do in their fields." The striving for the impossible goals of perfection and possession and the accompanying purge of great feeling perhaps explain why Van Gogh could write of the finished work as being calm.

Van Gogh wrote to his brother and friends that his paintings should be framed in white and hung in white kitchens or against plain backgrounds. This was both a sign of his humility and a realization of how his paintings could be shown to best advantage. They can be seen in the strongest sunlight, unlike those of Van Ruisdael or Poussin, and still surpass the intensity of the actual scene. Van Gogh wanted not an equivalence of nature, but its more intense re-creation. He wanted his drawing and color to smell of the earth. The fields that Van Gogh painted are disappointing. He made them exciting in the way that they were coded into his strong pure tones, boldly set against one another in a torrent of staccato touches. Always we are conscious of the life of the painter's hand, its obvious power, trained responsiveness, but unexplainable individuality. The painter himself wrote, "What a queer thing *touch* is, the stroke of the brush." Perhaps Van Gogh's wonder and uncertainty stemmed from his use of the brush as a direct and spontaneous extension of his internal state of being. He used the touch to disentangle the inner character of what he felt was the true soil of Provence. Wherever he went, Van Gogh absorbed through painting the sights and effects that alone could give him peace.

A common theme from nature is the closeup of a small segment of foliage in which the artist searches for the individuality of the part. With botanical accuracy, the German artist Albrecht Dürer in *Study of Plants* (Fig. 9.13) depicted the plant life in a tiny area of marsh. This was more than a purely secular scientific investigation for Dürer sought the minute and multiform evidence of God's creativity. Dürer's quantitative surface replication would have been anathema to Chinese and Japanese artists, who felt that optical accuracy concealed the essential quality of nature. Dürer, however, found provocative challenge and meaning in the multitude of shapes, colors, textures, the precise proportions, and degrees of erectness of which each plant form was composed. The clustering of the forms demanded different and less formal compositional solutions than his large religious and figural paintings. He did not impose an obvious stilted ordering on the plants but carefully preserved the appearance of overlapping disarray, seen in the lower center area, while unobtrusively contrasting and harmonizing the stalks and leaves against one another. He filled the range between the largest and smallest forms, but the tallest stalk informally stabilizes the whole within the picture area. Although painted and drawn in water color, the picture has a dry quality and flatness of surface. The cool precision of painting belies Dürer's ardor in studying nature. In his own words, "Art, however, is in nature, and whoever can draw it out, he possesses it."

To enact his fantasies on nature in such paintings as *Botanical Theater* (Fig. 9.14), the modern Swiss painter Paul Klee staked out a small uncontested territory of his own, one unavailable to such optical aids as Dürer's perspective or the modern microscope. Klee wanted a totally new and poetical point of view to give familiarity to the obscure and minute, such as the intimacy of the night world of the plants. His viewpoint is not that of a detached observer, but one that exists in the mind when the eyes are closed. Through his meditations, Klee's art became a fusion of the internal and external world in a way not

9.13 Dürer. *Study of Plants*, 1503. Vienna, Albertine Gallery.

9.14 Paul Klee. *Botanical Theater*, 1934. Bern, Klee Foundation.

seen previously in Oriental or Western art. His oil and watercolor *Botanical Theater* seems disarmingly familiar at first. There is no horizon line or sky, no definable light source or distance between the viewer and the plants. No means exist to measure the spaces and scales of the painting against one's self or a landscape. There is no botanical guide to catalogue the plant life. Klee's world seemingly has its own laws of size, light, growth, and species. Klee believed in the interrelation of all phenomena and his objects have a double image character, being part vegetal and part animal.

Identical gestures are shared by plants and humans. The pungent color that floats over and through the shapes, and the prickly textures in and around the plants recall experiences of sight, smell, taste, hearing, and touch. The fantasies are themselves derived from personal sense responses to varied stimulations. It is as if Klee were able to project himself into the subhuman night world and look at the scene through the senses of its occupants. Klee's sensitivity and imagination were so acute that he felt that the sounds of nature's growth, the movements of roots, snails, and planets were audible. The creative act sprang from inner watchfulness and listening and the uninhibited response to free associations induced by imagination as he worked. When a spiral was begun, it might emerge as a snail, or two leaves might change into a pair of eyes. Klee's painting was, perhaps, a serious parody of the old view that the world was a stage, and he recalls unseen dramas daily enacted.

Klee's drawing method was partially automatic; he let his pen and brush explore the surface guided by impulse, the feel of the materials. He was alert to suggestions from any source. He claimed that

> the work of art is above all a process of creation. . . . A certain fire, an impulse to create, is kindled, is transmitted through the hand, leaps to the canvas, and in the form of a spark leaps back . . . to the eye and further back to . . . the will, the idea. The beholder's activity, too, is essentially temporal. The eye is made in such a way that it focuses on each part of the picture in turn; and to view a new section, it must leave the one just seen.

So rich and intricate is Klee's composition that it must be taken in slowly, part by part. The drawing and textures form bridges between these parts. This slow reading evokes the realization that Klee was interested not in re-creating the visible world, but in

creating new and plausible organisms and their total environment. He once wrote, "Art is a simile of the Creation. . . . Today we reveal the reality that is behind visible things, thus expressing the belief that the visible world is merely an isolated case in relation to the universe and that there are many more other, latent realities." Klee felt that his art would comfort his viewers by reminding them that the mind itself is not confined to earthly potentialities.

To fulfill his imagery of fantasy, Klee transmuted all of the earlier modes of painting and drawing by exploring them afresh and in a personal way. He shared with Dürer and Leonardo a belief in disciplined form, but the latter's explorations were intellectually governed by the desire to give a vivid, accurate, and rational appearance to perceivable nature. Klee's art was based on the irrational, and his form study was open-ended and intended to permit the complete unlocking of the head and heart as sources of inspiration. Klee strove for union with what he called the "heart of creation. . . . in the womb of nature . . . where the secret key to the universe is safely kept." Klee's paintings were small, done within the radius of his elbow and the action of his wrist. This discrete scale encourages lengthy private discourse between viewer and subject, and it immediately frames the attitude of the beholder as well as the subject. The small scale is essential to his style, and again in Klee's words, "style is the ego."

The art of Paul Klee may be termed imagistic. It took form from his imagination, and the root of the word "imagination" is "image." Imagistic painting gives form to that which is unavailable to the outward senses. Klee felt that the artist's moral imperative was to search his inner being for inspiration and "to render visible those impressions and conceptions not in themselves visible." A second modern painter who responded to internal sensations and created private images nevertheless related to nature is the Chilean-born artist Matta Echaurren. His large *The Earth Is a Man* (Fig. 9.15) is an inscape, or landscape of the mind, a transformation of his experience with the volcanic landscape of Mexico. Matta's tropical palette of yellows, reds, and blues and his vague retention of a horizon line with its subsequent major divisions of sky and earth preserve some of the properties of the Mexican landscape. Matta's transformations extend, however, into a visionary fusion of genesis and apocalypse, coalescence and dissolution. Unlike Leonardo's visionary cataclysms, those of Matta are not susceptible to literary programming nor based upon scientific geological and climatic studies. Matta's turbulent imagery may reflect the tension of the times (the Second World War), as did Leonardo's drawings.

In his painting Matta created an untraversable, uninhabitable world in constant flux. There are fantasies upon flora, primeval birds, molten eruptive geology, and an eclipsed sun. In the upper area is the eclipse, which unexpectedly intensifies the light penetrating the entire painting. There

9.15   Matta. *The Earth is a Man,* 1940–1942. Collection of William Rubin.

are no straight lines or sharp angles or hard surfaces as every shape and area is in the process of changing. As a consequence, the shapes are smooth, undulant, and unstable. Most are disconnected but appear as mutual conjugations and are seen against what may be parent openings, or bodies, from which they may have evolved. Matta gave his shapes an insubstantial elusive quality by wiping the paint on with a cloth, dissolving one color area into another and obliterating any sustained reference to the pigment and its materiality. The poetic ambiguity of his space comes from soft transparencies of shapes, avoidance of logical recession, and unpredictable areas of phosphorescent brilliance or absorbent darkness. The over-all composition depends upon a roughly bipartite rectangular aggregate of shapes and directions that loosely parallel the axis of the frame. There is an ambivalence of direction so that lateral and vertical movements are reversible, thus enhancing the cyclical nature of the theme. Putting Matta's work into historical perspective, William Rubin wrote, "Whereas the rationalist Greeks had used the external image of man (microcosm) to represent the order, logic, and finite mechanical perfection of the universe (macrocosm), Matta invokes a vision of galaxies to suggest the infinity and mystery within man."

Until the twentieth century, sculptural themes from nature were usually decorative foliate motifs for architecture, synoptic landscape backgrounds for figures in reliefs, or personifications of the seasons, fertility, and the like. Two among many modern sculptors for whom nature has supplied important themes and a central focus for art are the Alsatian Hans Arp and the American Seymour Lipton. Arp's *Growth* (Fig. 9.16) is but one example of a lifetime of work that deals with the unseen forces and processes shaping life. In his

small bronze sculpture, Arp has imaged the internal fluid pressure of life's force in the soft serpentine ascension of the form and its multiple protuberances. The theme is generic, but the form calls to mind associations with various plant and human shapes, particularly the procreative areas of the body. Movement is achieved through the surface continuity, the absence of parts, and the smooth finish that permits unob-

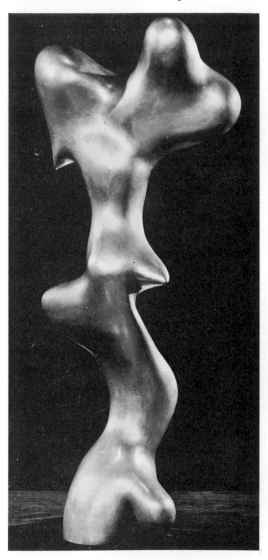

9.16 Arp. *Growth*, 1938. Philadelphia Museum of Art (Photo: A. J. Wyatt, Staff Photographer)

9.17 Lipton. *Earth Forge #2,* 1955. Brooklyn Museum. (Photo: Oliver Baker)

structed passage for light and shadow. The sculpture gives an impression of pulsation, enlargement, and upward striving. Arp has treated the lower area to suggest that it continues below the level of sight into root. To his abstract sculpture Arp gave a greater sensuality and grace than a Greek sculptor would have bestowed upon the figure of Venus. Like Klee's, Arp's purpose was to show the importance and relatedness of common, recurrent phenomena in nature and to combat human vanity which viewed the world as man-centered. A witness of wars and revolutions, Arp wanted an art to counter human bestiality and society's adulation of the rational and technological. He affirmed the peaceful, handmade, and irrationally conceived, longing for man's return to a more simple existence and "an elemental, natural healthy art" that would release men from cares and self-consciousness. "Works of art should remain as anonymous in the great workshop of nature as the clouds, the mountains, the seas, the animals and man himself. Yes! Man should once again become part of nature."

Lipton's *Earth Forge #2* (Fig. 9.17) is a type of sculptural emblem of nature's processes in the hidden areas where life is made. The sculpture's effect is that of a horizontal enclosure emerging from and enveloping a spiral core. The artist desired a form that held the promise of gradual, inevitable opening. He meant the work to convey a sense of what goes on in the bowels of the earth during the winter period of gestation. The regenerative process as viewed by Lipton is accompanied by great power and tensions, unlike Arp's view of growth's peaceful unblocked pressure. Their styles and biological preferences are accordingly different. Arp's forms seem shaped by cellular multiplication and are invertebrate when they are not vegetal. Further, Arp's surfaces are continuous and closed, showing only the external aspect of his growths. Lipton's sculptures show the internal and external aspects of his subjects simultaneously. His conceptions are of relentless conflicting drives, like outward and inward thrusts, uncoiling and recoiling motions. His shapes and silhouettes are crisper than those of Arp, and his curving, roughened surfaces envelop clearly defined areas of space. Existence and art meant for Lipton a continuous dialectic, or coexistence of contraries in uneasy relationships. Through art, Lipton sought to give this tension an intelligible esthetic form and to encourage men to live with the difficult nature of existence. Like Arp and Klee, Lipton relied on mental association, and the process of transferring insights and reflexes into sculpture evoked reminiscence of widely disparate objects. *Earth Forge #2* mingles mechanical, botanical, and sexual symbols. The sculpture is an example of the *compound image* frequently found in modern art. This type of imagery is greater than the sum of its parts and is unpredictable on the basis of any or all of its components. It requires a logic of form and an illogic of events, such as the bringing together in one work of plant and machine. The parts give up certain characteristics of their identity and share or fuse with the other motifs to create a unique total image. This compound image does not originate in conscious written or verbal programs but is irrational and intuitive. The beholder is not expected to try to break down the whole into its parts, but to expose himself to it in open fashion and to feel whether or not the broad theme has been given effective artistic form.

Art, like science, is a record of man's interaction with nature. Landscape art is not important because it gives geographical information about China, Holland, or Southern France. It has value because of the way these places were seen, felt, and thought of and then given esthetic form. For artists like Breughel, Dürer, and Leonardo, art had a cartographic function, but this was not its sole or primary purpose. Threading through all of the art discussed in this chapter has been the artist's desire to know about creation, his gods, and reality, where he and men stood in relation to the universe. The act of painting and mak-

ing sculpture from nature has been as important perhaps as the knowledge or answers imparted by the finished works of art. For it is through the art process that the artist felt most strongly his communion with nature. For some artists, painting from nature helped to fathom its order and to re-experience its genesis, but for others, it was the occasion to put nature into a more perfect and personal order.

Artists have derived from nature the means or motifs to externalize their feelings or images of themselves; an awareness of life not given to the eye, the reconstruction of an ideal past, understanding of the present, and prediction of the future; escape from the difficulties of daily existence, or terms on which to meet reality; satisfaction of a need for objective knowledge, or the stimulation of fantasy.

Every artist in history looked upon nature in terms of his art and that which preceded him. Within the limits and possibilities of their styles and traditions, artists have produced full and rich interpretations of nature, esthetically moving, often, precisely because of their limitations. The impossibility of the artist producing an exact and objective record of nature is explained in a statement by Klee in which he makes an analogy between the artist and a tree:

> He is like the trunk of the tree. Afflicted and moved by the forces of the stream he conveys what he has perceived into his work. The tree top expands in all directions and becomes visible in time and space and all the same things happen with his work. . . . It would never occur to anyone to demand of the tree that its top be shaped just like the roots. Everyone knows that what is above ground cannot be just a reflection of what is below. . . . The artist like the trunk of the tree is really doing nothing else than accumulating what comes from the depth and passes it on. He neither serves nor commands; he is an intermediary. . . . Beauty has merely passed through him.

CHAPTER 10

PAINTING AND OBJECTS

The largest surviving pre-Roman body of painting that concerns itself with objects is to be found in Egyptian tombs. The pictures of foodstuffs and their containers in Egyptian reliefs and wall paintings do not constitute still-life painting or rendering of objects for their esthetic value. They are accompanied by representations of the deceased, for whom these objects were to serve in the afterlife, of workers who were to make and gather the objects in the service of the dead man, or of gods who were to receive the objects as offerings. Their purpose in Egyptian art was utilitarian. As long as ancient art was god-centered and deeply rooted in magic and religion, no legitimate tradition of still-life painting could develop. But, by the fourth century B.C., ancient literary sources recount, urban Greek artists had achieved a highly illusionistic technique of representing objects in stage sets and on portable panel paintings and frescoes for homes and shops. Though none of this Hellenistic art has survived, its emergence in the fifth and fourth centuries accompanied a broadening

and increased secularization of artistic subject matter in both painting and sculpture. It was part of a public taste for the immediate material existence, and a growing religious and political relativism. Much of the still-life art produced by Greek artists dealt with food, and the bowls, vessels, plates on which meals were served, reflecting the tastes and social customs of the artist's patron and his guests and the delight of the city dwellers in products of the country. The Greek imitation of the fruits of nature and the connotations of sociability and connoisseurship had its parallels and influence in Roman painting and mosaics, many of which have survived.

One such mosaic, the floor of a Roman dining room, is known as "The Unswept Room" (Fig. 10.1). Dating from the second century A.D., it is probably a copy by Heraclitus of a lost work from the Greek City of Pergamum. It was not uncommon for guests at a fashionable banquet to litter or assault the floor with bits of food. The objects in the "Unswept Room" mosaic are table discards, the refuse of a

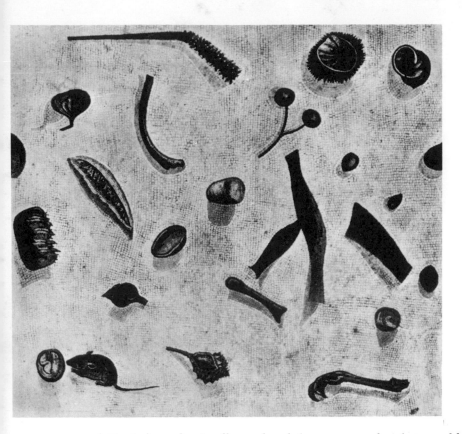

10.1 Heraclitus. The Unswept Room, second century A.D. Rome.

tastefully balanced, ritually ordered banquet such as would be held in the triclinium, or dining room. The artist's patron exercised wit and foresight in selection of the subject. The mosaic consists of small, roughly squared cubes of white and colored stone set into cement. The color range and intensity of the stones, or tesserae, used by Roman mosaicists surpassed the palette of the fresco and panel painters in antiquity. The minute size to which the stones could be cut permitted subtle tonal gradations and complex curvatures so that the artist's medium did not inhibit his choice of objects or illusionistic intent. Not only the shape and color of the objects, but their relief due to cast shadows and the mouse in the left-hand corner would impel an unsuspecting guest to tread carefully into the rooms or would serve for conversational diversion between the courses. The mosaic floor has the plausible appearance of dis-

order that would accompany the wiping of the dining tables between courses of a banquet. Study of the entire composition reveals the calculation and sensitivity to complex balance possessed by the artist. Objects do not overlap or touch. Nor are shadows tangent at any point. There is no single organizing axis or consistent light source. The mosaic is in perspective, so to speak, from any point in the dining room. The artist savored the full range of shapes and sizes of his forms. Guests reclining on couches would be close enough to partake of this experience. He was careful to refrain from setting one shape off as a dominant, and the whole is visually unclimactic. Unlike purely ornamental art, no segment of the mosaic repeats or predicts what is adjacent, and the eye is forced to engage the part as well as the whole. The careful spacing between shapes and shadows and the over-all density in each large quarter of the floor results in a harmonious ordering of a highly sophisticated type.

Contrast of this mosaic with Egyptian paintings of objects, illuminates the changes that had taken place in the relationship between man and his environment, from one of fear and the deeply felt need for security in the next world, to one of relaxed pleasure and confidence. The second-century A.D. Roman host who entertained his guests in the "Unswept Room" could pride himself on the creativity of his chef in artistically preparing the food, and at the same time, be honored in his choice of the mosaicist who had perpetuated the fate of the meal.

From the fourth through the fourteenth and fifteenth centuries in Western art, the Roman achievements in rendering of secular objects and in making them complete subjects for a work of art were forgotten or ignored. The object's life in art underwent important transformation. For about one thousand years in painting, mosaics, and sculpture, objects served as attribute, symbol, or accessory for Christian heroes. The throne for instance, occupies an important place in early Christian imagery. While the Bible records the magnificence of Solomon's throne, Christian imagery was influenced by the thrones of Roman emperors which the artists had before their eyes. Use of the throne as a venerated object and imperial substitute in art and life was also derived from pagan traditions. During the important Council of Ephesus in the fourth century, a throne, empty except for the gospels placed upon it, had the place of honor and signified that Christ chaired the conclave. A fifth-century mosaic (Fig. 10.2) from a church in Rome illustrates how an object could replace the image of Christ himself. The regal, authoritarian tone of the mosaic is due not alone to the sumptuousness of the throne with its inlaid precious stones, ele-

gant drapery, and brilliantly colored cushion beneath the scroll of sacred scripture, but also to the formality of the object's placement. Not unlike the mosaic images showing Christ in Glory (Fig. 2.9), the throne is frontal, placed centrally between symbols of the evangelists John and Luke, and dominates the whole with its size. The central axis of the throne is shared by the scriptures and the Holy Dove, which reveals to the eyes of the enlightened beholder the source and omnipotence of Christian law. By contrast with the whites, grays, and pastel tones of the "Unswept Room" mosaic, by the fifth century, Christian mosaics had acquired more consistently rich, dark, and luminous colors and surfaces. The border of the mosaic displays less caprice or spontaneity in design than did the decorative motifs in earlier Roman art, symptomatic of the formality and stylization developing in Christian art along with the codification of Church dogma and power.

Where the Christian mosaic of the throne was valued in its time for the exalted nature of the subject and preciousness of the medium, Van Gogh's late nineteenth-century painting of his own chair (Fig. 10.3) is valued today for its artistic power and revelation of the artist's feelings about himself and his relation to others. It is questionable whether Van Gogh was aware of the earlier tradition of the object as a symbol of a human or a god. Largely through instinct and the urgent need to attach himself to others, he came to endow objects—his own shoes, pipe and tobacco, books, gloves, and flowers—with human associations. The objects that moved him were modest, their physiognomy shaped by use. The companion painting to that of his own chair was one of Gauguin's chair, bought by Van Gogh when the former moved in for an ill-fated stay at Arles. Gauguin's chair was characteristically the better made, on a carpet, in a carefully

10.2 Rome. Early Christian mosaic of a throne with evangelical symbols, fifth century A.D.

10.3 Van Gogh. Chair, 1888. London, Tate Gallery.

decorated room, and bore the candle and book Gauguin used for reading late at night. Both the gift of the painting to Gauguin and the expense of procuring the better furniture were poignant gestures of friendship.

Although the subject is passive, Van Gogh's painting of his own chair can move the viewer to uneasiness. The heavy outlining of the chair aggressively asserts its object character as does the strong yellow and thick paint substance recreating the wood and straw. Van Gogh found the facture of the object and makes the viewer aware of how its parts fit together, just as one can sense the rightness of the painting's parts. Unlike the frontal throne of Christ seen from slightly below and eternally stabilized against the backdrop of heaven, Van Gogh painted from above the chair and turned it at a severe angle to the floor tiles and the corner of the room. He made no attempt to align the objects into a simple uncontested pattern. To hold the chair visually within the frame, Van Gogh joined the front right leg to the yellow frame of the blue door, and brought the top and bottom of the chair close to the picture's edge. Deepening the reds in areas of the floor tile countered some of the push of the yellow in the chair, just as the yellow interstices between the tiles mitigated the concentrated power of the chair's color. Force met with force, tilt with countertilt, the angle of one grid held in check by another. The tautness of equilibrium makes it impossible to visualize the chair in any other position. Each part of the whole vigorously appeals to the eye, prohibiting tranquil inspection, and it is here that the chair's power as an object and visual form is brought home to us—for to it we must constantly return. Where the throne in Christian art helped to relate man to his god, orient him to the universe, Van Gogh's chair was the artist's link with sanity and human love. The thirst to possess what he painted, whether objects, people, or trees and wheat fields, may have been increased by his awareness that attacks of epilepsy could be forestalled through the concentrated effort of painting.

Between the throne mosaic and Van Gogh's painting, there were critical developments in the painting of objects. By the end of the medieval period, the object, though marginal to the figures, had come to assume considerable symbolic and esthetic importance, as we have learned from such a fifteenth-century painting as the Merode Altarpiece (Fig. 5.2). The object became central to painting in the late fifteenth and sixteenth centuries. In seventeenth-century Holland, still lifes were an art form of esthetic rather than symbolic significance. In contrast to the situation in Roman Catholic countries, the Dutch Protestant Church was not an important sponsor of art, so still-life paintings were developed to satisfy the needs and taste of a secular clientele. The paintings were small, modest objects, intended for hanging in the home among other prized domestic possessions. Still lifes were also purchased as financial speculations, so that the artist, anticipating his modern counterpart, did not always know his future buyer. The passive, esthetic subject matter of the Dutch still lifes, free of moralizing, except for occasional inclusion of a candle or timepiece as mementoes of death, coincided with the insulated atmosphere of the middle-class Dutch home, and recalls the tranquilizing effect of objects and rural scenes painted in ancient urban Roman homes. The Dutch love of finely painted objects reflects their distaste for heroic oratory and dramatic images that would arouse the passions and make demands upon the viewer's learning. To the modern viewer, this still-life painting may suggest smugness, self-content with political and social security. In a sense, these still lifes are a reflection of Dutch culture and prosperity in the seventeenth century; they record that country's acquisition of material wealth and an overseas trade that returned to the home country exotic objects, foods, and wines. The fact that most Dutch still-life painting refers to meals makes of these paintings emblems of the Dutch pride in hospitality. They are fitting companion paintings to portraits of affable Dutchmen who invite us to share their wine and company. There was a wide variety of still-life painting, involving different types of meals and degrees of opulence or modesty, depending upon the different cities in which they originated and their date. Toward the end of the century, the still lifes show more precious, exotic objects, assume complex arrangements and a more feminine air.

The Dutch enjoyed seeing inanimate objects in stable compositions. Objects were placed close to the viewer, soliciting him to share intimately the discoveries and knowledge of the artist. Both the patient making and the patient seeing of the art was best done while seated. Experiencing a Dutch still-life painting de-

10.4 Claesz. Still life, 1643. The Minneapolis Institute of Arts.

mands the same savoring as required in the eating of a finely prepared meal. As illustrated in the work by Claesz (Fig. 10.4), artist and patron delighted in calculated chaos. The objects are represented in disarray, as they would be following a meal by someone who had just pushed back from the table. Before undertaking the painting, the artist spent considerable time thoughtfully arranging the objects in search of shapes that rhymed, means to link disparate forms and ease the eye's course through the painting, and an angle of illumination that offered a maximal range of values to set off both the materials and shapes of the objects. Just as the highlight of the meal often depended upon a single spice, such as that obtained from a partly peeled lemon, so is the painting's cuisine dependent upon perhaps one small brilliant tone set against a prevalent monochrome or narrow range of subdued tints. The span from vertical to horizontal forms, from near to distant, is accomplished through careful adjustment of objects and lighting.

Drama is ultimately that of light, which illuminates and anneals the multiple shapes and textures.

Unlike the specializing Dutch painters, the seventeenth-century Spanish artist Francisco de Zurbarán exhibited a duality of interests that produced official religious and royal imagery as well as still lifes. His art as a whole reflects the painter's existence at court and in the cloister, and the domestic environment of objects. That Zurbarán carried over attitudes from one mode of life to another can be seen in his *Still Life with Four Vessels* (Fig. 10.5). Four beautifully made, variously shaped, but relatively modest objects are disposed like a litany, in a line parallel to the picture surface, along a stone ledge. This arrangement simulates that of object offerings placed before the altars in Spanish cathedrals of the time. The mood of the whole echoes that of Zurbarán's images of humble monks. Unlike the Dutch paintings, this picture gives no suggestion of casual use or sociable situations involving the objects.

They are there for serious contemplation, not unlike the monk's practice of meditating at length upon a single passage of scripture. The symmetrical placement of the four vessels is deceptive. Zurbarán elicited a range of contrasts far beyond the number and superficial appearance of the objects. He turned each vessel to a slightly different angle. He contrasted earthenware to metal, placed metal and ceramic vessels on metal plates, set the tallest and smallest objects both at the left, but placed the objects with the tallest neck and the widest body at the right. Although the dramatic side lighting is consistent, no two objects receive the same amount of illumination. The cast shadows effect links between the vessels. Zurbarán was deeply aware of the individuality and worth of each object, and their importance in his art is different from the mundane references that satisfied the Dutch patrons.

Oriental painting does not include the Western category of still life. Despite the fact that Chinese artists produced magnificent objects with a history of important religious and esthetic use in temple, tomb, and home, they never created entire paintings devoted to inanimate objects. Closest to Western still lifes of fruit detached from the tree is *Persimmons* (Fig. 10.6), by the Chinese painter Mu Ch'i, who lived in the late twelfth and early thirteenth centuries A.D. Mu Ch'i's six persimmons, painted in ink on paper, are divorced from any setting or support; they hover as if suspended in consciousness. It is only their proximity to the lower edge of the hanging that suggests their normal encounter with a table or the ground. As the painting has been cut, it is impossible to comment on the relation of the objects to the total field.

The spiritual speculation of the artist is suggested by the fact that the persimmons are rendered in various stages of their life. (For this reason alone, the French term for still life, *la nature morte*, "dead nature," is inappropriate.) The Chinese painter dealt only with living things. He

10.5   Zurbarán. *Still Life with Four Vessels*, 1633–1640. Madrid, Prado Museum.

10.6 Mu Ch'i. *Persimmons*, late twelfth century A.D. Kyoto, Ryūkōin temple.

found the life-cycle of the persimmon as important as that of man. The Western Baroque hierarchical value classification and man centered prejudice were foreign to the artist and culture that produced *Persimmons*. Each fruit has a singular shape, tone, weight, density, and relation to adjacent fruits. Unlike Zurbarán's regular spacing, the occurrence of Mu Ch'i's persimmons seems naturally informal. They are related by overlap, tangency, and discrete intervals, yet do not share even an invisible ground line. No two stems are the same, nor are their proportions and direction predictable. To alter any of the foregoing relationships would be to disrupt their internal harmony. The many judgments made by Mu Ch'i in his study of the

lessons of the persimmons issued from sustained concentration and final revelation. Zurbarán's vessels and Mu Ch'i's persimmons remind us that an artist's life-view may be manifested through the smallest and most modest subjects.

By means of elegant objects, the eighteenth-century French painter Pierre Subleyras enhanced a portrait of Francis I, Duke of Este and one-time commander of the French army in Italy (Fig. 10.7). The objects indicate both attributes of the Duke and the early eighteenth-century ideal of a ruler. Francis I is represented in effigy by a handsome marble bust carved by Bernini between 1651 and 1652. Ironically the bust was made from two paintings so that we see the duke through the eyes of four artists. The white gloves and sheaf of red carnations resting on a finely embossed silver platter announce his courtly manners. The body of the exotic plumed bird refers to his participation in the aristocratic hunt and taste for gourmet food. The armor and astrolabe suggest his interest and prowess in military and astronomical science. The bronze sculpture of Hercules supporting the world remind the viewer of Francis' ethical guide. The frightened woman and children in the background may signify the terror of war and threat to the reproduction of life against which the Duke existed as protector. Subleyras' casual arrangement of objects seems to be in calculated contrast to the order of court life enjoyed by the ruler on state occassions. Bernini's bust, however, shows a subtle combination of loosely flowing forms contrasted with the firm self-assured pose of the man himself. Both the painting and the bust epitomize the eighteenth-century aristocratic ideal of intertwined formality and informality, seeming to be one thing, but in fact being another. The painting's beauty was in certain respects prepared before the work was undertaken by the quality of the objects

10.7 Subleyras. Still life, 1730–1745. The Minneapolis Institute of Arts.

moist elusive equivalences of his subjects. They take shape not from solid outlines, but from light values and the oil properties of his medium. The durable is created by the inconstant. With the exception of the works of Rembrandt, never in the Dutch still-life painting that Chardin admired are we made as conscious of the physical nature of the oil medium, the touches of the brush, and the sheer material substance of the painting's surface. Chardin coaxed from a few colors a rich gamut of tones such as those in the copper basin. When closely studied, these tones contradict the initial appearance of the basin's solidity and simplicity. Working without preliminary drawings, Chardin established each tone in response to small sensations of light and dark given directly to the eye; for example,

chosen. This is art about art. In another eighteenth-century still life, however, a superior work of art is made of inferior objects. The eighteenth-century French painter Chardin found in simple middle-class utensils sources for wonder and life-long exploration (Fig. 10.8). More than could religious or political objects, those chosen by Chardin reveal the strong morality of the painter. The sturdy household basin or pitcher, reshaped and recolored through daily use, was for Chardin evidence of frugality, temperance, and constancy. It served his passionate study of the mysterious effects of light upon substance, in other words, reality given to the eyes. Like Zurbarán, Chardin aligned objects on a shelf, out of reach and set apart for visual search. Unlike the cool, dry, and hard surfaces of Zurbarán, Chardin created warm,

10.8 Chardin. Still life, c. 1732. Los **Angeles** County Museum, Exposition Park.

see the ladle at the left. In addition, the artist expressed the force of the contrast between the pitcher's bulge and the concavity of the basin, the irregular against the regular perimeter of the cloth and pitcher, and the rhythmic continuity through tangencies of the handle, basin, lid, and pitcher. Unlike the interchangeable possibilities of Subleyras' composition, Chardin's progression from object to object is immutable, and we cannot rearrange or separate the shapes once they have been set into the final construction. The artist used a pyramidal climactic compositional device, favored by academic painters of the time for exalted figure paintings. Instead of mounting a goddess or king at the apex of the whole, Chardin ironically placed a succulent side of meat hanging from a hook.

Subleyras and Chardin exemplify the distinction between *picture makers* and *painters*. Picture makers, such as Subleyras, wish us to experience the object in a literal manner, observing their success in closely matching the several local properties of objects in an airless space. It is as if we could reach out and pluck a flower from within the picture frame and thereby perfume the air. Neither the oil medium nor the hand of the artist intrude into our awareness of the illusion before our eyes. Painters such as Rembrandt and Chardin create plausible illusions of objects, but also impart to them the visible evidence of artifice, their oil and brush facture, and the impossibility of the object's separation from what is a unique painterly environment.

Edouard Manet was a painter and not a picture maker. To enjoy his painting is to relish color nuance and the matching of tones, the tasteful dispersal of color accents over the field of the canvas, the bold address of shapes to the painting's surface. His paintings of objects were not intended to be inventoried nor philosophized over. Manet's construction of large, strongly edged, relatively flat areas of closely linked

tones appeal more quickly to the eye than do any of the previously considered paintings. The painted fabric of Manet's objects and background is more apparent and looser in weave than that of Chardin and the Dutch. There is a more consistent awareness of the flat picture surface. The span, direction, and twists of his brush call attention to this surface as well as to the object. Manet reserved the most brilliant tone for the small area of the lemon off to one side. Less brilliant, copper brown and pinks occur more frequently than the yellow, but less frequently than the grays. Manet made the grays and whites most susceptible to nuance, and they take up the largest area. The culinary concoction possible with the sea food is no less subtle and piquant to the tongue than is the painting to the eye. *Still Life with Carp* was painted for the cultured vision of a sophisticated, but at the time limited, audience. The objects were important not only in establishing tonal problems, but because in themselves they created a discriminating and pleasurable esthetic experience.

Where Manet was content to accept the shape, if not the tone of objects, Cézanne insisted upon re-examining all properties of what he painted as if seeing them for the first time. Cézanne could not passively repeat anything given to the senses, but was impelled to reform, recolor, and reorganize what entered within the boundaries of his canvas. Zurbarán and the Dutch could admire the craftsman's art in making handsome objects, but Cézanne felt no allegiance to the glassmaker, ceramicist, or the farmer whose apples he painted (Fig. 10.10). His reconstruction of objects was motivated by a desire to increase their visual interest and to meet the unique structural and expressive demands of the painting. Neither perversity nor ignorance of perspective techniques led him to reshape the compote dish into an asymmetrical, flattened oval, but rather the pictorial

10.9 Manet. *Still Life with Carp*, 1864. Courtesy of The Art Institute of Chicago.

need of additional coordination with the frame for increased stability and visual weight, high-valued tones at the upper left to balance the cloth at the lower right, and dislocation of the compotier's base to work in with the assembled apples and glass. This meant stretching the basin of the compotier. Every decision made during the painting solved a problem raised by preceding work on the canvas rather than one raised by fidelity to the known character of the object. Where previous painters allowed objects to compose the painting, Cézanne relied upon painting to compose the objects. The apples illustrate this point. Cézanne realized them in paint both from the outside edge inward, and from the inside out. The direction of their stroke-faceted surfaces must be seen against the directions of the knife, cloth, the pile of fruit itself, and ultimately all other movements in the painting. Each touch of the brush in an apple fixed the light value, hue, curve or flatness, warmth or coolness of a particular area of sensation. Any part of Cézanne's

painting yields to the pull of adjacent areas because of the thoroughness by which all have been fitted together. The distortion of the top of the glass is not exactly encountered again in Cézanne's art, as it depends upon the new shape of the compote dish and the imaginary ellipse created by the apples themselves. Cézanne used such blunted shapes as well as the ingenious connection of objects and bright color to achieve an ambivalent reference both to the picture's surface and to objects in depth. Cézanne repeated the objects, but never their painting. The importance of Cézanne's contribution and the value of his art has been stated by Meyer Schapiro:

At the threshold of our century stands the art of Cézanne, which imposes on us the conviction that in rendering the simplest objects, bare of ideal meanings, a series of colored patches can be a summit of perfection showing the concentrated qualities and powers of a great mind.

Fortified by Cézanne's assertion of the artist's obligation to re-form the visual

10.10   Cézanne. *Still Life with Compote Dish*, 1879–1882. Paris, Collection Lecomte.

world, the cubist break with the imitation of the object was a relatively quiet revolution. Picasso, Braque, Léger, and Gris did not select new subject matter or issue violent manifestoes attacking those who represented the perceived form of the object in three-dimensional space. At no time during the years of Cubism's most important painting did these artists completely renounce the object. Their objects, however, originated in a restricted and immediate part of their environment. More specifically, the objects derived from a favored café, the studio, and home, the latter two being frequently one and the same. Old photographs of Braque and Picasso in their studios between 1910 and 1916 show walls, tables, and floor covered with arbitrarily juxtaposed objects. The objects found in their paintings are not costly or rare, but were prized as esthetic objects or personal possessions, utilized in daily activity and having intimate associations of conviviality. Death, moralizing, personal crisis, world events, all are shut out from cubist paintings in favor of pleasure. The objects conveyed human sentiments, but were rendered in a way that showed the artists' unsentimental attitude toward the older tradition of still lifes. Never did the Cubists arrange objects in the sequence of their original setting. Within their paintings, however, is often found an object that suggests limited analogies with the unique syntax of the Cubist work of art—fragments of newspapers. The sequence of articles and photographs on a front page, for example, does not follow the original format. The layout of the page depends to some extent upon visual judgment as well as news-

worthiness. Articles about widely disparate subjects are found side by side. Just as
in Gris's painting (Fig. 10.11), there are
unexpected juxtapositions. Further, head-
lines involve contractions or cryptic abbre-
viations. The type itself consists of marks
to which we respond according to their
myriad combinations. In another still life
by Gris, *Tea Cup*, the artist included a pair
of photographs showing a public monument before and after a law was passed prohibiting defacement by advertisements.
The uncoordinated, random affixing of papers to the monument's stone base in an irregular patchwork was a witty comparison
with Gris's own painting, which involved
the attachment to the canvas of pieces of
paper carrying public announcements. In
Gris's *Breakfast*, a segment of a Parisian
daily has been cut out to provide the artist's
signature, characterizing the incompleteness of every object in the painting.

Segmentation, basic to Cubism's
ethic and esthetic, is explicable by the artist's insistence upon his ability to transform
meaningfully all that enters into the painting. The whole is made up entirely of
parts (in earlier periods this statement
would seem like an insignificant glimpse
into the obvious), and the parts are all interdependent. The cubist still life is not a
continuation of the viewer's world, as were
still lifes before Cézanne. It is an addition
to the visual world, a material esthetic object verifiable by the senses but enjoyable
through the intellect. Gris's *Breakfast* resulted from a series of adjustments, or intellectual acrobatics, by which the world of
three-dimensional objects was transposed
onto a rectangular flat surface bearing
crayon, paper, and oil paint. Many of the
objects' original properties—their appearance under certain lighting conditions, continuity and solidity, and often their color
and texture—were set aside. Color and texture may occur elsewhere in the painting,

or the object may be colored and textured
by some other form, such as wall paper or
wood grain. The decisions to keep, discard,
and redraw were not made beforehand but
were occasioned by the desire to make a
moving and strong pictorial structure without counterpart in the outside world. The
simultaneously rendered plurality of views
of one or several objects is caused not by
any cubist knowledge of or interest in theories of relativity, but rather by the search
for interesting and useful prospects that fit
or "work" into the design while preserving
reference to the object itself. The objects
no longer perform utilitarian services such
as the containment of wine or coffee, but,
what is more important to Gris, they satisfy

10.11 Gris. *Breakfast*, 1914. Collection Museum
of Modern Art.

10.12 Matisse. *Gourds*, 1916. Collection Museum of Modern Art.

esthetic demands. The volume of the objects is implicit rather than explicit, as the ambivalent flat-layered construction of the painting produces an ambiance different from the viewer's space. Gris's achievement cannot be corroborated by measuring and matching. Gris and the Cubists practiced a consistent inversion of properties so that the painting's final logic is visual. There is no area in which objects are habitually situated. They are disposed throughout the work, and an equivalence of design importance is given to intervals between and outside of objects. In other words, there is a breakdown between the distinction of object and ground, the priority of top, middle, and bottom. As with Cézanne, the final painting is judged in terms of how well the composition sits within the frame. Drawing, painting, and the manipulation of objects signify an important step toward an increased tolerance of means by which the artist might link the art object with its environment.

It is unnecessary to refer to the original objects in order to evaluate and enjoy Matisse's *Gourds* (Fig. 10.12). Line, color, and composition, though influenced by his contact with the visual world, are primarily personal inventions. The control and quality in his art were supplied by Matisse's exceptionally good taste and dependence upon artistic intuition. *Gourds* gives itself immediately and fully to the eye as a fresh sensual experience, the viewer being moved before reasoning is accomplished. The choice, limited number, and forceful rendering of objects eliminates questions of their meaning. Their clarity of shape and careful diffusion emphasizes their familiarity and durability. The objects' internal coherence within the frame and the large, bright, flat, pure color areas quickly establish within the eye the rightness and importance of the total harmony. (Compare Fig. 10.6).

Matisse "dreamed" of an art having "balance, purity and serenity." His imagery endures beyond the first moments because of the range and provocativeness of his contrasts. His shapes and colors possess a tenuous tie with the visual world. Painting from memory rather than direct perception, Matisse liberated drawing and color from the local properties of objects so that they in turn could release his feelings of joy and serve his views of expression in art. In 1908, Matisse wrote,

> What I am after, above all, is expressiveness. Expression to my way of thinking does not consist of the passion mirrored upon a human face or betrayed by violent gesture. The whole arrangement of my pictures is expressive. The place occupied by figures or objects, the empty spaces around them, the proportions, everything plays a part.

As with the term "espressivo" in music, we do not ask, "expressive of what?" Matisse's drawing is expressive because behind its execution are not only skill and taste, but also strong will.

The irregularity of objects in *Gourds* is occasioned by the subtle demands of the painting's surface construction, but it does not extend to the extremes of the Cubists' manipulations. Matisse delighted in the formal completeness of objects as well as in the entire painting. Instead of the linear armature of the Cubists, he set up an informal dispersal of shapes on a strong asymmetrical blue-black background, a daring balance of few against several. The painting uses the effectiveness of intervals as well as linear correspondences, the visual weight of a color when seen in areas of varying sizes and contexts. New color chords, such as blue-black-reddish brown, were sounded in *Gourds*. These chords did not originate in observed sequences before Matisse's eyes, but came instinctively as he responded with pleasure to a particular tone he had set down. "I cannot copy nature in a servile way; I must interpret nature and submit it to the spirit of the picture. When I have found the relationship of all the tones the result must be a living harmony of tones." Like the Cubists, Matisse felt that through art could be discovered the essential or decisive character and content of the world of appearances.

The Italian painter Giorgio de Chirico could not, however, accept the visual world as a basis for expressing his views of reality. In de Chirico's *Grand Metaphysical Interior* (Fig. 10.13), the painting of objects involves the art of fantasy, images not based upon what is given directly to the senses. The stimulus of external sensations is replaced by the artist's attentiveness to internal "strange sensations." The objects of de Chirico's painting can be inventoried and identified, but their context and connection elude definition. What is crucial for the painter is that they are enigmatic. The objects are set in an interior, but it is not a room in the sense that it knows human residence. It is an interior because behind a window shade suspended at the right is not a blue sky, but a green exterior. Within the interior is a naturalistic painting of an Italian villa; the familiar exterior world is dislocated and consigned to a picture frame as one more inexplicable object. Painted with equal illusionistic precision in an adjacent framed panel are normally unrelated objects. The framed panels are supported by drafting instruments, associated with rational design. De Chirico endowed these tools with obscure meanings that we can sense but not fix in precise terms. They have been used as part of a calculated irrationality. The light and shadow in the room, its depth construction are independent of traditional usage or the position of the viewer. Shadows, shapes, space, and silence make an uncanny ambiance that is all the more compelling because of the intense and convincing exactness with which it has been painted.

The word "Metaphysical" in the title refers to de Chirico's belief that the artist should paint a higher reality than that

10.13 De Chirico. *Grand Metaphysical Interior*, 1917. Collection James Thrall Soby.

of the senses. He therefore sought to restore mystery to art and to paint the obsessive hallucinatory images which he felt mirrored the state of his soul. He became alienated from the empiricism and logic of previous artists. De Chirico's world is that seen when the eyes are closed, a cool, dry, inert, and uninhabitable environment traversable only by the eye. The intimate nature of the choice of his objects is seen as a contrast to the social and hedonistic connotations of those in Cubism or Matisse's work. "I fill up the empty spaces in my canvas as the structure of the picture requires with a body or an object according to my humor." Objects in older still lifes had a unity of origin and use, and in-

volved shared experience. Perhaps influenced by Cubism and its collage, de Chirico's irrational dislocation and juxtaposition of objects from the everyday world he distrusted were important in releasing the inhibitions and fantasy of later artists who felt that to be true to one's self in art demanded response to the fringes of consciousness and the deepest recesses of the self. De Chirico and subsequent fantasist artists shared the conviction that their work could give pleasure and fulfillment to sensitive and intelligent audiences, that their art could interlock with the imagination of a sympathetic viewer.

For Marcel Duchamp the meaning and value of a work of art depended upon its interpretation in the viewer's mind. "The spectator brings the works in contact with the external world by deciphering and interpreting its inner qualifications and thus adds his contributions to the creative act." The painter of *The Bride Stripped Bare by Her Bachelors, Even,* or *The Bride* (Fig. 10.14) was against traditional meaning whereby the painting illustrates the title and is fully understandable on the basis of a pre-existing public body of knowledge. *The Bride* is a cynical commentary on art, the machine, reason, sentimentality, and sex. Duchamp's intentionally dry, academically precise painting of objects was intended to discourage praise of the virtuosity of his hand. He baffled attempts to trace the origin and meaning of the objects and deflated technology by producing irrational machines that do not produce. For those who love a love story, and something old, something new, something borrowed, and something blue, there is no empathy with Duchamp's *Bride* or her "Bachelors." Done during a period of personal crisis, *The Bride* is a complex metaphor or private myth, modern in its private origin, incompleteness, and ambiguity. Duchamp used his metaphor with wit to mechanize love and humanize the machine, to depersonalize art but personalize the act of viewing art. Duchamp was giving form to what he called a "world of unknown quantity," of which the visible world is only a shadow. Art should be made, he felt, only by intuition and revelation. "The artist acts like a mediumistic being who, from the labyrinth beyond time and space, seeks his way out to a clearing."

    The Bride consists of two glass panels mounted in an aluminum frame measuring roughly six by nine feet. The shapes were applied to the glass with paint, varnish, and lead wire. (The cracks, of which the artist approved, resulted from an accident in shipment.) Technically, the work is marvelously made and has the

grace of art. Objects are not represented on the glass surface; they are on the glass, knowing no other habitat. From Duchamp's notes it appears that the top panel is the "Bride" panel, and the lower the "Bachelor." At the upper left is the Bride, consisting of intricate and suggestive plumbing forms. To the right is a perforated cloud shape. At the lower left are nine objects recalling those used in dry-cleaning plants; Duchamp called these his "malic molds," or "Bachelor Machine." Below them is "the slide," or waterwheel on

10.14 Duchamp. *The Bride Stripped Bare by Her Bachelors, Even,* 1915–1923, (Unfinished) Philadelphia Museum of Art.

runners. Toward the top and center of the lower panel is an X or "scissors" shape supported by the vertical "bayonet" of the "chocolate grinder." Below the "scissors" is a series of funnel shaped "sieves" filled with dust. The radiating spoke forms at the right comprise the "ocular witness." In one version of *The Bride*, Duchamp wrote,

> As the bachelors are intended to serve as an architectonic base for the Bride, the latter becomes a kind of apotheosis of virginity. A steam engine on a masonry pediment. On this brick base, a solid foundation, the bachelor machine, all grease and lubricity (to be developed)—just where, as one still ascends this eroticism reveals itself (and it must be one of the major cogs of the bachelor machine), this tormented cog gives birth to the desire-part of the machine. This desire-part then changes its mechanical status, from that of a steam engine to that of internal combustion engine. And this desire motor is the last part of the bachelor machine. Far from being in direct contact with the Bride, the desire-motor is separated from her by a gilled cooler. This cooler is to express graphically that the Bride, instead of being a mere sensual a-sensual icicle, warmly rejects, not chastely the bachelors rebuffed offers. . . . In spite of this cooler, there exists no solution of continuity between the bachelor machine and the Bride. But the bonds will be electrical and will thus express her being stripped; an alternating process. If necessary, short circuit.

The plurality of interpretations advanced by Duchamp indicates that he invited the viewer's speculation and wanted him to make his own poetic or punning liaisons between objects. The absence of a simple rational and complete program of meaning for *The Bride* should not discourage looking at the large glass. A further irony of *The Bride* is that it is a painting done on glass, recalling the older view of the picture surface as a window through which one looked into an idealized extension of space. Duchamp painted his objects on the window, and looking through the glass we see our own world, not one imagined by the artist. Within an object-filled room, the forms on *The Bride* seem to hover and move, existing in ever-changing contexts when viewed from different angles.

The art of de Chirico used the dislocation of familiar objects and their relocation in unfamiliar situations. Duchamp invented objects that aggressively parodied objects, human situations, and the body itself. *Target* (Fig. 10.15), by the young American artist Jasper Johns, is *itself* the painted object. There is no illusionism. *Target* has no reference to anything outside itself. The subject of the painting is a two-dimensional target identical with the painted papered surface on which it exists. When the artist wished to introduce three-dimensional objects, he made plaster casts and closeted them in boxes with movable lids. He presented us with no riddle, but asked only that his work be taken at its face value. Johns took two-dimensional objects, in this case a target, in others the American flag or stenciled numbers, out of their customary surroundings and connotations. He did not, however, put them into de Chirico's uncanny enigmatic settings. Johns heightened the vividness of the object through size, color, and texture. In short, he wished the viewer to have "a direct painting experience." Johns's position reflects the current view of art as empirical experience for the viewer, with the work of art as an independent object of total surface importance brought into being by any means the artist may choose.

This permissive view of means is illustrated in Robert Rauschenberg's *Broadcast* of 1959 (Fig. 10.16). He culled from his New York environment a host of objects brought together into "combines."

The objects have a general character of personal souvenirs, entries in an autobiography of the artist and the city. There is no illusion of objects. They have been used before in their existence and are used directly again in the combines. According to Rauschenberg, "A pair of socks is no less suitable to make a painting with than wood, nails, turpentine, oil and fabric." He combined a stuffed angora goat with an automobile tire, a step ladder with a thermometer, scraps from billboards with photographs of celebrities, mirrors, baseball bats, and Coca Cola bottles, and in one instance, growing green grass. His selection of objects was not indiscriminate but involved judgments of the eye. In *Broadcast* he mounted two working radios, adjusting them so that each can be tuned into only one station. One transmits news and sports, the other music. Near the radios are appropriate photographs of racing, police beating a rioter, and the word "Help." The improvisation of parts and over-all structuring action of the paint produce a jazz

10.15 Johns. *Target*, 1958. Collection Leo Castelli. (Photo: Burckhardt)

10.16 Rauschenberg. *Broadcast*, 1959. Milan, Collection G. Panza di Biumo. (Photo: McNeeley)

quality in harmony with the sounds transmitted by the second radio. *Broadcast* is thus environment painting in a broader sense than we have heretofore encountered. Rauschenberg's combines are like fanciful time capsules bearing witness for the future to his life and times. Rauschenberg included smells and sounds along with sights, and the pathetic, ludicrous, comic, vulgar, and exuberant means by which modern society has expressed itself as brashly as the artist.

We began and end this chapter with art made from discards, those from a table and those from a city. Both share random and sophisticated composition while preserving the flavor of the subject. Both Heraclitus and Rauschenberg have given society's detritus a second, more durable life through art.

This introduction to the artist as a painter of objects has suggested the span of his performance, from imitator to creator to selector of objects; from fabricator of illusionistic familiar surroundings to inventor of new environments. He has ranged from playful deception through story telling, personification, moralizing and philosophizing, metaphor and emblem making, esthetic contemplation, and meaninglessness. The painting of objects reflects great changes not only in style but also in the content that reflects man's attitudes to his environment, be it one of fear, reverence, wonder, curiosity, pride, dependence, distaste, or pleasure.

CHAPTER 11

THE PORTRAIT IN PAINTING AND SCULPTURE

MEN

If all that remained of ancient Rome were the sculptural portraiture of its citizenry, we would still have an important record of that civilization. No people before or since the Romans indulged themselves so extensively in carved and painted portraits. Worship of and fidelity to one's ancestors and egotism accounted for countless death masks and portraits for Roman home, tomb, palace, and forum. The first century B.C. *Portrait of a Man* (Fig. 11.1) may have been a marble copy from a death mask, for the subject's cheeks are sunken and the flesh is pulled back in the mouth area as on the head of a dead man. Except with its leaders, the Romans of the Republican period made no attempt to flatter themselves and preferred the stark, hard evidence that living left upon the face. As so much has remained of Roman culture, the weight Romans placed on their values may be balanced against the testimony of the many surviving portraits. In theory, they valued honesty and frugality, self-re-

liance, simplicity, firmness of purpose, and a gravity that revealed a sense of what was important. They believed in toughness and discipline, organization and a pragmatic approach to daily life. Roman literature reveals many and spectacular exceptions to these values, but the Roman conquest of the ancient world and the *Pax Romana* reminds us that during the Republic and early Empire many Romans did live by them. The attitude of the sculptor toward his subject in the work illustrated shows a toughmindedness and desire to record honestly the man's facial individuality from the dented skull to his jowls. The simulation of flesh and bone are there for us to touch. The discrepancies between the two sides of the man's face have been retained. Even with the eyes painted in, as they were in the original state, there would not appear to be any discrepancy between the inner and outer man.

The third and fourth centuries A.D. saw the decline of the Roman Empire. In these centuries sculptors and painters gave to the human face a sense of crisis at

211

11.1 Rome. *Portrait of a Man*, first century B.C.

phers, the eyes were the gateway of the soul. Through them the sculptor could portray a turning inward and focus upon the spiritual life. No longer were men confident in their mastery of the physical world. There is now a conflict between the spirit and the body, the present and future life, not only in Christians, but in non-Christians. In art, esthetic physical attractiveness was reduced in order to impart more forcibly the metaphysical idea.

Eric Ambler once wrote,

A man's features, the bone structure and the tissue which covers it, are the product of a biological process; but his face he creates for himself. It is a statement of his habitual emotional attitude; the attitude which his desires need for their fulfillment and which his fears demand for their protection from prying eyes. He wears it like a devil mask; a device to evoke in others the emotions complementary to his

11.2 Rome. Portrait of a Roman Senator, fourth century A.D.

once individual and public. No comparable large body of portraiture exists in the history of art. The fourth-century portrait of a Roman Senator (Fig. 11.2) reveals how sculptors limned the consequence of a time of testing. The old material and religious values had fallen into disrepute, and there was a search for new ideals in life and art. Portraits of men, women, and children from a wide geographical area in the Empire reflect this change. Now the artist and his patron show little regard for sensuous or material likeness. No longer is the surface supple and highly finished. Hair is synoptically treated by shallow cuts. The axis of the head's structure has become rigidly geometric, lacking the flexibility or idiosyncrasy of earlier work. The face has lost traces or the potential of mobility except for one area— the enlarged eyes animate these sculptures and reveal the change in form that stressed an attitude new to the ancient world. The eyes are at conflict with the axis and set of the rest of the face. For Roman philoso-

own. If he is afraid, then he must be feared; if he desires, then he must be desired. It is a screen to hide his mind's nakedness. Only a few men, painters, have been able to see the mind through the face.

Jan van Eyck, one of the earliest and finest portraitists in European art, was a painter who grasped the difference between the biological and the psychological in the human face. In his portraits of the 1430's, which include some of the earliest easel portraits in art history, there is an amazing coincidence of technical virtuosity and powers of observation. In his portrait of The Knight of the Golden Fleece (Fig. 11.3), no physiognomic detail escapes the painter's eye. Even the capillaries of the eyes are rendered. The face is not unlike a microscopic map in which all of the inflections of the terrain have been thoughtfully recorded. All traces of its wear and use have been fixed immutably. Despite the impassive set of the face, there is drama in the visual intimacy achieved by Van Eyck with the flesh and its unique biography. The subject's individuality is not proclaimed by action or setting. Rather, his dress, pose, absence of setting, and even certain props, show that he conforms to an aristocratic ideal of self-composure and dignity. The face is a silent residue of a life of action. It is as if Van Eyck believed that the accumulation of an infinite number of details would provide the circumstantial evidence with which to identify the character as well as the appearance of his subject. The erectness of the figure and the unflinching face epitomize a Flemish ideal of will and alertness.

Van Eyck also displayed great sensitivity to the mass of the head, which he accentuated by lighting most intensely that part of the face farthest from the viewer. The near portion is in half-lights. Both the lighting and flesh treatment reveal the painter's empirical study of the

11.3   Van Eyck. *The Knight of the Golden Fleece, Balduyn Delannox,* 1430–1435. Berlin, Deutsche Museum.

head's structure, skeleton as well as musculature. The vividness and telling quality of the flesh are due to extremely subtle color tonalities achievable in part through the use of oil glazes which both capture and repel the light.

Four hundred years after Van Eyck's painting, the French artist Géricault portrayed a number of insane patients of his friend Doctor Georget. This series was a project to demonstrate Georget's belief that insanity derived from physical rather than spiritual causes, and that pathological evidence could be obtained by close study of the face. The same discerning scrutiny with which Van Eyck approached his sitter was thus employed for clinical purposes. The patients knew they were being painted and were allowed to dress and

11.4 Géricault. Portrait of a Kleptomaniac, 1821–1824. Ghent, Museum of Fine Arts. Copyright A.C.L.

act as normally as possible. Nothing in the background, dress, or general pose of the portraits reveals that the subjects had been hospitalized. Géricault's task was to study and record the mask into which the face had been set, but also to mirror the grinding impulses behind it. Figure 11.4 is the portrait of a man afflicted with a monomania for theft, a kleptomaniac. Géricault brought to bear all of his sensibility to subtle color and surface inflections in a painting that is a work of considerable esthetic beauty. The most obvious symptom of the man's malady resides in the eyes and tense relationships in the face.

Géricault's style and temperament were ideally suited for this project; he passionately probed the expressiveness of color and drawing along with situations involving individuals in distress. His focus

was often upon subjects who were without external anchorage and by force of circumstance were thrown back upon themselves. As a contributor to the nineteenth-century Romanticist movement, Géricault brought to art moving images of men in action and tense inaction, an oscillation that accompanied the emergence of severe political and social change after Napoleon's fall.

Géricault painted portraits of those who, in a sense, were victims of modern society; the Italian Renaissance artist Raphael painted portraits of those who made the elite society that flourished in the early sixteenth century. Raphael was himself admitted into this society, marking the artist's increased social stature at the time.

His portrait that best epitomizes the Renaissance social ideal in style and subject is *Baldassare Castiglione* (Fig. 11.5). In some respects the picture was made before Raphael took up his brush. The pose that largely determined the painting's composition was probably a joint decision of the sitter and painter. Castiglione was the author of a book, *The Courtier*, that set forth the requirements for the ideal Renaissance man, his skills, conduct, and objectives. Castiglione could have served as a model for his own book as he was a poet, a brilliant scholar, an outstanding ambassador and courtier. In his book, Castiglione comments as follows on his ideal: ". . . beside nobleness of birth, I will have him have not only a wit, and a comely shape of person and countenance, but also a certain grace that shall make him at first sight acceptable and loving unto who so beholdeth him." The perfect courtier was also expected to be capable of feats of arms and hardiness, to have ingenuity and fidelity. He was to be pleasant to every man, always witty and discreet, and everything that he did was to be accomplished with grace. On the clothing of the perfect courtier, Castiglione wrote,

A black color has a better grace in garment than any other color . . . and this I mean for his ordinary apparel. . . . He ought to determine with himself what he will appear to be and so to apparel himself, and make his garments help him to be counted such a one, even of them that hear him not speak, nor see him do any manner of thing. . . . Our Courtier ought not to profess to be a glutton nor drunkard, nor riotous and unordinate in any ill condition, nor filthy and uncleanly in his living.

Not only did Raphael faithfully record Castiglione's appearance and manner, but he also enhanced the man's grace and bearing by subtle shadows and lights. The pyramidal shape formed by the figure and locked within the frame insures its stability. The figure's left arm forms a restraining barrier between himself and the viewer, while the more frontal face permits a certain cordiality without excessive intimacy. The careful but unostentatious position of the hands further exteriorizes the man's inner grace—a matter of mind as well as physique. Both Castiglione's book and Raphael's painting, really a portrait of abstract concepts, considerably influenced later art and life. Raphael's portrait does not admit the ugly, principally because the painter would not choose an ugly subject.

An entirely different ethic of manliness and painting led to the seven-

11.5 Raphael. *Baldassare Castiglione,* 1510. Paris. (Caisse Nationale des Monuments Historiques)

11.6 Hals. *Portrait of a Man*, 1661–1664. Kassel, Staatliche Kunstsammlungen, Gemäldegalerie, Hessisches Landesmuseum.

teenth-century Dutch *Portrait of a Man*, by Frans Hals (Fig. 11.6). Quiet reserve has given way to warm and frank affability, a shared intimacy between the viewer and the man. Calculated composure is superseded by an appearance of spontaneous informality. The Dutchman's dress, unkempt hair, casual posture, and complexion ruddied by excesses of diversion make him not a perfect courtier, but an ideal masculine companion for his time and place.

Raphael's smooth, immaculate picture surface, so in keeping with his subject, has its analogy only in the underpainting of Hals's portrait style. After painstakingly detailing his subject in a relatively tight surface treatment, Hals rapidly repainted the entire work in slashing strokes and ragged patches of color. It is possible that by this late stage in his career, Hals had dispensed

with this underpainting. Raphael may be judged a superb picture maker, Hals a consummate painter. The material substance of Hals's paint and color is as vivid as the man's physical quality. Making no move to fuse his touches of the brush, Hals set down a few brilliant highlights, rawly exposed. Against these key values, he scaled his other lights and darks. Unlike Raphael, he created strong esthetic accents that draw the eye away from the man's face. These random spottings contribute, however, to the stability of the whole painting. No large, single-colored area is unrelieved by traces of energetic fabrication. The painter's gusto is apparent in the way he has avoided the architectural posture used by Raphael and twisted the hat, face, and body into angles opposed to those of the frame. Castiglione's composition directly relates him to an impersonal ethical coordinate system. Hals's man seems to provide his own moral and esthetic axis.

The history of portraiture includes images not only of the living, but also of the dead. The Spanish painter El Greco did a portrait of Saint Jerome (Fig. 11.7) over a thousand years after the saint had died. El Greco's portrait is also of an ethic, a spiritual rather than a secular one. El Greco abstracted the figure from any specific setting. As painted by the artist, the saint possesses the quintessential qualities of asceticism and inner vision. The coolness that emanates from the painting is due both to the frigid light with which El Greco clothed it and to the artist's focus upon the other-worldly reflections of the saint as he pauses to contemplate what he has written. The attenuated head and body exteriorize El Greco's concept of spiritual enlightenment. The portrait is an exhortation to pursue the contemplative life that ignores physical comfort. The head and hands of the saint are like magnetic poles, and El Greco does not let the eye tarry on what intervenes between them. Despite the figure's quiescent attitude, the painting is veined with tension rather than repose. The strong movement of the lights on the cardinal's robe, the angle of the beard in relation to the head, even the body in relation to the garment give a tautness to the whole.

Van Gogh's painting (Fig. 11.8) of an old French peasant, Patience Escalier, forms an interesting modern counterpart to El Greco's saintly image. Van Gogh wrote of this painting:

> Instead of trying to reproduce exactly what I have before my eyes, I use color more arbitrarily so as to express myself more forcibly. . . . I think of the man I have to paint, terrible in the furnace of the

full harvest, the full South. Hence the strong orange shades, vivid as a red-hot iron, and hence the luminous tones of old gold in the shadows.

Van Gogh, who did this portrait in the late 1880's, could never have painted a thing or person he could not see. He did not paint the saints of Church history, but he made holy the people he painted. As Meyer Schapiro has observed, his is the only great portrait of the peasant in the history of art. The area behind the old man's hat has the color not of the sky, but of the soil of Provence. He has been beatified through his lifelong contact with the earth. The arbitrary as well as local colors introduced into the face are the carriers of Van Gogh's love for the man. The identity of every fea-

11.7 (left) El Greco. *Saint Jerome, c.* 1600. Copyright The Frick Collection. 11.8 (right) Van Gogh. *Patience Escalier,* 1889. London, Collection Chester Beatty.

11.9 Giacometti. *Diego, c*. 1955. Walker Art Center.

ture is fiercely insisted upon through drawing as well as through color. The directions of the strokes in the face are like a magnetic field, pulling toward the eyes. In them are to be found summations of all the painting's passionate color and the man's humanity. The hands worn by travail are autobiographical, testimony to infinite patience and endurance of suffering. The painting is over life-size, in itself a gesture of love and friendship by the artist. Unlike El Greco's distant and unapproachable *Saint Jerome*, the old man absorbs the viewer by his personality and warmth. Van Gogh gave to a man on the lowest rung of the social ladder charismatic properties that in the Middle Ages were reserved for the saints and images of Christ.

The finest art of the twentieth century has included relatively little portraiture. The best that has been done has been of unstable individuals and is intimate and probing. Twentieth-century artists have generally turned from portraiture because of the traditional demands of fidelity to the subject and have turned instead to subjects or areas that fulfill their ideas of what art should be. The Swiss-born sculptor Alberto Giacometti is an exception. From his earliest works, he has studied the human face, almost exclusively that of his younger brother Diego (Fig. 11.9). To Giacometti,

> Sculpture, painting and drawing have always been for me the means by which I render to myself an account of my vision of the outer world and particularly of the face. . . . It is utterly impossible for me to model, paint or draw a head . . . as I see it, and still, this is the only thing I am attempting to do. All that I will be able to make will be only a pale image of what I see.

From this statement we learn that his sculpture is for Giacometti alone. His dilemma and inspiration lie in his fascination with his elusive vision of the external. Given his portrait of Diego, the complexity and precariousness of Giacometti's art is manifest. *Diego* has an almost Egyptian remoteness, like a world unto itself. The fixity of this state is paradoxically achieved through the inconstant surface; no part is literally matchable with the surface or features of the brother's real face. For Giacometti, each face has a double existence. The first is the face he sees; the second is the face that he sees in imagination and that constantly eludes him. To him, the finished sculpture is invariably an unhappy compromise.

Giacometti needs the sitter's isolation; he wants to grasp a man's whole being as seen from a distance. For this reason, his heads are extremely thin in frontal view. Each encounter with the interval between the nose and the upper lip, or the area beneath the eye is for Giacometti like exploration of an uncharted, awesome terrain. He seeks a frugal but expressive surface that evokes movement and life, joining at once the inner and outer man.

WOMEN

Portraiture includes many fine renderings of women motivated in commemorating their likenesses for eternity by desires identical with those of men. Until the last quarter of the fifteenth century, Italian portraits of men and women tended to be in profile. The Italian nobility preferred to have only half the face committed to posterity. This preference for the profile portrait was influenced by ancient coins and medallions that contained profile portraits of rulers. The significance of antiquity's attraction to Renaissance society is shrewdly put by Johan Huizinga:

If ever an élite, fully conscious of its own merits, sought to segregate itself from the vulgar herd and live life as a game of artistic perfection, that élite was the circle of choice Renaissance spirits. . . . The game of living in imitation of Antiquity was pursued in holy earnest. . . . The whole mental attitude of the Renaissance was one of play. . . . This striving . . . for beauty and nobility of form is an instance of culture at play. The splendours of the Renaissance are nothing but a gorgeous and solemn masquerade in the accoutrements of an idealized past.

This segregation and search for beauty and nobility of form is manifest in the design of fifteenth-century Florentine palaces as well as in profile portraits. Renaissance palace designs were inaccurate attempts to revive the principles of ancient Roman palaces. Both may be conceived of as the public, social façades of their owners. Neither permits a feeling of intimacy with the viewer. The relevance of this comparison is apparent in Alberti's Rucellai Palace (Fig. 11.10) and Pollaiuolo's *Portrait of a Young Lady* (Fig. 11.11). In the profile portrait the sitter remains permanently aloof and detached. A blue sky serves as a background and elevates the figure from earthly reference. The careful setting of the head into the picture area and the tapering broad base made by the pose add to the stability and dignity desired by the patron. While the profile pose eliminates the possibilities of a psychological investigation of the face, it encourages stress of the esthetic grace of the subject. Renaissance costumes and tastes share a certain cool, contained, surface elegance. The woman's tight-fitting bodice, upswept hairdo, and plucked eyebrows create a clear rhythmic series and a continuous graceful silhouette. There is no strong accent, modeling, or coloring of the face within its contours so that stress is

11.10 Alberti. Rucellai Palace, 1446–1451. Florence.

placed upon the edge. The expressiveness of the portrait relies heavily on its esthetic surface design rather than on the movements of the mobile features, the eyes and mouth. The cosmetic fashion favored an artificiality that obscured the natural potential of the flesh. The woman has herself reformed nature, and the artist continues in this spirit.

Rubens' ideal woman, seen in his portrait of Susanna Fourment (Fig. 11.12), pampered her natural gifts with graceful and revealing clothes whose sensual textures flattered those of her flesh. She neither affected an imitative role nor held herself aloof, but was desirable in mind and body. To give the fullest expression to the charms that delighted his eye, Rubens used a frontal, three-quarter pose, at once modest and alluring. The vitality of the woman and her outgoing personality are set off by the turbulent sky and magnificent hat which,

it has been suggested, was a flattering recollection of the canopies under which royalty was accustomed to stand. It is possible to enter into a private dialogue with Rubens' subject. This, unlike Pollaiuolo's portrait was a personal painting, one of a close friend, whose younger sister Rubens was to later marry. The artist indicated the pleasure of re-creating her warm moist flesh and the firmness of the exposed portions of the body against the large wavy silhouette. Rubens formed his subject from color tempered or heightened by soft shadows and brilliant light. The full range of the modes of his brush reveals itself in the broad treatment of the sky and large

11.11 Pollaiuolo. *Portrait of a Young Lady*, 1475–1500. Courtesy of the Metropolitan Museum of Art, Bequest of Edward S. Harkness, 1940.

11.12 Rubens. *Susanna Fourment*, 1620. Reproduced by Courtesy of the Trustees, The National Gallery, London.

areas in the sleeves, the more restrained formations of the feathers and hair, the propriety of matched strokes in the flesh, and the deft touches that created highlights in the earrings and eyes. Both the outpouring and restraint of feeling in the actual painting echo the mood of the woman.

Rubens' hedonism was shared by Henri Matisse in a portrait of Madame Matisse (Fig. 11.13) done at the turn of this century. Like Susanna Fourment, Madame Matisse wears a glorious hat piled high with flowers. Matisse did not insist upon the climactic facial focus as did Rubens. It is not the flesh nor intriguing mood that Matisse celebrates in this painting of his wife. He has painted her as a warm esthetic delight. Her face is handsome and sympathetic, a strong, quiet foil for the riot of color and movement enacted around her. Matisse painted ecstatically, unfettering

color from its previous obligations to modeling and textures. It is now the free carrier of his love both for the woman and for the painting itself. Rubens accentuated and modulated his bright colors by placing them next to subdued hues or setting them in partial shadow. The flat areas of bright color in Matisse's painting are modulated only by degrees of saturation; they range from pastel greens and pinks to full-bodied orange-reds and purples. The large color patches of the background complement those within the figure area and serve as blocks to set the form within the frame. Setting aside the finesse of brush stroke of which he was capable, Matisse applied his paint rapidly and rawly, scrubbing and

11.13 Matisse. *Woman with the Hat*, 1905. Collection Mr. and Mrs. Walter A. Haas, San Francisco.

striping to effect the immediate release of his exuberant feelings. He dispersed his color accents according to the needs of esthetic structure, thus making the painting, like Madame Matisse's hat, a beautiful bouquet of color sensations.

Sculpture as well as painting has recorded many faces of women, with some of the finest portraits as early as Egypt. From the ruined workshop of an Egyptian sculptor who lived in the fourteenth century B.C. has come an unfinished head of Queen Nefertiti (Fig. 11.14), the wife of Ikhnaton, the pharaoh who broke with the religious traditions of Egypt and acknowledged only one divinity, that of the sun. He also broke with tradition in demanding that his artists in their work humanize himself and his family. Consequently this sculpture is an image both of a queen and of a handsome woman. The upper portion of the sculpture would have been fitted with a crown which would have continued the diagonal tilt of the face. The lines on the stone indicate that the eyes and eyebrows were to be painted in and that the artist produced the face in perfect symmetry by dividing it exactly in half. Completed stone sculpture portraits were usually fully painted. Despite his recourse to such stylizations as that of the eye, the artist gave the obdurate surface of the stone sensitive undulations that imply direct observation of the Queen. A quiet sensuousness accompanies the serene dignity of the Queen. Whether seen full face or in profile, the portrait has an immutable self-containment and permanence of mood, the fulfillment of Egyptian art's purpose of providing the subject's soul with a tranquil eternal life.

At a great extreme from Nefertiti's portrait is Bernini's bust of his mistress, Costanza Buonarelli, done in the seventeenth century (Fig. 11.15). *Nefertiti* transcends the temporal world; Bernini's

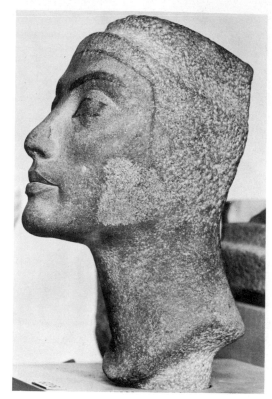

11.14 Egypt. *Queen Nefertiti*, fourteenth century B.C. Cairo Museum. (Photo: Hirmer)

woman is of the moment. She is in the process of movement and on the verge of speaking. Bernini re-created her as an impressionable, vital person. In removing extraneous stone, he also lifted off all that masks the private life of the unguarded and impulsive in woman's conduct. The violent and intimate nature of the relationship between the sculptor and the woman is hinted in her disheveled clothing and hair, extensions of her internal excitement. As form, the sculpture knows no symmetrical blocklike enclosure but boldly twists into the space about it. The silhouette is irregular and agitated but so controlled as to return the eye to what lies within it. The iris of the eye is incised to complete the surface's mingling with light. Bernini's figures presuppose some unseen presence outside

11.15 Bernini. *Costanza Buonarelli*, 1636–1639, marble. Florence, Museo Nazionale. (Photo: Alinari)

flective surface of which the metal was capable and which alienated the work of sculpture from the baroque ethic of intermingling art and visible reality. Brancusi worked through what he considered layers of superficial appearance in order to find in nature the real essence of things, seminal forms, like the egg, by which to prove his mystical belief in the underlying unity of living forms and to realize an absolute beauty of simplicity, purity, and equity of existence.

11.16 Brancusi. *Mlle. Pogany*, 1913, bronze. Collection The Museum of Modern Art, the Lillie P. Bliss Bequest. (Photo: Sunami)

of themselves to receive the out-pouring of their feeling and action. The portraits by Bernini and Rubens were bold personal gestures by which the artists embraced the living.

For Constantin Brancusi, sculpture became the means by which the artist reached for the mystical center of existence. He used reduction in facial detail and arbitrary redesigning of the features in his bronze portrait of Mlle. Pogany (Fig. 11.16). He stripped away those characteristics and idiosyncrasies of the woman's face which so delighted Bernini. The head has been contracted into an egg shape. Trained in a Budapest Academy, Brancusi adjured its surface virtuosity and fidelity that produced what he called "beefsteak" art. He insisted upon the hard, smooth, re-

11.17 Van Eyck. *Giovanni Arnolfini and His Bride*, 1434. Reproduced by Courtesy of the Trustees, The National Gallery, London.

Brancusi intended the evocative power of his design and shape to attune the sympathetic beholder with his ideals. Accordingly, he rearranged his subject to effect an impeccable clarity and continuity of rhythm and shape. He retained the woman's hands, for example, for their extension of her nature and as a means of augmenting the movement in the head. In later versions, he eliminated the darkened area of the hair and rough ending of the area below the neck to the right, giving the sculpture even greater closure.

The expressiveness of the head lies not in the life of the features and flesh but in its total gesture, the constantly changing reflections on the polished bronze surface, and the evocative power of the design. The self-containment of the composition harmonizes with the quiet, introspective withdrawal of the woman. The sculpture retains the quality of "likeness," but its measure is that of the work of art against the spirit of the woman and Brancusi's personal ideal of beauty.

MARRIAGE PORTRAITS

The double portrait, known in Roman times, has occurred fairly often since the fourteenth century. The type of double portrait to be considered here is the marriage portrait.

Giovanni Arnolfini and His Wife (Fig. 11.17) was painted in 1434 by Jan van Eyck. The painting shows a private wedding ceremony that took place in the bedroom of the bride of a wealthy Italian banker living in Flanders. Present are witnesses, one of whom is the painter himself, indicated by the inscription above the mirror, "Jan Van Eyck was here." Until the sixteenth century, two people by mutual consent could achieve a legitimate marriage outside of the church and its rite. Van Eyck's painting is more than a superficial document of the occasion; quite literally, there is more than meets the eye in this portrait. It exteriorizes all the implications of the union of man and woman; in order to create it, Van Eyck used a setting filled with objects whose symbols and connotations were well known to his clients and friends.

The bride and groom are shown full length, standing in the center of the room with hands joined. Showing the entire figure in a portrait requires a greater interval between the viewer and the subject; consequently, less area is devoted to the face. Despite this diminished area, the facial portraits are strong. Van Eyck did not attempt to flatter the groom, whose morbid sensuousness and equine resemblance come through strongly. The man is shown as the dominating figure by his pose and solemnity, while the bride turns in deference to him. Some mistake the proportions of the bride for those of pregnancy. Actually, she is holding the hem of the long skirt up to her waist.

The choice of the bedroom for the event and painting was symbolic, for it had a long religious tradition as a nuptial chamber. Northern medieval painting showed the Annunciation to Mary taking place in Her bedroom. The burning candle in the chandelier relates not only to a masculine symbol, but also to its use in marriage rites and its implications of God's presence. The dog is a sign of fidelity and, possibly, passion. (On medieval tombs, a dog was placed at the feet of its master to serve him in death.) The light passing through the window may have alluded to the purity of the bride. The mirror directly above the hands of the newlyweds was a symbol of the all-seeing eye of God, and its presence is like a celestial notary seal. Within the convex mirror are seen in miniature more of the contents of the room than in the format of the painting itself. Its

11.18 Kokoschka. *Hans and Erica Tietze-Conrat*, 1910. Collection Museum of Modern Art, Mrs. John D. Rockefeller, Jr. Fund. (Photo: Sunami)

spotless reflection of reality made the mirror a symbol of truth. This use of the reflected objects permitted a second wedding, that of the visible with the invisible. They are poetic extensions of the figures themselves. The objects serve to identify the locale and to symbolize the hidden spiritual and sexual relationships.

Oskar Kokoschka's portrait of the newly wedded *Hans and Erica Tietze* (Fig. 11.18), painted around 1910, does not depend upon symbols, place, witnesses, or prescribed gestures to show the bond that exists between man and wife. The picture is given no locale; the figures are seen as if through their own consciousness. The absorbent, but measureless space around them and the warm ephemeral colors are the painter's intuited extensions of their feelings and bodies. In Kokoschka's body imagery, the figures possess their space, and color and shape it by their psychic state. Wiry, scribbled lines are etched into the paint surface around and beyond the

figures by the hard ends of his brushes.

The gestures of the hands make a bridge between the man and woman, but it is an incomplete span. Significantly, the hands do not touch. Kokoschka seems to have sensed an unbreachable gulf between the two, an essential isolation. In contrast to Arnolfini, Hans Tietze is the more dependent member of the couple. His profile pose, slightly shorter height, lack of his wife's relative self-containment bring to the surface certain private weaknesses. This was not a posed portrait; Kokoschka studied the movements and actions of his subjects, searching for the moment that permitted him to pierce the social veneer. His subjects are rendered vulnerable. What he presents is more private than what would find outlet in his subjects' diaries, and yet less decipherable than what could be put into a written autobiography. Kokoschka suggested, but never circumscribed, the ultimate complex depths within individuals in their relations to themselves and others.

Kokoschka sought the naturalness achieved in moments of obliviousness to an outsider or realized in the most intense self-consciousness. He prized gestures impelled by inner forces, tangible surface evidence of the existence and power of the subconscious. Working in Vienna while Freud was teaching there, Kokoschka's findings were his own and illustrated an instance of modern artists' independence of scientists in the study of man.

SELF-PORTRAITS

Portraits fulfill myriad functions. The rendering in painting and sculpture of the human face has been linked with religion and the need to secure ties between the living Romans and their dead. For Egyptian royalty, the portrait was assurance of immortality through the provision of the soul's abode in an effigy. Status in a world of exalted political and social rank could claim the right to portraiture in many societies. The likeness and pose of an important figure could perpetuate an ethic of ideal social conduct. Concepts of manliness and femininity found important interpretation in Renaissance and Baroque portraits. Implementation of inquiry into human nature as expressed through the biological and psychological evidence of the face was another function of portraiture. The desire to convey intimate personal sentiments motivated many artists. The problem of finding a mystical essence of the human matched with the quest for personal absolutes of beauty and perfection attracted others. In all instances of portraiture, a major function was one of building a bridge between the artist and his human environment.

Having seen examples of the artist's purpose to serve others, we may conclude with the artist's study of himself. At sixty, Leonardo da Vinci approached the drawing of his own countenance with the same curiosity and discernment he brought to his observation of nature. In many respects his drawing (Fig. 11.19) is an objective likeness, but Leonardo accentuated his eyes. The eye was an endlessly fascinating organism for Leonardo, who was amazed that within its small size could be perceived all of the external world. Within the drawing is a graduated focus from the cursory outline of the top of the head and the broad undulant treatment of the beard, through the darkening and increased detailing of the brows, mouth, and nose, to the deeply recessed and shaded eyes. A life spent in the study of light and shadow has its residue in this drawing. The head is a summarizing of studies of bone and muscle structure as well as curiosity about the operation of the mind behind the face. The beard recalls Leonardo's development of new modes of drawing to capture the movement of flowing water and the upheavals of dust. Just as he made scrupulous studies of the action of weather upon the earth's surface, so Leonardo frugally set down in closely matched sequences of thin parallel lines the effect of age upon his face. He made no attempt to elicit sympathy or enter into a personal interchange between himself and the viewer. Significantly, he omitted reference to his hands and the upper part of his body. He drew exclusive attention to the fountainhead of his extraordinary ideas and visions.

The modern painter Joan Miro, drawing partially from a reflection in a convex mirror, gave free play to fantasies induced by irritability at the sight of his own features (Fig. 11.20). Miro could not be neutral toward any part of the head. He found in each feature of his face deeply personal as well as playful associations expressible only by his unique pictorial language. He did not superpose his invented forms on the face, but made them part of its new structure. He exaggerated the asymmetry not only of the face, but of each part or pair of features. Weight, texture,

11.19 (left) Da Vinci. *Self-portrait*, red chalk. 1510–1513. Turin. 11.20 (right) Miro. *Self-portrait*, oil and pencil, 1937–1938. The Museum of Modern Art, Collection James Thrall Soby. (Photo: Sunami)

shape, and tangibility have been consistently reworked. He inverted or parodied functions. He was drawn to openings in the head, accenting their existence, as in the mouth, suggesting their relatedness to other parts of the body. Lines, hair, and eyelashes excited his interest and led to their transformation into knifelike projections. Miro used the muscles of the face as a point of departure for self-involved, fanciful configurations. The forehead erupts into flamelike formations that destroy any sense of the head's closure. The head itself could not contain the wealth of sensations and ideas that it induced, and there is a sharing of textures and shapes between the areas inside and outside the face. Miro permitted his hand to move automatically across the surface, responding to impulse as if he were in a trance. His previous habits of drawing and the shapes themselves come through nevertheless, for much in this portrait is traceable to his earlier art. Leonardo's self-portrait was an affirmation of the control of art by the intellect joined with perception. Miro celebrated the irrational and emotional basis of art and life. His rendering of the eyes transformed their role as receivers of sensations from the external world to that of objects of internal sensation.

In the twentieth century, the span of portraiture has been extended from that of idealization and fidelity to external appearance to the exteriorization of an internal body image of others and the self.

CHAPTER 12

THE FIGURE
IN SCULPTURE

THE FIGURE IN OLDER
SCULPTURE . . . .

The appearance and development of the nude in Greece, from the seventh century down to the Classical period of the fifth century B.C., constitutes one of the finest legacies of Greek civilization. Its development implies a civilizing process not encountered earlier in the ancient world. It signifies an overcoming of the duality between man and the world, a gradual subsiding and mastery of fear, or cosmic dread.

Particular needs, associations, experiences, and ideals went into the formation of the nude, making of it a collective expression of an important aspect of Greek culture. *The Spear Carrier* shows that the relation of man to the world was one not of fear, but of self-confidence. *The Spear Carrier* has come down to us only in Roman copies and a German reconstruction. It was made by Polyclitus in the fifth century

B.C. Its identity is not known; the figure may represent Hermes, Achilles, a messenger of the gods, a soldier, or a hero of the gymnasium. The Classical nude represents a frank extension into art of man's own ego. The world is seen in man's image and ruled by his ideals of orderliness. This art form is not motivated by fear and desire for self-preservation, as is primitive African sculpture, for example. The Greek Classical nude signifies its creator's concern with the here and now, with no speculation on vague, mystical subjects or death. What had been in Homeric times remote, distant, and to be feared was brought within the orbit of man's knowledge and perception. The Classical nude reflects a man-centered world, one where man is the middle and measure of all things and is in felicitous equilibrium with nature.

The Classical Greek figure without clothing must be termed "nude" rather than "naked." The latter term suggests shame, self-consciousness, an unfamiliar state. The nude figure is one at ease without garments. For the Greeks, nudity separated them from the barbarians. They had no sense of sin or shame. Through the perfectly formed nude body the Greeks expressed and re-experienced their ideals of eurhythmics. *The Spear Carrier's* rhythm signifies not only control of the body but training of the mind and its dominance over the physical. The Classical nude epitomizes Apolline values of moderation and avoidance of excess. This proper measure of human conduct is partly paralleled in art by the Classical sculptor's love of mathematical measure as an insurance of perfection in the appearance of his art. Polyclitus recorded his perfected canon of proportion. He based it upon a division of an ideal body, whereby each part could be expressed as a fraction of the whole, the head as one-eighth of the body's total height, for example. The application of mathematical proportion to the nude human figure evidenced the Greek's propensity for giving tangible and sensual form to abstract concepts, of making rational abstractions a delight to the senses. The Greeks gave form to virtues by means of the unclothed figure. *The Spear Carrier* embodies the ideas of hygiene, courage, and dignified self-composure.

The Classical view of beauty depended upon subtle manipulation of antithetical conditions. The fifth-century "beauty pose" showed rest tempered by movement, a balance between perfect energy and perfect repose. The artistic device that permits the imaging of this dualism is counterpoise; for every movement in one direction, there is a countering movement in another. Like the Parthenon, the Classical nude expresses the Greek ideal of wholeness. All of the parts of a human sculpture or building are patently clear in themselves and in their relationships to each other and the whole. Nothing can be altered, added, or taken away without disrupting the total unity and over-all beauty.

The Greeks of the fifth century

believed that everything had an ideal form of which the phenomena of experience are more or less corrupted replicas. It remained for the artist to see through this imperfection and to perfect what nature had disguised or left unfinished. Classical sculp-

12.1 Greece. Polyclitus. *The Spear Carrier*, reconstructed by Römer, *c.* 450 B.C. Munich, Antikensammlungen, Glyptothek und Museum antiker Kleinkurst. (Photo: Kaufmann)

ture was not a mere juxtaposition of limbs and bodily parts that the artist had observed in his models. The Greek view of the ideal form was a balance of functional necessity and an ideal schema. What makes Classical art so effective is the continued presence of imagination and positive design.

One of the best summations of the achievements of Classical Greek culture as expressed through its art of the human form has been provided by Erwin Panofsky:

> As the system of Greek architecture lends exemplary expression to the properties and function of inanimate matter, so does the system of Greek sculpture and painting define typical forms of the character and behavior of living creatures, particularly man. And not only the structure and movement of the human body, but also the active and passive emotions of the human soul were sublimated, in accordance with the precepts of "symmetry" and "harmony," into noble poise and furious battle, sweetly sad parting and abandoned dance, Olympian calm and heroic action, grief and joys, fear and ecstacy, love and hate. All these emotional states were reduced to . . . "pathos formulae" which were to retain their validity for many centuries and appear "natural" to us precisely because they were "idealized" as compared to reality—because a wealth of particular observations had been condensed and sublimated into one universal experience. Thus to have captured and ordered the multitude of phenomena is the eternal glory of classical art: at the same time, however, it was the insurmountable barrier. Typification necessarily implies moderation; for where the individual is accepted only in so far as it corresponds to those "general laws" which . . . define the "natural", there is no place for extremes.

The limits of this chapter permit only a few illustrations of the historical wealth of sculptural interpretations of the human body. The examples have been chosen on the basis of their intrinsic worth and diversity of approach.

Large-scale stone sculpture declined after the fall of Rome, reflecting Early Christian apprehension about carved images. It revived only after A.D. 1000. Following *The Spear Carrier* by over fifteen hundred years is a Romanesque sculpture of the Old Testament prophet Isaiah, from the southern French church of Souillac (Fig. 12.2). This relief sculpture is based on contemporary carving and manuscript painting rather than on a living model and the long tradition of free-standing sculpture. Further, the Isaiah figure is seen in connection with architecture. These factors account for the relative flatness of the form and its orientation parallel to the rear wall and an invisible surface plane. Isaiah is shown in what appears to be a type of ecstatic dance, holding at arms' length a scroll on which was originally written an excerpt from his prophecies. In form and meaning, *Isaiah* is the antithesis of *The Spear Carrier*. In purpose, however, the two are similar. Both were concretizations of human beliefs, presenting the viewer with ideal modes of being through heroes greater than himself. The Christian figure testifies to the existence and superiority of a spiritual world that transcends that of the viewer. The Classical ideal was universal; that expressed at Souillac is hieratic. The Romanesque Christian sculptor, unlike Polyclitus, did not recognize a single proportional norm for an ideal figure based upon constant numerical ratios. He varied his proportion with the rank of his figure and the expressive needs of his design.

The elongation of Isaiah's proportions, which de-emphasizes his material weight and volume, permitted a complex countermovement of the axes of his form. The prophet's body has assumed a violent variation upon the Greek Classical ideal of tranquil counterpoise. The prophet's many joints and the lack of synchronization of the arm gesture with the multiple directions of the rest of the body are stressed. The spear carrier has weight and volumes so disposed as to permit infinite retention of the pose, but it is difficult to conceive of Isaiah's tiptoe balance as permanent. Yet while it is not hard to conceive of the spear carrier shifting his stance, it requires a stronger effort of imagination to see Isaiah altering his posture. The reason is that the Greek sculptor used a physiological

basis for the body structure while the Romanesque artist used an abstract linear armature. There is no celebration of muscular coordination in the latter. The spear carrier is an athlete of the body, Isaiah an athlete of the spirit. The movement and proportion of the Isaiah was directed in its appeal less to the eye than to the mind. There is an excitement in the prophet's pose, a type of spastic and unself-conscious total gesture that mirrors his spiritual intensity. The Romanesque crisscrossed oppositions create a more drastic self-involvement than is found in the Greek design. However, where the spear is an expendable design accessory, the scroll is needed to complete the balance of the prophet. This suggests the relatedness of the Christian figure to elements outside of himself and his existence in a complex universal hierarchy.

To understand the appropriateness of *Isaiah's* costume for the figure itself and to gain further understanding of the remoteness of this Romanesque interpretation from that of Classical Greece, one may compare this sculpture to the fifth-century relief *Nike Adjusting Her Sandal* (Fig. 12.3), from the Acropolis. (It is possible that Nike is not tying her sandal but is dropping it. This was an ancient Greek practice not unlike the dropping of a handkerchief.) The Greek garment, the chiton, clings to the woman's form in revealing fashion, this because of the practice of oiling the body prior to donning a robe. The drapery folds depend on the modeled articulations of the body. The veiled appearance of the feminine form does not reduce its sensual appeal. There is a flattering reciprocation between skin and garment that heightens the physical charms of the woman. The Romanesque drapery, like the treatment of the hair, shows a taste for strong abstract linear surface design that shares no dialogue with the body. The Greek drapery carving is deep and produces strong light and shadow rhythms,

12.2   Souillac. *Isaiah, c.* 1120–1130 A.D. Church of Notre Dame.

while the medieval French cutting is shallow, in keeping with the reduced sensuality of the whole. The rich designs and angular stylized hem of the prophet's robe pull the eye away from thought of the flesh; the curving folds of the *Nike* make the flesh apparent.

The mid-twelfth century jamb figures of the Royal Portal at Chartres Cathedral demonstrate another medieval ideal of the human figure (Fig. 12.4). It must be remembered that simultaneously with these Old Testament figures, Gothic sculptors were called upon to do a variety of other subjects and treated the human form in several ways. The artists demonstrated repeatedly that they could render the human form in movement with a surprising degree of naturalistic observation. In other words, not all twelfth-century Gothic cathedral sculpture demonstrates the properties seen in this example. The jamb figures have been given a columnar rigidity and verticality. The adjective is appropriate, for their axis is bound to that of the building to which they are attached. The antithesis of this assimilation to a nonhuman structuration is to be found in Greek caryatids (Fig. 12.5) from the porch of the fifth-century Erechtheum, on the Acropolis, in Athens. These Classical maidens, who serve as a vertical support for the roof of the porch, still display freedom of movement. One leg is stiffly poised, indicating that weight is carried on this member; the other is relaxed. Each maiden is allowed a degree of mobility, an unarchitectural freedom, that demonstrates the sculptor's view of the essential autonomy and integrity of the human form. He could not conceive of an inorganic basis for her construction. The Gothic sculptor willingly subsumes this liberty in the case of the saints in order to enhance the impression of the power and superhuman attributes of his subjects. The drapery of the Gothic saints has its own vitality and expressiveness independent of

the bodies. It is an important supplementary expressive device. The expression of an ideal through the body did not mean to the Gothic artist an imitation of reality. It meant a reorganization and invention of nonnatural devices. The jamb figures are dematerialized in part by their elongated proportion. In contradistinction to the caryatid who stands confidently upon a base, or ground, the Gothic saints are poised suspended upon their toes, announcing their spiritual transcendence of corporeality. The jamb figures manifest no awareness of each other, no visual or gesticular interchange. Each is shut off from the material world. There is no joy in their bodies or in human relationships. The rational and sensuous knowledge available to the Greek artist with which he animated his optimistic figures was unknown or untenable to his Gothic counterparts. The bodies of the

12.3 Athens. *Nike Adjusting Her Sandal, c.* 410 B.C. Acropolis Museum. Courtesy Royal Greek Embassy.

Gothic saints are refuges from the uncertainties, tensions, and anxieties of the natural world. There is no appearance or hint of repose and relaxation emblematic of man's concord with himself, society, or the world. The Gothic world could not accept the outlook of the Greeks.

The art of India, too, reflected a world outlook irreconcilable with the Gothic. The warm, ripe Indian tree goddess (Fig. 12.6), or Yakshi, who entwines herself with a tree on the east gate of the Great Stupa at Sanchi, has no place in the medieval Christian constellation of sacred personages. Her swollen, curving body with its globular breasts belongs with the hemispherical stupa rather than amidst the pointed arches and rectilinear towers of Chartres. The Yakshi also knows nothing of the columnar associations or inhibition of the Greek maidens. She recalls her role

12.4 (left) Chartres Cathedral. Jamb figures from the Royal Portal, mid-twelfth century A.D. Courtesy of the French Cultural Services.

12.5 (below) Athens. Caryatids from the porch of the Erechtheum, c. 420 B.C.

as fertility goddess. The abandon of her posture accentuates the sensuality of her form. No internal skeleton impedes the suggestive torsion of her inflated "Subtle Body." The Yakshi was symbolic in both Buddhism and Hinduism, which through their teaching and art convert the human erotic instinct to higher purposes than being an end in itself. The exaggeration of the Yakshi's sexual parts had religious motivation and was intended to arouse those who looked upon her to initiate their spiritual communion with the gods. The proportions, sequences of curves, and shaping of the parts did not proceed from a system based directly upon the actual human body, but shared some of the arbitrariness of Romanesque design. Far more than painting, the three-dimensional and tactile potential of sculpture successfully embodied the spiritual eroticism of Indian artists.

To turn from the Sanchi Yakshi to Donatello's *Mary Magdalen* (Fig. 12.7) creates an interesting juxtaposition. Al-

12.6 Sanchi. Yakshi, first century B.C. East Gate of the Great Stupa. (Photo Elisofon)

12.7 Donatello. *Mary Magdalen*, 1454–1455. Baptistery of Florence, Italy. (Photo: Brogi)

12.8 Donatello. *Saint George*, 1417. Florence, National Museum. (Photo: Brogi)

though Donatello is referred to as a Renaissance sculptor, his life-sized, painted wooden image of the Magdalen is the expression of an essentially medieval Christian attitude toward the incompatibility of body and soul. Art history is like a river with many branches and oxbows. Styles and attitudes may lessen in breadth, depth, and force, but they continue to influence and participate in the stream of history. Although Donatello often carved healthful and cosmetically attractive figures in an age that admired physical beauty, he retained the penitential spirit of the late Middle Ages. Intended for the Baptistery of Florence, his sculpture is a merciless study of the body made less than human, first through self-indulgence and then through a self-denying asceticism. He renewed the late medieval dichotomy between truth and surface beauty. Magdalen has become a living corpse, a medieval reminder of death and the wages of sin. Only the inflamed spirit of the converted woman powers the leathery flesh-covered skeleton and holds out the same hope as baptism. The spiritual intensity imparted to the sculpture by Donatello transcends its physical repellence and makes the work esthetically compelling. The slight interval between the hands is a life-giving tension that complements the psychological force emanated by the head. Essential to this focus is the rigidity of the body, which differs from that of the Chartres jamb figures in that Mary Magdalen's is self-imposed. No sculpture in Western art is further from the Greek Classical ideal of eurythmy. And yet, Donatello did make sculptures of the body which share certain Classical ideals.

The development of a naturalistic or lifelike rendition of the human body was not the exclusive achievement of the Italian Renaissance. The later Middle Ages witnessed many sculptures in which the sculptor and the painter who finished the sculpture achieved striking resemblances to the external appearance of the human form. This precedent does not detract from the value and power of Donatello's sculpture of St. George (Fig. 12.8), carved in 1417. To the citizens of Florence this was a heroic image with which they could identify themselves. Donatello's knight became, in fact, a type of city symbol. It embodied ideals of vigilance, courage, strength, and youthful manliness. The figure's humanity can be seen in the way its weight presses against the ground. The upward movement of the stance simultaneously suggests a countering thrust as if the figure resists gravity. Although he sheathed it in armor, Donatello created the illusion of the body's possession of volume and bone structure. Donatello's sculpture is informed by actual observation of the body as well as by ancient sculpture and a reticence to repeat medieval formulas in the body's rendition.

Interest in depicting human psychology by means of the body reached a climax in the work of the baroque sculptor Bernini. His *David* (Fig. 12.9), done in 1622 to 1624, shows the body in a mobile position, a contrast to the usual Italian Renaissance preference for the figure in repose. Like other Renaissance art, however, the *David* had one viewpoint from which it was most completely seen in terms of disclosing the full, uninterrupted sweep of the gesture. The theme is tension. The body is coiled, spiraling in space, as David prepares to loose the stone against Goliath. The stance, contraction of the muscles, and set of the face set the figure's mood and purpose. It is impossible to question Bernini's understanding of anatomy and the movement of the body. He was heir to the great discoveries and achievements of the Renaissance and Michelangelo. Dissatisfied with the static, self-contained, aloof aspect of most Renaissance figures, Bernini moved the body in corkscrew fashion and mo-

12.9 Bernini. *David*, 1622–1624. Rome, Borghese Museum. (Photo: Anderson)

bilized the spectator to move about it. Bernini sought to unite the work of art with the space and reality of the viewer and to extend art into the world of the living. He represents the apogee of the sculptor's interpretation of what might be called the outer life of the body. Not until Rodin in the nineteenth century would the direction of sculpture change.

TRANSFORMATIONS OF THE FIGURE IN MODERN SCULPTURE . . . .

Since Rodin is credited with being the father of modern sculpture, his *John the Baptist* (Fig. 12.10) is an appropriate work to keynote a discussion on the subject. The sculpture emerges from the past, for Rodin's conception of the human form was based upon a continuous tradition that began at the end of the medieval period. The body, which rests firmly on a base, is recreated as a continuously enclosed, solid mass. Structure and movement are dictated by anatomy and physiology; expression derives from the artist's observations of psychology, and the title comes from a literary source. The human form was modeled by Rodin as it was given to his eye and hand, and as his mind recalled its inner structure. But Rodin passionately loved the body as a marvelously expressive organism of balance and counterbalance. To make his art lifelike, he gave to his sculpture the appearance of being a resumé of successive motions. Movement was to Rodin the necessary link between the flesh and the soul. In his view, man, not the saints, was holy, and the body was the temple of the spirit. It was not John's message nor what he symbolized that moved Rodin so much as the model's instinctive urgency to express himself and his resulting bodily tension. The vigor of the figure's stance and gesture was matched by the energy of the sculptor's fingers as he built up the surface to suggest organic growth and animation. The body is realized through Rodin's studies of thousands of profiles perceived from all points of view, a technique he claimed to have

12.10 Rodin. *John the Baptist*, 1878. Collection The Museum of Modern Art. (Photo: Sunami)

learned from the study of Greek sculpture. The surface reception and rejection of light give pulse to the bronze, making the flesh a mirror of the figure's psychological existence. The bold stride and thrust of the arms bring the sculpture into our space and detach it from the cold and remote existence of academic sculpture. In his best work, Rodin created disturbing presences that live in the world of the viewer.

Rodin's art both attracted and repelled young artists at the beginning of the century. To some, it seemed melodramatic and deficient in strength of form. In a statement made in 1908 and previously quoted, Matisse spelled out this criticism without reference specifically to Rodin: "What I am after, above all is expression. . . . Expression . . . does not consist of the passion mirrored upon a human face or betrayed by a violent gesture. The whole arrangement of my picture is expressive." For the word "picture" Matisse could have substituted "sculpture."

Matisse himself made important contributions to sculpture, and his statement was prophesied by his own work, *The Serf* (Fig. 12.11), done around 1900. Although it reveals the influence of Rodin's bronze figures, it is an outright rejection of Rodin's marble sculpture. The surface of both sculptures received accents of modeling not totally dictated by the outer character of a masculine body; Matisse's figure is more densely compact than the *St. John*. Both sculptors at some point set aside rational knowledge to create expressive changes which return to the eye new esthetic experiences. Certain shapes and surface finish are more expressive than others. While the serf is passive, the sculpture becomes dramatic through the activity of the sculptor. The totality of *The Serf*, rather than its facial expression, makes it visually moving. But Matisse had sought in the face and body of the model evidence of a deep

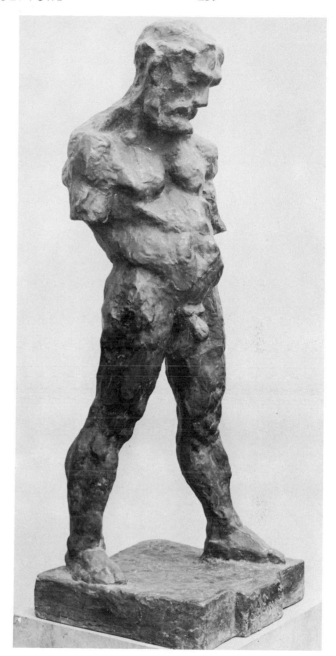

12.11 Matisse. *The Serf*, 1900–1903. Gerson Gallery. (Photo: Studley)

gravity that he felt existed in every human being. For both Matisse and Rodin, the body conveyed their near-religious feelings towards life, predicting the replacement of

religious sculpture by spiritual sculpture in
modern art.

A younger contemporary of Ro-
din, the sculptor Aristide Maillol, created
an art that differed in both its human ideal
and its form from that of the older sculptor.
Maillol's *Mediterranean* (Fig. 12.12) set the
norm for his sculpture of the next forty
years. The contemplative, amply proportioned woman became Maillol's fixed idea.
Just as her personality seems free from
nervousness or tension, so are the modeled
surfaces of her body purged of agitation,
the unexpected, and irregular. There is an
aura of cleanliness, of sun-insured health
to her body. The form is almost boneless,
inflated into soothing volumes that repose
solidly upon the base. Traces of the sculptor's fingers, that in the work of Rodin and
Matisse often scarred the surface with

ridges and depressions, were erased by
Maillol. His hand never intrudes into the
viewer's awareness. Maillol chose to under-
see the body, rejecting its wrinkles and
bony joints in favor of an unperturbed,
continuous covering whose firm closure reflects the withdrawn state of mind of the
subject. The silhouettes and intervals between the limbs are cleanly shaped, and
there is nothing to surprise the eye or
feelings. Maillol's women have the simple
beauty of freedom from shame, existing as
outposts of serenity in times of turbulence.

Maillol's disdain for the complexity and elusiveness of Rodin's sculpture was
shared by the young Romanian sculptor
Constantin Brancusi. Although he won first
prize in a contest to reproduce an anatomi-
cally correct figure in sculpture, scientific
accuracy did not long remain his concern.
Not long after his arrival in Paris, he was
asked to carve a gravestone for a dead
countryman. Ancient Greek gravestones
showed the tender parting of the living and
the dead. Brancusi chose to show their eternal union. Rejecting the surface data of the
body in *The Kiss* (Fig. 12.13), Brancusi
sought an elementary quality in both form
and content. Rather than suggesting a succession of movements, Brancusi's bodies are
conclusions, conceived in a few suggestive
shapes essential to the theme. Brancusi
avoided interlocking limbs and the play of
the flesh. His figures take and preserve the
form of the block from which they have
been cut, intimating Brancusi's mystical
sentiments about the relation of life to matter. Influenced by primitive sculpture, the
artist reduced and re-formed the details of
the body to increase expressive force. *The
Kiss* is not a sentimental ode to love or a
comic charade, but the fixing of a basic
human gesture for fulfillment. For Brancusi, sex was a motivating force of existence, and he could not veil such strong instinct with sentiment and surface distrac-

12.12   Maillol. *Mediterranean*, 1901.

tion. There is wit, however, in the double image of the bodies beneath the arms. Brancusi's gift to later sculptors was demonstration of the shaping power of the artist.

Part of Rodin's positive legacy to the German sculptor Wilhelm Lehmbruck was the vision of the heroic in human suffering. Lehmbruck's solemnization of the body in *Standing Youth* (Fig. 12.14) was a result of his equating the leanness of the human figure with the spiritual. The body is made monumental through meticulous measure, without loss of growth or development. The youth is not posed in the assertive stride of *John the Baptist*, but is in a set stance that nevertheless elevates him. The statue's visual power comes from the lack of physical movement and the implied strain it would require. The willful reduction of the body conveys Lehmbruck's concern with the tense effort of striving by the human spirit. It is not a trained, lithe body that permits Lehmbruck's figure to survive. This youth is a naked man whose body has been shaped by his individual character. In the manner of *Isaiah*, he is an athlete of the spirit, not the flesh. The gestures lack the more obvious rhetoric of Rodin's art and seem to turn back upon the man, suggesting his essential isolation and need to know and master himself. The large feet that press against the ground show Lehmbruck's sentiments about man's roots in the earth, his past and future. The difficult track of his life is suggested by the abrupt thrusts and changes of direction in the silhouette of the body. Done on the eve of World War I, this sculpture carries Lehmbruck's hopes for youth. In Lehmbruck's sculpture during and after the war, the body seems to break down, and with it the artist's confidence in man's mastery of his fate. Lehmbruck is one of the few modern sculptors to seek and achieve pathos in the human body.

Relative inaction gave drama and dignity to Lehmbruck's concept of the body, but the Italian sculptor Boccioni saw the human form only in terms of vibrant force. Reacting against academic sculpture with its insistence upon imitative modeling, sublime poses, and ennobling subjects, Boccioni recast the body in terms of the science and technology of his day. He was obsessed with the visible and invisible movement and interpenetration of all matter. In *Unique Forms of Continuity in Space* (Fig. 12.15), the previously closed shell of the body is ripped open and pene-

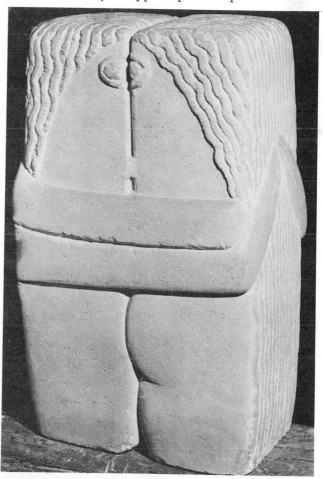

12.13 Brancusi. *The Kiss,* 1908. Philadelphia Museum of Art, Collection Louise and Walter Arensberg.

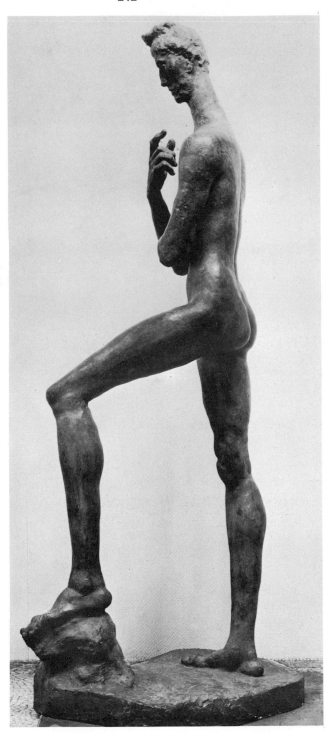

12.14 Lehmbruck. *Standing Youth*, 1913. Collection The Museum of Modern Art. (Photo: Sunami)

trated by the space about it. The solid portions of the body that act upon space acquire an undulating molten flow that adds to the fusion of the irregular silhouette with its environment. Boccioni even considered painting the edges to enhance the impression of a continuum. Although Boccioni contributed to futurist publications enthusiastic writings that extolled the machine and dynamism, he was committed to the human body and bronze. Where academic sculptures showed science by having a Classical figure hold a scientific instrument, Boccioni imparted to the body itself qualities of what it represented.

Sculptors from the Renaissance to the present time have transformed a studio model into a god, a general, a lover, or a virtue. While academic sculptors changed the identity of the model, Lipchitz and the Cubists acknowledged his identity, but revolutionalized his appearance. Lipchitz' *Man with a Guitar* (Fig. 12.16) perhaps first impresses the viewer by those things it is not. This is not a sculpture into which the viewer can project himself or that exhorts him to be a better citizen. The body lacks flesh and feeling, has not been "imitated from nature," and does not correspond to the sense experience of our eyes and hands. The label "Cubism," is also misleading as there are no cubes in the sculpture, nor is the work the cube root of the body. It was the intention of Lipchitz and the Cubists to establish the sovereignty of the mind of the artist, not "nature," over the work. The human body has not been deformed, but reformed by the artist's intellect and esthetic judgment. Anatomy and physiology, the traditional vocabulary and grammar of the sculptor, have given way to what might be called a new sign language—a language not inherited from the ages, but one which Lipchitz thought was of his time. Flat surfaces of varying shapes and thicknesses set at a variety of angles to one another construct an arbitrary armature for the general verticality of a figure. The body is transposed into an esthetic object. The basic change in cubist art is from the body seen to the body made. There is no separation of inside and outside; we see through, not into, the sculpture.

The sculpture has its own spirit and logic of organization, dictated by needs for visual coherence, variety, and interest. These properties, along with structural rightness and expressiveness, become the sculptor's criteria. Though mathematical formulas do not rule the work, there are general characteristics and constants in sculpture of this type. No segment is a complete form independent of its adjacent shapes (the circle being the exception that proves the generality), nor are the successive views of the sculpture predictable on the basis of any one view. The expressiveness of the sculpture resides not in figural gesture, but in the character of the shaping and joining. In arriving at this type of art, Lipchitz did not do violence to sacred subjects. His figure is anonymous and is involved in what is itself an esthetic activity. Lipchitz detached himself from notions of heroicism and correctness.

Modern sculpture is not a single movement as we have already seen. The American Gaston Lachaise, far from giving up the outer image of the body, accentuated its firm and sensuous shapes. Lachaise's

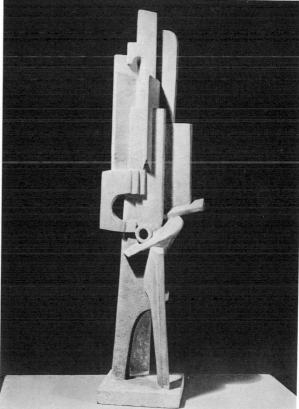

12.15 Boccioni. *Unique Forms of Continuity in Space*, 1913. Collection The Museum of Modern Art. (Photo: Sunami)

12.16 Lipchitz. *Man with a Guitar*, 1915. Collection The Museum of Modern Art. (Photo: Sunami)

12.17 Lachaise. *Standing Woman*, 1932. Collection The Museum of Modern Art. (Photo: Sunami)

ripe, robust, full-blown feminine forms recall statues of prehistoric fertility goddesses. *Standing Woman* (Fig. 12.17) possesses simultaneous references to masculinity and femininity, weight and grace, repose and energetic movement. Unlike Classical art, the proportion is not dictated by abstract numerical relationships; the relation of the parts to each other and the whole is a qualitative one in which the artist's personal associations with parts of the body and demands of a visual balance predominate. The tapering of the extremities and disposition of the weight enhance the dignity and ease of the body. There is

health not simply in the woman herself, but in the honest attitude of the artist who avoids contrived eroticism. Lachaise frankly presents a strong and handsome image of woman as the source of life.

In his *Figure* (Fig. 12.18) done between 1926 and 1931, Jacques Lipchitz showed a new concern with art and life. This work began a new direction both in his own art and in modern body imagery in sculpture. Lipchitz created a new sculptural metaphor for a state of being. His interpretation of tension is a chainlike configuration climaxed by a concave oval in which are set two small cylinders. For moments of mental crisis we have such verbal images as, "My stomach is tied in knots." What Lipchitz gives us is not a view of a tormented individual, such as Rodin's *Thinker* (Fig. 12.19), seen as if by someone else, but rather an imaginative self-image of the individual in distress. A poetical internal anatomy is revealed, not the contents of an x-ray plate. Lipchitz' form suggests the pulls and unresolved forces to which a human being may be submitted and, as signified by the weld of base to the link forms, the resultant immobility of spirit and body. The oval suggests internality by its reversal of the normally convex head, its elimination of the useless features, and immobilization of the eyes. Photographs of people in states of shock show a kindred suspension of consciousness, the eyes useless for sight, and the entire form rigidified under immense but invisible pressure. Lipchitz was concerned with the effects rather than the cause of this paralysis. Man is here not a hero, but a victim. Cubist painting and sculpture had effected a suspension of older habits of seeing and rendering the human body and had provided unlimited alternatives. The esthetic concerns of *Man with a Guitar* were enriched by the sculptor's involvement with the inner life and feelings not dealt with in earlier sculpture.

The decades of the 1920's and 1930's saw the introduction into sculpture and painting of exciting fantasies on the human body. The body was conceived in terms of the artist's inner senses, permitting him to express private feelings of desire or distaste. It was not performed in the shape of the studio model but grew from the excited imagination of the artist. The source of the artist's image cannot be found in either a living body or the artist's own biography. Dreams were not the primary source of the new conceits, but new forms were often induced by the artist's irrational associations with body parts.

The Spanish sculptor Julio Gonzalez sought to restore to sculpture properties of mystery, fantasy, and even the diabolic. *Woman Combing Her Hair* (Fig. 12.20) resists the old criteria. There seems to be no principle by which he projected

into sculpture his image of the woman. Gonzalez' fantasy on the body is not simple design by substitution. He ignored the three-dimensional and somewhat rectangular coordinate system of cubist sculpture. He evoked and re-formed the woman's body and movement by a series of contraries—open instead of closed forms, sharp as opposed to round shapes, hard and rough versus soft and smooth surfaces. Space does not exist outside of the body, but is its intimate possession, something to be shaped and pierced and set off by what Gonzalez considered his "drawing" of strong shapes. This union of space and solid is for Gonzalez the equivalent of the coexistence of the soul and the flesh. At a time, in the 1930's, when plowshares were being beaten into swords, Gonzalez wrought iron into a lyrical and civilized object. In his own words, "It is time this metal ceased to be a

12.18 Lipchitz. *Figure*, 1926–1931. Collection The Museum of Modern Art. (Photo: Sunami)

12.19 Rodin. *The Thinker, c.* 1880. Philadelphia Museum of Art.

murderer and the simple instrument of a super mechanical science. Today the door is open for this material to be, at last, forged and hammered by the peaceful hands of an artist." Iron and welding, new and exciting media for the modern sculptor, gave Gonzalez inexpensive means by which to achieve shapes, angles, and projections impossible in wood, stone, or cast metal. The toughness

12.20 Gonzalez. *Woman Combing Her Hair,* 1936. Collection The Museum of Modern Art. (Photo: Sunami)

of iron yielded, under his hands, the most delicate as well as strenuous constructs of his imagination. Gonzalez found it impossible to sustain this type of imagery and later returned to more naturalistic works, but his personal example and art created an important influence on many later sculptors in metal.

Giacometti's *Woman with a Severed Neck* (Fig. 12.21) literally and figuratively takes woman off the pedestal. Instead of the languid posture of a fulsome nude, we see the body dissected and recomposed. It is a frankly sadistic image. Giacometti could not render dispassionately a model to which he was indifferent. He saw the body not in its exterior reality, but in the way it affected his life and moved him within. Here he created a pointed and violent configuration, antipodes to round and calm forms. The figure lost all of its compactness, and in its skeletalizing in space became a transparent construction. The body resembles an aggressive landscape whose tensions are created by movement in opposing directions. The moral imperative in Giacometti's art is his belief in the primacy of fantasy and the conviction that abstract forms are true forms for sculpture.

Woman receives a new life and serenity in the work of Henry Moore (Fig. 12.22). Moore transformed the body to show more satisfactory visual relationships. When Moore reduces the size and definition of the head, eliminates the feet and hands, fuses normally unconnected body parts, and introduces a great hollow in the middle of the torso, he is not motivated by a perverse desire to shock. His rephrasing of the body and endowing of a tissuelike surface created strong continuous rhythms that for Moore link man and nature. His reclining forms of wood and stone seem shaped by the corrosive and abrasive action of the elements. The re-

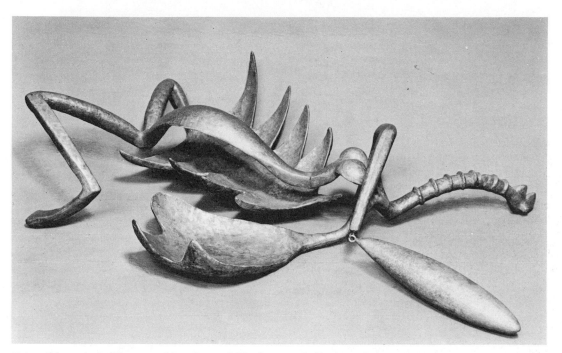

12.21   Giacometti. *Woman with a Severed Neck*, 1932. Collection The Museum of Modern Art. (Photo: Sunami)

12.22   Moore. *Reclining Figure*, 1946. Cranbrook Academy of Art.

clining pose has been traditionally associated with tranquillity and dignity, and these properties are still honored. The living body possesses many openings, and Moore's use of hollows derives from mixed associations, esthetic and sexual reveries on the inner cavities of the body, womb, and cave fantasies. Moore contributes a personal image that exalts qualities and processes sensed, if not seen, in the body.

By the Second Word War, modern painting and sculpture had seen unprecedented developments in form and content. The artist was able to express his most intimate thoughts and feelings about the human body in a direct and honest manner. For centuries, sculptors had interpreted the outer man, but within our own century the means and incentive to reveal his previously unsculptured inner life came into being. It is from such fertile beginnings that sculpture since World War II has been conceived.

Giacometti turned to the creation of thin, hermetically isolated figures after 1945. All that Moore valued, the body's relaxed voluptuousness, placid rhythms, stability, and equanimity, Giacometti disavowed. As in *Pointing Man* (Fig. 12.23), his people possess a fragile being, bordering on dissolution. He sought a maximum of expression with a minimum of means. The silhouettes of his figures are unstable and without appeal to the touch. Standing rigidly or walking through space, his figures are like isolated peninsulas. Giacometti attempted to express the essential solitariness of man. In his search for truth, he shaped his art according to discoveries made by his mind as well as by his eyes. The thin, vertical proportions of his figures stem from observance of the way people actually look at a distance. A six-foot figure across the street may appear to be a few inches high. Furthermore, the distant figure lacks volume and distinct separation of parts. Giacometti pointed out that the Greeks always carved their figures as if the viewer were about six feet away from the model. No matter how close to a work by Giacometti the viewer comes, the figure gives the impression of being seen from a great distance. Giacometti did not seek to enter the body or turn it inside out. The remoteness of the viewer is related to the remoteness of his sculptured figures from contact with other human beings.

Perhaps the most powerful sculpture based upon the human body since 1945 is Seymour Lipton's *Sentinel* (Fig. 12.24). Despite the lack of reference to the familiar external anatomy of the body, the sculpture possesses a strong human presence. *Sentinel* is in the tradition of twentieth-century imaginative metaphorical sculpture.

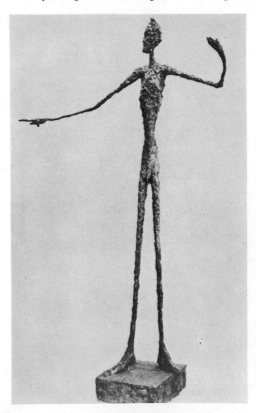

12.23 Giacometti. *Pointing Man*, 1947. Collection The Museum of Modern Art.

Lipton conceived of a sculpture to signify brooding power and demonic force. His metaphor is compounded of reminiscences of a helmeted figure in armor, a battering ram, a fortress battlement, Chinese calligraphy, and the orchestration of feelings of push and pull, human dignity, and mystery. Lipton's metaphor exists as part of a personal depth language and is open-ended. The work is not meant to be dissected nor to have its components traced. The feeling inspired by the sources is rationally translated.

The sculpture is about eight and one-half feet tall; it is possible to approach it and stand under the arrow-visor-battlement shape at the apex. The sculpture has both an inside and an outside. It deals with fantasies on internal anatomy; it is an attempt to exteriorize the inner struggle and defiance in the life of man. Using cut-out sheets of monel steel, brazed with nickel, silver, or bronze, Lipton carried out his conceits and created a new psychological depth and physiology for the body.

The foregoing examples of twentieth-century sculptures of the human form give scant indication of the existing breadth and depth of interpretations accorded this subject in the last fifty years. Along with modern painters, sculptors have opened up seemingly limitless areas of human experience and esthetics for exploration.

12.24 Lipton. *Sentinel*, 1959. Collection Yale University Art Gallery. (Photo: Baker)

CHAPTER 13

MICHELANGELO

Michelangelo Buonarroti was born in the Tuscan town of Caprese in 1475 and died in Florence in 1564. At the end of the 1480's, he studied painting for a year in Florence with the brothers Domenico and David Ghirlandaio. He then studied sculpture with Bartoldo, a former pupil of Donatello, who taught in the magnificent sculpture garden of the Medici family in Florence. Michelangelo's youthful work attracted the eye of Duke Lorenzo de' Medici, who, invited the young artist to join his household. There Michelangelo was introduced to the most brilliant group of intellectuals in Europe, contact that had a deep influence upon Michelangelo's attitude toward ancient sculpture and the purpose of art. During these years in Florence Michelangelo made drawings of the work of Giotto and Masaccio as well as of Roman and Greek sculpture. In 1494, when the house of Medici fell from power, Michelangelo made the first of several flights in his search for the security and tranquillity he needed for his work, but was never to find. After two years in Venice and Bologna

he went to Rome in 1496, there to carve his first *Pietà*, now in St. Peter's. He returned to Florence for four years, beginning in 1501, to work on several civic commissions, including the *David*. In 1505 Michelangelo was called to Rome by Pope Julius II, one of the first great and troublesome sponsors of Michelangelo's art. It was the sculptor's fate to be frustrated and harassed by powerful patrons who encouraged grandiose schemes and then capriciously diverted the artist from completing them. From 1505 to 1513, against his wishes, Michelangelo painted the Sistine Ceiling and worked intermittently on the enormous project for the pope's sepulcher, of which only the *Moses* and *Bound Slaves* saw realization. Between 1520 and 1534, Michelangelo divided his time between Rome and Florence, sculpture and architecture. For Pope Leo X, he worked on the Medici Chapel in Florence. In 1529 he served as a military engineer on the Florentine fortifications. From 1534 until his death, Michelangelo lived in Rome, painting the Last Judgment, 1532 to 1541, and the Pauline Chapel,

250

1541 to 1550. In 1547 he became chief architect for the rebuilding of St. Peter's Cathedral, a project which excited his last thoughts and energies. During the 1530's and 1540's he wrote many religious sonnets, dedicated to his friend Vittoria Colonna, who deeply influenced his spiritual direction. Busied with a number of architectural projects, such as the redesigning of the Capitoline Hill in Rome, in the last years of his life, Michelangelo did only two incomplete sculptures, both on the theme of Christ's death.

The history of art shows many examples of artists who brought major talents to bear upon minor subjects. Vermeer and Matisse come to mind as examples of men whose greatness lay in the *way* they interpreted the commonplace, giving to it the quality of the uncommon. Michelangelo brought great art to great ideas. He was the most brilliant technician and one of the great intellects of his time and place. The fact that his places were Florence and Rome and his time the Italian Renaissance, gives some idea of Michelangelo's measure. He was obsessed with the extent and endless mystery of God and His creation Man. Never did Michelangelo show an interest in the rendering of objects or landscape. His was a man- and God-centered art. Nor did he paint and carve in terms of living men. His aim was to depict the universal fate of humanity, but, so far as is known, he made only one pencil sketch of a contemporary. He was loth to be bound to an earthly material model. He felt impelled to work from divine inspiration in order to spiritualize his experience of reality and to obtain eternal and transcendent truth.

Michelangelo saw his destiny in the chisel and stone. Sometime between 1536 and 1547 he wrote, "The greatest artist has no conception which a single block of marble does not potentially contain within its mass, but only a hand obedi-

ent to the mind can penetrate to this image." Elsewhere, Michelangelo defined the art of sculpture as "the taking off that puts into the rough hard stone a living figure grown most great just where stone had grown most small." The bringing forth of life from base matter was a spiritual act for Michelangelo, one sympathetic to God's creation of life. He once referred to God as the "Divine Hammer." Great art, he believed, depended upon the artist's first possessing within himself a perfect God-given conception or Idea, whose first-born was a simple clay model. Its second realization was in "the rugged living stone" and possessed "such beauty that none may confine its spirit."

It would be futile in the limits of this chapter to attempt a total history of Michelangelo. A few examples that contain seminal ideas and lend awareness of the scope and depth of their maker's art will be discussed.

Begun when Michelangelo was twenty-six, *David* (Fig. 13.1) was carved between 1501 and 1504 at the request of the city of Florence, partly to commemorate the completion of a new civic constitution and partly to demonstrate that city's artistic leadership and vigor. David was famous not only as the slayer of Goliath, but also as a ruler, and his association with justice made him an appropriate figure to celebrate a new governmental reform. Originally intended to stand on top of a buttress of the cathedral, the eighteen-foot-high statue was placed in the main square of the city as a type of civic emblem. In the finely muscled, alert, and somber youth, the citizens could see an embodiment of what they felt were their own virtues. Michelangelo may have shared these ideas, but he also wished *David* to confirm his establishment as the greatest living sculptor. In his contracts at

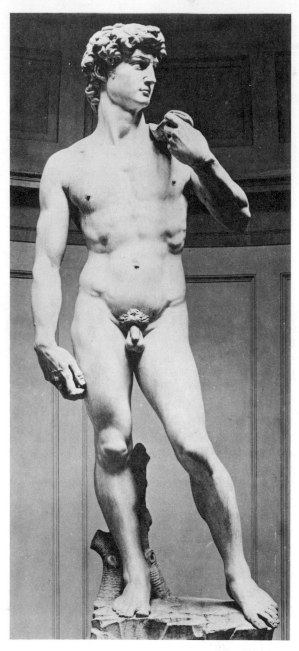

13.1 Michelangelo. *David*, 1501–1504. Florence, Academy. (Photo: Alinari)

the time, Michelangelo specified that his sculpture be of unsurpassed beauty. Not only did he demonstrate to the satisfaction of all his knowledge of ancient Greek art and the science of anatomy, but he was also able to give form to a deep personal vision of a hero. In Michelangelo's view, only a handful of human beings in the history of the human race qualified as heroes. These were primarily Old Testament prophets or rulers who perfectly embodied the active and contemplative life. In his youth, when *David* was created, Michelangelo equated truth with beauty, and to *David* he gave the body of a Greek Apollo, but not that god's temperamental equanimity. By the time of the *David*, the nude form in art had been largely divested of its medieval sinful associations, partly because of the acceptance of ancient art and thought as compatible with Christianity. Michelangelo believed that the nude male body was divine and that its ideal rendition in art would approximate the prototypal image conceived by God. He wrote: "And who is so barbarous as not to understand that the foot of a man is nobler than his shoe, and his skin nobler than that of the sheep with which it is clothed."

The quality of repose suggested by a front view of the youth's stance is not sustained, for there is a faint suggestion of a tensing of the muscles in the torso, more obvious in the neck and vehement in the angry visage. This psychological climactic element and contrast of the states of mind and body is alien to Greek Classical ideals. There is also an asymmetry in the right and left sides of the body. The figure's right side is protected by the downward-hanging arm holding the stone. The left side is more vulnerable. Significantly, David looks to his left. From the Middle Ages there had been a tradition which associated divine protection with the right and the origin of evil with the left. It has been suggested that David is "frowning" at the sight of Goliath, assuredly the symbol of evil. It would be a mistake, however, to conceive of this work as the illustration of a specific event or moment. David is, above all, a symbol of force and anger. The stone and sling signify the need for alert and courageous defense of principle. Like the Barletta sculpture of a Byzantine emperor, the militant and defiant attitude of David is a warning to the enemies of the right and a comfort to those he protects. The angry concentration of the face reflects displeasure with human weakness. Michelangelo was a Christian sculptor who could satisfy his religion with the idea of a Hebraic hero in the body of a Greek god.

No artist before Michelangelo possessed such complete mastery of the human body and ability to render its richness as a material organism and its emotional and intellectual span of mind and spirit. Possessing natural gifts as a craftsman and observer of his subject, Michelangelo was also a great student of art. The sculpture of ancient Greece and Rome and that of the fifteenth century, in which he was born, provided ideas and forms that he welded to his personal style. The greatest master to influence Michelangelo, however, by the sculptor's own words, was God. To the Greeks and certain Renaissance sculptors, beauty was achievable by means of proportion or mathematical measure, but for Michelangelo, proportion was qualitative, not quantitative. Proportion meant the extent to which his image corresponded to the "Idea" inherent in it. Furthermore, the physical beauty of his figures was not an end in itself. It was intended as a reflection of a spiritual beauty and was meant to elevate the thoughts of the beholder above material things. True beauty could not be obtained by mere copying of the visible world. Michelangelo's art proceeds from the mind, in which he believed he could more perfectly comprehend the perfect form.

Michelangelo despised Raphael's optimism in the ability of his contemporaries, such as Castiglione, to achieve grace.

The sculptor felt that Raphael had a naïve and incorrect faith in simple formulas of human conduct as a means of achieving true earthly happiness and excellence. The differences between these two men can be seen in Raphael's portrait (Fig. 11.5), considered earlier, and Michelangelo's *Moses* (Fig. 13.2), of about 1514, intended for a tomb of Julius II that was never completed. To Michelangelo, Moses was a moral and physical giant, a man whose imposing physical frame was the instrument of heroic physical action—the leadership of his people on the great exodus. The enormous and vital head of Moses is the locus of divine visions, the fountainhead of law. This is the moment when Moses sees the Jews dancing around the golden calf. In the manner of the *David*, Moses is caught in the passion of anger when confronted by the vision of human depravity. Like David, Moses sees evil coming from his left. The horns derive from an apocryphal tradition that had beams of light sprout from his forehead at the moment of his vision of the Lord. Michelangelo could conceive of only superhuman bodies for those gifted with supernatural vision who could rise above human fallibility by tremendous moral effort.

Unlike that of Castiglione, the seated posture of Moses does not signify complete repose. The sculpture's drama comes from the unlike forces and movements of rest and action contained within a single form. The whole is formed by a rectilinear blocklike ordering in depth. Any movement that diverges from frontality or the vertical and horizontal is given exaggerated emphasis. The right and left sides of the body and drapery are calculated contrasts. Moses' right leg and arm, which clutches the tablets of the law to his side, still evoke the idea of repose. The withdrawal of the left leg as if to support the rising figure and the gesture of the left arm sig-

13.2   Michelangelo. *Moses*, 1513–1516. Rome, San Pietro in Vincoli.

nify the transition from immobility. The head is violently twisted away from the frontal direction of the chest. In the lower area, the drapery coordinates and frames the divergent positions of the legs. The virile beard is a recapitulation of the arm and chest axes and effects the transition to the head. Like the sculpture of David, that of Moses rises from a quiescent base through the pillarlike right leg to the intermediary zone of the chest and climaxes in the fiercely intense area of the eyes and brows. The heroic proportions and physique of Moses are the only conceivable containers for the magnitude and depth of his supernatural excitement and agitation of spirit. *Moses* helps us to understand why Michelangelo's contemporaries saw in his style qualities of the terrible.

The antithesis of *Moses* is Michelangelo's misnamed *Dying Slave*, or *Bound Slave* (Fig. 13.3). It, too, was intended for the tomb of Pope Julius II. Although based upon a late Greek sculpture of one of Niobe's dead children, the figure is not a political slave, nor is he dying. His prison is not that of chains nor even of the cord across his chest, but that of the body itself, which incarcerates the spirit. If he were dying, the figure would express joy, for it would mean that his spirit was about to rejoin God. Behind the figure is a half-finished ape, which to an educated viewer of the time would have signified the dominance of lust or the passions over reason. The human dilemma celebrated by Michelangelo is the mortal life of torment away from the Creator. The fate of man is to have joined within himself a temporal body and an immortal soul. As expressed by a contemporary philosopher, Marsilio Ficino, whose ideas often paralleled those of Michelangelo,

Our mind, as long as our sublime soul is doomed to operate in a base body, is thrown up and down with permanent disquietude, and it often slumbers from exhaustion and is always insane; so that our movements, actions and passions are nothing but the vertigos of ailing people, the dream of sleepers, and ravings of madmen.

This sculpture puts into tangible form ideas that Michelangelo was later to express in his poetry. Between 1547 and 1550 he wrote in a private lament to God: "For Thou not only gavest to time my divine soul, but didst imprison it in this frail body and weary flesh and must hand it over to its cruel destiny. How can I escape living thus. Without Thee."

To convey pathetic restlessness of the soul, Michelangelo drew upon Greek principles of expressive body posturing. The *Slave* employs Classic counterpoise in which the lines of the shoulders, hips, and knees parallel neither the ground nor each other. Moving upward from the feet of the slave, each direction taken by the body is countered by another immediately above, so that the whole is a self-adjusting mechanism in a soft, serpentine formation. The relation of the shoulders to the knees exists in crisscross fashion, so that to understand Michelangelo's construction the figure's right shoulder should be seen in relation to his left knee, for example. Despite the mobility imparted to the body, Michelangelo's figures always seem capable of sustaining the pose and outline the shape of the original stone block from which they were cut.

In his painting of the Sistine Ceiling (Fig. 13.4), Michelangelo executed a humanistic-religious program of almost unparalleled magnitude. The ceiling painting was commissioned by Pope Julius II against the wishes of Michelangelo, who longed to devote his energies and life to sculpture rather than painting. For four years, between 1508 and 1512, Michelangelo lay on his back, covering the more than seven hundred yards of ceiling with the outpourings of a fired imagination. The strain of

13.3 Michelangelo. *Bound Slave*, from the tomb of Julius II, 1514–1516. Paris, The Louvre.

13.4   Michelangelo. Ceiling of the Sistine Chapel, 1508–1512. Rome, The Vatican. (Photo: Alinari)

working while lying supine under the dripping plaster wrecked his health and frame.
At the end of his project, he wrote a poem
describing his condition:

> I've grown a goiter by swelling in this
> den—
> As cats from stagnant streams in Lom-
> bardy,
> Or in what other land they hap to be—
> Which drives the belly close beneath the
> chin;
> My beard turns up to heave; my nape
> falls in,
> Fixed on my spine: my breast-bone visi-
> bly
> Grows like a harp: a rich embroidery
> Bedews my face from brush drops thick
> and thin.
> My loins into my paunch like levers
> grind:
> My buttock like a crupper bears my
> weight;
> My feet unguided wander to and fro:
> In front my skin grows loose and long;
> behind
> By bending it becomes more taut and
> strait:
> Crosswise I strain me like a Syrian bow.
>
> (From Goldwater and Treves,
> *Artists on Art*, p. 59)

Despite his plaints and protesta-
tions, it seems likely that Michelangelo
viewed this painful task as a form of penance and that the ardor of his creative
labors was an expiation for his sinful guilt.

The iconography of the Sistine
Ceiling is an amazing fusion of Hebrew
and Christian theology with Neoplatonic
ideas. In all likelihood, Michelangelo had
papal assistance in the formulation of the
extensive program, and it seems certain
that although the Pope gave him license to
do as he pleased, the project satisfied the
spiritual and political desires of the patron.
At the time the ceiling was being painted,
the papacy was waging war against foreign
troops and heretics within the faith itself.
The Sistine Ceiling was touched by these
contemporary events, and by means of com-

plicated theological metaphors, the Pope
had Michelangelo assert the former's confidence in his ultimate triumph over his
enemies. The subject of the ceiling is osten-
sibly that of the Old Testament God who
created the world and punished Man for
denying his Lord. In the triangular spandrels are the ancestors of Christ, such figures as David, who is shown killing Goliath, and Judith, who has beheaded Holofer-
nes. Flanking the central rectangles that
contain scenes from Genesis are the Sibyls
and Prophets who foretold the Creation
and punishment. The agitated nude figures
holding garlands and large golden Eucharistic wafers are human souls, or acolytes.
The secondary motives of the ceiling were
to assert the theological ancestry of the
Pope and to imply that he was a messiah
acting as the earthly agent of God to
punish the heretics. The Pope's family
name in English was "Oak Tree," and there
are references in the ceiling to oaks. The
spandrels depict the deliverance of the
chosen people, perhaps a prophecy of the
actions of Julius II.

The main scenes on the ceiling are
depicted in rectangular frames. The order
of the scenes does not follow the chronology of Genesis. Above the head of the
visitor entering the Chapel are "The Re-
vilement of Noah," "The Flood," "The
Sacrifice of Noah," and "The Fall of
Man." The common theme of all these subjects is God's punishment by means of the
elements—earth, water, fire, and air. They
illustrate how God chastises a world that
betrays Him and the sacrifice of Christ
through false offerings and the partaking of
the forbidden fruit.

The fulcrum panel of the ceiling,
originally directed above the partition that
divided the Chapel in half, is the scene of
God's creation of Eve from the side of
Adam. Eve at this time symbolized the
Church. In the ceiling's sequence, the
Church stands as the mediator between

man and God, and is the means of man's redemption.

The second half of the ceiling is above the sacred section of the chapel, the altar. The theme of the remaining four subjects, "The Creation of Adam," "The Separation of the Waters from the Earth," "The Creation of the Sun, Moon, and Planets," and "The Separation of Light from Darkness," is the creative power of the Divinity.

As in Michelangelo's earlier work, the figures are preterhuman in size and action. God is the Old Testament divinity who roars out of a whirlwind and speaks with a voice of thunder. (His visage, seen in "The Creation of Adam," was strikingly similar to the bearded profile of Julius II.) The purpose of the program was to strike fear and awe into the minds of the mortals who looked upon it—awe of God, and of the Church, and of His earthly representative.

While some of the figures in the Ceiling may be traced to artistic prototypes realized by Michelangelo's predecessors, the whole is a magnificent personal construct. It testifies to the range of Michelangelo's imagination and his great sense of human guilt. It is one of the greatest products of a human mind, eye, and hand that civilization has witnessed.

The Sistine Ceiling is a marvel of skill and dexterity, but the power of Michelangelo's art transcends virtuoso effects. There is a philosophical justification for all aspects of his style. He put his knowledge of the form and workings of the body into the service of spiritualizing human anguish and exaltation. The agitated athletic figures of the sibyls and prophets mirror the profundity and excitement of visions inaccessible to ordinary mortals. In the scene of the creation of Adam (Fig. 13.5), Michelangelo infused Adam's form with the mingled experience of a body awakening with reluctance at the separation of the spirit from its Creator. Adam is not joyful

at his earthly birth; the languid posturing of his arms and torso reveal his melancholy state, and the face has an expression of ineffable longing. Significantly, Michelangelo stressed the hands of Adam and God and the slight interval between them that signified the measureless gulf that now separated man and his Creator. Attention is drawn repeatedly to the contrasts and similarities between the bodies of Adam and God, fitting accompaniment to the sculptor's poem written possibly during the years of work on the Sistine Ceiling. "He who made the whole made every part; then from the whole chose the most beautiful, to reveal on earth, as he has done here and now in His own sublime perfections. The human figure is the particular form in which beauty is most clearly manifested."

Small indication can be given in this brief space of the intellectual wealth Michelangelo mined to construct the program of his ceiling. Scholars such as De-Tolnay and Hartt have, in impressive and often conflicting studies, begun to unravel the many levels of meaning and alternative interpretations of its content. That such scholarly approaches are essential to the full understanding and appreciation of Michelangelo's art is borne out in the sculptor's own views on painting:

At its best nothing is more noble or devout, since with discreet persons nothing so calls forth and fosters devotion as the difficulty of a perfection which is based upon union with God. For good painting is nothing but a copy of the perfections of God and a recollection of His painting; it is a music and a melody which only intellect can understand, and that with great difficulty. And that is why painting of this kind is so rare that no man attains it.

The Medici Chapel, on which Michelangelo worked from 1520 to 1534, like the Sistine Ceiling must be conceived of not only as an artistic interpretation of a humanistic program, but also as a monumental attempt at propaganda. The official

13.5 Michelangelo. *The Creation of Adam*, detail from Sistine Chapel Ceiling. Rome, The Vatican. The Metropolitan Museum of Art. (Photo: Anderson)

purpose of the designs was to create a sepulchral chapel to house the bodies of Lorenzo and Giuliano de' Medici. The Chapel is attached to the Church of San Lorenzo in Florence. The date of the Chapel's commencement is an important one as it coincided with a decline in the power and aspirations of the House of Medici due to the death of two of its most important members. They too were to have been buried in the Chapel, but this plan was subsequently discarded. The Chapel may have been intended as a grandiose allegory of princely and papal power, as the Medici were allied with the Pope. It was to glorify the deceased occupants of the Chapel by using them as examples of the ideal conduct of rulers, this conduct being the observance of certain Neoplatonic ideals. The rewards beyond the tomb of such an exemplary life were interpreted by Michelangelo in the sculptures that surmounted the wall sepulchers (Fig. 13.6).

There are four reclining figures on the two sepulchers. Below the figure of the Duke Giuliano lie the figures of Night and Day. Beneath the seated form of Lorenzo are the recumbent figures of Twilight and Dawn. The times of day signify the temporal life which is one of ceaseless despair and restlessness, unremitting move-

ment and pain. The agonies of the temporal life are given form in the ample, contorted torsos of the times of day. On a sketch for the tomb over which are Night and Day, Michelangelo wrote,

> We have with our swift course brought to death the Duke of Giuliano, it is just that he take revenge upon us thus: that we have slain him, he thus dead has taken the light from us and with closed eyes has fastened ours so that they may shine forth no more upon this earth. What would he have done with us while he lived?

The moral of this lament was that in death the Duke had conquered the temporal life and time. He was now outside of time. Michelangelo also planned to insert a mouse on the tomb to symbolize the gnawing, destructive action of time.

The faces of the two dukes (Figs. 13.6 and 13.7) show that Michelangelo did not create portrait likenesses of his subjects. He gave them a greatness and dignity that seemed to him a fitting commemoration for posterity. Without question, these "portraits" are of abstract ideals, as Giuliano did not live up to the principles glorified in his sculptural effigy. The figure of Giuliano embodies the Neoplatonic ideal of the active life, one of vigorous physical administration, shown by his overt pose, the mar-

13.6 (left) Michelangelo. Tomb of Giuliano de' Medici, c. 1524–1534. Florence, Medici Chapel. (Photo: Roger-Viollet) 13.7 (above) Michelangelo. *Lorenzo de' Medici*, c. 1524–1534. Florence, Medici Chapel.

shal's baton, and the coins in his hand, symbolizing a man who expends himself in outward actions. Lorenzo, his finger to his lips and head partly in shadow, epitomizes the contemplative life and saturnine disposition. In his meditative, introverted pose, he sits with his left elbow on a closed money box, which signified miserliness.

Both lords look towards the Virgin and suckling Christ at the end of the Chapel (Fig. 13.8). She incarnates the Church, which took to its bosom the exiled House of Medici when it had been previously expelled from Florence. She is also the prophetic mother who gives her breast to the Child, but also draws back with the premonition of His sacrifice. The Medici Dukes are garbed in Roman armor, recalling their posthumous (1514) election by the Pope as militant Captains and defenders of the Church. According to Fred Hartt, the sculptural ducal effigies were in one sense a call to the leaders of Italy to rally to the defense of the Church in her time of need.

Standing in the Medici Chapel, the visitor has the impression of being an intruder. Michelangelo's architecture is scaled to the sculpture and not the human being. The light entering from high up in the ceiling falls onto cold marble surfaces. The room itself is of exaggerated height and gives the impression of a deep, well-like space, unearthly, amicable only to the sculptural effigies.

Michelangelo's great fresco of the Last Judgment (Fig. 13.9) must be viewed as part of the program of the Sistine Chapel, only two-thirds of which was actually carried out. It was proposed that Michelangelo execute a great fresco over the chapel doorway having as its subject the fall of the rebel angels. "The Last Judgment" fresco was to terminate this cycle. It is recorded, perhaps apocryphally, that when the Pope first saw the finished judgment fresco he fell on his knees in prayer. Michelangelo's painted vision is an awesome sight, calculated not to console the viewer with the promise of ultimate justice, but to make him pause and reflect upon the adequacy and profundity of his personal faith. Michelangelo never intended his style to edify the eye. He aspired to devotional images that would incite those with little devotion to contemplation and tears, reverence and fear. The subject of the great fresco over the chapel's altar is of the moments before the judgment. Some of the biblical sources, according to DeTolnay, who has made the best analysis, were Matthew 24:30–46, Revelations 1:7, 20:12, Daniel 7:13–14, John 3:19, Isaiah 13:6–9, Ezekiel 37:1–9. The seething groups of figures that comprise the great fresco do not fall into easily definable compartments or classifications, and there is some doubt at first as to who are the angels, the citizens of Heaven, who are the damned, and who are the saved. Beginning with the Resurrection in the lower area, directly above the altar of the chapel, the agitated and turbulent tone of the final day is established. The dead are literally pulled from the tombs. There is a persistent element of tension, or rebellious strength in the bodies of those to be adjudicated, and a fierce determination by the damned to resist their fate. Michelangelo sees man as an independent spirit capable of defying God and universal laws even in the last hour. Christ the Judge responds to the feeling of the moment in a militant, almost wrathful gesture, as He vigorously enacts his role as supreme judge. His pose recalls that of ancient sculptures of Zeus and Roman emperors, or of generals riding triumphantly in the hunt or battle on the old sarcophagi. There is no mitigating the sentence or mood of Christ. The Virgin turns away as if acknowledging her inability to sway Him. Around Christ are numerous figures of martyrs, who brandish instruments of their martyrdom as if demanding justice. Soaring in the heavens are

13.8 Michelangelo. *The Virgin and Child, c.* 1524–1534. Florence, Medici Chapel.

the wingless angels who transport the symbols of Christ's own martyrdom, as recorded in the Revelations according to St. John. Late in the century, the Counter-Reformation was to look askance at Michelangelo's daring in depicting the angels with no visible means of support, and much of the nudity of the figures was painted over. To Michelangelo, the angels and the saved rose in the heavens because of their faith, not needing the assistance of wings or a staircase. The ascent to Heaven is a difficult process for the elect, and a figure being hauled up by a rosary suggests that prayer

13.9 Michelangelo. *The Last Judgment*, 1534–1541, Sistine Chapel. Rome, The Vatican. (Photo: Alinari)

and intense faith achieve divine elevation. In sympathy with reformers within the Church itself who questioned the indiscriminate sale of indulgences, Michelangelo felt that faith, more than good works or the intervention of celestial advocates, was responsible for man's salvation. The composition of the whole has a rotary movement of energetic figure clusters about the form of Christ. The circular design may have carried for Michelangelo symbolism related to that of the rose window of the Gothic cathedral—solar or cosmic symbolism, the wheel of fortune, eternity, and judgment.

The damned plummet or are dragged forcibly to the depths and Charon's bark. In the lower right corner stands Minos, the chthonian judge of Dante's *Inferno*. Michelangelo does not, as Dante did, depict him half man and half minotaur. He has the head and body of a man and the tail of a serpent, which winds around his body, perhaps as a sign of the depths of Hell to which sinners are consigned. Michelangelo signified the area of the damned not only by its location on the left side of Christ, but also by the powerful downward glance of God as He peers directly into Hell. Just below Christ, to His left, kneels St. Bartholomew, holding in his left hand the skin of a man whose face is unmistakably Michelangelo's. The head of the saint is that of Pietro Aretino, one of Michelangelo's most severe critics. The *Last Judgment* provided the opportunity for Michelangelo to profess his own sense of unworthiness and guilt.

During the last thirty years of his life, Michelangelo experienced a deep spiritual and artistic change. He grew dissatisfied with physical beauty, pagan subjects, philosophic truths, and art itself: "Thus I know how fraught with error was the fond imagination which made art my idol and my king." His last drawings and sculptures were all of the same theme, the dead Christ.

The reason for this concentration lay in Michelangelo's belief that faith and salvation were dependent upon one's attitude toward the sacrifice of Christ, that the soul's grace came only through a complete faith in the meaning of Christ's death on the cross. "No brush, no chisel will quiet the soul once it is turned to the divine love of Him who upon the cross, outstretches His arms to take us to Himself."

In perhaps his last drawing, he showed Christ on the Cross (Fig. 13.10) flanked by the mourning figures of Mary and John. The encompassing gesture of Christ's arms is emphasized by the contraction of the figures at the base of the cross. The features of Christ's face as well as those of the mourners are only hinted at. The multiple outlines of the forms impart a trembling appearance. Many years before, Michelangelo had given up the hard, incisive, sculpturesque edge in his drawings in search of means to body forth the inner life of his subjects. Light and shadow replaced contorted musculature as the carriers of pathos and Michelangelo's spiritual sentiments. The more deeply felt the content, the more frugal became the artist's means. In sculpture, this frugality may be seen in one of his last works.

Until the time of his death in 1564 Michelangelo worked intermittently upon the *Rondanini Pietà* (Fig. 13.11) begun in 1550. Carved from what may have been an old Roman column, the vertical form of the Virgin supports the dead Christ, just removed from the cross. Incomplete as it is, the late style of the Pietà obviously eschewed the supple, muscular, high-surface finish of the early sculptures. In its place were coarse textures, harsh junctures of limbs, and angular interlocking of shapes. Michelangelo sought to draw the beholder's attention away from the surface toward a contemplation of the internal meaning of the subject. His late vibrant forms seem built from the inside out, affirming the im-

13.10 Michelangelo. *The Cruci-fixion, with the Virgin and Saint John,* drawing in black chalk, 1550–1556. Courtesy of the Trustees of the British Museum.

portance of what the eye cannot see—the life of the soul and the Virgin's final spiritual communion with Christ. The earlier sure placement of gestures gave way to changes during the carving, as if the artist sought symbolically to fuse the man and woman.

As part of his conversion to medieval mysticism, Michelangelo turned away from the Renaissance's achievements in depicting a vigorous, healthy and beautiful body. It was not for lack of inspiration that Michelangelo struggled at the end. Though solemn in form and theme, Michelangelo's last work expresses the spiritual joy he felt in the meaning of his subject. Reputedly his last words to a friend were, "Remember the death of Christ."

The most gifted artist of his age, Michelangelo was also the most tormented. With all his endless fascination with the mysteries of creation, redemption, and salvation, he was conscious of human frailty and fallibility. In short, Michelangelo's affliction was to possess magnificent visions that he felt achieved only a pale and inadequate expression in his art. His fate lay in the quest to grasp the infinite while knowing his own finitude. His attempt took the form of brilliant and daring paintings, sculpture, and architecture which still inspire awe and wonder. The irony is that Michelangelo felt that he was a failure. By the 1540's he had given up painting. His last sculptures were left unfinished. At the end, he had turned to architecture, the most abstract medium, to achieve his lifetime need for a union with the Creator. What makes Michelangelo in some respects a modern personality is the extent to which his personal growth and change were mirrored in his art. His drawings, sculptures, and painting reflect great bursts of inspiration, upheavals of superhuman energy, and the weight of his disillusion. No artist before or during his time exhibited so intimate a bond between his personality and art. No artist before him so fiercely insisted upon maintaining his individuality.

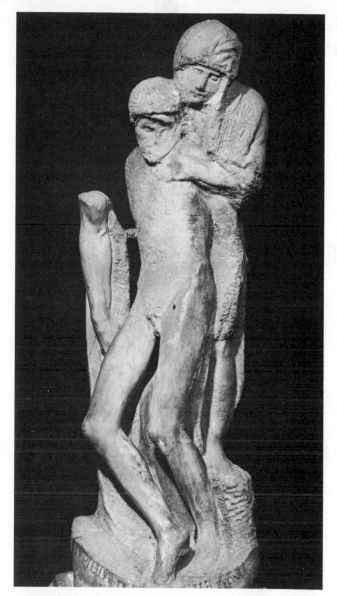

13.11 Michelangelo. *Pietà*, 1550–1564. Rome, Castello Sforzesco. (Photo: Anderson)

CHAPTER 14

REMBRANDT

Rembrandt Harmensz van Rijn was born in 1606 and died in 1669. His father was a miller who wanted his son to be a scholar and sent the boy to a humanist school from his seventh to fourteenth years. For a short time, Rembrandt was enrolled at the University of Leyden. His early contact with great literature was to influence his later art. In 1620, he entered the studio of an unimportant Leyden artist and remained for three years. At seventeen, he went to Amsterdam, where he studied for half a year with a well-known artist named Lastman. In 1632, he moved permanently to Amsterdam, where he began to have success as a portrait painter. In the same year he married the wealthy Saskia van Uylenburgh. They had four children, but three died; only Titus reached maturity. Saskia died shortly after Titus's birth. By 1649 Hendrickje Stoffels was living with Rembrandt. Her willingness to become the painter's common-law wife brought her social hardship and actual persecution, a fact that makes Rembrandt's repeated interpretations of Christ and the woman taken in adultery all the more poignant. She stayed with Rembrandt through increasing financial difficulties brought on by his omnivorous appetite for antiques and other objets d'art, many of which he used as props in his paintings. By 1657, Rembrandt was bankrupt and had lost his house and collection; two years later his graphic art was dispersed to satisfy his creditors. Contrary to the popular notion that Rembrandt was then exiled to a terrible life of poverty and neglect, he continued to receive good commissions and to devote himself to problems that interested him. In 1663 Hendrickje died, and in 1668, Rembrandt lost Titus.

In his personal and artistic life, Rembrandt defied convention. For most of his life he recognized none of the accepted canons of social conduct, monetary management, adherence to the state Calvinist religion, flattery of potentially wealthy and influential clients, and most of all, what and how a Dutch painter should paint. From documentary evidence it appears that Rembrandt considered himself a revolutionary in art because he did not acknowledge academic rules and followed only nature and art of his own choosing. When Rembrandt was at work, one historian has pointed out, he would not have stopped for a king.

His lifelong quest for freedom prevented Rembrandt from affiliating with any orthodox religion or political party. He cannot be catalogued, as can so many painters of his time, as a painter of portraits, genre, or religious subjects. No other artist of his time was identified simultaneously with the different media of painting, etching, and drawing. He drew freely from literature, history, subjects before his insatiable eye, and older art. Though he relied heavily upon the written word for inspiration, he distrusted writing about art, and the vast corpus of his work manifests his displeasure with artistic theory. His varied sources served his search for the ties that bound humanity throughout history. Compelled to individualize every subject in his art, Rembrandt never lost sight of mankind for its men. He saw life as a historical continuum from cradle to grave. With his view of the continuity of all life, travel was unnecessary, and Amsterdam became for him the microcosm of history. Rebel that he was, Rembrandt accepted the role of the artist that had developed in the Middle Ages: to move, delight, and instruct.

Simeon in the Temple (Fig. 14.1) is in many respects typical of Rembrandt's early paintings of religious subjects. This is not, it should be noted, religious painting, for it was not intended for use in a church. Rembrandt was a founder of what might be called private, nonecclesiastical, devotional painting. He did not illustrate dogma nor propagandize organized religion. His was a private religion without theology, and his paintings, drawings, and prints constituted a spiritual art. From his Roman Catholic mother, Rembrandt, a Protestant, had derived his love and knowl-

edge of the Bible. His interpretations of biblical stories have the freshness of personal discovery. The style that produced *Simeon in the Temple* was partly influenced by the Scriptures, particularly the frequent references to the symbolism of light. Against the looming backdrop of the formidable synagogue architecture, Simeon kneels with the Christ Child and his parents before Anna, standing with outstretched arms. The small group is illuminated by a strong shaft of sunlight. The faces of the Child and the "just and devout" old Simeon are most strongly lit, recalling the passage from Psalms, "God is the light of their countenance." Simeon, who knew that he could die in peace with the coming of the Messiah, appears to be looking above the head of Anna and saying, "O Lord . . .

14.1 Rembrandt. *Simeon in the Temple*, 1631. Copyright The Hague, Foundation Johan Maurits van Nassau, Mauritshuis. (Photo: Dingjan)

my eyes have seen thy salvation, who thou hast prepared before the face of all peoples; a light of revelation to the gentiles, and a glory for thy people Israel." (Luke 2:22–34)

Rembrandt knew the chief rabbis in the Jewish quarter of Amsterdam and had visited the synagogues. In his ardor to re-create the true image of the Scriptures, he ignored the archeology of the Italians and his Flemish contemporaries and drew his inspiration from his immediate surroundings. The small painting is filled with observations of types, costumes, gestures and postures, contrasts between intense concentration of the group occupying the center of the stage, and casual indifference of bystanders on the stairs to the right. The figures and architecture are so disposed in depth as to make the viewer, too, a bystander off to one side in the shadows. The large, deep recessional movements are made by diagonal dispositions of the figures and arcades of the synagogue. The darkened areas were given luminosity by Rembrandt's device of underpainting his canvas with warm bright colors and then scratching through the layers of darker overpainting of the architecture. The whole painting has a theatrical aspect with the principals subordinated to the great space and strident contrast of light and dark. The mystery in the painting resides more in the setting than in the people. The faces as yet do not reveal Rembrandt's later deep understanding of human motivation. What we see is a drama of place rather than of persons.

Rembrandt's development as an individual and as a painter is reflected in a single painting that he began early in his career but felt compelled to rework as he grew older. His painted sketch of *John the Baptist Preaching* (Fig. 14.2) was begun around 1636 or 1637 and worked upon in-

termittently until 1650. In this sketch, the subject is biblical, but the theme is that of an inspired individual addressing a group. At the time of the sketch's conception, Rembrandt was sympathetic to the Mennonites, a sect that decried a formal church and the ritual and sacraments of the Roman Catholics. Its ministers were laymen who preached not dogma, but mercy and charity, humility and obedience. Stress was laid upon the impulses of the heart, conscious, silent prayer, and simple, warm spirituality. The Mennonites sought to return to the basic truths of the Bible instead of using it to construct an elaborate theology. They championed respect for the poor of spirit and love of one's brethren in Christ. Their sentiments may have influenced this conception of John the Baptist.

In loose array, all strata of society are gathered to hear John speak from the heart of salvation. Rembrandt's later reworking of the sketch tended to concentrate the light upon John and those closest to him. As in the painting of Simeon, the illumination is appropriate not only for reasons of style, but also to the moment when the ascetic prophet John announced the Messiah as light coming into the world. John further spoke of the importance of fellowship, the need for brotherly love. Like the word of Christ, John's word is as a light to the path of the faithful. Rembrandt showed the crowd divided in its attention, atomized into those who hear, are moved, and understand, those who daydream or doze, and those who bicker or content themselves with trivial diversions. In the lower center of the scene, just to the left of the obelisk crowned with Caesar's portrait, three Pharisees stand in partial shadow having turned their backs on John and disputing among themselves. Rembrandt did not resort to the obvious device of illuminating only those who are enlightened, for

14.2 Rembrandt. *John the Baptist Preaching*, c. 1636–1650. Berlin-Dahlem Museum. (Photo: Steinkopf)

the enactment of vanity and folly can be found in both the light and dark areas of the crowd.

The sketch was epic in its intent, for with the large crowd and rich observations of the living, Rembrandt included a deep landscape. By muting its tones and underplaying its definition, he was able to restore focus to the figure of John. The obelisk and vague natural backdrop for the prophet frame his gestures and subordinate other areas. In the bright sections can be seen the earlier style of figure construction with the more opaque faces, heavy reliance on drawing, and attentiveness to picturesque detail. The later style treated figures and costumes in broader, less complicated strokes and fewer, more somber tones.

Rembrandt never traveled as did other famous artists of his century in northern Europe, but his imagination and taste for the remote filled the painting with archeological monuments, rugged panoramas unlike those around Amsterdam, and such opulent exotic accessories as turbans, bridles, monkeys, and camels. The small sketch is charged with almost an overabundance of ideas and esthetic means; the later changes were in the direction of great clarity and stability.

Rembrandt's constant restlessness and relentless self-criticism are also apparent in two states of his etching of *The Three Crosses* (Figs. 14.3 and 14.4). These etchings also show his great divergence from the early style of *John the Baptist*

14.3 Rembrandt. *The Three Crosses*, 1653. (Etching third state.) London, Courtesy of the Trustees of the British Museum.

14.4 Rembrandt. *The Three Crosses*, 1653. (Etching fourth state.) London, Courtesy of the Trustees of the British Museum.

Preaching, a style that had brought him considerable commercial and critical success. Each painting, drawing, and print seemed to open new possibilities for the artist, who set personal goals of artistic perfection above financial gain.

In itself, the third state of *The Three Crosses* seems to have a moving completeness. It is a readable drama whose subject is the Passion of Christ and whose theme is the loss of a man. In centrifugal fashion, Rembrandt detailed the several reactions to the execution, ranging from the indifference of the mounted troops, the satisfaction of the Pharisees at the lower left, the anguish of Christ's followers, to the conversion of the centurion. The hard barrenness of Golgotha intrudes into the scene in the rocks and scrub vegetation. The tortured bodies of the thieves flank Christ, and the descending light divides its focus among the three crosses. This division of interest and surfeit of action impelled Rembrandt to make the fourth state. The successive states are like the chronology of the last hours of Christ on the cross. The final etching shows the world in near darkness except for the torrential shaft of light above Christ's head. As in Genesis, the separation of light and dark suggests creation of new life. The solemn centurion is the principal subordinate figure, stressing the significance of conversion and comprehension of the meaning of Christ's death. It is not the inaction and rigidification of the few accessory figures still perceivable that alone alter the mood, but also the rugged, stiff outlines of their bodies and their reduction to obscure presences floating in a sea of darkness. Black was felt and savored by Rembrandt as a tangible substance. Etching ink and the hatchings and close striations of the etcher's needle imparted the special qualities of soft absorbent black that he could not reproduce in his paintings. Its appeal may also have been that it permitted emphasis of the contrast between the polarities of light and life and darkness and death.

Photographs tend to dull the surface of Rembrandt's etchings. In the original the blacks come to life through their varying brilliance and depths, and the untouched white areas of the paper have a full range of intensities depending upon the character of the lines and shaded areas adjacent to them. In the final state of *The Three Crosses*, the etched lines are constricted into series of straight verticals or diagonals, layers of cross-hatchings that veil the scene and disconnect the figures from any coordinate system other than that of the light and dark. The deep cutting of the etching tool and the erosion of long acid exposure has given the paper's surface layers of relief with which to catch and channel the light that falls on it. The mobility and character of the light rather than the figures create the final supreme drama in the etching, which conveys Rembrandt's intuitions about the nature of death.

Rembrandt's conception of Christ Himself is notable. Hanging from the cross is the taut but meager body of an ordinary human being. Musculature did not achieve sublimity for Rembrandt. Christ's strength and spirit issue from erect posture, the head and radiance about it. More than Michelangelo, Rembrandt was drawn to the flesh as evidence of Christ's suffering manhood.

Rembrandt avoided pathetic struggle in the figure of Christ. In a small secular painting, *The Slaughtered Ox* (Fig. 14.5), done two years after the Crucifixion series, however, Rembrandt evoked the violence of brutal execution. In the early Middle Ages the ox symbol of St. Luke was thought to prefigure the sacrifice of Christ. It is not impossible that, with the Crucifixion theme so much in his mind during the time of this painting the two subjects may have overlapped. Further, Rembrandt's famous paintings of anatomy dissections in which dead bodies are cut open and explored may also have conditioned his se-

14.5 Rembrandt. *The Slaughtered Ox*, 1655. Paris, The Louvre.

lection and treatment of the theme. The painting shows the spread-eagled carcass of the ox hanging from a rude wooden frame. The gutted animal seems self-illuminated with an almost phosphorescent glow. Massing his pigment in thick viscous surfaces, Rembrandt created an equivalence of the moist, greasy, richly nuanced muscle, fat, and bone of the animal. He showed with wonder the partially hollow interior of the flayed animal, filled with complex substance and color. Allowing it to dominate its gloomy setting and the timid woman peering around the corner, Rembrandt transfigured and heroicized the slaughtered ox and affirmed his fascination with the mystery of life and death.

To juxtapose an etching of the Crucifixion with a scene from an Amsterdam butcher shop is to bring together the poles of Rembrandt's interests. The past and present, the imaginary and the real, alternate and interweave throughout his art. Rembrandt was a rebellious Dutchman who could not follow his fellow artists in documenting and praising their time and place. With grandiose projects half-formed in his head, he would take the time to draw whatever immediately attracted his eye in the street or along the canals. It is likely that his drawing from life provided him with the inspiration to paint subjects from the Bible, which, when realized, often retained their secular origin. Such a painting is a late version of *Bathsheba* (Fig. 14.6) although no preliminary drawings exist. Possibly Hendrickje, who was the model for many drawings, posed for Bathsheba. Her pose in the painting may have been inspired by Rembrandt's encounter, through seventeenth-century engravings, of classical Roman sculptures that showed seated women such as Venus in profile. Recall Michelangelo's synthesis of David; that of Rembrandt was to take a Dutch housewife, pose her in the manner of a Roman goddess to re-create the character of a tragic Hebrew woman.

In his later years, when this painting was done, Rembrandt painted fewer crowd scenes, preferring to isolate individuals. He tended to immobilize his subjects, placing emphasis upon their inner rather than outer reactions to events. The great mysteries for Rembrandt were not those of theology, but those of humanity. His painting of Bathsheba shows the wife of Uriah, chosen by David for himself, in a moment of troubled reflection. The theme is typical of Rembrandt, for it reveals the individual's passive submission to fate. Bathsheba is attended by a servant, or David's messenger, who prepares her for the fateful meeting with the king. In Bath-

14.6 Rembrandt. *Bathsheba*, 1654. Paris, The Louvre. Anc. Coll. Vizzavona-Druet, Musées Nationaux.

sheba's hand is the note that begins the tragedy. The expression given to the face, the limp quality of the arm holding the letter, the unthinking compliance with the actions of the maid construct a story of an individual caught in a web of circumstances over which she has no control, though she knows the outcome. Rembrandt reconstructed the Bible in human terms. He was most moved by the vulnerability of people, their unwitting involvement in tragedy. While the painting initially gives the impression of factual account, Rembrandt added an aura of elusive, lyrical revery. Professor Julius Held identified this type of painting as Rembrandt's formula "of making his models appear both physically present and psychically remote."

Rembrandt's nudes were not in the Italian Renaissance tradition. They lack classical proportions, cosmetic perfection, and litheness. They are naked rather than nude, and the revelation of the body becomes an invasion of privacy. With his intense empiricism, Rembrandt could not submit the naked body to norms superimposed by other styles and cultures. His nudes are not generalized types; each body seems shaped by the character of its possessor. The body still shows the impress of clothes, diet, and relatively sedentary as opposed to athletic activity. Gravity of mind and the pressure of conscience is sustained by the heaviness of the body.

Few of Rembrandt's paintings deal with miracles. Rembrandt saw the Bible in terms of men and women with distinct personalities, problems, and hopes not unlike those daily encountered in Amsterdam. When he painted *Christ at Emmaus*

14.7 Rembrandt. *Christ at Emmaus*, 1648. Paris, The Louvre. Anc. Coll. Vizzavona-Druet, Musées Nationaux.

(Fig. 14.7), he set the scene in an austere high stone room that dominated the figures by its scale. Only the radiance emanating from Christ assigns to Him the property of divinity and separates the painting from genre art. To evoke the apparition of Christ, Rembrandt set Him directly before a hollow niche which looms like a dark void, echoing His miraculous emergence from death. The niche also relates the figures and encloses the area of dramatic but underplayed action. By temperament unsympathetic with Catholic theology and its link with the formal centrality of Renaissance compositions, Rembrandt shifted the focus of the painting to the left of center. He had made copies of Leonardo's painting, and the general arrangement of forms in a shallow space, the framing of Christ, and the orientation of the table and figures roughly parallel to the surface show his adaptation of Renaissance design. Unlike Leonardo, Rembrandt bathed the room in deep but transparent shadows and a powerful warm light which the figures absorb in varying degrees of intensity. He gave to Christ an unaristocratic personality, stressing his sweetness of spirit, capacity for love, and ability to be at home with the humble. No painter before Rembrandt came as close to fathoming the Jesus of the Gospels or the historic Jesus referred to in Chapter 2, *Images of Gods*. Rembrandt did portrait studies of Christ, probably based on a bearded young Jew from the Jewish quarter near his home. In the

14.8   Rembrandt.
God and Abraham,
c. 1655.

Emmaus scene, the bearded Christ retains the soft gentle qualities with which Rembrandt endowed him in scenes showing his earthly ministry. Only the area around the eyes suggests the suffering and fatigue of the Passion. Significantly, one of the disciples studies Christ's face for signs of the miracle, rather than his gesture of breaking the bread. Rembrandt avoided Caravaggio's rhetoric of gestures and object accessories. Rembrandt himself had said that he searched for "the greatest inward emotion."

Rembrandt wished his paintings to be seen in a strong light and from a distance. Only under these conditions may we sense the calculated positioning of figures in depth and their relatedness to each other and the setting. In a photograph, these things are lost, and the whole becomes opaque and shallow. In the original, the figure of Christ is seen in suggestive and forceful relation to the niche. The thin strip of light on the right foreground unobtrusively enhances the recession of the middle area and grounds the verticals of the rear walls. This stiff, rectilinear scaffolding

permitted the painter to show subtle and restrained movements in the figures while drawing attention to their internal response.

Another epiphanal subject is the drawing of God announcing His covenant to Abraham (Fig. 14.8), done about eight years after *Christ at Emmaus,* in the mid-1650's. As recounted in Genesis 15 and 17, God promised to give the ninety-nine-year-old Abraham a son and to make him the father of nations. Both themes had a deep attraction for Rembrandt, who was preoccupied with the family all his life and believed that the Jews were the chosen people. Rembrandt saw the community as an extension of the family unit and such rituals as Christ's presentation in the temple as a linking of the two.

In the Bible it is written that at God's appearance Abraham fell flat on his face. This was a sign of fear and an indication of his unworthiness to look upon the face of the Lord. Rough as the sketch is, Rembrandt gave enough attention to the face of the Lord to recall His kindly admonition, "Fear not, Abram, I am thy protector." Rembrandt did not look upon Jehovah as the wrathful force of Michelangelo, but gave to Him the same benevolence seen in the images of Christ. He flanked the Lord with two angels and above His head drew the dove, thus incorporating the trinitarian symbolism that recurs when the three men appear to Abraham and Sara and the Lord again promises them a son.

Rembrandt's hundreds of biblical drawings show the flood of inspiration the Scriptures unleashed in his imagination. Some drawings were part of studies for paintings; many others emerged from the sheer love of drawing and of creating images of favored stories. His drawings form personal glosses on the Bible, for they impart ideas and information not found in the Scriptures.

The rhythms of Rembrandt's hand as it moved over the grainy white paper, holding the reed pen, form an intimate revelation. *God and Abraham* was not done from posed models, but the information and shorthand acquired from long study served him when he drew from imagination. He used his strokes to establish the broad gestures and the limits of movement for figures of the angels. These strokes do not fashion continuous constrictive outlines, but overlap or leave gaps in the silhouette which indicate the fusion of the body with the atmosphere about it. In the prostrate form of Abraham, several of the lines begin or end within the body's outline and have a hooked termination. With a single pen flourish, Rembrandt established where a limb was joined to the body and where and to what extent it projected from the body. The body and its clothing were conceived of as directions and weights. Note, for example, the area of the Lord's head and shoulders, the silhouettes of the angels, and the weighted outline of Abraham's back. With the paper as a light source, a few touches of dark establish the mood and detail of the Lord's

face. For such accessories as the clouds and the room, Rembrandt's hand swept over the surface in quick series of parallel lines. Despite what seems speed of execution, Rembrandt pondered over his drawings, and the vertical lines above Abraham have a precision of placement that anchor his body and play against the movement of the group at the right. The properties of the reed pen and years of drawing had made it impossible for Rembrandt to draw a line that did not vary in thickness and thinness, direction and intensity of value. At this stage, however, his lines tended to group themselves into fewer numbers, raw connections, broader and less serpentine curves. They had acquired a stiffer and coarser quality that accelerates the readability of the whole without loss of dramatic force.

One of Rembrandt's last paintings is *The Return of the Prodigal Son* (Fig. 14.9). Perhaps because of his own close ties with Titus, Rembrandt repeatedly interpreted the theme of father and son. In the picture, the wordless but profound reaction of all to the homecoming signifies the indivisible ties of the family. The sons who remained with the father display no jealousy or recrimination. They are sympathetic witnesses to a sacred moment. Just as Rembrandt understated the drama, his frugal means add to the force of the painting. There is no action nor elaborate interweaving of figures and background. The individual forms are somewhat rectangular and blocklike. This suggestion of self-containment is balanced by the dissolution of the edges of the forms and the meld achieved with their luminous ambiance. There is a simple scale of emphasis with the greatest wealth of color lavished on the rags of the son. With the reduction of the figures to a static condition, Rembrandt solemnized the human being and achieved a supreme drama of persons. This image of forgiveness and pity is a form of last artistic confession that may show the artist's resolution of conflicts with the world.

Rembrandt's early prominence, even before his arrival in Amsterdam in 1632, was based upon his talents as a portrait painter. Like his fellow Dutch painters, he responded to the demand of the well-to-do middle class for portraits. Personal friends—writers and doctors—and interesting-looking individuals he pulled in from the streets of Amsterdam also sat for their likenesses. In later years, Rembrandt experienced difficulties with clients who claimed that their portraits were not good likenesses, as they were accustomed to the slick, extroverted, often smug images that fashionable painters achieved. After his bankruptcy, Rembrandt continued to receive important portrait commissions, one of which was from the Board of the Drapers Guild. It resulted in a group painting known as *The Syndics* (Fig. 14.10).

One of Rembrandt's important contributions to group portraiture lay in his successful solution of the problem of achieving an informal, unself-conscious, and convincing union of all of the sitters. Since portraits were paid for on the basis of the amount of the figure shown, it was essential that all of the faces be clearly in evidence and that priority be given to the Guild president. Rembrandt chose a moment during a meeting of the board with its stockholders, immediately after a query had been made from the floor. Within the painting, the figures are subtly united by their relationship to the president, who is rising to respond. The interlocking groupings and positions of the bodies give a sense of the official relationship. The device of directing all attention outside the picture in the direction of the viewer unites the figures externally. The sobriety and similarity of their apparel—they have been described as resembling ominous black birds—and the heavy warm atmosphere of the room, suffused with rich brown and gold tone on the walls and near

edge of the table covering, further weave the painting's harmony. As in the best of Rembrandt's work, there is an underlying conflict between the apparent and the real. The subjects were, in fact, men of status and solid achievement who, on the occasion of the board meeting, presented the image of unshakable probity and solidarity. To the far right, however, is set into the molding of the wall a painting of a burning city, which, DeTolnay has shown, in Rembrandt's time signified the ephemerality of worldly power. It was a commentary on vanity and a warning to those of wealth to be not proud. The faces of the men betray their inherent individuality and those human qualities that do not always jibe with official roles. Rembrandt did not caricature these men, nor can their faces be simply read in a program. But to

14.9 Rembrandt. *The Return of the Prodigal Son,* c. 1665. Leningrad, Hermitage Museum.

14.10   Rembrandt. *The Syndics*, 1662. Amsterdam, Copyright Fotocommissie Rijksmuseum.

absorb each face is to remove oneself from the room and matters at hand, for the private history of each figure cannot be masked out. As prosaic an event as a business accounting has been transformed into a work of art and a probing psychological study of the price and nature of power through Rembrandt's assay.

In 1662, the same year that he painted *The Syndics*, Rembrandt worked on a painting for the Amsterdam town hall. Its subject was the ancient conspiracy of the Batavians, ancestors of the Dutch, who rebelled against Roman rule. *The Conspiracy of Julius Civilis* (Fig. 14.11) was the largest painting Rembrandt undertook. When it was rejected, he removed it from the town hall and cut it down to the area he liked the most, which was of mar-

ketable size. The date of its painting makes the contrast between the group portrait and the historical work all the more interesting. Rembrandt's visionary inclination came forth to the fullest in the midnight meeting of the conspirators. He was inspired by the swearing of allegiance until death upon the sword of Julius Civilis, an ironic contrast to the dispute in the stockholders' meeting. The confident reserve of the fiscally wise guild president makes an equally interesting comparison to the heroic presence of Julius Civilis, who was to take on the legions of the Roman Empire. The quiescent sunlight of the board room with its connotations of security and permanence gives way to the brilliant, unstable, and concealed radiance emanating from the conspirators' table, lighting and transfiguring their varied, rugged features and then fading into the gloom. The faces of the conspirators belong with their costumes, roles, and the moment; the intriguing double life of the syndics is absent. Each figure has freedom of movement within a restricted space, preserving his individuality without weakening his relation to the group. Layers of glazes built up the surfaces into thick crusts. No color area is of pure single tones. Characteristic of Rembrandt's late style, as the paint became richer and more mobile, the outward actions of the figures was reduced, and they became more submerged within themselves.

Rembrandt knew Raphael's portrait of Castiglione and made a drawing of it. *Jan Six* (Fig. 14.12) epitomizes Rembrandt's ideals—dignified masculinity, a

certain amount of cool correctness mingled with an irrepressible human warmth. Rembrandt endowed the living subject of his art with qualities of an active and contemplative life. Jan Six was both a successful poet and a politician. Significantly, Rembrandt did not portray the great contemporary Dutch political and military heroes. The most compatible subjects in his later life were men such as Jan Six who, like the painter himself, fully indulged their worldly and intellectual appetites. Personal rather than civic accomplishment seems to have impressed Rembrandt.

This admiration for men who lived by strong individual codes was natural for a painter who resisted the formulas of painting. Jan Six stands to the right of center, takes no notice of the viewer, and does not assume a stable pose arranged by

14.11 Rembrandt. *The Conspiracy of Julius Civilis*, 1661–1662. Stockholm, Copyright National Museum.

14.12 Rembrandt. *Jan Six*, 1656. Delft, Six Collection.

the limbs. Part of his face is concealed in shadow. He is not shown as the extroverted affable or the prim type favored at the time.

The portrait of Jan Six, like Rembrandt's most inspired work of any period, is a summing up of all that the artist had learned about the craft of art and the nature of men. By 1654 when the portrait was done, Rembrandt could produce elegant and profound painting in which budgeted means achieved liberal expressive power. The painting of Jan Six is in a sense a double portrait, a blend of studied contrasts, giving simultaneous insight into the public and the private identity of Jan Six. The automatic gesture of putting on the glove prefaces his going out into the streets. The tan gloves, scarlet cape, green-gray coat, and black hat are part of the gentleman's public face. The actual face has not as yet been "put on" or arranged, but is relaxed into a momentary unawareness of others while the mind is absorbed in soft revery. Through the tilt of the head and the oil pigment's affirmation of the flesh, the weight of the man's thought can be felt. The collar and row of buttons have a firm tangibility that restores the viewer to the external man. Rembrandt did not try to dazzle with the virtuosity of his brush. He used a studied casualness in the single strokes of the gold braid and the vertical streaking of shadows in the cloak. Within the critical areas of focus, such as the hands and head, the strokes increase their accent and direction, and group firmly together to suggest the rough and nuanced substance of flesh against smooth cloth.

Rembrandt's ability to tell a story and to widen the narrative beyond its literal meaning was not restricted to group scenes, but can be seen in a painting with but two figures. *The Jewish Bride* (Fig. 14.13) was done in 1668; though possibly based upon the Biblical story of Rebecca and Isaac, its theme was marital concord. The models were probably Titus and his wife. Into this painting the artist extended his sentiments of family and erotic love. It

is a frank, sensual attitude, one of sharing, unlike any in Renaissance paintings of the family. The story is unfolded in delicate and subtle gestures and can be compared to the marriage portraits by Van Eyck and Kokoschka. The gestures of the man suggest love and possession, while the bride's convey feelings of submission and encouragement. A gamut of loving feeling finds expression in this one painting. Economy and restraint of style makes the slightest movement count. Colors emerge from shadow, the strongest reserved for the area in most intense light. This light significantly does not fall upon the faces, but

14.13 Rembrandt. *The Jewish Bride*, 1668. Amsterdam, Copyright Fotocommissie Rijksmuseum.

14.14 Rembrandt. *Self-portrait with Saskia*, c. 1635. (Deutsche Fotothek, Dresden)

upon the man's sleeve. The lightest parts are most thickly painted, so that in some places the pigment actually forms a relief that catches shadows and lights from the room in which the painting hangs.

Rembrandt was one of his own favorite subjects. He painted a great many self-portraits from all periods, leaving one of the most important personal histories in art. The two selected for study here (Figs. 14.14 and 14.15) demonstrate the range in both style and private life. The first is a portrait of himself and Saskia, done around 1640. It portrays what was then Rembrandt's ideal of a man and a successful artist. This ideal includes woman and wine in hand, good clothes, with a bold suggestion of the cavalier, a fine table and surroundings. Rembrandt shows himself as a sociable extrovert, proud of his material possessions and willing to share them. This painting helps to explain his later bankruptcy. It also shows his conversion from a coarse miller's son to an elegant Amsterdam gentleman. It provides a personal inventory, giving a visual richness to the sword hilt and glass that rivals his own face. The painting mirrors a type of materialist greed that precludes any serious human revelation.

Rembrandt's self-portraits after 1640 reflect the succession of crises that overtook him and show a more critical and understanding self-appraisal. Where the early self-portraits were based in part upon his own convenience as a model, his ostentation and self-esteem, the portraits after 1640 demonstrate his increasing desire to know himself. A self-portrait from the 1660's summarizes the late alter-images. There is no setting or elaborate costume, and for this painting Rembrandt chose not to play a role. There is a total self-consciousness. Although his life had been veined with suffering and bitterness, there is no resentment or self-pity in the portrait.

It is a calm and supremely understood study of the evidence that age gives to the flesh—the flesh has become a human poem. For Rembrandt, man is ultimately a solitary being. The world is in his brain; the eyes now mirror introspection rather than the outward alertness of the early portraits. The greatness of the intellect is unrelated to exterior beauty. While no one knew better than Rembrandt the insecurity of existence, his last portraits show wonder and enthusiasm for life.

The principal means by which Rembrandt expressed his human consciousness was light. Early in his art, he used light as a device to organize the painting, to achieve melodramatic effects, and as a transparent symbolism. As he grew older, he became aware of its more profound potential. He studied it deeply and took on new principles. The luminosity in his paintings was no longer the illumination of the room in which the viewer stands; it was no longer subject to theories dependent upon the particular relation of solids to voids. The light in his mature works is an intangible surrounding, independent of local colors. Its qualities depend upon the nature of the subject. Rembrandt used light to play upon the polarity of the inner and outer world, to bridge the surface and depth of these he painted. Along with his use of light, he used incrustation of paint with a richness and materiality previously unknown. He achieved a spectrum of substances as well as infinite gradations of light and shadow. A great synthesis in Rembrandt's art is that of a basic materiality and a spiritualizing of forms.

Rembrandt has not always been acclaimed as a great artist. He was "rediscovered" in the nineteenth century, but it was not until our own century that the magnitude of his achievement was realized. Today it is recognized that no painter surpassed Rembrandt in sensibility to paint

14.15 Rembrandt. *Self-portrait, c.* 1660. Aix Museum. (Photo: Taurgo)

and the ability to develop its expressive potential. His ideas and feelings about man rank him with the finest humanists. These two gifts were joined and interdependent in his art. His art is one of human beings. He saw their destiny through the body.

In Rembrandt's paintings, graphic work, and drawings, man appears in both historic and private moments, as hero and victim. To the figures of the Bible, legend, myth, and history, remote from Rembrandt's sight, he gave a personality and humanity unprecedented in the history of art. He showed rulers in their fallibility, biblical heroes and businessmen in their frailty, the King of Kings as a gentle human being. Moral expression, for Rembrandt, took precedence over physical beauty.

CHAPTER 15

PICASSO

More than any other artist, Picasso symbolizes to the public the revolutionary aspect of modern art. A census of his subjects, however, reveals that for the most part they conform to those of older art—portraits and self-portraits, still lifes, landscapes, animals, studio images, mothers and children, lovers, illustrations of literature and myths, war and combat between men and animals, themes of pleasure and suffering, and even the interpretation of past works of art. The extent and variety of subjects demonstrates the artist's tremendous range of interests and his sensibility to the esthetic, social, psychological, emotional, and physical makeup of life. Picasso is one of the few modern artists who has not specialized. This may be explained by his attitude toward what the artist is:

> The artist is a receptacle for emotions that come from all over the place: from the sky, from the earth, from a scrap of paper, from a passing shape, from a spider's web. . . . Where things are concerned there is no class distinctions. We must pick out what is good for us where we can find it.

Despite Picasso's seemingly encyclopedic interests, he has not concerned himself with religious problems and biblical literature. Picasso is close to Rembrandt in his spiritual concerns with man as he exists outside of the Church and its laws. Unlike Rembrandt, however, Picasso does not attach a deep philosophical importance to flesh, light, and pigment, though his strength lies in the way he has been able to interpret the human body.

Accompanying the variety of Picasso's subject matter is an equally diversified series of modes to his style, many utilized in the same period. Again the artist's own words are relevant: "If the subjects I have wanted to express have suggested different ways of expression I have never hesitated to adopt them. . . . This does not imply either evolution or progress, but an adaptation of the idea one wants to express and the means to express that idea." There is an ethical basis, then, for Picasso's modal system and his recourse to such diversified media as painting, graphics, drawing, and sculpture.

Picasso returned throughout his

life to certain basic themes and problems, feeling that as he grew older he brought to bear new insights and superior means of realization. There coexists with his pride in craft and concern with its problems and potential a humanistic inquisitiveness and sympathy.

It is here possible only to sketch the importance and excellence of Picasso's work, and his contributions to, if not revolutions in, art's history.

Even the outlining of statistics of Picasso's personal history, travels, outstanding projects, and the people who have influenced him would take up this entire chapter. There were no important and famous teachers in his youth, no sponsors of the stature of the Renaissance, which casts light on conditions under which many modern artists work. The many books on Picasso make his interesting biography easily accessible. Let it suffice to say that Picasso was born in 1881, in Malaga Spain, the son of an art teacher with whose assistance he passed with distinction and amazing speed the entrance examinations for two Barcelona academies in 1895 and 1897. In Barcelona, he came in contact with an important group of artists and intellectuals and with advanced European art. By his third trip to Paris in 1904, he decided to settle in that city; critical success was beginning to come to his work after early years of neglect and privation.

Picasso's art of around 1900 is filled with images of poverty. They are a sincere expression of his own personal economic plight and that of his Spanish and Parisian friends. His subjects were the bohemians, artists, personal acquaintances, the part of society forced to live a difficult marginal existence. *The Frugal Repast* (Fig. 15.1) is one of Picasso's first prints, a virtuoso performance of his technical precociousness and ability to wed modes of drawing to the mood of his subjects. The seated figures reflect Picasso's early search

15.1 Picasso. *The Frugal Repast,* etching, 1904.

for pathos in postures. Joined by the arrangement of their limbs, the bodies make a stable closed composition that contrasts with the instability and divergency of their attention and personalities. Their bony attenuation is an expressive device; it conveys privation and permits extreme and elegant distortion. Picasso stressed the many joints of hands, arms, and shoulders. This may be a self-portrait. The grays and blacks of the etching are appropriate to the morbid subject. At this time Picasso was exploring the use of single colors, such as blue and green, with wide latitudes of nuance to set the mood of an entire work. Remarkable as is the sensitive reconstruction of the faces and hands, of greater importance artistically is the way Picasso interrelated the figures with the objects on the table. The structure, placement, and weights of the vessels can be felt in relation to the emaciated bodies. The curve in the neck of the bottle has its response in the shadow at the upper left and in the man's elbow. Adding to the depressing quality is the hollow of the empty bowl, seen against the declivity of the man's torso as if a metaphor of its internal state. The lights and darks of the bottle and bowl repeat those of the man and woman. The composition of the objects is as studied as that of the figures and is characterized by overlap, tangency, and discreet intervals between shapes. The remoteness of the objects from the figures permits the spacing necessary to play off the two groups against each other and to stabilize the lower area. Picasso pulled down into the table the gray shadow between the bottle and the man's arm, bridging the bulge and concavity of the two shapes. The man's wrinkled shirt is a concentrated repeat of the folds and textures of the tablecloth. In his first etching, Picasso accommodated his style to the potential of needle, acid, and ink. The silhouettes appear as if the etching needle were actually touching inflections of the arms; no nuance is missed and some are added. The exquisite softness of the gamut of shaded tones evokes flesh, cloth over bony flesh, and bottle glass. This etching is rich in the number, disposition, size, and means by which Picasso used his blacks and moved through a full scale from the deepest to lightest tones. The over-all intensity of exposed white of the paper is held in check by light touches of the needle in the fan-shaped clusters of strokes on the wall area behind the figures.

Two years after *The Frugal Repast*, Picasso painted a vigorous self-portrait (Fig. 15.2) revealing his changed attitude toward the human body and art. The elimination of pathos and social consciousness coincided with Picasso's improved financial and artistic success. Throughout his work, the painter's life and art intermingle in confessional, playful, or boastful tones. In the portrait Picasso avowed a

new willfulness that joined altered conceptions of what was manly and what was art. There is no melodrama or plea for sympathy. The portrait exudes self-confidence; Picasso keeps no secrets. His power comes from the will, the eye, the hand, and the colors of the palette. Years later, Picasso was to remark that it was above all the hand that determined the painting. In the self-portrait, Picasso stripped away those details that would mitigate or be extraneous to the concentrated and immediate effect. He had become aware that expressiveness resides in the way the means of art are used, reflecting the urgent feeling and intelligence of the artist. Picasso used drastically fewer means than in the etching. A contrast of the eyes and ears of the man in both works is revealing, but one of their right arms is the most effective. The right arm of the man in *The Frugal Repast* is one of the most beautiful in Picasso's art. It was born from a thousand tiny openings incised in the metal plate. In the painting, two major strokes establish the arm's shape, weight, direction, and robust strength. What Picasso was after was a reduction of means, not necessarily simplification. This reduction leaves few strokes, colors and shapes, but the residue is here unsimple. The self-portrait has a forceful instantaneous effect but reveals more after slow and thoughtful reading of its part-to-part construction. No arc or curve in the painting is purely geometrical; each contains irregularities that come from Picasso's feeling for the nature of the shape and his need to preserve vitality and interest of the line. The two lines of the arm, those of the neckline, the brows and edges of the face are descendents of the thousands he had drawn earlier, as in the etching. The silhouette of the white shirt developed from the contour-probing of the tablecloth and arms in *The Frugal Repast*. Accumulated experience provided the basis for the judgments that distinguished the black lines which appear in the shirt, for example.

Picasso admired the intensity of expression in primitive masks, but he admired more the asymmetrical constructions of symmetrical features and objects of Cézanne's art. Also from Cézanne, Picasso received the idea of creating in art continuity where in nature there was discontinuity, and the reverse. The palette is locked into place by its juncture with the sleeve and bottom of the shirt. (The portrait is related as a whole to a Cézanne self-portrait.) Cézanne's reduction of myriad shapes to multiples of each other found understanding in Picasso's conjugation of the ovoid in the head and neckline and the multiplication of the arcs in the same area. The young artist was learning to create and manipulate the emotive power of certain shapes in various combination. He made of himself an object of esthetic rather than psychological study.

The militant masculine mood of the self-portrait is enhanced by the colors —rugged earth tones in coarse pigmentation. Whites, browns, and blacks are the basic triad with which Picasso evoked tough, solid forms that aggressively assert themselves in space, allowing the figure to dominate the painting's format. Picasso explored tones susceptible to nuance. He worked white against white, white against black, white against orange-brown. Evidences of another and critical side to the painting are the soft, discreetly shaded folds in the right sleeve that temper the over-all harsh severity. For some reason Picasso removed the brush from his hand in the painting. The heaviness of the paint's application suggests that he might just as well have worked the paint with his fingers. In these years Picasso was after a new feeling of what the primal nature of art was and could be. He preserved a certain rawness of means and gave the totality a rugged, hand-made look. Picasso had even eliminated the use of a mirror, shown by the place-

15.2 Picasso. Self-portrait, 1906. Philadelphia Museum of Art.

ment of his right arm on the left side of the painting.

The *Demoiselles d'Avignon* (Fig. 15.3) is one of Picasso's most notorious but by no means most esthetically successful paintings. The ideas and energies unleashed and its failures make it important in the history of Picasso's art. The painting, the largest undertaken by Picasso until that time, was fated to incompletion and inconsistency because of the rapidity and excitement with which his art was changing from month to month and painting to painting. In 1906 and 1907, psychologically, emotionally, and esthetically, Picasso could not produce a large, complex, and homogeneous canvas. In a single year his production of drawings, and paintings equaled or exceeded the lifetime output of many artists of the past. It was not only energy, but Picasso's compulsion to work out every idea and impulse as it flooded through se-

15.3 Picasso. *Les Demoiselles d'Avignon*, 1907. Collection The Museum of Modern Art. (Photo: Sunami)

ries of drawings and paintings which overlapped or were tangent to each other, but never stood in isolation.

The *Demoiselles d'Avignon* was both a battleground and a nursery for Picasso's art. On its surface he seemed to wage war with the accumulated traditions of western painting, accepting solely the demands of expressiveness and order. The tearing down was partially balanced by what were born as new and fruitful alterna-

tives, for it took him additional thousands of drawings, canvases and sculptures, in fact his lifetime, to realize and fulfill all that was near its beginning in this one painting. The painting's subject began in sketches as an allegory: the wages of sin is death. Prostitutes in a brothel paraded before a sailor and, in one instance, a death's head. Accompanying the departure of the skull and sailor from the designs was also moralizing intent. The painting passed through stages until it lost any programmatic meaning and would have been an awkward fit into the old category of genre. What Picasso was heading for was painting primarily as an esthetic object intended to move and delight the beholder. This meant stripping away the sentiment of the female nude as well as conventions of drawing, coloring, and composing. Brutal as are its conceptions and execution, the *Demoiselles* descends from a long line of genteel and robust paintings of nudes. In retrospect it seems like a parody of suave sensuous paintings by such baroque painters as Rubens. The demoiselles elbow against the woodland nymphs, goddesses, and innocent bathers who for so many generations symbolized concord with nature and sinless fertility. Picasso seemed undecided whether to stage the women indoors or out; the woman at the left seems to have a farmer's tan, unlike the indoor pink complexion of the woman next to her. Picasso's women are objects of display transformed by the instincts of the artist, which enter freely onto the canvas. The Spanish prostitutes are given a mixed ethnological parentage, reflecting Picasso's new excitement with Iberian and ancient art (the central two figures) and with African art (those on the flanks). Picasso's primitivizing adopted certain models of distortion, insistence upon parts, and what he may have felt was the sexual intensity of African sculpture. These are grafted onto the Greek classical beauty pose in the center, the rigid vertical Egyptian stance at the left, and the seated studio model at the right. In the figure at the left Picasso used the Egyptian frontal eye, and in the next two figures put a profile nose on a frontal face.

The green-striped face of the woman at the upper right may have derived from primitive masks showing scarification, a process echoed in Picasso's painting. Each figure is either an ethnic or esthetic hybrid, and only the still life of the fruit is finished and consistent. Too many fragments and ideas forced him to suspend his growth to complete the whole.

Within the frame of the painting traces of Picasso's struggles to destroy and reconstruct are plainly visible, even to notations such as the rough blue outline superposed on the leg at the lower left. Picasso had set aside traditional means of uniting a group of figures. Common focus, activity, moods, viewpoint, setting, light and shade, and limb arrangement no longer met his needs. To give his canvas its own autonomy, the figures and setting had to relinquish theirs. The body contours were broken into, and parts were made almost interchangeable by their reduction to such basic shapes as the V form found in crotch, breast, elbow, and jagged background shapes. Cohesion and expressiveness of the surface demanded flat rather than voluminous bodies, obscuring of the figure's means of support, making space relationships inconsistent, and assigning accents and visual importance that rivaled the bodies themselves to intervals between figures. The rhythms and force set by reformations of the body spill over into the background.

The painting's pinks, blues, whites, browns, and blacks are a recapitulation of all Picasso's previous periods. The blue between the central and right figures is glacial and shrilly appealing to the eye. Picasso's conflicting impulses led him to mix outline and edge, modeled and flat surfaces, black, white, and blue silhouettes. He could not resolve so much color and so many modes into a single dominant harmony of contrasts, but ironically, much of the painting's initial appeal derives from the freshness of color and raw juxtapositions. Picasso probably intended a painting with shock value, to stab directly at the emo-

15.4 Picasso. *Head, Apple and Box*, 1909. Collection Douglas Cooper.

tions rather than the intellect. With Matisse and others of the time, Picasso shared an ethic of the primacy of feeling in art as well as life. His dilemma as a painter was to possess the instinct for lucid control and linear armatures; he could not liberate both color and drawing as could Matisse.

Picasso's development was rapid and extremely varied. There was no simple continuous progression toward his completely cubist paintings, but this latter direction will be briefly illustrated. *Head, Apple, and Box* (Fig. 15.4), shows a more consistent style than the *Demoiselles*. It illustrates the extension of the cubist mode to objects as well as to the human form. The head's anatomical structure and the shapes of the objects do not predict the basis of Picasso's drawing. His design does not follow, say, the musculature of the face, the natural curves of the features, nor the proportions of the box. He increased the complexity and expressiveness of the face through new angles and facets. Though passive, the woman's face is activated by the energized drawing in such in-

ventions as the peaked eyes and the arbitrary and increased frequency of shadow. There is no dominant symmetrical vertical axis to any of the forms; the artist preferred disconnected sequences. The box with its inverted perspective and multiplication of planes moves toward a crystal form of increased weight and stability. At this stage of Cubism, Picasso was still interested in light and shadow, mass and volume, and the sensual swelling of flesh. Characteristic of his drawing was the swinging rhythm of repeated parallel movements by which he worked from light to dark, re-created the swelling of the apple, or found a continuity between the right side of the woman's face and the arc under the chin. No large flat surface remained uninflected, no parallel lines were of the same length, no two features identical. Yet with all this richness of treatment, he restricted his means to simple straight and curved lines.

Ma Jolie (Fig. 15.5) was a painting of Marcelle Humbert, with whom Picasso was deeply in love and who died during World War I. "Ma Jolie" was both the name he gave to her and the title of a popular song. With his ideas of the years of 1911 and 1912, Picasso could not paint her in the traditional portrait manner. In part he "inscribed" his love, as he put it, on the canvases devoted to her with the words, "J'aime Eva" and "Ma Jolie." In the past, such sentiments had not been so literally a part of the work of art. The fact that Picasso did so without disrupting the integrity or logic of the painting is itself a sign of Cubism's break with the past. From the Renaissance through the nineteenth century, art was the making of a similitude to the visual appearance of nature. With Cubism, empirical verification lay only within the painting itself. The similitude is that of the final painting to the emotions of the artist who produced it. Put another way, Picasso in *Ma Jolie* did not deal directly with the world of appearances with its distinctions and logic. He wanted *equivalences* of his love for Eva in drawing and color in the same way that the words "Ma Jolie" are equivalences of a song and a woman without looking or sounding like either. It might be said that painting had become an addition to reality. Picasso's vision of and emotions induced by Eva, he translated into problems of form and color; the solutions in terms of lines, planes, and brushstrokes, increasingly blur but do not eliminate her presence. In one sense the pulse of warm and cool color alternations and the shimmer of countless touches of the brush give a presence to the "vibrations" of her life as Picasso felt them. Still, Picasso did not want the appearance of a woman, but of a painting, a unified, moving, beautiful object. The anatomy is the painting's linear armature fleshed out in tones of brown, pink, white, and gray. The diagonals and vertical massing of the planes are vestiges of the seated human figure. On the wooden stretcher of the canvas, Picasso

wrote, "Woman with a Zither," probably the original title. Part of a hand at the lower right is in position to hold the instrument. The zither's design has analogies to the painting's vocabulary; music did not supply the theory or model for cubist painting, but it was a bond by which the artists and in this case the woman Picasso loved were joined. While the resulting order of the painting reflects intellectual precision, the whole was done with passion. The drawing and painting of *Ma Jolie* is disciplined and of great beauty.

15.5 Picasso. *Ma Jolie*, 1911–1912. Collection The Museum of Modern Art. (Photo: Sunami)

15.6 Picasso. *Mandolin*, 1914. Collection the artist.

Picasso's own statements on Cubism, made in 1923, are important in understanding the artist's conception of its nature and relation to the past.

> Cubism is . . . an art dealing primarily with forms, and when a form is realized it is there to live its own life. . . . Drawing, design and color are understood and practiced in Cubism in the same spirit and manner that they are understood and practiced in all other schools. . . . We have kept our eyes open to our surroundings and also our brains. We give to form and color all their individual significance. . . . The fact that for a long time Cubism has not been understood . . . means nothing. I do not read English, an English book is a blank book to me. This does not mean that the English language does not exist, and

why should I blame anybody else but myself if I cannot understand what I know nothing about.

Picasso's inexhaustible creative energy and the fertile ideas of Cubism led him to work in sculpture in a manner as unprecedented as his painting. One of Picasso's most influential works is the twenty-four-inch-high *Mandolin* (Fig. 15.6). Its making and appearance appear to resist the label of sculpture for it has not been cast, modeled, or carved; it does not sit upon a base, and its subject is a musical instrument. Picasso used scraps of wood from boxes and canvas stretchers, discards that lay in his study. The wood Picasso employed had been processed and shaped to fulfill a utilitarian function before being put to purely esthetic purposes. His selection of the scraps was not haphazard, for he was attracted by the grain, size, and shapes. Some pieces may have been used without reworking; the "found object" is preserved intact in the sculpture. Most of the scraps had something done to them, either painting or sawing. The curved white piece, like the planes in cubist paintings, reveals the rough marks of its formation, for none of the forms was sanded. The rude facture is essential to Picasso's ethic and esthetic sense. The sculpture has been put together, constructed, assembled, literally manipulated; this method of joining along with the expanded tolerance of materials was to have a strong effect on later modern sculpture. Picasso, like other advanced artists of the time, was rebelling against the academic conception of "noble media," such as marble and bronze, and "noble subjects," such as the human figure in heroic action. If heroism is present in the *Mandolin*, it resides in the courage and daring of the artist's defiance of tradition. Literally and figuratively, Picasso helped to remove sculpture from the pedestal of tradition. His is not relief sculpture in the old sense. It has no rectangular frame to contain the sculpture or balance and co-ordinate the shapes within. The frame's absence also introduces the possibility of play of irregular shadows cast onto the wall by the projecting parts, and these shadows give added depth and vibrancy. There is no consistent or uniform rear plane to which successive relief planes can be referred. Even more than cubist painting, the sculpture's planes advance into the space of the beholder and yet exist in an inconsistent overlapping which maintains an ambivalence of inward and outward movement. Picasso painted some of the construction, reversing the trend begun with Michelangelo, one of the first to give up painting sculpture.

The still life of the *Ram's Head* (Fig. 15.7) testifies to the viability of the cubist style and Picasso's alertness to new subject matter. There is far less decomposition of objects than in *Ma Jolie*, and fa-

miliar textures and shapes facilitate reading the contents. What is new and unfamiliar in Picasso's art is the range of sensations to which the objects address themselves. The objects are foods in their raw unedible state, unlike the contents of earlier cubist still lifes with their sociable connotations and objects that appealed to the touch. Picasso contrasted the horn and hair of the ram, fish scales, and shells with sharp edges against moist, pulpy substances like the squid at the lower left. Violence is to be seen in the subjects themselves—in the saw-severed head of the ram and the arsenal of teeth in the gaping fish mouth—consonant with the abrupt conjunctions of textures. Yellow from the blue-veined lemon to the left of the ram's head, a rectangular patch cut by the circular lemon, spices the dominant blues, whites, and browns of the painting. The black linear scaffolding of the *Ma Jolie* period paintings has disappeared; the composition includes large,

15.7 Picasso. *Ram's Head*, 1924. New York, private collection.

15.8 Picasso. *Three Dancers*, 1925. Collection The Museum of Modern Art. (Photo: Sunami)

free-swinging curved lines and planes that alternate and join with rectilinear passages in tight cohesion. The colors and textures lie flat upon the surface, affirming its two-dimensionality. The objects are tautly grouped and held within the frame by such inventive drawing as the free repeat of the serrated edge under the ram's head and in the spine of the fish.

Another area of sensations into which Picasso's sensibilities forcefully expanded in the mid-twenties was that of internal body imagery, seen in *Three Dancers* (Fig. 15.8). Traditionally, naked figures in an interior meant that the artist was studying anatomy and postures. By 1925, Picasso had become interested in the art of fan-

tasy as exhibited by Miro and Arp, whose work was touched on earlier. What appealed to Picasso were bold incursions into the irrational and the unlocking of inhibitions with respect to form and content. Rather than creating a studio study of the way three naked models look to someone else, Picasso imagined their own inward sensations as their bodies are given over to the abandon of a frenzied dance. Each dancer possesses a phantom double, a second and even third self. This is obvious in the black areas, not literal projected shadows but poetic extensions of each figure's consciousness of the body area in which the strongest feelings are localized. The figure at the left is given an extra breast, that to the right a second and larger head of different silhouette and expression. In an unclinical, intuited way, Picasso showed how, in moments of great physical exertion and erotic stimulation, a new self-consciousness comes into being. Affected by these conditions may be the emphasis, size, weight, color, shape, location, and even orientation of the body parts. All of the figures seem to be boneless, for example, and much of the distortion occurs in the most fleshy areas. Cubism's breakdown of the body as a continuous closed vessel was the foundation for this new imagery in Picasso's art. Picasso and other artists could now extend their most intimate sentiments to the entire internal as well as external reconstruction of the body in art. Picasso gave his figures a fictive transparency so that we see simultaneously the pink of the flesh and the suggestions of inner organs.

In *Three Dancers* there is an outpouring of feelings and visions. The dancer to the left has received the most inspired treatment. She is given a third breast by shaping of the interval between her right arm and her body, and her eyes are interchangeable with the pink and black breast. Fiery red outlines the shadow of her left arm. The legs of the tall central figure change in color from pink to light gray; the third dancer is made up of a white, brown, and black silhouette. All three dancers have their physical and psychological images ingeniously interlocked with each other and the setting behind them. The painting thus takes place in an interior in a double sense.

An etching with a subject revealing the way Picasso worked is *Painter with Model Knitting* (Fig. 15.9), an illustration for Balzac's *The Unknown Masterpiece*. The short story is of Frenhofer, a seventeenth-century painter who devoted his life to achieving a perfect balance, within a single painting, of drawing and color. In Balzac's time, Poussin and Rubens were considered rivals championing, respectively, drawing and color. The artist's final masterpiece is a chaos of drawing and color out of which emerges a small but superb woman's foot. The old artist, recognizing his failure, destroys himself and his art.

In the etching, the artist's work bears no resemblance to the external appearance of the woman, but it does catch the spirit of Frenhofer's dictum that in drawing a hand it is not enough to show its attachment to the body, it must also be shown as a continuation or extension of thought and feeling. The drawing on the canvas is a form of knitting in which the woman is translated into a series of interwoven rhythmic configurations. Unlike the painting in process in Vermeer's *The Art of Painting*, the outcome of the drawing is unforeseeable on the basis of the model. In 1935, Picasso said, "A picture is not thought out and settled beforehand. While it is being done, it changes as one's thoughts change. And when it is finished it still goes on changing according to the state of mind of whoever is looking at it."

In other works, Picasso reversed the mode of the drawing and the model and even the artist, indicating the interchangeability of his style and the myriad

15.9 Picasso. *Painter with Model Knitting,* 1927. Collection The Museum of Modern Art. (Photo: Sunami)

15.10 Picasso. *Minotauromachia*, 1935. Philadelphia Museum of Art, gift of Henry P. McIlhenny.

approaches to life and art, all based upon the artist's willful transformation of that from which he works. It is unwise to try to label Picasso's modes or to call the drawing of the model in his illustration "abstract." On the use of this word Picasso said,

> There is no abstract art. You must always start with something. Afterward you can remove all traces of reality. There's no danger then, anyway, because the idea of the object will have left an indelible mark. It is what started the artist off, excited his ideas, and stirred up his emotions [that] will in the end be prisoners in his work. . . . They form an integral part of it even when their presence is no longer discernible. Whether he likes it or not, man is the instrument of nature. It forces on him its character and appearance.

During the 1930's Picasso was strongly attracted to ancient Greek mythology, partly as a reaction to the futility of rational conduct in the face of the rise of fascism. There resulted in Picasso's art, notably his *Minotauromachia* etching (Fig. 15.10), the formation of private myths, rather than literal interpretations of such Greek legends as Theseus and the Minotaur. In many drawings, prints, and paintings preceding this etching, Picasso had created fantasies based upon the Minotaur, the bull and the bullfight. These, coupled with prior themes in his art, are brought together in the *Minotauromachia* with no rational plan or decipherable story. The whole is a paradigm of the illusionistic surrealist image built upon instinctive creation. The artist responded to obsessive themes which mingle the bizarre, erotic, violent, and innocent in free association.

Both in previous interpretations and the *Minotauromachia*, Picasso deviated from the original story of the Minotaur. In antiquity, the Minotaur was a creature with the body of a bull and the head of a man. Picasso's hybrid is reversed, and in un-

Greek fashion the seat of reason is the head of the animal, not that of the man, which may relate to the importance the artist placed on feeling. Further, the Minotaur was severally shown as a pathetic victim, a tender abductor or object of love, and confounded with the person of Theseus. In the *Minotauromachia* the Minotaur does not constitute a menace but is shown reaching for the light held by the young girl whose history goes back to Picasso's early paintings. Just to the left of the Minotaur's legs is a white sail instead of the black sail which in the Theseus myth was erroneously kept, resulting in the suicide of Aegeus. The horse and woman toreador emerge from the earlier bullfight series, and as before, the woman shows the evidence of violation. In her dreamlike state she menaces the gored horse with the sword rather than the Minotaur, who had also been fused with the bull in the bullfight series. The figure ascending the ladder at the left, who looks over his shoulder in the direction of the light, is Christ. Picasso had done a small painting of the Crucifixion in the late twenties; the theme of Christ mounting to his death is an old one in Spanish art. Above the scene, in the niche of a blockhouse, are two young girls, seemingly witnesses, but whose attention is upon two doves. These witnesses also derive from earlier studies of arena combat. The two birds standing before a niche occur in a painting done by Picasso's father before 1900. Much of the etching's fascination comes from the myriad references and ambiguous interrelationships of time, place, and action.

Picasso admired Rembrandt's work, and his etching reflects a comparable sensitivity to the tonal gradients of the paper and ink, particularly in the range of whites beginning with Christ and traversing to the Minotaur at the right. A noteworthy transition takes place from the daylit background at the right to the semidarkness at the left which makes the candle's flame the most brilliant area.

In the spring of 1937 Picasso began work on studies for a large canvas to commemorate the bombing of the Spanish town Guernica by Franco's planes. This was his first painting directly inspired by a specific historical event. Nevertheless, the studies and completed painting were a logical outlet and summation of his imagery of the late 1920's and 1930's that had dealt with brutality and fantasies upon the body. One brilliant sketch (Fig. 15.11) shows how Picasso became deeply engrossed in the nonpolitical aspects of the project—notably the theme of the human deranged by pain. The woman's head has been completely detached from the body, and each feature's response to pain is shown separately. Even the normally neutral areas of eyelashes, brows, and hair aggressively participate. The eyebrows do not lie passively on the forehead but cut into it like deep scars. The hair pulls away from the head resembling rawly exposed nerves such as those suggested in the lines from the right eye running down the cheek. The eyes have been pulled apart and transposed into teardrop forms filled and surrounded by splintering shapes. A large dark patch between the eyes localizes another area of heated aggravation. The nostrils, one almost detached from the nose, are swollen and flared. The entire head seems divested of its cranial skeleton as it is twisted into soft and angular contortions. The climactic feature is the mouth burst open in a scream, the lips peeled back revealing the irregular, precariously rooted teeth, the lining of the palate, the black cavity of the throat, and the rigidification of the tongue into a sharp, cutting instrument. Grunewald's *Isenheim Crucifixion* was a source of this drawing. From children's art, Picasso took the use of crayon, and deceptively childish scribbling within the facial contours achieved a graduated series of vaguely defined irritated spots. The drawing betrays the fierce pressure with which the crayon was dug into the paper, particularly in the brow and hair. Picasso's sadism, extended to the means as well as subject, is frankly manifest. Older artists, such as those of the Counter-Reformation, had found sadistic outlets in themes of the martyrdoms of saints. By the time of the *Guernica*, modern artists had more direct outlets for these sentiments.

In the final painting of *Guernica* (Fig. 15.12), Picasso eliminated all political reference to the fascist aggressor and modern warfare, focusing upon the agonies of the noncombatants. No cipherable links between the figures and groups exist, and while Picasso may have had private symbols in mind, he has refused to spell out his intent. At various times in Picasso's art, the bull signified Franco and the Spanish people. To assign to the bull at the left the role of aggressor is to overlook that the bull is also a victim. In the center is the distended head of the dying horse, its body pierced by a spear. Beneath the horse are segments of a man whose arm clutches a broken sword and a flower. In older art the figure fallen beneath a galloping horse was a victory symbol, but this tradition was ended in the *Guernica*. From his student days in the Barcelona Academy, Picasso had made drawings of figure casts, introducing them into still lifes during the 1920's. The figure who runs in from the right is a descendant from earlier paintings of gigantesque nudes running along a beach, but now the woman's form is swollen and constricted in flagrant exteriorization of her internal distress.

Other reminiscences of earlier work are the mother and child, and the woman who leans from the window holding the lamp, who may have vague con-

notations of justice. There is ambiguity as to the interior or exterior locus of the action and a puzzling redundancy of light sources. *Guernica* is a study in panic; the two women at the right, deprived of all reason, are drawn to rather than repelled by the center of the disaster.

The great scale of the *Guernica* was new for Picasso and he made many drawings for the composition and ended by reducing the number of textures and colors. The use of blacks, grays, and whites not only eliminated a number of color problems, but also created suitable and dramatic accompaniment to the nightmarish theme. The stippled texture in the horse and the over-all black and white further resemble the qualities of newsprint and journalistic photos of violence during the turbulent

15.11 Picasso. Study of a woman in pain, for *Guernica*, May 24, 1937.

15.12 Picasso. *Guernica*, 1937. Collection The Museum of Modern Art.

years before the painting. (He did not work from photographs in *Guernica*, however.) Picasso's recourse to the classical pyramidal composition is not out of character, for he had taken many motifs and devices from classical art in the previous years. He could not, however, accept the classical insistence upon the pyramid's centrality, symmetry, and stability, and the climax of the pyramid is not an idealized human but a terrorized beast. Further, the pyramid is interlocked with the flanking areas through continuities and discontinuities of colors and shapes. The part thus predicts the whole, as no single figure is shown in the same tone nor can its shape be detached from that to which it is adjacent.

So many ideas emerged in the painting's process, evidenced by changes in the final work, that their momentum carried over into additional studies even after the painting was exhibited.

Since *Guernica*, Picasso seems to have become content to cultivate his own garden. Few of his later works match his earlier profundity and sustained inventive-ness. His became more playful and re-creative, less self-critical. He chose to re-work his own earlier themes and the art of the old masters and modes, particularly as they related to his love of his own children, women, and animals. After World War II Picasso exerted little influence on the important younger painters, for new problems and possibilities were introduced into art. Many important developments occurred in the early art of this century for which Picasso was not responsible, as will be seen in Chapter 17. Nonillusionistic art, for example, was a peripheral interest with Picasso whose thinking was always centered on the human form. The notoriety of his highly publicized private life and carefree ageless appearance due to revitalization by incessant creation make difficult a serious appraisal of his recent work. Few can disagree that before 1940 his protean energies, intelligence, attention to feeling, and sheer technical skill produced art of the highest quality in astonishing abundance. Not the least inspiration to Picasso at all times was his curiosity, concern, and delight with the face of art and humanity.

CHAPTER 16

THE CITY IN MODERN PAINTING

On many occasions before the late nineteenth century, artists painted the city either as a backdrop or as a central focus in their work. One of the most beautiful such paintings is Vermeer's *View of Delft* (Fig. 16.1). So accurate is Vermeer's painting that his location and the section of the city that he painted can be traced. From within a cottage that no longer exists, Vermeer looked out about four hundred feet across the Schie River to the Rotterdam and Schiedam gates and their connecting bridge. Behind them are the towers of the Old and the New Church. The city is seen at noon on a summer day; a slight wind is blowing from the southwest. Vermeer's picturesque home city of Delft lent itself to such sedentary contemplation. It was a city to be walked through slowly. Its countless delightful prospects and details revealed themselves only to the unhurried discriminating eye, like Vermeer's own. The leisurely pace of life is suggested by the women in the left foreground, patiently awaiting a boat. The painting records Vermeer's joy in the shapes and light of the city and the ineffable calm they induced. Each reflection of light on tile, glass, and brick has been set down, as have the fluid shadows of the buildings on the canal. The painter pointedly contrasted the shapeless inconstancy of the sky and water with the firm materiality of the city. The triangular strip of shoreline visually stabilizes the water area. So calculating was Vermeer that he painted out a small figure of a man on the shoreline near the center, perhaps to prevent foreground distraction from the city above. The city's solid, varied architecture and tranquil daily life seem to have a visual and ideological relationship to Vermeer's art. *View of Delft* is more than a documentary image. It is the fulfillment of the wish for an ideal, untroubled earthly existence.

The form and content of modern art have likewise been influenced by the cities in which they developed. In late nineteenth- and twentieth-century painting however, there is wider, more direct, and personal range of interpretation of the artist's urban environment. The esthetics, psy-

16.1 Vermeer. *View of Delft, c.* 1658. The Hague, Copyright The Foundation Johan Maurits van Nassau Mauritshuis. (Photo: Dingjan)

chology, technology, and sociology associated with the modern city have received rich artistic transformation. The changing form of modern cities has also accompanied the development of modern painting styles, and though affinities between the two can be sensed, it is not easy to pinpoint exact influences.

Paris of the 1870's was vastly different from seventeenth-century Delft. Paris was the pleasure capital of the world, a city redesigned to provide the Parisians' all-consuming eye with endless optical spectacles. With its boulevards it accommodated the moving eye, the spectator who rode in carriages, promenaded, or like Monet, overlooked the avenues from high up in buildings. As we have seen previously, the new buildings lining the boulevards lacked the picturesque individuality of houses along the Delft streets. The great mobility and dense traffic of the boulevards contrasted with Dutch preference for life

lived behind garden walls. When Henry James was describing the new Paris in his novel *The Ambassadors*, he could have been writing about Monet's painting of a Parisian boulevard (Fig. 16.2):

It hung before him this morning, the vast bright Babylon, like some huge iridescent object, a jewel brilliant and hard, in which parts were not to be discriminated nor differences comfortably marked. It twinkled and trembled and melted together, and what seemed all surface one moment assumed all depth the next.

In Monet's painting what seems all depth when viewed from afar becomes all surface when examined in detail. The figures, trees, and buildings have been reduced to touches and patches of one or two colors. Intimate viewing of the painting brings James' words to mind—"iridescent, twinkled, melted together." Unlike Vermeer, Monet underinterpreted forms

16.2 Monet. *Boulevard des Capucines*, 1864. Collection of the late Marshall Field.

under light, suspended knowledge of their volume, detail, and edge in order to achieve greater fidelity to what was optically given. Under the mist-filtered light, differences have not been "comfortably marked," and Monet achieved a wonderful fusion of the scene's components. The visual climax of the painting comes from a bright patch of orange at the right. The unfocused activity of the crowd is ideal for Monet's style of over-all dispersing of tonal accents. Like those of the top-hatted figures on the balcony at the right, our eyes may wander throughout the painting enjoying its facture without missing any story or dramatic event on the street below. The diagonal view of the street allows the stream of traffic to ebb and flow within the frame. To achieve this sustained esthetic image required a certain detachment of the artist from the scene, and one result was a depersonalization of the crowd. What Monet did personalize was the sheer act of esthetic seeing.

Seurat's vision transformed the prosaic into the poetic. The subject of his *Sunday Afternoon on the Isle of the Grande Jatte* (Fig. 16.3) was the holiday outing of lower-middle-class Parisians on an island in the Seine. What seem at first to be familiar persons and setting become the source of a haunting paradox. While appearing to share the enjoyment of the place and moment, the figures do not communicate. The gaiety of the moment comes not from the figures' expressions, but from the warmth and brightness of the colors. Ignoring the potential for movement, Seurat chose to image stilled life. The landscape is painted from a single viewpoint, but each figure within it is rendered from an individual perspective, as if the artist were directly opposite his subject. Maintaining the Impressionists' detachment, Seurat restored to

16.3 Seurat. *A Sunday Afternoon on the Island of the Grande Jatte,* 1884–1886. The Chicago Art Institute. Courtesy of the French Cultural Services, New York. (Photo: Vizzavona)

painting monumental size and volume of the figure. The shadows cast by the sun do not accord with a single light source. Convincing as is the intensity of sunlight, the painting was done in the studio by artificial light. Despite the informal dispersal of the figures, none can be shifted. A taut compositional armature is contrived by the relation of silhouettes and aligned shapes that link fore, middle, and background. The whole painting has the fresh appearance of instantaneous execution, but each silhouette was meditated upon in preliminary studies and purged of the superfluous. Seurat's edges are more expressive than the faces. The large, solemnized, and static figures are ironically constituted by minute, mobile touches of color. A systemization of impressionist color style, Seurat's esthetic of divided touch insured each color's brilliance by joining it with its optical complement, yellow with violet, red with green. His touch varied in size and direction, depending on the shape he was painting and the canvas' scale. Seurat achieved the casual through calculation. From the recurrent, uneventful moments in the life of mundane city dwellers, Seurat created the impression of the eternalized and heroic. Significantly, *The Grande Jatte* is one of the last major paintings in modern art to show the community united in a pleasurable situation.

Even in the late nineteenth century some artists did not look to the city with sympathy and optimism. The moral cost of city life, never assessed by Monet or Seurat, is measured out in paintings by the Belgian James Ensor and the Norwegian Edvard Munch. Ensor's *Entry of Christ into Brussels* (Fig. 16.4) is a bitter commentary upon a city's perversion

16.4 Ensor. *Entry of Christ into Brussels*, 1888. Collection Casino Communal, Knokke-le-Zoute, Belgium. Courtesy of The Museum of Modern Art. (Photo: Sunami)

16.5 Munch. *Evening on Karl Johan Street*, *c.* 1892. Bergen, Collection of Rasmus Meyer.

of a religious event into a vulgar carnival. The painting also reflects Ensor's personal disillusion and feeling of alienation from society. The actual events that Ensor saw in the streets of Ostend and Brussels, in which political factions verbally and physically assailed each other, became the basis of a personal metaphor. The figure of Christ in the painting's center is drowned by waves of grimacing masks and commercial slogans. The airy openness of Monet's boulevard has been replaced by a claustrophobic compacting of the street. The subtle touch and fleck of Monet's brush contrasts with Ensor's assaults on the surface, his violent twisting and streakings of thick pigments. Ensor brought to his paintings sharp insights into the psychology of crowd behavior under conditions of extreme stimulation and loss of inhibition. The masks become intimate reflections of the depravity inherent in those who chose them. Each mask is compelling in both the intensity of its expression and the sensitivity with which Ensor painted it. Coupled with this social lucidity was Ensor's awareness of his own repressions and neurotic anxiety. He was incapable of Monet's aloofness before a crowd. Consequently, Ensor compulsively jammed every inch of the painting with hostile figures, weakening the total composition. The painting is important for the beauty and power of its parts and the means by which Ensor brought to art an honesty of self-realization.

In his painting of *Evening on Karl Johan Street* (Fig. 16.5), Edvard Munch imaged the city through the eyes of someone in mental distress. The crowd is divested of identity and given no recognition of warmth. Through psychological over-interpretation, the faces are dehumanized, having less expression than the blank windows that are exaggerated in intensity. While the street pulls the eye into depth, physical passage is blocked by the phalanx of the crowd. This is a painting whose subject is anxiety over one's place in a world that is inhospitable and menacing. Seurat's distortions were mainly rational esthetic devices to control the world of his paintings. Munch imparted to his paintings psychotic distortions of the color and shape of familiar objects, faces, the tree at the right, the rooftops, the street's angle in depth. In art before Munch, the distressed individual was seen within the painting as if observed by a rational onlooker. With Munch, Van Gogh, and the German Expressionists, the total environment of the painting was colored and shaped by the subjective state of the artist. Although influenced by Scandinavian writers of the time, such as Strindberg, Munch's insights, like Ensor's, derived in large part from personal crises.

While Munch saw the city as a place in which to lose one's sanity, the Italian Futurist Boccioni looked to newly industrial cities at the turn of the century as the hope for society and his own art. Even before painting *The City Rises* (Fig. 16.6), Boccioni had written in his diary, "I feel that I want to paint the new, the fruit of our industrial time. I am nauseated by old walls and old palaces, old motives, reminiscences. . . . I want the new, the expressive, the formidable." Wrestling with preliminary studies, he finally composed a large "synthesis of labor, light, and movement." Although he claimed to cancel all previous values, ironically it is not modern machinery and architecture that Boccioni celebrates, but old-fashioned driving energy of human and horse power. The process by which the city is formed enervated Boccioni's style to such a point that the electric passages of intense color and light obliterate the separation of shapes and their surroundings. Boccioni was obssessed with the ideas of painting the vibrant interchange of matter and of idealizing movement at all levels. Where mobility was part

16.6 Boccioni. *The City Rises*, 1910. Collection Museum of Modern Art, Mrs. Simon Guggenheim Fund. (Photo: Sunami)

of an esthetic spectacle enjoyed by Monet, for Boccioni it was a militant life force, urgently associated with the violence needed to rouse Italy from its lethargy.

The cities painted by Boccioni's contemporary and countryman de Chirico are memorable for their mysterious stillness. While living in Paris between 1911 and 1914, de Chirico nostalgically recreated elements of old North Italian cities. Constant in his images are exaggerated perspectives of arcade-lined piazzas. The impenetrable shadows of the arcades and those projected by unseen statues impart an uneasy quality. *The Melancholy and Mystery of a Street* (Fig. 16.7) is filled with unanswerable questions. Is the railway van empty, and why has it been derailed and set into the square? Is the situation one of innocence or menace? The girl with the hoop is like a phantom image of the little girl in Seurat's *Grande Jatte*, just to the left of the large couple standing at the right. Placing her in a new context filled with

objects, de Chirico set up intriguing elliptical relationships between the girl and the open van, the girl and what lies beyond, around the corner. The thin painted surfaces and precise delineation removes de Chirico's hand from our absorption in the image and these questions. The city here is not ground for esthetic sensations nor commentary on social problems. De Chirico could not directly confront his time and place, but withdrew into a painted world of his own invention and private meaning.

The Parisian painter Robert Delaunay, painting in the same years as De Chirico, found in the Eiffel Tower an optimistic sign of man's courage, energy, and ability to construct rational works of use and beauty (Fig. 16.8). His serial paintings of this symbol of Paris were motivated by his love of the city and the appropriateness of the tower to his ideas about art. To Delaunay, color was form and subject. Rhythms and contrasts of color are the expressive backbone of his paintings. The arrangement of these colors, however, required advance calculation not unlike that used by Eiffel to construct his tower. Delaunay wrote, "This art can identify itself with architecture, it carries within itself the architectural laws of color." Among these laws is one encountered in Seurat's art, namely, that complementary colors juxtaposed appear more intense than in isolation. The red-painted tower is not a completely arbitrary gesture by Delaunay, for during its history it was painted speckled, gold, and orange-red. So completely did Delaunay possess the tower in his mind that his paintings were done from memory. The unstable, eruptive appearance of the tower resulted from Delaunay's fantasies about the disintegrating action of light on the tower's form and his urge to vivify its ma-

jor areas. The esthetic nature of the Eiffel Tower lends itself to fantasy. It has no separation of inside and outside, its crisscross grid breaks up whatever is seen through it, and from any angle its struts are exposed to shifting illumination and shadow.

Delaunay's admiration for the work of the engineer was shared by an Italian immigrant to America, Joseph Stella. In John Roebling's starkly elegant Brooklyn Bridge, Stella saw the symbol of the new world and the carrier of his hopes (Fig. 16.9). Casting off his early style of the old masters, Stella sought fresh means to translate into art the new panoramas created by steel and the polyphony of electric lights that "violated the city's darkness." The suspension bridge was the con-

16.7 (left) De Chirico. *The Melancholy and Mystery of a Street,* 1914. New Canaan, Connecticut, Collection of Mr. and Mrs. Stanley Resor. 16.8 (right) Delaunay. *The Eiffel Tower.* Amsterdam, Copyright Gemeente Museum.

16.9 Stella. *The Brooklyn Bridge*, 1917–1918. Yale University Art Gallery, Collection Société Anonyme.

junction of worlds for Stella. Its obsessive growth in his imagination forced him to devote the entire painting to the bridge, so that the viewer is overwhelmed by its size and depths. The urgency of realizing his ecstatic vision was so strong that during his poverty in 1917 and 1918 Stella painted on a bed sheet. The richness of his image is matched by his own words:

To realize this towering imperative vision in all its integral possibilities I lived days of anxiety, torture and delight, trembling all over with emotion as those railings in the midst of the bridge vibrating at the continuous passage of the trains. I ap-

pealed for help to the soaring verse of Walt Whitman and to the fiery Poe's plasticity. Upon the swarming darkness of the night, I rung all the bells of alarm with the blaze of electricity scattered in lightnings down the oblique cables, the dynamic pillars of my composition, through the green and red glare of the signals I excavated here and there caves as subterranean passages to infernal recesses.

The visionary art of the seventeenth century followed the artistic laws of rational seeing. Stella preserved the hallucinatory nature of his inspiration by the discontinuity of his perspectives and unexpected spottings of light and dark. So much a part of the painting was the bridge that in his writing Stella interchanged the pillars of the bridge and the composition. Skyline and suspension cables mesh, confounding attempts to isolate the bridge from the city beyond.

The first two decades of the twentieth century saw Manhattan transformed by clusters of skyscrapers. Paris had been the city of light; New York became the city of height. New England-born John Marin shared with Stella a romantic attraction to the physiognomy of the city and the connotations of its growth. His watercolors and prints of new skyscrapers, like the Woolworth and Telephone buildings, and his view of *Lower Manhattan* (Fig. 16.10) illustrate his written sentiments:

> These buildings move me, they too must have life. Thus the whole city is alive, buildings, people all are alive, and the more they move me the more I feel them to be alive. . . . I see great forces at work, great movements; the large buildings, the small buildings; the warring of the great and small; influences of one mass on another greater or smaller mass.

Marin squeezed the panorama of lower Manhattan into a small area and then exploded it outwards. The sun burst was achieved by collage, the sewing of cut-out yellow paper onto the watercolor. Rather than a literal detonation, the burst is the reflection of the sun from the gold dome of the now-destroyed Pulitzer Building. The image conveys the unleashing of the city's energy and the violent interchange that Marin intuited between the massive structures. The shapes that fracture the buildings are tightly fitted into a complete and expressive design. The watercolor medium permitted Marin to fix his revelation

16.10 Marin. *Lower Manhattan*, 1922. Collection Museum of Modern Art, the Lillie P. Bliss Bequest.

16.11 Leger. *The City,* 1919. Philadelphia Museum of Art, A. E. Gallatin Collection.

and to impart the necessary range of firm to elusive and opaque to transparent qualities.

In 1919, Fernand Leger painted *The City* (Fig. 16.11), the culmination of a long, unsentimental love affair with Paris and the machine. Realizing that the modern city was too big and complex to be imaged from one view, Leger continued his cubist style which permitted the juxtaposition of those urban qualities he most admired. (Painting such as his has influenced montage photography.) Leger's mechanized metropolis is an optimistic vision. Trained first as an architect, then during the war as an artilleryman, Leger was a life-long admirer of the machine. Leger re-engineered the city in terms of the products and beauty of technology. His colors are the pure hues of commercial advertising, cement, and metal. The textured patterns were inspired by railings, stairways, and the Eiffel Tower. Segments of the mass-produced, stenciled letters and billboard figures, replace anything that might suggest the handmade object. The smooth surface and regular edges were painted impersonally. The robotic figures on the stairs are the ideal inhabitants of Leger's metropolis. The light so important to Vermeer and the Impressionists plays no part in *The City*. The shapes are self-illuminating, rarely tempered by shadings, always clear, clean, and hard in their edges and joinings. Where Vermeer and Monet delighted in the painting of soft clouds, Leger mechanized smoke into a globular sequence above the figures on the stairway. Leger looked upon smoke as a symbol of civilization and its harnessing by hard lines as an affirmation of his own masculine command. The visual spice of *The City* comes from unpredictable contrasts, such as the rare rounded volumes that seem to bulge in front of the surface, and the single tall column that stands against so many medium and small forms. There is a visual rightness to the scale of each shape in relation to the painting's large format. This is a big painting, one step from mural art, handled in large forceful rhythms and bold color that would lose in impact if reduced in scale.

Piet Mondrian's *Broadway Boogie*

Woogie (Fig. 16.12) gave form to his love of American music and the rhythms of New York, where he spent the last years of his life. The entire composition is made up of elementary units, variations upon a rectangle, orchestrated to achieve a maximal richness and variety. Set against a white ground, the colors are pure tones of red, yellow, gray, and black. There is precision but also unpredictability in Mondrian's structural analogue of jazz with its discipline and improvisation. His intentions were set forth in writing:

> The art of the past established rhythm . . . veiled by subject matter and particular forms. . . . In our time, rhythm is more and more accentuated, not only in art, but in mechanized reality and in the whole life.

The feel and visual concept of music were important to Mondrian, not the imaging of musicians, instruments, and dancers. Privately he admired the city's youth and the sensual manifestations of the city's vitality. His writings show that he conceived of the city as the basis for a new style of art:

> The genuinely modern artist sees the metropolis as abstract living converted into form: it is nearer to him than nature. . . In the metropolis the natural has already been stiffened up, ordered by the human spirit. The proportion and the rhythm of patch and line in architecture will speak a more direct language to him than the capriciousness of nature. In the metropolis beauty expresses itself more mathematically.

Mondrian's own style, however, had origi-

16.12   Mondrian. *Broadway Boogie Woogie,* 1942–1943.   Collection Museum of Modern Art. (Photo: Sunami)

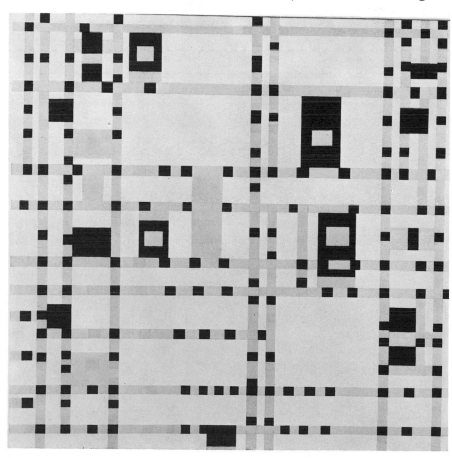

16.13 Kline. *New York*, 1953. Buffalo, New York, Albright Art Gallery. Gift of Seymour H. Knox.

nated in the paintings and drawings that he did in rural Holland, discussed in the next chapter. He could make the foregoing statement because it was his conviction that what he had found in art was applicable to all forms of life.

The city was seen by Monet and Seurat as the source of esthetic delight and relaxed diversion. To Ensor and Munch, the city meant fateful encounters, habitation by depravity, and the inducement of suicidal alienation. For Boccioni the regeneration of cities signified healthful expenditure of energy and portended revolutionary changes in society. De Chirico's

silent city held cryptic omens, but also sanctuary for a troubled spirit. Delaunay and Leger responded to the calculation and unsentimental makeup of their Parisian environment and saw affinities between the laws of architecture and engineering and those of painting. Marin and Stella experienced joyful hallucination before the city, with Stella seeing the bridge as the poetic pathway to the promise of the future. The tempo and mathematics of the modern metropolis were passionately fixed by Mondrian into dispassionate squares.

With these few examples of the city, one can begin to understand the variety in modern art. For those who look upon modern artists as being indifferent to what goes on around them, here is evidence to the contrary. That the artist is only interested in esthetic problems is contradicted by the painting and written statements of Boccioni, Mondrian, Marin, and Stella. Both older art and the visible urban world have gone into the form of their paintings, and the form and content are indivisible. An artist need not paint faces and buildings or what he directly confronts to have been directly influenced by the city. Working and living in it, the artist constantly absorbs through his thoughts and feelings what is around him. In a sense, anything that a present-day artist paints while working in the city is, consciously or unconsciously, a reflection of his urban environment.

Such is the case in *New York* (Fig. 16.13) by the artist Franz Kline. "When I look out the window—I've always lived in the city—I don't see the trees in bloom or mountain laurel. What I do see or rather not what I see but the feelings aroused in me by that looking is what I paint." When this work was begun, Kline presumably had no conscious intention of painting the city. The title probably came when the painting was finished and the artist reflected on it and perhaps recalled the visual and emotional stimulus that had worked its way into the image during the process of painting. Kline's painting style, which consists of a taut equivalence of black and white areas given a personal calligraphic form, may also have prepared his imagination for the city with its rugged monochromatic shapes and contrasts against the sky. The commercial paints and broad house-painter's brush that permit rapid release of momentary impulses on a large scale further link the painting to its urban origin. For Kline, the success of the final painting is not imitative properties but whether or not he has communicated his feelings. While *New York* and *View of Delft* are poles apart in form, it would be a mistake to disclaim for Vermeer the emotional values prized by Kline. To convey his love of a tranquil ordered world, Vermeer had to paint in accurate and detailed manner, taking relatively small license with light and shapes. But the cumulative power resulting from this license-taking raises his painting far above the value of documentary reproduction.

CHAPTER 17

NONILLUSIONISTIC MODERN PAINTING

In the preceding chapters we touched upon the relation of art to man's attempt to come to terms with his religious, spiritual, political, physical, economic, social, and esthetic environment. In this final section we move from concern with the external world to modern art's relation to the self. No clear-cut distinction exists, and no one can say with surety where the self ends and the outer world begins. The works treated in this chapter have in common the lack of illusion of the familiar visible world. The paintings are personal visions, conceits of the artist's inspired imagination, concrete evidences of his thought and feeling. Their meaning and all that is needed for experiencing them is on the surface.

The artist's decision to move away from illusionistic painting frequently entailed important decisions and commitments that extended beyond the world of the studio. The implications of the way a man paints reach into his psychological and emotional makeup, and style is part of the artist's world view. Furthermore, the artist will preserve in his nonillusionistic work a certain residue of his earlier imagery based upon his perception of nature. This can be seen by juxtaposing works from both styles of a single painter. In all cases to be considered here, the artist's gravitation toward pure surface painting was motivated by a search for increased spiritual freedom or self-liberation.

As a young painter in Holland at the turn of this century, Piet Mondrian was inclined toward passive settings in the Dutch countryside with no action or figures. Mondrian searched for solitary prospects, those small segments within the vast panorama of nature that reflected an inherently stable and tranquil world. Mondrian's painting of the windmill (Fig. 17.1) shares qualities of De Hooch's painting of the Dutch interior (Fig. 6.17). Both utilized painting to make more explicit life and nature put into order. Mondrian selected a viewpoint which permitted him to align principal axes, those of the bridge and mill, within the scene with those of the picture frame, thus permitting stable pic-

17.1 (above) Mondrian. *Landscape with Mill*, 1904. Collection Muscum of Modern Art. (Photo: Sunami)

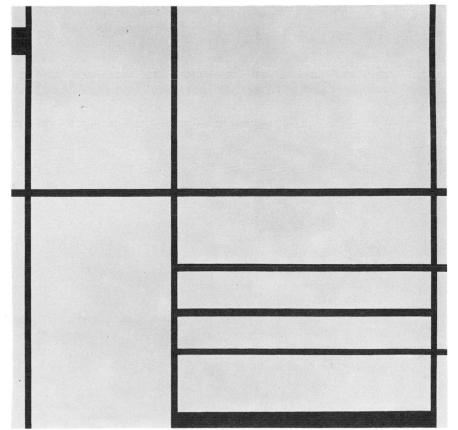

17.2 (right) Mondrian. *Composition in White, Black, and Red*, 1936. Collection Museum of Modern Art. (Photo: Sunami)

torial construction. The shadows in the placid water echo and reinforce the directions of the mill and bridge, and a grid pattern is repeated in seven areas. Many brushstrokes, such as those at the left and in the pond, are uncommitted to literal movements within nature but stiffen the design armature of the whole. Many of the original details of the scene have been screened out and replaced by a steno-language of the brush and reduction to a few colors. The artist's viewpoint with the large area given over to the reflecting surface of the water has contributed to a perceptible flattening out of space, which, coupled with an obvious contrivance of repeated motifs, gives a strong surface rhythm to the painting. During Mondrian's subsequent growth as an artist and in his writings his obsession with the implications of rhythm became patent. Rhythm was a critical link by which Mondrian hoped to unite "the individual with the universal."

Hundreds of paintings intervened between the *Landscape with Mill* and *Composition in White, Black and Red* (Fig. 17.2) of 1936, but the latter is in mood and design, a condensation of the former. The constructive components of the later work, straight lines in rectilinear conjunction, are in the mill painting. Junctures are now crisp, all shapes and the pure colors lie completely upon the surface; irregularities traceable to the hand are absent. Crucial to the continuity of form and meaning between the two paintings is the relation of the asymmetrical composition to the frame, as if what is within its borders were an incomplete, fragmented view of a greater order. The irregular quadrature of the later painting is controlled not by directly perceived shapes in nature, but by the artist's intuition of balance between black lines, small red, and large white rectangles. Mondrian's compositional reflexes had been conditioned by his paintings of land, sky, wa-

ter, and trees. The painting's title accurately describes what is *on*, not in the painting's surface. Mondrian believed this type of painting was important for humanity because it presented in purified artistic form a model of equilibrium, imperfectly experienced in nature, but eternally sought in all forms of life. Seeing as the painter's task the expression of a vision of reality, Mondrian desired the purest expression of life through the freeing of color, rhythm, and form from their particularized appearance in nature. In the varying dimensions of the rectangular areas, with perfect balance of tension, he felt such a liberation could be accomplished. "Space becomes white, black or gray; form becomes red, blue or yellow." The hermetic, self-denying qualities latent in the mill painting emerged through the years with a puritanical severity as Mondrian followed a personal artistic and moral ethic intended to enlighten and uplift viewers of his painting.

The years between 1910 and 1915 were critical in the history of modern art, for then a number of artists working simultaneously in different countries gave up the concept of pictorial illusion. The new nonillusionistic art continued to be burdened with reminiscences and feelings engendered by the artist's contact with the visual world. In 1913 the Russian painter Kasimir Malevich did a series of pencil drawings (Fig. 17.3) in which first one, then two squares, a circle, and cross forms replaced his earlier images for peasants and alternated with his cubist collages. Of Malevich, as for Mondrian and other insurgent artists of the time involved in the quest for new and more personal expressions of the spirit and esthetic, the break with the rendering of the visible world was not immediate, total, nor without difficult adjustment. Like Mondrian, Malevich wrote about the moral imperatives in his art, an indication of his insecurity and urgency. In a series of essays begun in 1915 and pub-

17.3 (right) Malevich. *Suprematist Elements: Two Squares*, 1913. Museum of Modern Art.

17.4 (below) Malevich. Charts designed to show the mundane sources of Cubism, Futurism, and Suprematism. Museum of Modern Art. (Photo: Sunami)

lished in 1927, *The Non-Objective World*, Malevich reconstructed the circumstances in which he created imagery induced by the feeling of objectlessness:

> When in the year 1913, in my desperate attempt to free art from the ballast of objectivity, I took refuge in the square form and exhibited a picture which consisted of nothing more than a black square on a white field, the critics and, along with them, the public sighed, "Everything which we loved is lost. We are in a desert. . . . Before us is nothing but a black square on a white background!" But this desert is filled with the spirit of non-objective sensation which pervades everything. Even I was gripped by a kind of timidity bordering on fear when it came to leaving "the world of will and idea," in which I had lived and worked, in the reality of which I believed. But a blissful sense of liberating non-objectivity drew me forth into the "desert" where nothing is real except feeling . . . and so feeling became the substance of my life. This was no "empty square" which I had exhibited but rather the feeling of non-objectivity. . . . The black square on the white field was the first form in which non-objective feeling came to be expressed. The square = feeling, the white field = the void beyond this feeling.

In his search for new forms to express feeling Malevich had been excited by the airplane and the sensations of speed and flight. In interesting charts (Fig. 17.4) designed to show the mundane sources of Cubism, Futurism, and his own art, Suprematism, Malevich chose for aerial photos, including one of a desert, to illustrate his idea of the recession of object identity as one achieved the heights of detachment from ground level-coordinates. Malevich's drawing shares with the modern technology that produced these new views and sensa-

17.5 Kandinsky. *Landscape*, 1910. The Solomon R. Guggenheim Museum.

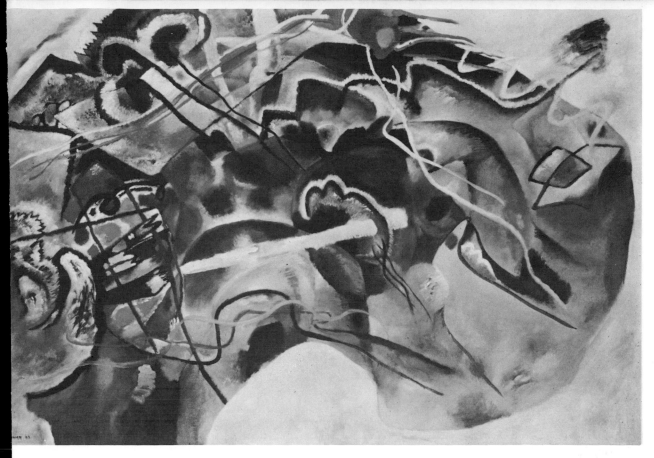

17.6 Kandinsky. *Picture with White Edge*, 1913. The Solomon R. Guggenheim Museum.

tions properties of precision and calculation, and like Mondrian's, his imagery has the "feel" of geometry.

The form and mood of modern nonillusionistic painting and the diversity of temperament that produced it are reflected in a comparison of the art of Mondrian and Malevich with that of the Russian Wassily Kandinsky. Kandinsky's early art, too, shows his attraction to the countryside. The human figure was marginal to his art, and objects were excluded. By 1910, when he painted a landscape with a factory chimney (Fig. 17.5), Kandinsky had moved to a point where it was increasingly difficult to match his painting with an actual landscape. He had reduced distinctions between land and sky, trees, hills, and buildings, near and far; his paintings coalesced into strong arbitrary color harmonies less and less dictated by perceived sequences of hues. He did not seek a stable viewpoint

or geometrically based order, but imaged a turbulent heaving earth. Against broad sweeping curves of the hills are ragged and diffuse color patches, producing intense color sensations and contributing to the excited mood of the whole. Unlike the impressionist painter, Kandinsky did not paint the mood induced by his contact with nature, but rather superimposed upon the landscape an already existing emotional state. Kandinsky's predilection was for wild, hilly terrain laced with precipitous diagonals, adequate carriers of his feeling. These properties flood over into a later painting *Picture with White Edge* (Fig. 17.6). Although not consciously intended as a landscape, it shows that the movements of his hand and thought could not expunge his earlier experience; there is a pictorial sign language of wavelike hills and jagged series of peaks and trees.

Taken as a whole the *White Edge*

has an apocalyptic mood; dating from the eve of World War I, it may have been indirectly inspired by Kandinsky's response to the tense atmosphere in Germany, where he was working. Its brilliant color evokes sensations of clashing sounds. Kandinsky believed that sense experiences overlapped and that each color had its equivalence in sound so that painting was an orchestration of elements having inherent expressive associations with which the painter could strike chords in the soul of the viewer. Framing the dense and saturate color mass in the painting is an irregular white edge, a color which Kandinsky wrote of as a pregnant stillness. Like Balzac's Frenhofer, Kandinsky sought a perfect fusion of drawing and color and, like the fictional painter, achieved exquisite but nevertheless controlled chaos. There is no sustained way by which shapes are joined; they clash head on, overlap, grow, and dissolve, persistently defying enumeration and measure. The painting has an irregular pulse of congestion and expansion and clear traces of large and small movements of a hand dominated by impulse and strong rhythmic movement. Neither Cubism nor the nonillusionistic constructions of Mondrian or Malevich have the variety and strenuous interweaving of Kandinsky's pictorial means.

Kandinsky's departure from illusionism was gradual, hesitant, backsliding, and rarely complete in the years between 1910 and 1914. His writings show a deep awareness of and misgivings about a possible important loss to art in the giving up of the familiar. What impelled him in the direction of the *White Edge* was a growing distrust of modern materialism, science, organized religion, and illusionistic art, all of which he came to regard as impediments to the free expression of the human spirit. Inner freedom was for Kandinsky the sole criteria for ethics and esthetics. The creative process ideally meant suspension of consciousness and purely

spontaneous and intuitive work, but Kandinsky did in fact impose critical judgment. He wrote,

> I have painted rather subconsciously in a state of strong inner tension. So intensely do I feel the necessity of some of the forms that I remember having given loud-voiced directions to myself, for instance, "But the corners must be heavy." The observer must learn to look at the picture as a graphic representation of a mood and not as a representation of objects.

In his painting of *The Farm* (Fig. 17.7) done in 1921 and 1922, while he was in Montroig, Spain, and Paris, the Spanish artist Joan Miro used beloved souvenirs of his homeland. The identity of every item of this extensive inventory is fiercely insisted upon. The intense particularization of all objects in an airless space contributes to their charm and eventual ambiguity. Simultaneously, we are given the diversity and unity of a staggering number of objects, so that we become aware of conjugated series—those of holes and circular patches, scalloped and peaked shapes, radial spoke forms in the trees and grass, parallel diagonals and horizontals in roof and earth areas. The vividness and interest of the painting come from the relatively even dispersal and avoided overlap of a wide gamut of forms running from the infinitesimal pebbles to the large buildings, larger trees, and infinite sky. *The Farm* is a brilliant memory image in which the painter reconstituted an ideal environment. Miro had grass from Montroig brought to his Paris studio in his search for accuracy. The drawing, coloring, and shading of each object was the occasion for willful transformation rather than mechanical duplication. The various containers, for instance, are attractive for their shapes and black interiors rather than their utility. The proximity and discontinuity of multiple textures, directions, and shapes, for instance, at the base of the tree, fill the canvas with surprises

17.7 (above) Miro. *The Farm*, 1921–1922. Museum of Modern Art, Collection of Mrs. Ernest Hemingway.
17.8 (below) Miro. *Catalan Landscape*, 1923–1924. Collection Museum of Modern Art. (Photos: Sunami)

and visual wit. Concomitant with the rational planning of the composition, there has been the intrusion of fantasy in the giving of a double life to each shape (that of familiar function and slightly unfamiliar form), multiple views to create depth, surface pattern, and a chain of associations.

The fantasy incipient in *The Farm* was unchecked in Miro's *Catalan Landscape (The Hunter;* Fig. 17.8). Suspended upon a flat surface of yellow above and pink below is an aggregate of lines and shapes derived from the earlier painting. Now, however, the drawing has suggested the object, so the undulating line lives a ubiquitous life as a mustache, the horizon, an animal body, waves, birds. Certain shapes and lines obsessive to Miro are now disassociated from the objects that occasioned them. There is a playful mocking of geometry in the use of the ruled line and the triangle, seen in its more familiar state at the lower left, but then made part of the rabbit's tail just to the right and the hunter's head above. The pipe-smoking hunter has a large ear, not inappropriate for the chase, an exposed heart, a scraggly beard whose shapes appear in the farmhouse of the earlier painting. The dotted

trail that he follows twists playfully against the lines of his body and arms. Influenced by his contact with Cubism, Miro detached a large eye from a head and the letters "S A R D," perhaps from the Spanish word *Sardana*, a Catalan folk dance. The earlier disposition of elements has become more random and whimsical. The span from minute to large is retained from the earlier work, but here Miro magnified and reconstituted certain objects, such as the rabbit and insect forms, more arbitrarily, according to their weight in his consciousness and the dictates of fantasy. While vestiges of a scene or subject remain, they are accompanied by less decipherable elements, and the painting's poetry is more obvious in its rhymes, more arcane in its meaning. There is no longer an intent to follow the logic or syntax of nature's appearance. Miro's creatures live only on the painting's surface. Miro's full conversion to an art that was not based upon the restraint of reason, but which encouraged instinctive or automatic outpouring of fantasy was a moral one, like that of Kandinsky who sought artistic spiritual release.

The American Jackson Pollock's early *Seascape* (Fig. 17.9) is a moody image

17.9 Pollock. *Seascape*, 1934. Collection of Lee Krasner Pollock.

of a storm-tossed boat seen against a disquieting sky. The canvas is filled with an over-all dense pigmentation, rugged shapes, and strong motions. The subject was selected for its appropriateness to the strong and aggressive feelings of the young artist. From his first works, Pollock asserted his rebellious nature and his need to impose his will and muscular energies on both nature and art. The small format and limits of the canvas are strained to contain the violence of his painting.

Created sixteen years and hundreds of paintings and drawings later, Pollock's *Autumn Rhythm* continues, refines, adds to, and subtracts from the seminal qualities of *Seascape*. From the easel painting Pollock had gravitated toward what might be called the "portable canvas mural," roughly eight and one half by seventeen feet. In 1947 the painter wrote:

I prefer to tack the unstretched canvas to the hard wall or floor. I need the resistance of a hard surface. On the floor I am more at ease. I feel nearer, more a part of the painting, since this way I can walk around it, work from the four sides and literally be *in* the painting.

Vermeer's painting of the artist in his studio demonstrated a system ideal for wrist painting. The artist's subject was reduced to the scale of a traditional easel format. In Pollock's work of the late 1940's, scale was not strongly predetermined but resulted from the interaction of the artist and his evolving image, which finally set the finished size of the painting. Further, Pollock was desirous of arm as well as wrist painting; the rhythms and energies of his entire body found outlet in the creative act. He gave up oil for enamel paints for both technical and esthetic reasons. He was freed of oil paint's historical associations, and the more viscous media permitted greater spinning out of the linear fabric, the heart of Pollock's mature style. The dripping and spattering of paint as Pollock walked around and over the horizontal canvas was a technique thoughtfully and deliberately arrived at as the inevitable means by which to impose his visions and feelings on the painting's surface and the viewer's eye.

17.10 Pollock. *Autumn Rhythm*, 1950. Courtesy of The Metropolitan Museum of Art, George A. Hearn Fund, 1957.

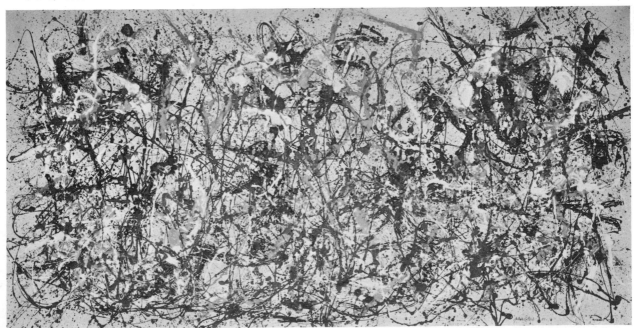

Accidents and chance were encouraged, but controlled and corrected. "I *can* control the flow of paint: there is no accident, just as there is no beginning and no end." The automatism of Kandinsky and Miro continued in Pollock's colored drawing but with less disposition to repeat landscape and object forms. Pollock literally wished to be *in* his painting, more deeply involved in its creation than previously physically or psychologically possible.

> When I am *in* my painting, I'm not aware of what I'm doing. It is only after a sort of "get acquainted" period that I see what I have been about. I have no fears about making changes, destroying the image, etc. because the painting has a life of its own. . . . It is only when I lose contact with the painting that the result is a mess. Otherwise it is pure harmony, an easy give and take, and the painting comes out well. . . . I want to express my feelings rather than illustrate them.

The expression rather than illustration of feeling is therefore the content-form of *Autumn Rhythm* (Fig. 17.10).

Just as Pollock felt that he must not lose contact with the painting, so must the beholder give it full and continued attention, and not look for an image of leaves and clouds. Seen in its own terms, *Autumn Rhythm* is a new, unfamiliar, physically impenetrable, unstable environment. It consists of a tangled web or netlike configuration, possessing inconstant densities, suspended in ambiguous relation to the surface. The eye is permitted to look through the web as if into a tinted void given atmospheric properties by the spattered color. The web is woven by the intimate calligraphy of the artist. The composition is punctuated by nodes of coagulated color, congested tangles, and open and airy passages. Like a graph, the surface is a record of the artist's hand responsive to his internal state as he worked over the entire surface,

the lines serving as traces of impulse and decision. There is no beginning nor end, but at the four sides the configuration tends to turn back upon itself as if signifying the limits of the nucleus. The parts and their relation are unpredictable and no segment is duplicated. The key to the color harmony of the painting is the predominance of the blacks, against which are browns and whites in lesser number, and the pervasive color of the canvas itself, a positive element in the artist's thought. The title was supplied after the painting was done when, perhaps, Pollock found a relevant correspondence of qualities or mood between the two. He placed his finished works outside his barn in a field to study not their similarity to nature, but whether or not they held their own as autonomous objects.

Dutch-born Willem de Kooning is another American painter whose art has helped make New York the center of important, daring, interesting, and viable painting. The violence of de Kooning's art lies not in the action content of the painting, but in the action of painting. In his *Woman, I* (Fig. 17.11), the first of a savage series, the woman, who seems all eyes, teeth, and breasts, is passive. Her form materializes from and is menaced by the painter's slashing assaults upon the canvas. *Woman, I* does not intentionally or directly allude to any single person or public concept. She belongs to the painted surface; she is a hallucination of the painter's. De Kooning described his obsessional image and suggested the intervention of his inner feelings and subconscious in its formation: "I always started out with the idea of a young person, a beautiful woman. I noticed them change. Somebody would step out—a middle aged woman. I didn't mean to make them such monsters." And on another occasion he said, "Women irritate me sometimes. I painted that irritation in the Woman series, that's all."

17.11 De Kooning. *Woman I*, 1950–1952. Collection Museum of Modern Art.

17.12 De Kooning. *Gotham News*, 1955. Albright Art Gallery, Buffalo, N. Y. Gift of Seymour H. Knox.

De Kooning is a reactive artist, irritated by a wide variety of sensations and visual suggestions from all over, and in one sense his painting is antidotal to the emotionally insincere in society. His powerful shocks overcome the viewer's emotional inertia.

De Kooning's method was to build up an image from scraps of his earlier drawings, cutouts from newspapers or photographs, freehand drawing of letters, emotions, or technical preoccupations. Like Frankenstein's monster, *Woman I* was a synthetic concoction of used parts. "Whatever I see becomes my shapes and my condition. The recognizable form people sometimes see in the picture after they are painted I see myself, but whether they got there accidentally or not, who knows." The creative process for de Kooning was open-ended, seemingly contradictory, an intense intimate dialogue between painter and paint. His painting is a dialectic in permanent process. He worked in alternating moments by paroxysms of energy and lucid calculation. Simultaneously, he infused the image with deep feeling and made its complex parts work as a unit. He constantly built up and then destroyed his images, so that on a single canvas dozens of older paintings lie beneath the fluid surface. Occasionally they "work up" to the surface, so that the painting takes on the form of a personal diary of partially eradicated entries.

In 1955 when he painted *Gotham News* (Fig. 17.12), the Woman seems to have vanished, but in fact she is present in phantom, albeit fragmented forms. The same gross, flashy pinks, breast and triangular shapes, and jarring junctures elbow into the later composition. A second, more literal after-image is the reversed printing made by the transfer of printer's ink on the canvas. De Kooning pasted bits of newspaper on to the canvas, when they were pulled off, bits of "stale news" were left. Like Kline's *The City*, *Gotham News*, no matter how indirect, bears the imprint of Gotham, or New York. The whole painting is de Kooning's signature, for it is forcibly brought and held together by his unique calligraphy and color sense. It is a piece of de Kooning, as much the style of his life as his painting.

To turn from the painting of Pollock and de Kooning to Mark Rothko's is to leave drawing, coarse textures, and pigmentation, the mark and energetic movement brought by the sweep of the brush, congested abrupt confluences of shapes, and noisy violence of the canvas as a battleground. Rothko's art is one of drastic reduction to a silent, almost immobile type of painting which might be described as that of open color, or color sensation. Color and scale are the two basic ingredients of such canvases as *Tan and Black on Red* (Fig. 17.13). The large size of Rothko's surfaces is necessary to the power of the color sensations he creates. Tan, black, and red in a smaller area do not evoke the same emotional responses as on the large scale Rothko used. The great size allows the beholder to become absorbed in the painting. There are no allusive elements in the painting, only soft, vaporous-edged, rectangular patches hovering against and in front of one another. Color is unconstrained by drawn or hard boundaries; it breathes and finds its own shape. Rothko soaked or stained the canvas as well as brushing on the color, so that the final effect is not that of opaque color lying *upon* a surface, but one of absorbent color's indefinite suspension. Color is Rothko's form and content, the sole carrier of his idea which varies from painting to painting and may crudely be expressed as a mood, or feeling of, say, tragedy, exhilaration, or withdrawal. In the painter's words, he wanted "the elimination of all obstacles between the painter and the

17.13 Rothko. *Tan and Black on Red*, 1957. The Museum of Modern Art. Collection of Mr. and Mrs. I. D. Grossman. (Photo: Sunami)

idea, and between the idea and the observer." Objects, forms, marks of the artist's hand would be "obstacles." The variety and drama in Rothko's art comes from the way large color areas interact so that, as an example, redness and blackness may induce anguish without being translated into a specific situation.

With much of modern painting, we may be assured of the artist's sincerity. The burden of sincerity often rests with the beholder and the way he chooses to receive the painting. There is an ethic to seeing as well as painting, and the observer must adapt himself to the new experiences this art affords. Just as for the artist, there must be decisions, openness, and risks taken by the viewer. Rothko expressed his feelings about the life of a painting: "A picture lives by companionship, expanding

and quickening in the eyes of the sensitive observer. It dies by the same token." The maximal exposure that the paintings in this chapter require involves the viewer's achievement of a state of concentration or communion with what is directly given to the eye. Direct painting requires direct experience. In the process the viewer may make discoveries about himself. Many artists do not seek to share their work with all men; Michelangelo said that great art was only for the brilliant in mind. Much of the modern art is for those who are emotionally attuned to the artist.

Modern nonillusionistic art is accused of not communicating. Literary subjects, descriptive imagery, or verbally transcribable ideas, it is true, are absent from this form of painting. The artist seeks an emotional truth. The imperative of this art is self-expression, not description or interpretation of one's time and place. Style and technique are means, not ends, by which expression is achieved. Recognizing the individuality and intimacy of what they have to express, such artists as Mondrian, Pollock, Kandinsky, and Miro evolved their own means and form in order to permit direct and complete self-revelation.

In no previous period has such a burden fallen to the artist, in terms of what he must extract from the self to achieve the form and content of what he paints. Michelangelo and Rembrandt found complete and true self-expression through the Bible and the human body; their techniques and not a little of their styles were acquired from the history of art. Nonillusionistic painters must reject tradition and research the properties of color, line, space, shapes, textures, scale, and composition, to extract just those essences that convey their mood or "inner necessity." In an age and civilization that has come to value and reward those activities which involve group decisions and mass production, the individually conceived and handmade work of art is all the more to be cherished. What is heroic in modern art is not the large-scale imaging of historical or literary heroes. The artist must face intellectual and emotional chance-taking, consuming demands upon moral and physical stamina, gamble with material security, and possess unflinching self-confidence in order to make his contribution to art and the culture to which it is so vital.

Nonillusionistic art makes the visual experience primary, because of the artist's full exercise of intellectual and moral judgments. The reality with which the artist is concerned is that of the emotions, the artist's very being.

BIBLIOGRAPHY

The following books and articles were consulted and used in the preparation of the text. This bibliography is by no means an attempt to list all of the material available on these subjects.

SUGGESTIONS FOR READING IN THE HISTORY OF ART:

Gombrich, Ernst: *The Story of Art.* Phaidon, 1960. One of the most lucid and intelligent general introductions to the chronology of art history for the layman.

Gombrich, Ernst: *Art and Illusion; A Study in the Psychology of Pictorian Representation.* Pantheon, 1960. An important and interesting treatment of the subject, beautifully illustrated and intelligible to the educated layman.

The Great Ages of World Architecture series published by George Braziller. Well illustrated and written by scholars for the general public.

Hauser, Arnold: *The Social History of Art,* 4 vols. Knopf, 1957. An important sociological approach to the history of art.

Janson, Horst W.: *Key Monuments of the History of Art.* Abrams, Prentice-Hall, 1959. An excellent selection of over one thousand photographs drawn from eastern and western art.

The Pelican History of Art series, edited by Nikolaus Pevsner, published by Penguin Books, Baltimore, Maryland. A series of scholarly monographs on the history of art. Many of the volumes already published in the series are cited in this bibliography.

1. ART AND MAGIC

Adam, Leonard: *Primitive Art.* Pelican Books, 1949.

Carter, Dagny: *Four Thousand Years of Chinese Art.* Ronald Press, 1948.

Elisofon, Eliot; Fagg, William; Linton, Ralph: *The Sculpture of Africa.* Thames and Hudson, 1958.

Frankfort, Henri: *Art and Architecture of the Ancient Near East.* Penguin, 1954.

Groenewegen-Frankfort, Helen: *Arrest and Movement.* University of Chicago Press, 1951.

Hauser, Arnold: *The Social History of Art,* Vol. 1 of 4 vols. Knopf, 1957.

Laming, Annette: *Lascaux.* Pelican, 1959.

Miki, Fumio: *Haniwa. The Clay Sculpture of Protohistoric Japan.* Tuttle, 1960.

Noma, Seiroku: *Haniwa.* Asia Society, 1960.

Payne, Humfrey and Young, Gerard W.: *Archaic Marble Sculpture From the Acropolis.* Cresset, 1956.

Sickman, Laurence and Soper, Alexander: *The Art and Architecture of China.* Penguin, 1956.

Von Simson, Otto: *Sacred Fortress,* University of Chicago Press, 1948.

Willetts, William: *Chinese Art,* 2 vols. Pelican, 1958.

2. IMAGES OF GODS

APOLLO

Hirmer, Max, and Lullies, Reinhard: *Greek Sculpture*. Abrams, 1955.
Guthrie, W. N. C.: *The Greeks and Their Gods*. Beacon, 1955.
Malraux, André: *The Metamorphosis of the Gods*. Doubleday, 1960.
Murray, Gilbert: *Five Stages of Greek Religion*. Beacon, 1951.
Kitto, H. D.: *The Greeks*. Pelican, 1951.

BUDDHA

Bowie, Theodore, ed.: *The Arts of Thailand*. Catalogue of the Exhibition, 1960–1962, 1960.
Coomaraswamy, Ananda: *A History of Indian and Indonesian Art*. Weyhe, 1927.
Coomaraswamy, Ananda: *The Transformation of Nature in Art*. Dover, 1956.
Goetz: Hermann, *India*. McGraw-Hill, 1959.
Kramrisch, Stella: *The Art of India*. Phaidon, 1954.
Rowland, Benjamin: *Art in East and West*. Harvard University Press, 1954.
Rowland, Benjamin: *The Art and Architecture of India*. Penguin, 1953.

CHRIST

Grabar, André: *Byzantine Painting*. Skira, 1953.
Hauser, Arnold: *The Social History of Art*. Knopf, 1957.
Kayser, Stephen S.: "Grunewald's Christianity," *Review of Religion*, November, 1940.
Malraux, André: *The Metamorphosis of the Gods*. Doubleday, 1960.
Muller, Herbert: *Uses of the Past*. Oxford, 1957.
Pevsner, Nikolaus; and Meier, Michael: *Grunewald*. Abrams, 1958.
Schapiro, Meyer: "The Romanesque Sculpture of Moissac," parts I and II, *The Art Bulletin*, September-December 1931.
Von Simson, Otto: *Sacred Fortress*. University of Chicago Press, 1948.

3. RELIGIOUS ARCHITECTURE

THE STUPA

Bowie, Theodore, ed.: *The Arts of Thailand*. Catalogue of the Exhibition, 1960–1962, 1960.
Goetz, Hermann: *India*. McGraw-Hill, 1959.
Kramrisch, Stella: *The Art of India*. Phaidon, 1954.
Louis-Frédéric: *Indian Temples and Sculpture*. Thames and Hudson, 1959.
Rowland, Benjamin: *The Art and Architecture of India*. Penguin, 1953.

THE PARTHENON

Dinsmoor, William Bell: *The Architecture of Ancient Greece*. Batsford, 1950.
Lawrence, Arnold: *Greek Architecture*. Penguin, 1957.
Muller, Herbert: *Uses of the Past*. Oxford, 1957.
Stevens, Gorham Phillips: *Restorations of Classical Buildings*. American School of Classical Studies at Athens, 1958.
Yalouris, N.: *Classical Greece, The Elgin Marbles*. New York Graphic Society, 1960.

THE GOTHIC CATHEDRAL

Bowie, Theodore: *The Sketchbook of Villard de Honnecourt*. Indiana University Press, 1959.
Branner, Robert: *Gothic Architecture*. Braziller, 1961.

Crosby, Sumner McKnight: Review of Von Simson's *The Gothic Cathedral* in the *Art Bulletin*, June, 1960.

Dow, Helen: "The Rose Window," *The Journal of the Warburg and Courtauld Institute*, July, 1957.

Frankl, Paul: *The Gothic*. Princeton University Press, 1960.

Gilbert, Kathryn; Kuhn, Helmut: *A History of Esthetics*. Indiana University Press, 1960.

Gimpel, Jean: *The Cathedral Builders*. Grove, 1961.

Harvey, John: *The Gothic World*. Batsford, 1950.

Holt, Elizabeth: *A Documentary History of Art*, Vol. 1. Anchor, 1957.

Horn, Walter: "On the Origin of the Medieval Bay System," *Society of Architectural Historians Journal*, Summer, 1958.

> (The material in this article will appear in a book by Walter Horn and Ernest Born: *The Aisled Medieval Timber Hall, A Study of Its Origins, Development and Survival*.)

Johnson, James R.: "Art History and the Immediate Visual Experience," *The Journal of Aesthetics and Art Criticism*, Summer, 1961.

Katzenellenbogen, Adolph: *The Sculptural Programs of Chartres Cathedral*. Johns Hopkins Press, 1959.

Knoop, Douglas and Jones, G. P.: *The Medieval Mason*. Manchester, 1949.

Krautheimer, Richard: "Introduction to an Iconography of Medieval Architecture," *Journal of the Warburg and Courtauld Institute*, 1942.

Muller, Herbert: *Uses of the Past*. Oxford, 1957.

Panofsky, Erwin: *Scholasticism and Gothic Architecture*. Meridian, 1957.

Panofsky, Erwin: *Suger*. Princeton, 1946.

Smith, Baldwin: *Architectural Symbolism of Imperial Rome and the Middle Ages*. Princeton University Press, 1956.

Von Simson, Otto: *The Gothic Cathedral*. Pantheon, 1956.

4. THE SACRED BOOK

Goldschmidt, Adolph: German Illumination, 2 vols. Harcourt Brace, 1928.

Grabar, André; Nordenfalk, Carl: *Early Medieval Painting*. Skira, 1957. Both this and the succeeding volume have excellent bibliographies.

Grabar, André; Nordenfalk, Carl: *Romanesque Painting*. Skira, 1958.

Hinks, Roger P.: *The Carolingian Renaissance*. Sedgwick and Jackson, 1935.

Metz, Peter: *The Golden Gospels of Echternach*. Praeger, 1957.

Rickert, Margaret: *Painting in Britain in the Middle Ages*. Penguin, 1954.

Swarzenski, Hanns: *Early Medieval Illumination*. Oxford, 1952.

5. THE SYNTHESIS OF HEAVEN AND EARTH IN FIFTEENTH-CENTURY ART

FLEMISH ART

Flanders in the Fifteenth Century, Art and Civilization. Catalogue of the Exhibition: Masterpieces of Flemish Art. Detroit Institute of Art, 1960.

Friedländer, Max: *From Van Eyck to Bruegel*. Phaidon London Press, 1956.

Held, Julius: Review of Panofsky, Erwin, *Early Netherlandish Painting*, *The Art Bulletin*, September, 1955.

Meiss, Millard: "Light as Form and Symbol," *Art Bulletin*, September 1945.

Panofsky, Erwin: *Early Netherlandish Painting*, 2 vols. Harvard University Press, 1953.

Rousseau, T.; Freeman, M.: Articles on Campin's Merode Altarpiece, *Bulletin of the Metropolitan Museum of Art*, December, 1957.

Schapiro, Meyer: " 'Muscipula Diaboli,' The Symbolism of the Merode Altarpiece," *The Art Bulletin*, September, 1945.

Van der Elst, Baron: *Last Flowering of the Middle Ages*. Doubleday, 1954.

Von Simson, Otto: "Compassio and Co-Redemptio in Roger Van der Weyden's Descent From the Cross," *The Art Bulletin*, March, 1953.

ITALIAN ART

Clark, Kenneth: *Piero della Francesca*. Phaidon, 1951.

De Wald, Ernest T.: *Italian Painting 1200–1600*. Holt, 1961.

Hendy, P.: *Masaccio, Frescoes in Florence*. New York Graphic Society, 1956.

Janson, Horst W.: *The Sculpture of Donatello*, 2 vols. Princeton University Press, 1957.

Offner, Richard: "Giotto or Non-Giotto," *Burlington Magazine*, June–July, 1939.

Olschki, Leonardo: *The Genius of Italy*. Cornell University Press, 1954.

Thompson, J. W.; Rowley, G.; Schevill, F.; Sarton, G.: *The Civilization of the Renaissance*. Frederick Ungar, 1959.

White, John: *The Birth and Rebirth of Pictorial Space*. Faber and Faber, n.d.

6. The Synthesis of Heaven and Earth in Sixteenth- and Seventeenth-Century Painting

ART AS RELIGIOUS PROPAGANDA

Blunt, Anthony: *Artistic Theory in Italy 1450–1600*. Clarendon Press, 1940.

Burckhardt, Jacob: *Recollections of Rubens*. Phaidon, 1950.

Dvorak, Max: "El Greco and Mannerism," *Magazine of Art*, January, 1953.

Friedlander, Walter: *Caravaggio Studies*. Princeton University Press, 1955.

Hinks, Roger P.: *Michelangelo Merisi da Caravaggio*. Beechhurst, 1953.

Holt, Elizabeth: *Documentary History of Art*, Vol. 2. Anchor, 1957. (This was the source of the excerpt on the trial of Veronese.)

Mâle, Emile: *L'Art Religieux de la Fin du XVIe Siècle au XVIIe Siècle*. Colin, 1951.

Meier-Graefe, Julius: *The Spanish Journey*. Harcourt Brace, 1927.

Wittkower, Rudolph: *Gian Lorenzo Bernini*. Phaidon, 1955.

Wittkower, Rudolph: *Art and Architecture in Italy, 1600–1750*. Penguin, 1958.

Wittkower, Rudolph: "El Greco's Language of Gestures," *Art News*, March, 1957.

Wölfflin, Heinrich: *Principles of Art History*. Dover, n.d.

THE TABLE IN BAROQUE SECULAR ART

Blunt, Anthony: *Art and Architecture in France, 1500–1700*. Penguin, 1954.

De Tolnay, Charles: "Vermeer's 'The Artist's Studio'," *The Gazette des Beaux Arts*, April, 1953.

Friedländer, Max: *Landscape, Portrait, Still Life*. Cassirer, 1949.

Furness, S.: *Georges de la Tour of Lorraine*. Routledge and Kegan Paul, 1945.

Held, Julius: *Flemish Painting*. Abrams, 1953.

Highet, Gilbert: "Bruegel's Rustic Wedding," *Magazine of Art*, November, 1945.

Puyvelde, Leo van: *Jordaens*. Elsevier, 1953.

Trapier, E.: *Velasquez*. Hispanic Society of America, 1948.

7. Images of Kings

Blunt, Anthony: *Art and Architecture in France, 1500–1700*. Penguin, 1954.

Frankfort, Henri: *Art and Architecture of the Ancient Near East*. Penguin, 1954.

Frankfort, Henri: *Kingship and the Gods*. Chicago University Press, 1948.

Grabar, André: *L'Empéreur dans l'art byzantin*. Les Belles Lettres, 1936.

Groenewegen-Frankfort, Helen: *Arrest and Movement*. Chicago University Press, 1951.

Hamberg, Per G.: *Studies in Roman Imperial Art*. Munksgaard, 1945.

Jenkins, M.: *The State Portrait*. Art Bulletin Monograph, 1947.

Lehman-Haupt, Hellmut: *Art under a Dictatorship*. Oxford, 1954.

Lewis, W. H.: *The Splendid Century, Life in the France of Louis XIV*. Anchor, 1957.

Liudprand of Cremona: *The Works of Liudprand of Cremona*. London, 1930.

Sickman, Laurence; Soper, Alexander: *The Art and Architecture of Japan*. Penguin, 1956.

Strong, Eugenie: *Apotheosis and After Life*. Constable, 1915.

Wittkower, Rudolph: *Gian Lorenzo Bernini*. Phaidon, 1955.

Yûzan, Daiduji S.: *Bushido*. Kokusai Bunka Shinkokai, 1941.

8. THE PROVISION FOR PLAY

Anderson, John; Spiers, R. P.; Ashby, T.: *The Architecture of Ancient Rome*. Batsford, 1927.

Atkinson, R. J. C.: *Stonehenge*. Pelican, 1960.

Bieber, Margaret: *The History of the Greek and Roman Theater*. Princeton University Press, 1939.

Brown, Frank E.: "Roman Architecture," *College Art Journal*, XVII, 2, 1960.

Carcopino, Jerome: *Daily Life in Ancient Rome*. Yale University Press, 1960.

Coffin, David R.: *The Villa d'Este at Tivoli*. Princeton University Press, 1960.

Dinsmoor, William B.: *The Architecture of Ancient Greece*. Batsford, 1950.

Drexler, Arthur: *The Architecture of Japan*. Museum of Modern Art, 1955.

Fujikawa, Sako: *Cha-no-yu and Hideyoshi*. Hokuseido Press, 1957.

Huizinga, Johan: *Homo Ludens, A Study of the Play Element in Culture*. Beacon, 1955.

Huxtable, Ada L.: *Pier Luigi Nervi*. Braziller, 1960.

Kuck, Loraine E.: *The Art of Japanese Gardens*. John Day, 1940.

Lavedan, Pierre: *Histoire de l'Urbanisme*, Vol. 1. Laurens, 1926.

Lawrence, Arnold: *Greek Architecture*. Penguin, 1957.

Mannix, P. P.: *Those About to Die*. Ballantine, 1958.

Marks, Robert. W.: *The Dymaxion World of Buckminster Fuller*. Reinhold, 1960.

MacKendrick, Paul: *The Mute Stones Speak, The Story of Archaeology in Italy*. St. Martin's, 1960.

Mumford, Louis: *The City in History*. Harcourt Brace, 1961.

Robertson, Donald: *A Handbook of Greek and Roman Architecture*. Cambridge, 1943.

Smith, G. C. Kidder: *The New Architecture of Europe*. Meridian, 1961.

Sitte, Camillo: *The Art of Building Cities*. Reinhold, 1945.

Wittkower, Rudolph: *Art and Architecture in Italy, 1600–1750*. Penguin, 1958.

9. THEMES FROM NATURE

Blunt, Anthony: *Art and Architecture in France, 1500–1700*. Penguin, 1954.

Clark, Kenneth: *Leonardo da Vinci*. Penguin, 1954.

Collins, Leo C.: *Hercules Seghers*. Chicago, 1953.

Giedion-Welcker, Carola: *Hans Arp*. Thames and Hudson, 1957.

Elsen, Albert: "Seymour Lipton," *Art International*, February, 1961.

Friedländer, Max: *Landscape, Portrait, Still Life*. Cassirer, 1949.

Grohmann, Will: *Paul Klee*. Abrams, n.d.
Haftmann, Werner: *The Mind and Work of Paul Klee*. Faber and Faber, 1954.
Klee, Paul: *On Modern Art*. Faber and Faber, 1940.
McCurdy, Charles: *Leonardo da Vinci's Notebooks*, 2 vols. Reynal and Hitchcock, n.d.
Panofsky, Erwin: *The Life and Art of Albrecht Dürer*, 2 vols. Princeton University Press, 1955.
Rowley, George: *Principles of Chinese Art*. Princeton University Press, 1947.
Rubin, William: *Matta*. Museum of Modern Art, 1957.
Schapiro, Meyer: *Paul Cézanne*. Abrams, 1952.
Schapiro, Meyer: *Vincent Van Gogh*. Abrams, n.d.
Sirén, Osvald: *Chinese Painting*, Vols. 1, 2. Ronald Press, 1956.
Sickman, Laurence; Soper, Alexander: *Art and Architecture of China*. Penguin, 1956.
Soper, Alexander: "Early Chinese Landscape Painting," *Art Bulletin*, June, 1941.
The Complete Letters of Vincent Van Gogh, 3 vols. New York Graphic Society, 1958.

10. Painting and Objects

Barr, Alfred H.: *Matisse*. Museum of Modern Art, 1951.
Friedman, B. H., ed.: *School of New York*. Grove, 1959 (Essays by Ben Heller on Jasper Johns and David Myers on Robert Rauschenberg.
Friedländer, Max: *Landscape, Portrait, Still Life*. Cassirer, 1949.
Lebel, Robert: *Marcel Duchamp*. Grove, 1959.
Rowley, George: *Principles of Chinese Painting*. Princeton University Press, 1947.
Rubin, William: "Reflexions on Marcel Duchamp." *Art International*, December 1, 1960.
Schapiro, Meyer: *Paul Cézanne*. Abrams, 1952.
Schapiro, Meyer: *Vincent Van Gogh*. Abrams, n.d.
Soby, James Thrall: *Giorgio de Chirico*, 2d ed. Museum of Modern Art, 1955.
Soria, Martin: *Zurbaran*. Phaidon, 1953.
Sterling, Charles: *Still Life Painting from Antiquity to the Present*. Universe Books, 1959.

11. The Portrait in Painting and Sculpture

Ambler, Eric: *A Coffin for Dimitrios*. Dell, 1957.
Giedion-Welcker, Carola: *Constantin Brancusi*. Benno Schwabe, 1958.
Friedländer, Max: *Landscape, Portrait, Still Life*. Cassirer, 1949.
Held, Julius: *Peter Paul Rubens*. Abrams, 1953.
Hirmer, Max: *Egypt*. Phaidon, 1956.
Hoffman, Edith: *Kokoschka, Life and Work*. Faber and Faber, n.d.
Lipman, Jean H.: "The Florentine Profile Portrait in the Quattrocento," *Art Bulletin*, Vol. XVIII, 1936.
Meiss, Millard: "Nicholas Albergati and the Chronology of Van Eyck's Portraits," *Burlington Magazine*, May, 1952.
Miller, D.: "Géricault's Portraits of the Insane," *Journal of the Warburg and Courtauld Institute*, 1940–41.
Panofsky, Erwin: *Early Netherlandish Painting*, 2 vols. Harvard University Press, 1953.
Selz, Peter: *New Images of Man*. Museum of Modern Art, 1959.
Soby, James Thrall: *Joan Miro*. Museum of Modern Art, 1959.
Schapiro, Meyer: *Vincent Van Gogh*. Abrams, n.d.
Wittkower, Rudolph: *Gian Lorenzo Bernini*. Phaidon, 1955.

12. The Figure in Sculpture

THE FIGURE IN OLDER SCULPTURE

Clark, Kenneth: *The Nude.* Pantheon, 1956.

Janson, Horst W.: *The Sculpture of Donatello,* 2 vols. Princeton University Press, 1957.

Kramrisch, Stella: *The Art of India.* Phaidon, 1954.

Panofsky, Erwin: *Meaning in the Visual Arts, The History of the Theory of Human Proportions as a Reflection of the History of Styles.* Anchor, 1955.

Schapiro, Meyer: "The Sculptures of Souillac," *Studies in Memory of Arthur Kingsley Porter.* Harvard University Press, 1939.

Wittkower, Rudolph: *Gian Lorenzo Bernini.* Phaidon, 1955.

TRANSFORMATIONS OF THE FIGURE IN MODERN SCULPTURE

Barr, Alfred H.: *Matisse.* Museum of Modern Art, 1951.

Elsen, Albert E.: *Rodin's Gates of Hell.* University of Minnesota Press, 1960.

Elsen, Albert E.: "The Humanism of Rodin and Lipchitz," *College Art Journal,* Spring, 1958.

Elsen, Albert E.: "Seymour Lipton," *Art International,* February, 1961.

Rewald, John: *Maillol.* Hyperion, 1939.

Ritchie, Andrew C.: "Julio Gonzalez," *Museum of Modern Art Bulletin,* Vol. XXIII, Numbers 1–2, 1955–56.

Ritchie, Andrew C.: *Sculpture of the Twentieth Century.* Museum of Modern Art, n.d.

Sartre, Jean-Paul: *Alberto Giacometti.* Pierre Matisse, 1948.

13. Michelangelo

Blunt, Anthony: *Artistic Theory in Italy, 1450–1600.* Clarendon Press, 1940.

Condivi, A.: *The Life of Michelangelo,* trans. by D. B. Updike. Merrymount Press, 1904.

DeTolnay, Charles: *Michelangelo,* 5 vols. Princeton University Press, 1943–1960.

Dvorak, Max: "El Greco and Mannerism," *Magazine of Art,* Jaunary, 1953.

Goldscheider, Ludwig: *Michelangelo Drawings.* Phaidon, 1951.

Goldwater, Robert; Treves, Marco: *Artists on Art.* Pantheon, 1945.

Hartt, F.: "The Meaning of Michelangelo's Medici Chapel," *Essays in Honor of Georg Swarzenski.* Chicago University Press, 1951.

Hartt, F.: "Lignum Vitae in Medio Paradisi, the Stanza d'Eliodoro and the Sistine Ceiling," *Art Bulletin* 32:115–45, 181–218, June–September, 1950.

Olschki, Leo: *The Genius of Italy.* Cornell University Press, 1954.

Panofsky, Erwin: *Studies in Iconology.* Oxford, 1939.

14. Rembrandt

Benesch, Otto: *Rembrandt.* Skira, 1957.

Benesch, Otto: *Rembrandt's Drawings,* 5 vols. Phaidon, 1954.

DeTolnay, Charles: "The Syndics of the Drapers' Guild," *Gazette des Beaux Arts,* Vol. 23, January–June, 1943.

Fromentin, Eugene: *Masters of Past Time.* Dutton, 1913.

Held, Julius: "Debunking Rembrandt's Legend," *Art News,* V. 48, February, 1950.

Held, Julius: "Rembrandt, Self-Education of an Artist," *Art News,* V. 40, February, 1942.

Munz, L.: *Rembrandt.* Abrams, 1954.
Munz, L.: *Rembrandt's Etchings,* 2 vols. Phaidon, 1952.
Roger-Marx, Claude: *Rembrandt.* Universe Books, 1960.
Rosenberg, Jakob: *Rembrandt,* 2 vols. Harvard University Press, 1948.
Schapiro, Meyer: "Fromentin as a Critic," *Partisan Review,* January, 1949.
Simmel, Georg: *Rembrandt.* Kurt Wolff Verlag, 1919.
Slive, Seymour: *Rembrandt and His Critics, 1630–1730.* Nidhoff, 1953.

15. Picasso

Barr, Alfred H.: *Picasso, Forty Years of His Art.* Museum of Modern Art, 1939.
Golding, John: *Cubism, A History and Analysis, 1907–1914.* Wittenborn, 1959.
Greenberg, Clement: "Picasso at Seventy-Five," *Art and Culture.* Beacon, 1961.
Penrose, Roland: *Picasso; His Life and Work.* Harper, 1959.
Rosenblum, Robert: *Cubism and Twentieth-Century Art.* Abrams, 1960.
Zervos, Christian: *Pablo Picasso,* Vols. I–XI. *Cashiers d'Art,* 1932–1960.

16. The City in Modern Painting

Deknatel, Fred B.: *Edvard Munch.* Museum of Modern Art, 1950.
Goodnough, Robert: "Kline Paints a Picture," *Art News,* December, 1952.
Mondrian, Piet: *Plastic Art and Pure Plastic Art.* Wittenborn, 1945.
Rodman, Selden: *Conversations with Artists.* Devin-Adair, 1957.
Rosenblum, Robert: *Cubism and Twentieth-Century Art.* Abrams, 1960.
Schapiro, Meyer: "Seurat and 'La Grande Jatte'," *Columbia Review,* 1935.
Soby, James Thrall: *Giorgio de Chirico,* 2d ed. Museum of Modern Art, 1955.
Swillens, Johannes: *Vermeer.* Spectrum, 1950.
Taylor, Joshua C.: *Futurism.* Museum of Modern Art, 1961.
Stella, Joseph: "Discovery of America; Autobiographical Notes," *Art News,* November, 1960.

17. Nonillusionistic Modern Painting

Goldwater, Robert: "Reflections on the Rothko Exhibition," *Arts,* March, 1961.
Greenberg, Clement: "Modernistic Painting," *Arts Yearbook 4.* Art Digest, 1961.
Hess, Thomas R.: *Willem de Kooning.* Braziller, 1959.
Hunter, Sam: *Modern American Painting and Sculpture.* Dell, 1959.
Hunter, Sam: "Jackson Pollock" (catalog preface). Museum of Modern Art, 1956–1957.
Hunter, Sam: *Miro; His Graphic Work.* Abrams, 1958.
Janis, Harriet; Blesh, Rudi: *De Kooning.* Grove, 1960.
Malevich, Kasimir: *The Non-Objective World.* Theobold, 1959.
Mondrian, Piet: *Plastic Art and Pure Plastic Art.* Wittenborn, 1945.
Kandinsky, Wassily: *Concerning the Spiritual in Art.* Wittenborn, 1955.
Robertson, Bryan: *Jackson Pollock.* Abrams, 1960.
Schapiro, Meyer: "On the Humanity of Abstract Painting," *Proceedings of the Academy of Arts and Letters.* National Institute of Arts and Letters, Second Series #10, New York, 1960.
Schapiro, Meyer: "The Liberating Quality of Avant-Garde Art," *Art News,* Summer, 1957.
Schapiro, Meyer: "The Younger American Painters of Today," *The Listener,* January, 1956.

INDEX